PERSPECTIVES ON ADULTS LEARNING MATHEMATICS

Mathematics Education Library

VOLUME 21

The titles published in this series are listed at the end of this volume.

PERSPECTIVES ON ADULTS LEARNING MATHEMATICS

Research and Practice

Edited by

DIANA COBEN
University of Nottingham,
Nottingham, England

JOHN O'DONOGHUE
University of Limerick,
Limerick, Ireland

and

GAIL E. FITZSIMONS
Monash University,
Victoria, Australia

KLUWER ACADEMIC PUBLISHERS
DORDRECHT / BOSTON / LONDON

Library of Congress Cataloging-in-Publication Data

ISBN 0-7923-6415-5

Published by Kluwer Academic Publishers,
P.O. Box 17, 3300 AA Dordrecht, The Netherlands.

Sold and distributed in North, Central and South America
by Kluwer Academic Publishers,
101 Philip Drive, Norwell, MA 02061, U.S.A.

In all other countries, sold and distributed
by Kluwer Academic Publishers,
P.O. Box 322, 3300 AH Dordrecht, The Netherlands.

Printed on acid-free paper

Contents

Contents   vii

Acknowledgements

The editors wish to acknowledge the following people who contributed to the production of this book:

- members of the international community, of *Adults Learning Mathematics – A Research Forum (ALM)*, several of whom are represented as authors or co-authors of chapters in this book, including those who participated in the series of annual conferences since 1994 and who provided support and inspiration,
- Peter de Liefde, Joy Carp, and Irene van den Reydt of Kluwer Academic Publishers for their professional support and advice,
- Jackie O'Shaughnessy for preparing the camera-ready copy for printing,
- the University of Limerick for supporting this project,
- the anonymous reviewers for their constructive suggestions regarding the structure of the book, and providing a fresh look at our strengths and weaknesses,
- Alan Bishop for his unobtrusive yet steadfast support, encouragement, and belief in this project.

Finally, the editors have made every effort to ensure that all text reflects the authors' intentions, but final responsibility lies with the authors for their individual contributions.

Preface

Alan J. Bishop
Monash University, Victoria, Australia

I had the honour to write the Introduction to an earlier book (FitzSimons 1997) on 'Adults returning to study' which has paved the way for this volume. In that introduction I commented that the excitement of seeing a new growth in a research field is like seeing a new leaf growing from a bud on a tree. Now, to continue the analogy I could perhaps say that this particular leaf has developed into a full branch which is also starting to bear fruit. This is equally exciting!

This new volume represents the range of interests in the developing area of research into adults learning mathematics. As the new millennium unfolds we can be sure of one thing, and that is that there will be an increasing number of adults continuing their education. Moreover, as society becomes more and more dependent on technology there can be no doubt that continuing mathematics education is going to be a necessity in every country. This is not only because of employment needs, which has tended to be the only way in which adult mathematics education has been conceived by many people, not least by those educational bureaucrats and politicians who link education with employment and economic output. But the continuing mathematics education of adults is also going to be a necessity because of needing to educate society about the increasingly widespread uses and abuses of mathematics.

However it is certainly not clear what form this continuing mathematics education should take, nor how to judge its benefits and effectiveness. Researching the field of adult mathematics education is a much more complex task than researching school mathematics education. In the latter the learning situation is often concisely circumscribed, the goals are usually made explicit, it takes place in a specified location, the materials are usually publicly available, the teachers are certified and easily recognised, and the assessment results can often be readily accessed.

In adult mathematics education however, the situation is not so simple. There are many kinds of activities that can take place under that heading. It can be a part of Formal mathematics education, as in the case of some university and college qualifications. It can be a part of Non-Formal mathematics education, as in the case of adult courses that are taken purely for interest and with no qualification attached. It can also be part of Informal mathematics education, which can happen anywhere, at any time, and which doesn't involve a course of any sort. It is therefore certainly not clear what the goals of adult mathematics education should be, nor who should determine them. Adult mathematics education takes place in a variety of locations and structures, with materials ranging from papers and texts to TV and Internet-based productions. The teachers can be formally qualified or not, and indeed may not even be referred to as teachers, and assessment can exist or not, depending on the formality of the education.

This then is an important but highly complex area to research, and this book aims to lay many of the foundations for studying the area. It is clear that with such a complex area no one research paradigm will suffice and so the four sections of the book each contain chapters which represent the variety of approaches currently being adopted. There is a very long way to go before the field becomes as well documented as school mathematics education, but this book's strength is that it shows us some of the more promising avenues to explore and theoretical perspectives to develop.

As well as being sure that the book represents the kind of foundational writing that was hoped for when this book series was proposed, I hope also that it will encourage other researchers and research students to enter this field and help it develop. In the last millennium mathematics education research contributed significantly to helping understand and develop mathematics education in school. Mathematics educators now need to turn their attention to the issues and problems associated with the field of adult mathematics education. In this new millennium this field presents a far greater challenge, and this book represents a significant beginning to meeting that challenge.

REFERENCES

FitzSimons, G. E. (Ed.) (1997). *Adults returning to study mathematics: Papers from Working Group 18, 8th International Congress on Mathematical Education, ICME 8.* Adelaide: Australian Association of Mathematics Teachers.

Chapter 1

Introduction

Diana Coben, Gail E. FitzSimons & John O'Donoghue
School of Continuing Education, University of Nottingham, UK; Monash University /
Swinburne University of Technology, Victoria, Australia; University of Limerick, Ireland

> Adults are not like school students but they too are mathematics learners. So we
> can expect to find from research on adult learners, data and thoughts which will
> inform and extend our constructs and concepts of mathematics learning in
> general. (Bishop 1997:3)

This book is about adults learning mathematics wherever and in whatever
circumstances they do so. It grew out of Adults Learning Mathematics
(ALM), an international research forum founded in 1994 to advance adult
mathematics education through disciplined inquiry. Since 1994 ALM has
held a series of international conferences bringing together researchers and
practitioners in the field of adults learning mathematics. The purpose of this
book is to draw attention to the emerging field of adults learning
mathematics through the dissemination of scholarly work in the field, much
of which was first discussed at ALM and other national and international
conferences. It is the first attempt by anyone to move beyond conference
proceedings and address specifically adults' mathematics education as a
research field. The individual contributions stand on their merits and speak
well for the field as a rich source of significant research questions and
possibilities.

This book also aims to situate adults learning mathematics within the
wider field of lifelong learning and lifelong education, along the lines
proposed by Malcolm Tight (1996). He states that lifelong education: builds
on and affects all existing educational providers, including schools and
Higher Education Institutions; extends beyond the formal educational
providers to encompass all agencies, groups and individuals involved in any
kind of learning activity; rests on the belief that individuals are, or can
become, self-directing, and that they will see the value in engaging in

1

D. Coben et al. (eds.), Perspectives on Adults Learning Mathematics, 1–11.
© *2000 Kluwer Academic Publishers. Printed in the Netherlands.*

lifelong education (Tight, 1996). Lifelong education does not begin nor does it end with school. Accordingly, neither should mathematics education be defined exclusively in terms of school mathematics. Historically, discussion of 'mainstream' mathematics education has focused on school mathematics and related issues, to the virtual exclusion of all else. But mathematics learning, whether involving children or adults, also takes place in a variety of non-school settings, including the home, various professional practices and cultural and workplace activities. This mathematics learning (and teaching) needs to be accommodated in any discussion of mathematics education research and practice. Paul Ernest (1998:72) seems to offer an embracing conception of research in mathematics education when he argues for a postmodern perspective which sees mathematics education as a field constituted by a multiplicity of practices including:

- the teaching and learning of mathematics at all levels in school and college;
- out of school learning (and teaching) of mathematics;
- the design, writing and construction of texts and mathematics learning materials;
- the study of mathematics education in pre-service teacher education;
- the graduate study of mathematics education texts and results;
- research in mathematics education at all levels.

Such views are welcome and timely as increasingly we are seeing that school mathematics cannot stand apart from considerations of the adult domains of 'everyday mathematics' and mathematics at work - and other issues which can only be fully explored in the context of adults learning mathematics. Some of these issues are examined in these chapters and show promising lines of inquiry for the future, for example, adult problem solving, mathematics life histories investigations, discourse theory, ethnomathematics approaches to curriculum development and research on numeracy teaching and teacher training. Together the contributors to this book give a fascinating glimpse of a journey-in-progress being negotiated by practitioners and researchers working with adults as they define a whole new research domain. The excitement attendant upon new developments and insights is evident as researchers from all over the world make common cause with like-minded colleagues and discover common ground.

Common ground may be difficult to traverse in the absence of common terms with which to discuss research and practice in adults learning mathematics. In particular, the field is bedevilled by the vexed question of what is (adult) numeracy and how does it differ (if at all) from (adult) mathematics learning and education? According to FitzSimons, Jungwirth, Maaß and Schloeglmann (1996) adult numeracy and mathematical education are two terms for one subject although the choice will probably depend on the socio-cultural surroundings in which the research takes place. In the German speaking countries, for example, only the term 'mathematics' is used in scholarship and in public discussion. FitzSimons et al. (1996) suggested that for a person to be mathematically well-educated (or numerate) requires three attributes. Firstly, to have a sound mathematical knowledge, that is, to know important concepts and methods and to be able to apply them appropriately. Secondly, to have knowledge about their power and their limitations (see also Keitel, Kotzmann & Skovsmose, 1993). Such knowledge about mathematics is very important; for example, when the outcomes of mathematical modelling have to be evaluated, such as forecasts of the economic situation, or the outcomes of opinion polls. Thirdly, to have an overview of, and a critical stance towards, the discipline. This includes consideration of subjective experiences with mathematics with all its emotional involvement, its utility values, and its meaning in our society (see also Ernest, 1998b).

World Mathematics Year 2000, sponsored by UNESCO, comes at a time when concern about standards of achievement in mathematics is high on the international agenda following the International Adult Literacy Survey (IALS) (OECD, 1997; see also Houtkoop & Jones, 1998) and the Third International Mathematics and Science Study (TIMSS) (Beaton et al., 1996). In these and other reports 'adult numeracy' has varying meanings. In some, there is a societal focus, primarily related to the socio-economic change and the technological development of society. In others, the focus is on the individual's development of skills for work and everyday life. Some emphasise a functional role (e.g., Withnall, 1995); others consider numeracy as a means to gain insight into the structures of society and to enable people to take an active part in political decision-making, enabling 'critical citizenship' (Evans & Thorstad, 1995) or democratic competence in the workplace (Noss, 1997; Wedege, this volume). The International Adult Literacy Survey (IALS) defined what it called 'quantitative literacy' in terms of arithmetic and reading, as follows:

> The knowledge and skills required to apply arithmetic operations, either alone or sequentially, to numbers embedded in printed materials, such as balancing a check-book, figuring out tip, completing an order form, or determining the amount of interest on a loan from an advertisement. (OCED, 1997:14).

This somewhat narrow definition reflects the focus on reading and writing in the survey and the survey team had some difficulty in finding quantitative literacy tasks for assessment at a low level of attainment

(Houtkoop & Jones, 1999:33). Numeracy also pertains to another IALS category, 'document literacy', defined as

> The knowledge and skills required to locate and use information contained in various formats, including job applications, payroll forms, transportation schedules, maps, tables and graphics. (OECD, 1997:14)

Education for document literacy in this sense is discussed by Iddo Gal in his chapter on 'statistical literacy'.

The follow-up to the IALS survey, the International Life Skills Survey (ILSS), will assess performance in four skill domains; prose literacy; document literacy; numeracy; and problem-solving. The focus in the numeracy part of ILSS will be on

> The ability to interpret, apply, and communicate mathematical information in four domains: everyday life, work situations, societal and community situations and further learning. (Houtkoop & Jones, 1999:39)

It is hoped that this broader definition will yield useful data for further analysis.

It is widely accepted that the numerate aspects of everyday activities cannot be separated from their general purposes and goals, nor from the social dimension of acting. The situation as a whole has to be taken into account. This implies that numeracy can only be learned and developed within specific contexts (cf. Lave, 1988; Lave & Wenger, 1991). Besides, the question arises whether it is possible to transfer numerate ideas and skills grounded in one context to another (see Billett, 1998; Ernest, 1998a; Evans, this volume, for further discussion of issues of transfer). In any case it is questionable what purpose would be served by teaching numeracy concepts in isolation, even if they could be taught that way. Finally, it should be mentioned that there is no agreement as to whether numeracy includes attitudinal or emotional factors (see Duffin & Simpson, this volume, for a discussion of the need to explore the link between the cognitive and the affective aspects of mathematics learning).

Protagonists of the duality between mathematics education and numeracy (including many politicians) often argue that numeracy is (or ought to be) a restricted mathematical education. It is seen as a low-level mathematics, often taught by non-mathematicians, to people who have no aspiration to be mathematicians. At first sight it seems obvious to reduce numeracy to elementary skills or abilities, and in practice being numerate is often understood in this way (that is, as having a good command of the four processes (addition, subtraction, multiplication and division with whole numbers), common and decimal fractions, and percentages; being familiar to some extent with descriptive statistics or the interpretation of simple (Cartesian) graphs. This approach often appears to be motivated by the need to overcome perceived educational deficits of the adult learner.

But numeracy need not necessarily be restricted to the skills or abilities mentioned above. If the thesis of its dependence on context is taken seriously, in certain cases even an understanding of rates of change might be classed with numeracy. For example, in discussions about economic issues certain facts, such as marginal rates, can be described exactly by the use of the concept of the derivative (see also Noss & Hoyles, 1996). Approaches to teaching which take up this broader view include those which focus on the role of mathematics in our society. Adult educators who wish to see society change use an emancipatory approach to guide the curriculum (e.g., Benn, 1997; Frankenstein, 1996), and attempt to combat inequalities through a stress on adequate mathematical education for all.

According to the German philosopher Hülsmann (1985), mathematics is basic to the integrative structure of the 'Technological Formation' - a dynamic system combining government, capital, labour, and research. In contrast to earlier times, present society is constituted by the technology being produced and applied in it. Mathematics is a social phenomenon, firmly embedded in social context, a functional form of communication. Two aspects can be discerned - the means aspect and the system aspect.

> Mathematics provides a means for individuals to explain and control complex situations of the natural and of the artificial environment and to communicate about those situations. On the other hand, mathematics is a system of concepts, algorithms and rules, embodied in us, in our thinking and doing; we are subject to this system, it determines parts of our identity. (Fischer 1993:113-114)

Fisher argued that we have not learned to recognise the reciprocity of this duality, focusing on the former and accepting the latter without question or reflection. Thus, adult numeracy when understood as a socially constructed phenomenon, has the potential for empowerment, even emancipation. Whether this occurs will depend on interpretations made by politicians, curriculum developers, and practitioners.

Difficulties in tracing activity by adults learning mathematics also occur because adult mathematics education may be subsumed within literacy or other community development programmes, where mathematics learning is seen as a secondary concern.

Against this background, this book begins with a look at perspectives on research on adults learning mathematics, starting with a review by Gail FitzSimons and Gail Godden of recent research published in English. The review spans different disciplines and covers various sites of research and practice, including the classroom, the workplace, community settings and distance education and a wide range of issues including teaching styles, technology, gender, and the assessment and evaluation of mathematics learning. Relevant research is reviewed in terms of both 'background' and 'foreground' considerations. The latter term is borrowed from Ole Skovsmose (1996:1) and it is used to mean "the set of opportunities which the student's interpretation of her socially determined opportunities reveals as 'real' opportunities... [which is] an important source for understanding an action". 'Foreground' considerations include individual considerations such as motivation to learn, as well as classroom and workplace considerations in teaching and learning. These include, for example: pressures on adult students; teaching styles; institutional and broader social considerations; the special needs of adults studying at university, focussing on topics such as course requirements and institutional responses and evaluation issues; research activity, including the activities of research forums and publications. 'Background' considerations include: the role of influential institutions, such as government and education systems; consideration of mathematics as a discipline; the classroom and workplace considered as social sites of mathematics activity; and socio-psychological considerations such as attitudes and beliefs about mathematics and mathematics anxiety.

While the review aims to be as comprehensive as possible in its coverage of a notably diverse field, it inevitably reflects the fact that the majority of research studies published in English take as their reference point relatively prosperous populations in technologically advanced societies. The review accordingly highlights areas where further research is needed and the authors echo the conclusion of Tine Wedege, Roseanne Benn and Jürgen Maaß (1999) that adults learning mathematics is an under-theorised domain which needs to draw upon as many relevant disciplines as possible in order to develop.

The three chapters following the review are offered as examples of different approaches to research on adults learning mathematics and draw on political, anthropological, psychological and educational theory in turn. In the first of these, Diana Coben discusses one of the issues that make research in this area problematic: the 'invisibility' of mathematics in many adults' lives and its elision with 'common sense'. Drawing on her research, with Gillian Thumpston, on the meaning of mathematics in adults' lives - their 'mathematics life histories' - she explores concepts of common sense developed by the Marxist theoretician and political leader Antonio Gramsci and the anthropologist Clifford Geertz, in an attempt to render the 'invisible' mathematics in adults' lives more visible to researchers and practitioners in the field.

In the next chapter, Juan Carlos Llorente describes his investigation, in Argentina, of the way housewives and domestic helps with little formal education constitute mathematical knowledge. He uses Piaget's theory of equilibration and the Piagetian technique of clinical exploration and his research indicates that these may offer a powerful tool for research in this area. Llorente's evidence suggests that adults (including those with little formal education) are able to transfer mathematical understanding from one context to another (a theme discussed further by Jeff Evans in this volume). In methodological terms, his research indicates that Piagetian clinical-critical exploration may offer a powerful and hitherto neglected tool for research in this area.

Section I concludes with Adrian Simpson and Janet Duffin's exploration of the tension between the cognitive and the affective in adults' thinking, based on their research with adult learners in England. They outline their attempt to classify learners' experiences and their response to those experiences, drawing on the work of the educationalist Richard Skemp, amongst others, and argue that the tension between the learner's cognitive and affective domains may be released by appropriate teaching.

In Section II, each contributor advances a social view of mathematics education for adults either explicitly or implicitly. A social perspective acknowledges as valid questions of values, power, social justice and responsibility. These concerns are evident in the individual chapters. Roseanne Benn is clearly motivated to achieve social justice and empowerment for adults through mathematics education. The notion of empowerment and greater beneficial participation in the information - laden society by adults is also a central issue for Iddo Gal. Statistical literacy is a key here. Social justice for Brazilian peasants is an explicit goal of Gelsa Knijnik's work using her ethnomathematics approach. Respect for learners in their everyday situations, and for their local knowledge is central to an ethnomathematics perspective, and plays a fundamental role in situated cognition. Dhamma Colwell discusses structure in everyday problem solving of adult women and how this structure is influenced by the feelings of the problem solver. Looking at this section as a whole one is struck by what might be described as the authors' desire to create more equitable forms of mathematics education for all adults.

Section III focuses on mathematical education for the workplace from both learners' and system perspectives. Mary Harris has shown that work carried on outside of the official labour market, particularly women's work, both productive and reproductive, although not factored into economists' models has nevertheless contained a great deal of mathematical knowledge, providing social as well as economic value. Tine Wedege's chapter argues that reforms in adult education must address the social nature of work, including the capacity to understand and modify technology. Considering objective as well as subjective perspectives on adult numeracy, she differentiates between the *a priori* definitions of qualifications and the notions of competency which are inextricably linked to people in a given context. Gail FitzSimons noted that the human capital paradigm has replaced that of social and personal development in recent decades, resulting in functionalist competency-based curricula in many Anglophone countries. Mathematics curricula appear to be based on rationalistic frameworks which are biased towards essentialism and fail to reflect both the changing nature of workplaces and recent research in mathematics education such as situated cognition (Lave, 1988; Lave & Wenger, 1991). Unlike countries such as Denmark there appears to be little official research interest in mathematics education for the workplace.

The final section, Section IV, confronts a variety of issues that arise in teaching mathematics to adults. There is a clear recognition that what works for children may not work for adults. In fact one is struck by the centrality of adults' interests and their needs in determining pedagogical approaches. These approaches are learner-centred, relate to learners' life experience, are heavily contextualized and appeal to learners' critical faculties. This selection of chapters deals with what may prove to be universal problems in adults' mathematics education namely, teaching specific topics, for example, algebra, developing appropriate assessments, applying mathematics. In any learner-centred pedagogy one would expect to see some signs of constructivism, so we are not surprised when Kathy Safford's research is based on a constructivist pedagogy. Barbara Miller-Reilly borrows from mainstream mathematics education and uses a realistic mathematics approach with her adult returners. John O'Donoghue, mindful of the pitfalls of traditional assessment approaches, seeks to adapt standard approaches for use with adult learners. Jeff Evans switches the focus from teaching to learning and explores issues surrounding the transfer of learning. Teaching mathematics to adults presupposes appropriate teacher education, but Diana Coben and Noyona Chanda reveal the parlous state of affairs in that respect in England. Their comparison with numeracy teacher development in Australia gives a glimpse of a more positive way forward. It is clear that practitioners and researchers have discovered that adult learners are indeed different in a multitude of ways that need to be recognised and harnessed for the improvement of adults' mathematics education. Finally, as a postscript, Diana Coben discusses the legacy for research and practice in the field of adults learning mathematics of the late Brazilian educationalist Paulo Freire.

It is evident that the researchers whose work appears between these covers are busy defining a new research domain through their individual and concerted efforts. It is early days yet to speculate on how this new field or sub-field of adults learning mathematics will develop. It is not the intention of the editors in this volume to impose a shape on this emerging field but rather to show how it is developing and to indicate some of the directions it is taking. However, it seems clear, even at this early stage that this new field cannot be other than interdisciplinary in nature, offering as it does, multiple perspectives on adults learning mathematics. This attribute places a special onus on researchers to explain their respective platforms so that there can be informed debate on their work. On the other hand the enormity of this global enterprise, adult mathematics education, and its diversity demands a very broad interpretation of education and mathematics education in particular. But such an interpretation must be given form if it is to be useful as an organising framework. There may be potential in adapting Alan Bishop's (1993) framework for mathematics education, in which he separates Formal Mathematics Education (FME) from Non-formal Mathematics Education (NFME) and Informal Mathematics Education (IFME). Such frameworks, if they gain currency, would provide 'tools to think with' for researchers working with adults learning mathematics. It is hoped that readers will find just such 'tools to think with' in this book.

REFERENCES

Beaton, A., Mullis, I., Martin, M., Gonzalez, E., Kelly, D., and Smith, T. (1996) *Mathematics Achievement in the Middle School Years: IEA's Third International Mathematics and Science Study (TIMMS)*. Boston: International Association for the Evaluation of Educational Achievement (IEA).

Benn, R. (1997). *Adults count too: Mathematics for empowerment*. Leicester, UK: National Institute of Adult Continuing Education (NIACE).

Billett, S. (1998). 'Transfer and social practice'. *Australian & New Zealand Journal of Vocational Education Research*, 6(1), 1-25.

Bishop, A. (1997). Introduction. In G.E. FitzSimons (Ed), *Adults returning to study: Papers from working Group 18, 8th International Congress on Mathematical Education, ICME 8*. Adelaide, SA: Australian Association of Mathematics Teachers, 3.

Bishop, A. J (1993). 'Influences from society'. In A. J. Bishop, K. Hart, S. Lerman & T. Nunes, *Significant influences on children's learning of mathematics*. Paris: UNESCO. (Science and Technology Education, Document Series No. 47), 3-26.

Ellerton, N. F. & Clements, M.A. (1998).' Transforming the international mathematics education research agenda'. In A. Sierpinska & J. Kilpatrick (Eds*), Mathematics education as a research domain: A search for identity*. Dordrecht: Kluwer Academic Publishers, 153-173.

Ernest, P. (1998) 'A postmodern perspective on research in mathematics education'. In A. Sierpinska & J. Kilpatrick (Eds), *Mathematics education as a research domain : A search for identity*. Dordrecht: Kluwer Academic Publishers, 71-85.

Ernest, P. (1998a) 'Mathematical knowledge and context'. In A. Watson (Ed.), *Situated cognition and the learning of mathematics*. Oxford: Centre for Mathematics Education Research, University of Oxford, 13-31.

Ernest, P. (1998b) 'Why teach mathematics? - The justification problem in mathematics education'. In J. H. Jensen, M. Niss & T. Wedege (Eds.), *Justification and enrolment problems in education involving mathematics or physics.* Roskilde: Roskilde University Press, 33-55.

Evans, J. & Thorstad, I. (1995) ' Mathematics and numeracy in the practice of critical citizenship'. In D. Coben (Comp) *Proceedings of the Inaugural Conference of Adults Learning Mathematics - A Research Forum* (ALM-1). London: Goldsmiths College, University of London, 64-70.

Fischer, R. (1993). 'Mathematics as a means and as a system'. In S. Restivo, J. P. van Bendegem & R. Fischer (Eds.), *Math worlds: Philosophical and social studies of mathematics and mathematics education.* New York: State University of New York Press, 113-133.

FitzSimons, G. E., Jungwirth, H., Maaß, J. & Schloeglmann, W. (1996). 'Adults and mathematics (Adult numeracy)'. In A. J. Bishop, K. Clements, C. Keitel, J. Kilpatrick & C. Laborde (Eds.), *International handbook of mathematics education.* Dordrecht: Kluwer, 755-784.

Frankenstein, M. (1996).'Critical mathematical literacy: Teaching through real real-life math world problems'. In T. Kjærgård, A. Kvamme, & N. Lindén (Eds.), *Numeracy, race, gender, and class: Proceedings of the third international conference on the Political Dimensions of Mathematics Education* (PDME III).Landås, Norway:Caspar Forlag,59-76.

Houtkoop, W. & Jones, S. (1999) 'Adult Numeracy: an international comparison'. In: M.van Groenestijn & D. Coben (comps) *Mathematics as Part of Adult Learning. Proceedings of the Fifth International Conference of Adults Learning Maths – Research Forum (ALM-5),* held at Utrecht, The Netherlands, 1-2-3 July 1998. London: Goldsmiths College, University of London in association with ALM, 32-40

Hülsmann, H. (1985). *Die technologische Formation-oder: Lasset uns Menschen machen.* Berlin Verlag Europaeische Perspektiven.

Keitel, C., Kotzmann, E. & Skovsmose, O. (1993) 'Beyond the tunnel vision: Analysing the relationships between mathematics, society and technology'. In C. Keitel & K. Ruthven (Eds.), *Learning from computers: Mathematics education and technology.* Berlin: Springer Verlag, 243-279.

Lave, J. (1988). *Cognition in practice: Mind, mathematics and culture in every day life.* Cambridge: Cambridge University Press.

Lave, J. & Wenger, E. (1991). *Situated learning: Legitimate peripheral participation.* Cambridge: Cambridge University Press.

Noss, R. (1997). *New cultures, new numeracies.* Inaugural professorial lecture. London: Institute of Education, University of London.

Noss, R. & Hoyles, C. (1996). 'The visibility of meanings: Modelling the mathematics of banking'. *International Journal of Computers for Mathematical Learning,* 1(1), 3-31.

OECD and Human Resources Development Canada and Minister of Industry, Canada (1997) *Literacy Skills for the Knowledge Society. Further Results from the International Adult Literacy Survey.* Paris: Organisation for Economic Co-operation and Development (cited as 'OECD, 1997')

Skovsmose, O. (1996) Meaning in mathematics education. BACOMET Research Report No. 4: Meaning and Communication in Mathematics Education.

Tight, M. (1996). *Key concepts in adult education and training.* London & New York: Routledge.

Wedege, T., Benn, R. & Maaß, J. (1998). '"Adults learning mathematics" as a community of practice and research'. In M. van Groenestijn & D. Coben (Comp), *Proceedings of the*

Fifth International Conference of Adults Learning Mathematics : A Research Forum (ALM-5*)*. London: Goldsmiths College, University of London, 54-63.

Withnall, A. (1995). 'Towards a definition of numeracy'. In D. Coben (Comp), *Proceedings of the Inaugural Conference of Adults Learning Mathematics - A Research Forum* (ALM-1). London: Goldsmiths College, University of London, 11-17.

Chapter 2

Review of Research on Adults Learning Mathematics

Gail E. FitzSimons & Gail L. Godden
Monash University/Swinburne University of Technology, Victoria, Australia / Central Queensland University, Australia

INTRODUCTION

This chapter will comprise two major sections, taking perspectives from the adult learner's background and more particularly their foreground. It will be structured by a focus on the knowledge interests intended to be served in the mutually interdependent arenas of decision-making which concern the adult learner of mathematics. These are analytically: (a) the macro- or institutional level, including political, social, economic, and cultural interests of government, also educational and mathematical institutions; (b) the meso- or structural level, including sites of learning and using mathematics, such as classroom, workplace, home; and (c) the micro- or personal operational or subjective level (Kogan & Tuijnman, 1995). A special section on the needs of adults enrolled at university will also be included.

This review of research is limited, for reasons of space, to English-language publications, the majority of which relate to studies conducted in the richer, more industrially developed parts of the world, especially North America, Europe and Australasia. The picture of research on adults learning mathematics that results is inevitably partial and incomplete. Nevertheless, we have attempted to be as comprehensive as possible in our coverage of extant research published in English, while highlighting areas where further research is needed. For reasons of space, it will be assumed that the reader is informed about general adult education issues. Thus this chapter will focus primarily on issues which impact on the *mathematics* education of adults.

D. Coben et al. (eds.), Perspectives on Adults Learning Mathematics, 13–45.

Who is an Adult Learner?

FitzSimons, Jungwirth, Maaß, and Schloeglmann (1996) characterised the field of adults and mathematics as having "great heterogeneity." Consistent with postmodernist discourse (e.g. Harvey, 1989), Wedege (1998) asserted that this is due to lack of a "grand narrative" concerning adults and mathematics and the great complexity of the subject.

The definition of an adult learner is nebulous, and revolves around the student, not the level of mathematics being studied, varying from country to country. Knowles (1990) argued that there are four definitions of the term *adult*: biological, legal, social, and psychological. The last occurs at a point where self-direction comes into operation and is, he claimed, the most crucial from the viewpoint of learning. In this chapter adults are taken to be those persons who are of an age or status where education is post-compulsory in their particular society. For some adults, this may be their first formal experience of mathematics education; for others there may be a break of at least one year, possibly decades, since their last formal study of mathematics. For some it may be a matter of choice, even of completing 'unfinished business'; for others there may be some coercion.

THE ADULT LEARNER OF MATHEMATICS: BACKGROUND

Influential Institutions

In countries around the world governments are experiencing the pressures of a globalised economy; many are informed by neoliberal ideologies associated with economic rationalism. Industries are beginning to appreciate the need to move from outdated Fordist production-line work practices and Taylorist management practices to a new work order where value is placed on human capital as well as plant and equipment. Accordingly, there is a renewed focus on the education of adults in conjunction with workplace reform.

Although the institution of education is seen, especially in recent decades, as a means of increasing the economic (and social) wealth of a nation (e.g. Faure et al., 1972; Delors, 1996), it has also served other purposes related to social (re)production (see Harris, this volume). Positionings impact on the histories of adult learners who are returning to study, and may be linked to the gatekeeping role of mathematics.

Mathematics is seen by many as an exclusive discipline. The public image of mathematics is as cold, abstract, inhuman, and related to absolutist, infallible philosophies (Ernest, 1995). It is regarded by sections of business and industry as well as governments as a high-status commodity, ultimately convertible into profits and control (Apple, 1992). The discipline is seen as a masculine domain suitable for those who are "rational, emotionally detached, instrumental, and competitive" (Martin, 1988/1997:165), and it is these aspects which appear to give added credibility to mathematical models. It is frequently assumed to be value- and culture-free, and yet the three pairs of values (rationalism/objectism, openness/mystery, and progress/control) discussed by Bishop (1988) have been valorised by those within the discipline while alienating many of those external to it. Certainly the role of mathematics underpinning technology has not been unproblematic and, as Jungwirth (1993) pointed out, women's distancing themselves from it is not necessarily irrational. Mathematics ability is often taken as proxy for intelligence (Cockcroft, 1982); the subject is frequently seen as an obstacle (often dreaded), as hard work and as having relevance only to itself.

Social Sites of Mathematics Activity

Although it is recognised that there is an interplay between agency and structure, this section will focus on the latter. Throughout their prior experiences of formal education, adult learners have been positioned by practices of curriculum (Popkewitz, 1997), pedagogies and psychologies about mathematical reasoning and learning (Popkewitz, 1988; Walkerdine, 1994), and textbooks (Dowling, 1998). These practices are not neutral but reflect larger economic, cultural and political considerations which contribute to individuals' memories of social divisions (e.g. class, race, ethnicity, gender) amplified in classroom experiences, and reflected in mathematics learning histories (e.g. Coben, this volume; FitzSimons, 1994b; 1995). Learners come into the mathematics classroom with multiple, overlapping subjectivities, with different aspects of these called up by a range of classroom practices (Evans, 1995, (2000); Lerman, 1998). At the same time new subjectivities are created by the activities of the classroom (Klein, 1998). According to Walkerdine (1994), the tradition of suppressing reference in formal education has encouraged learners to disembed context and forget meaning in an attempt to universalise logical reasoning. For many adult learners mathematics in school was characterised instead by low-level activity and rule-following, with tragic results.

Social structures continue to play a pivotal role in the education of adults (Godden & Pegg, 1993b; Kasworm, 1990). Methods of instruction which focus on technique and lack any overview, connectedness or historicity, together with an absence of community and manifestations of competitiveness rather than co-operation are discouraging to adult learners (Tobias, 1990). In the Adult basic education (ABE) and vocational education and training (VET) sectors there is ample evidence of innovatory practice appropriate to the needs of adult learners (e.g. FitzSimons (Ed.), 1997; annual proceedings of ALM, e.g. ALM-1, 1995 to ALM-5, 1999). Nevertheless, adult classes pursuing a narrow focus on explication, rote-learning, drill and practice, divorced from real-world relevance and ignoring the learners' experiences are also common (Cumming, in press; Nesbit, 1995). It has been argued that teaching approaches which attempt to incorporate the learner's perspective, such as constructivism and activity theory (e.g. FitzSimons, 1993 March; 1993a; Gordon, 1993, 1995) can help to provide adults with self-confidence. However, Klein (1998) warned that constructivist epistemologies may not take into account the socio-cultural and political contexts in which the learning takes place.

Research carried out by Lave (1988), Lave and Wenger (1991), and others illustrates dramatically the effect of context on mathematical tasks. Yet, in the workplace, as in everyday life, it is commonly reported that, from the perspective of mathematicians, adults are using complicated mathematical ideas and techniques, but seemingly unaware of their signification in mathematical terms (AAMT, 1997; Coben, this volume; Cockcroft, 1982; Foyster, 1988; Harris, 1991; Masingila, 1993; Zevenbergen, 1996). The social domain, together with workplace artefacts, is critical in providing support for the successful accomplishment of tasks (Kanes, 1997a, 1997b; Pozzi, Noss, & Hoyles, 1998). There is a large difference between the application-based, problem-solving approach required on the job and the usual tightly focused set of basic skills in training curricula (Buckingham, 1997; FitzSimons, 1998; Foyster, 1990; Harris, 1991; Straesser, 1998; Strässer, Barr, Evans & Wolf, 1991). O'Connor (1994) claimed that definitions of innumeracy in the workplace are ideologically loaded, and further add to the disadvantage of certain groups in terms of gender, race, class, and so on. Skills audits which include mathematics testing could further exacerbate existing inequities (Lord, 1991). Harris's work (1987; this volume) with women in the textile industry provides an example of how workers' (invisible) skills may be recognised. See also Gowen (1992) for discussion of politics and complexities in a workplace and their effect on delivery of programmes.

Having briefly addressed some institutional and structural considerations, we turn to focus on the personal, subjective concerns of the adult learner, particularly in relation to mathematics.

Socio-psychological Considerations

There is a plethora of general research into adults returning to study; for example, that related to role conflict (Kasworm, 1990), timing (Mohney & Anderson, 1988), and triggering life events (Sewall, 1982, 1983, cited in Kasworm, 1990). Many studies have focused on implied deficiencies of adult learners (e.g. Kasworm, 1990; Fredrick, Mishler & Hogan, 1984; Lunneborg, Olch & de Wolf, 1974; Sewall, 1984; Suddick & Collins, 1984, 1986; Swindell, 1995). Prior educational experiences are important for levels of performance (Fagin, 1971) and as the single best predictor of late life participation (Swindell, 1995). Not surprisingly, Galbraith (1990), Miller-Reilly (1997), and Wolfgang and Dowling (1981) observed different patterns of study and motivation between younger and older adults. Summarising the findings of her meta-analysis on adult undergraduates in higher education, Kasworm (1990:364) stated that: "Chronological age is the not the key variable." Rather, life experience (including education) reflecting sociocultural contexts and psychological development and expectations are more important.

Apart from considerations of age, underpreparation (or ill-preparation) of adult students is a serious issue, especially at the tertiary level (Boylan & Bonham, 1994; Godden, 1992; Stonehocker, 1985; Tomlinson, 1989). Fragmented curricula and the teaching-learning styles at school tend to encourage memorising techniques (especially for examinations) and rule-based learning (Barnes, 1990; Blackburn, 1984; Coady & Pegg, 1991; Hubbard, 1986; Narode, 1989) - as shown by diagnostic testing results (e.g. Berenson, Best, Stiff & Wasik 1990). (See also Coben, 1997, this volume; Noss, Hoyles & Pozzi, in press.)

Mature-age females are often reported as low in confidence (e.g. Crawford-Nutt 1987), coming from backgrounds lacking in educational opportunity (see also, FitzSimons 1993 March, 1993a, 1995 July). Clearly the affective domain is a critical influence on adult learners, and their background experiences have helped to construct their attitudes and beliefs (Taylor, 1994, 1995, 1997). Other surveys of attitudes and beliefs of mature-age students have been conducted (e.g. Agar & Knopfmacher, 1995; Crawford, Gordon, Nicholas & Prosser, 1994; FitzSimons, 1994a; Gordon & Nicholas, 1992).

Related to confidence is the self-perception of the learner about their own ability to learn. Davis (1996) argued that it may not be possible for many people to ever learn mathematics easily and effectively, or to find it interesting. Leder (1991, 1993) provided an example of the difficulties faced by competent adult learners when processing teachers' explanations in mathematics. Wedege (in press) used Bourdieu's concept of 'habitus' to analyse the contexts for knowing and learning mathematics from adults' experiences and perspectives, in order to make sense of the apparent contradiction between many adults being blocked in relation to mathematics in formal settings while being competent in their everyday life. However, Skovsmose (1996) argued that dispositions may change (see next section). For research in relation to older people see also Swindell (1995) and Withnall's (1995) pilot study.

Linked to attributions to success (Lehmann, 1987) are the concepts of self-efficacy and mathematics anxiety (Pitney, 1991). Hembree's (1990) meta-analytic study found that mathematics anxiety seems to be a learned condition, more behavioural than cognitive in its nature. Dossel (1993) suggested a range of contributing factors related to previous educational experiences (see also FitzSimons, 1994b, 1995 July). Following the seminal work of Tobias (1978/1993) there have been many successful programmes directly or indirectly helping to overcome mathematics anxiety, for example: Burton (1987), Buxton (1981), Crawford-Nutt (1987), Narode (1989), Shaw (1993), and Tobias (1987).

Having examined the literature which provided perspectives on the background of the adult learner in mathematics, we now turn to considerations of foreground from individual, learning site, and broader institutional considerations.

THE ADULT LEARNER OF MATHEMATICS: FOREGROUND

Introduction

'Foreground of the student' is described as the set of opportunities which the student's interpretation of her socially determined opportunities reveals as 'real' opportunities. In this way, a foreground is a subjective mediated socially determined fact. The foreground of the acting person is an important source for understanding an action. In a similar way, the foreground of a learning person is an important parameter in understanding the learning process. (Skovsmose, 1996:1)

Skovsmose continued that in a cyclical process, dispositions become changed through reflections on intentions and actions, and their consequences (intended and unintended).

Individual Considerations

The decision to return to study is intentional, and is made for a complex range of reasons which are not always articulated and which may themselves be in tension. Adults attending college or university do not see this as an end in itself but as a means of achieving future change or coping with changes that have already occurred (Spanard, 1990). Adults have "reasonably high educational aspirations and a relatively strong commitment to higher education" (Smart & Pascarella, 1987:319).

The concept of lifelong learning has been espoused by many governments. For lifelong education to become a reality it is critical that people have the ability to learn how to learn - something which cannot be taken for granted from the schooling adults may have received in the past. In a review of literature, van Aardt and van Wyk (1991: 316) identified three categories of learning strategies: "cognitive, metacognitive and resource management strategies". Students need assistance to develop learning strategies, as well as with the tasks and content itself. Surman and Galligan (1993) concluded that adult students require the opportunity for careful reflection, analysis, and reporting on mathematical knowledge and behaviours in order to develop deep approaches to learning, personal construction of knowledge, and explicit metacognition strategies. Cantwell and Beamish (1994) identified three belief systems of higher-order self-regulation in nursing and education students, finding: (a) a positive correlation between identified active metacognition of planning and processing (adaptive self-regulation), and academic success; (b) a negative correlation between identified inflexibility of approach (even in the presence of conflicting information) and academic performance; and (c) a negative correlation between inability to attempt something new and the presence of learning outcomes (see Simpson & Duffin, this volume).

Adults' motivation to learn is a crucial component of their foreground. A number of authors have noted that adults who have begun to learn mathematics again at an older age, even if they were not thoroughly enjoying the experience, were proud of their capabilities and progress. From their study of one set of ABE classrooms, Mullinix and Comings (1994) concluded that the high level of motivation in the students as full partners in the process should be used as a basis on which to improve their learning, grounded in their rich experiences. Enjoyment and achievement are often mentioned as necessary, as well as experiential learning (e.g. Tout & Marr, 1997). According to Nordstrom (1989) a major theme in the continuing education literature is that adult learners are concerned with maintaining a positive self-concept; although adult learners tend to be highly motivated to learn, they lack confidence in their ability to do so and require continuing encouragement. Hashway, Duke and Farmer (1993) found that, for young adults, goal-oriented self-determinism is the most important factor in their personal approach to education.

Sometimes adults unintentionally experience a change in attitude towards mathematics or form new study intentions after confidence-boosting exposure to programmes such as Family Maths (Horne, 1998) or return-to-study courses. There exists anecdotal evidence of mature age students continuing on with mathematics degrees and lecturing in mathematics teacher education, reflecting changes in study or career goals.

Mature-age students have family and work pressures complicating their studies, and possibly financial worries contributing to the anxiety many already feel because of their return to study - bringing on self-doubts in some (e.g. Boylan & Bonham, 1994; Wall, Sersland & Hoban, 1996). Situational barriers, especially for older students, include lack of mobility, insufficient knowledge of educational opportunities, and possible costs (Cross, 1981, cited in Swindell, 1995).

The practice of adult education has to a large extent been associated with a humanistic approach. Typical recommendations are for the educator to provide an atmosphere conducive to learning including a warm, supportive environment; identify the learner's needs and interests; emphasise interaction among participants; de-emphasise or eliminate grading; and to try to accommodate individual learning styles. However, this approach has been criticised (e.g. Benn, 1997) for failing to be emancipatory, merely changing the form of regulation while maintaining the power, knowledge, and authority of the discourse. Critical theorists, focusing on social and institutional structures, attempt to provoke change to overcome forms of oppression as they see it (e.g. Evans & Thorstad, 1995; Frankenstein, 1989, 1996; Yasukawa, Johnston & Yates, 1995). However, Ellsworth (1989) argued in a critique of critical pedagogy for college students that it may ultimately fail to be empowering if teachers fail to contextualise issues historically or politically. She maintains that the discourse of critical pedagogy is based on rationalist assumptions that give rise to repressive myths. Freire (1976) recommended that educators refrain from imposing their values on learners, and see themselves as co-learners, learning about the culture of the people among whom they are working, mutually responsible for growth and change.

We now turn to the meso- or structural level of the social sites of mathematics teaching and learning.

Teaching and Learning: Classroom and Workplace Considerations

In these sites of learning, it is important to consider adults' participation in the discourse of mathematics through continuous learning; and the possibilities for participation in democratic decision-making processes, both in the workplace and in society at large.

According to Knowles (1990), the term *andragogy* was coined in Europe in 1833. He first understood it as the "art and science of helping adults learn" (1990:54) and differentiated it from *pedagogy*, the theory of youth learning, where the teachers tend to assume full responsibility for decisions about learning thereby placing the learner in a state of dependency. More recently his model of andragogy has become a system of assumptions which *may* include those drawn from the pedagogical ideology, but not vice versa. Knowles recommended that teachers of adults be aware that there are differences in adults' educational and other backgrounds, formative experiences, self-concept, readiness to learn, orientation and approaches to learning, and motivation. Cranton (1992:16) exhorted:

> it is essential for all professionals to reflect critically on their practice, to be aware of their own values and assumptions, to make responsible choices based on their expertise and values, and through critical thought, become aware of and develop their philosophy of practice.

Lerman (1998), however, was critical of the notion of reflective practice, suggesting that it perpetuates the notion of an autonomous teacher, free of coercion from external influences such as government rhetoric. As discussed above, this is not necessarily a valid assumption in times of economic rationalism. Lerman (1998:41) recommended that, in a postmodernist society, teacher education should "encourage the expression of difference; teach methods of critique of orthodoxies of mathematics and mathematics education; and encourage theorising about the teaching and learning of mathematics". It could be argued that much of teacher education is about teaching adults, and Lerman's words find resonance with many papers on adult education (e.g. Bagnall, 1994).

Teaching styles are crucial in the education of adults. Gordon (1993) warned that the traditional lecture approach and assessment practices for teaching statistics in universities were precluding some mature-age students from being able to learn effectively. According to Gordon (1993, 1994, 1995), activity theory differs from constructivism in that it emphasises the interdependence of socio-cultural and cognitive perspectives. Barnes (1994: 1) also suggested taking into consideration the student's goals, values, and beliefs about the nature and purpose of mathematics: "If the student believes that mathematics is not meant to make sense, s/he may not be surprised or concerned about conflict". She advised educators to deliberately seek to find out where their students' misconceptions are, in a non-threatening environment, through listening and reflecting on what we hear - "and to 'de-centre', that is, put ourselves in the student's position and try to see things from her or his perspective" (1994:9). To address the problem of compartmentalisation by students, Hubbard (1994) suggested helping students to relate different topics in as many ways as possible reflecting the practice of problem solving where frequently several different topics need to be integrated to produce a solution.

Statistical literacy is one area of knowledge in the broader mathematics arena visible in everyday life. Gal (1997; this volume) advocated moving beyond basic descriptive statistics topics, which remain largely irrelevant to learners, to demonstration of techniques which enable students to be better informed citizens who are confident to challenge assertions made by public figures. Ginsburg and Gal (1997) stressed the importance of developing adults' interpretive skills, building on their substantial informal knowledge, and suggested the use of authentic texts with genuine purposes.

With nursing education no longer based in hospitals but in universities in a number of countries, there has been an increasing effort to assist trainee nurses to cope with needed mathematics skills (e.g. Coben & Atere-Roberts, 1996; Gillies, 1991). Gillies (1994) has strongly advised that the use of demonstration and "hands-on" experience are essential before teaching of formulae for drug dosage. An experiential approach, together with assistance given to students struggling with these skills, is necessary to prevent the errors occurring in this important practical field (see also Noss, Pozzi & Hoyles, in press). On-the-job experience is necessary, according to Billett (1998), to overcome problems which arise from the assumption that knowledge provided to students at the socio-cultural level is inherently transferable across a range of communities of practice (see also Wolf, Silver & Kelson, 1990).

Assessment is a major issue, particularly in the case of mathematics, in relation to competition to obtain and retain jobs and careers (Wall, Sersland & Hoban, 1996). In Ireland O'Donoghue (1997; this volume) developed a self-paced mastery system of learning which is assessment-driven. Learners can sit the mastery test if they believe they know the material and, if successful, move on. Thus the student has a degree of control over what and when they are learning. Whilst the idea of self-paced mastery learning is not new, its use appears to have increased with adults in recent years. For example, Coady's students studying a service statistics subject at tertiary level have benefited from this approach (Godden & Coady, 1997).

Taylor and Mander (1997) described the use of diagnostic tests, in a self-paced programme, to screen and sort students in bridging mathematics programmes before entering the mainstream courses. However, Johnson and Elliot (1998) warn that the widespread use of diagnostic tests, intended to target appropriate mathematics support, represents a deficit model which can be potentially disempowering for students when the control over their engagement actually rests firmly with the institution, not the learner. In this case, "the emphasis remains on the need to acquire the specific mathematical knowledge and skills, rather than on the development of independent learning skills which might enable students to regain control of their own learning of mathematics". (Johnson & Elliott , 1998:119)

McRae (1995) described a contextually based method of assessing students entering ABE programmes, on a one-to-one basis. Her method reflected a radical constructivist view and allowed for active participation by the student, acknowledging their prior knowledge and experience, while at the same time providing information to the student about the class (see also Cumming, in press). Wedege (1997) discussed a Danish project *Profile in Mathematics* designed to develop appropriate guidance material for students and teachers, enhancing capacities in everyday and working life.

Cumming (1995:6) noted that "the most important factors relating to assessment are the recognition of complex reasoning, the complexity of content for both learning and performance and the need to match assessment with learning and purpose." Clarke and Helme (1993) highlighted the distinction between the situation and the context of a mathematics task. When presented with a typical 'school mathematics' task of designing a five-room apartment with a given area, an adult male responded by drawing a large rectangle enclosing five similar rectangles. His construal of the task was as a test-like situation, and he freely admitted that this was not the way he would think of planning an extension to his house. Following Evans's (1995) discourse analysis, it could be argued that he felt positioned as a student in the practice of academic mathematics, and had focused on the practice of school mathematics. Had he felt positioned as the prospective client of an architect he would have chosen to call up the practical mathematics (and other) skills at his disposal in this assessment task.

Technology issues are assuming increasing importance in the foreground of students. Boers and Jones (1992) investigated the use of graphics calculators in examinations, and found that females performed better than males where there was an expectation that graphics calculators would be used in some questions. Boers and Jones (1994) found that there was a difficulty for students in having algebraic, graphical, and numeric approaches viewed together; students' conceptual levels were actually required to be at a (rather high) relational level in order to deal with all this information at once, thus favouring the more able, flexible thinkers. There is a clear warning that appropriate questions need to be set when using technology and that possible implications must be considered beforehand.

Maaß (1998) explored some of the issues associated with technology transfer at the university level. Taking into account social and economic contexts, the question becomes one of transfer of meaning: mathematical theories must be transformed into other technologies (e.g. computer programmes) before they can be useful in industry. Drawing on the work of a 1988 conference in Austria, he emphasised that the relationship between mathematics and technology faces the problem that mathematics is not an empirical science. Hülsmann (1989, cited in Maaß) believed that the formal aspects of technology rather than the formative aspects tend to be stressed. Thus, Keitel, Kotzmann and Skovsmose (1993:271) recommended that:

> understanding technology and evaluating or criticizing its impact and function, demands . . . *a meta-level of knowledge*. . . . Reflective knowledge does not have its epistemological basis in technological and pragmatic knowledge. Neither can technological knowledge be reduced to mathematical knowledge, an idea which is expressed in an educational context as: when you learn mathematics you also learn how to apply it.

They distinguished analytically six different levels of reflective thinking, ranging from a focus on the mathematical tool, through the relationship between means and ends, to the global impact of using formal techniques and about the evaluation process as such.

Clearly the use of technology will become more pervasive, and the issues are complex and far reaching - more than space will allow in this chapter. Adult educators need to be discerning in their appropriation of its artefacts, not only in terms of access and equity for students. As indicated by Keitel et al. (1993), a critical approach is needed to determine whether the use of technology is necessary in the first place. Secondly, the didactical values need to be assessed against teachers' goals and more broadly against research on pedagogical content and reasoning (Balacheff, 1993).

Related more and more to the use of technology, a student's literacy level is important to their mathematical expertise (Pitney 1991). Galbraith (1990:142) advised that "reading ability, mathematical readability of text material, the nature of mathematical language, and the way learners process information" were important to a student's (mathematics) learning potential. Much research in the literacy arena is also applicable to mathematics. Cope and Kalantzis (1998) emphasised three factors contributing to the need for increased levels of written, visual and numerate communication skills in vocational education and training: (a) newer systems of training replacing the hands-on, apprenticeship model, (b) technological and organisational developments in the workplace, and (c) the increasing use of flexible delivery and distance education modes generating new forms of texts. Groenestijn (1998), O'Donoghue (1997, this volume), Pickard and Cock (1997), and Vanhille and D'Halluin (1997) provide examples of research-based approaches to open learning situations for adults returning to study mathematics.

Journal writing has been used in a number of areas of mathematics instruction in recent years (e.g. FitzSimons 1993a, 1994b). Assessment of journals is a further step which some teachers have used as a metacognitive tool to elicit their students' reflection on the mathematics and their learning of it, thus furthering students' cognitive and affective understandings.

Recognising the substantial accomplishments of illiterate and semi-literate adults, Groenestijn (1997) articulated two important principles for their teaching: (a) it must be based on and applicable to actual real life situations, especially in the beginning of a course; and (b) the starting points must be the informal strategies already developed by these students. She outlined four phases of the didactical process to enable these students to progress towards coping with assignments on paper, leading to functional and flexible knowledge and skills. These are to: (a) begin with an actual situation, or at least to use real materials in the classroom to enable students to verbalise and explain their mathematical thoughts; (b) enable students to combine representations of real life material with their informal formulae; (c) enable students to replace representations of actual situations with visual, cognitive, more abstract models as they learn to develop functional notation systems; and (d) ensure that students can use formulae independently of visual supports in functional, actual situations.

At university, Wood and Perrett (1997) asserted that, in particular, students from certain gender, class, and national backgrounds which in earlier times would have made university entry difficult are likely to need to be helped with manipulating the discourse of mathematics while developing a deeper understanding of the concepts.

Not all education takes place in regular classrooms or community settings. Newman, Lewis and Beverstock (1994) reported that there is evidence to suggest that dealing with the illiteracy problem in prisons would contribute to counteracting the increasing level of crime, and limit prison costs. Adult teaching approaches should be linked to other aspects of education (i.e., social) in an holistic manner. Learning contracts and peer-tutoring have been flagged as effective in this setting. Halliday (1997) described her experience of setting up a mathematics refresher course for the inmates of a New Zealand prison in a way that was sensitive to the needs of the mix of ethnic groups. In particular, *"The basic principle in Maori thought is that the group is all important*" (quoted in Halliday, 1997:85; italics in the original).

Ward (1997) described her experience as a literacy teacher taking on the teaching of numeracy in the system of vocational education and training available to people who have learning impairments, physical disabilities, mental health difficulties, or any combination of these. She was critical of the tendency to impose a hierarchical curriculum structure on students in this group and restricting their education to manual computations. Her study showed that learning disabled students who had never encountered higher order thinking skills in a formal setting were able to master these in the required time as part of an holistic programme. Education systems need to recognise that all students need access to skills necessary to function as adults, according to Ward. Elsy (1995), discussing some of the issues confronting those who wish to undertake research in a special hospital, noted that although the respondents were very positive about their second chance to learn mathematics, they faced other problems such as the effects of medication on thinking and memory. As with all non-educational closed institutions, a major problem is lack of continuity due to factors beyond the control of the student.

Investigating the workplace culture and views of workers (many of whom were immigrants) in a light-metal manufacturing plant, Buckingham (1997) found that most had a strong sense of their work environment developed over time. They were generally keen on learning, especially when they realised major changes were imminent in their industry's structure. Functional mathematical skills in the workplace ranged from (a) routine basic numeracy, through (b) monitoring and maintenance, to (c) problem solving, planning and projection. Institutional barriers to participation by workers were identified by Buckingham as arising predominantly arising from the selective listening by management who made prior assumptions about the capability of each to make a useful contribution.

Institutional and Broader Social Considerations

Although the notion of lifelong learning was posited by Dewey, together with the importance of experiential learning, the concept was first given prominence by the UNESCO commissioned report (Faure et al., 1972) which emphasised the dual ideas of lifelong education and a learning society. Whatever the previous educational uptake and intellectual abilities of the person, the rapidly changing economic and social circumstances of our society require that education be seen as a lifelong endeavour, removed from particularities of time and location. It recognised the need for optimisation of professional mobility as well as the development of personal interests in education of the self, in order to develop and maintain a sense of personal agency in areas such as reason, creativity, democratic competence, and a spirit of social responsibility. However, over the last three decades the concept of lifelong learning has been increasingly appropriated by the discourses of economic rationalism (e.g. Marginson, 1997; Rubenson, 1995).

Discussing foregrounds for workplace education, Wedege (1995, this volume) defined three kinds of technological competence required in the workplace: professional, social, and democratic. These are resonant with Onstenk's (1998) notion of broad occupational competence. Workplace education and training calls for a complex array of skills and invites a more integrated and connected process than the current hierarchical, linear, modularised courses common in many countries (Achtenhagen, 1994; Brown, 1998). (See also FitzSimons, this volume.)

A serious institutional issue confronting adult education in mathematics is the provision of qualified staff. For example, in the US, Mullinix and Comings (1994) found that in ABE there was a very high proportion of part-time teachers, with little experience in teaching mathematics and/or adults (see also Gal & Schuh, 1994). In addition teachers' experiences of mathematics at school were often quite negative. Collaboration in teaching (i.e. with other instructors in a similar position) and in learning were found to be issues important to future progress. In Australia, Tout and Marr (1997) claimed that most of the ABE workers in Australia have been female, and that there has been very little professional development in the past, although this is beginning to change. They asserted that literacy teachers, although often poor in mathematics background themselves are often effective basic mathematics education teachers because of their empathy with the students. By contrast, qualified mathematics teachers may need to become aware of how they were taught themselves (usually following a transmission paradigm), and to work to find new ways. Ongoing professional development is essential, not only for teachers of ABE, but for all who work with adult learners of mathematics. Coben and Chanda (this volume) report problems with the training and qualifications available to adult numeracy teachers in England.

Special Needs of Adults Enrolled at University: Bridging Mathematics

The literature reviewed thus far has been compiled from studies pertaining to adults at all educational levels. However this section will focus on a subgroup which faces a particular set of issues: adults enrolled at university.

Mathematics is so pervasive that most university courses require, often implicitly, at least basic algebra and often more. Many students are literally shocked to find that a degree such as nursing or human resource management not only assumes pre-requisite mathematics but makes actual explicit demands in the course, including statistics (e.g. Australia: Gillies 1991, Gordon 1994, Taffe 1984; South Africa: Crawford-Nutt 1987; UK: Watkins 1997; US: Capps 1984; Germany: Kurz 1990). Students who may well have avoided mathematics in choosing their area of study are now forced to confront it.

Godden (1992), in a comprehensive synthesis of the international literature (English language only), showed that responses by institutions are as varied as the personalities within the institutions themselves. Bridging (or developmental) programmes, foundation or access years (e.g. Beilby, 1990), drop-in centres (e.g. Barnes, 1990), concurrent assistance within the course itself (e.g. Barling & Jones, 1991), math(s) labs (e.g. Brown, 1975, Guedes & Zandonadi, 1998), and peer tutoring systems are just some of the myriad of ways assistance is offered to students struggling with pre-requisite and on-going mathematics. Some come under separate administrative structures within the university; others may be linked to a mathematics department, literacy, or counselling bodies. A centre must have great strength to remain viable as a separate entity. However, many of these settings suffer from inadequate resources, including time and personnel.

A major reason for these individualised approaches is the marginal nature of this entire area of teaching and learning mathematics. Literacy education led the move to consolidated assistance efforts (Wepner, 1986); a common approach was, and remains, to deal with mathematical and literacy weaknesses together, and sometimes to provide assistance with general learning skills as well. Thus until recently most papers on mathematics at a basic or developmental level were buried in journals and conference proceedings of literacy and other disciplines, not mathematics teaching *per se*. The term *remedial* is now regarded as limiting and not used extensively in the literature - it has even been removed from the title of one journal (Ross & Roe, 1986) and therefore not often used as a descriptor for literature searches.

Students and staff in the centres and programmes find themselves in marginalised circumstances, tending to be stigmatised (Wepner, 1986) or ignored as an apparently taboo topic (Godden & Pegg, 1993b). The attitude of other mathematics educators and researchers suggests that those in the bridging field are not working in "real" mathematics (Coffey, 1983; Wepner, 1986); they are not prepared to give support or be involved (Bers, 1987). As with ABE, there is an extremely high proportion of part-time staff, often at the lower academic pay-scales (e.g. Boylan & Bonham, 1994), and mostly female (Godden & Pegg, 1993b). Obtaining appropriate staff is a constant issue. Until recently academic qualifications have come from minimally related areas (Wepner, 1986). In the US training has been recognised as requiring a consolidated approach, and one effort has been through telementoring at a distance (McCorkindale, 1987).

Often students are seen just once, only wanting an immediate problem 'fixed.' Others only partly complete a bridging programme. Students' perceptions of their needs may vary as they progress through the courses for which they are enrolled; their stated desires may be for immediate, instrumental understanding and hence at variance with the teacher's goals for longer term relational understanding. Nicholas (1994:109) stated:

> What is clear . . . is that learning is affected as much by the personal and affective elements; the student's goals, perceptions of the subject, approaches to learning, interest and desires and prior experiences, as by the rational elements; the course content, the knowledge base of the student.

Capps (1984) warned that drop-in assistance on its own may not really meet the students' needs because it deals only briefly with a small part of a larger problem. Godden (1992) expressed the concern that students who might otherwise have never considered attending university may begin a process which for some is doomed to fail.

Surman (1993) presented a learning model with three intersecting domains: (a) content knowledge in the cognitive area of mathematics; (b) self knowledge, where self-esteem is raised through increased self-confidence and self-awareness of the learning processes; and (c) social knowledge, that is, knowledge of the institutional culture of higher education. Griffin (1994) argued that most adult students enter university with an inadequate understanding of the values and beliefs of the university sub-culture. She concluded that the greater the number and difference of diverging beliefs and values, the greater the negative impact on the student's chances of achieving academic success.

However, many individuals strive and survive, with the successes seeming to justify the difficulties encountered. In fact, Boylan and Bonham (1994:7) found that "research conclusively indicates that special intervention for underprepared students increases their chances for success," and the earlier the better. The glowing comments from students on evaluation forms, and in personal cards and phone calls provide the momentum to proceed further and search for even more effective strategies. Patterson and Sallee (1986:724) commented:

A solid commitment to remediation as a relatively permanent necessity in the institution is the first, and maybe most important, component required to establish an effective remedial programme. This commitment must include a reasonable and permanent funding base, administrative backing from high levels and an appropriate physical environment.

The features most highly associated with programme success are to have a centralised or at least coordinated structure, training of tutors, and regular comprehensive evaluations (Boylan, Bliss & Bonham, 1997).

Highly individualised student-centred approaches are a hallmark of these programmes and centres, as is their spontaneity in providing a range of learning media. Godden and Pegg (1993a) concluded that the strength of bridging mathematics programmes, their great flexibility and student-centredness, was the very reason they were unable to be evaluated in the traditional manner of educational programmes generally; they called for a new approach to evaluation in this important arena. Lack of effective evaluation of such programmes also results in very little publishable work. Time is usually already a critical factor for daily activities, so research is a low priority. According to Wepner (1987:6), "the relatively few available evaluations provide minimal or no statistical or longitudinal data to establish programme effectiveness in terms of the primary goal of mathematics remediation." This is supported by McDonald (1988) who found that, in her study of 'exemplary' mathematics programmes, only about a quarter of the courses were being formally evaluated.

Discussing the validity of test items, Berk (1981, in Kinsler & Robinson 1990b:350-351) noted:

> If the instruments chosen are insensitive to or inappropriate for the outcome variable, an educational intervention that, in fact, is producing effects may appear to be failing. . . For example, a test intended to assess basic skills in mathematics may require the student to read the directions and even to read the problems themselves before any computation can be attempted. Such items lack construct and content validity.

Kinsler & Robinson (1990b) addressed the issue of pre-test/post-test designs, and provided a very comprehensive coverage of research techniques, not only those applicable to developmental education, but more generally.

> In summary, researchers have been attempting to move evaluative efforts towards more comprehensive processes. For this to occur, these investigations should involve: more than one facet of the program; be of a longitudinal nature; and, without ignoring the risk of producing impractical models, be comparable with

studies on programs elsewhere. Planning for evaluation is a necessary preliminary to conducting the program. Only by being aware of the problems and pitfalls, can adequate evaluation occur. Comparisons between different assistance mechanisms are difficult, but essential. One reason is a need to establish which method optimises the presentation efforts of staff and the learning efforts of students. (Godden, 1992:156)

Issues of evaluation apply across the entire sphere of adult education in mathematics, and further research is necessary in this regard.

Research Activity

Research fora are of enormous importance to both the practitioners and associated researchers. In the last 10 to 15 years, a number of organisations have been initiated to provide a much needed common focus for discussion and dissemination of research, making the area more publicly visible.

Adults Learning Mathematics (ALM), an international forum, commenced in the UK in 1994. The Bridging Mathematics Network (BMN) covering Australasia and beyond has existed formally since 1991. Both have annual conferences and networking, from which they were generated, is continually being extended. The BMN maintains an explicit focus on mathematics education for adults from Aboriginal, Maori and other indigenous cultures. The international symposium on bridging mathematics (Jones, 1990) arose from a government-funded programme, and attracted a range of participants from the VET sector as well as higher education, including mainstream mathematics educators. Other international groups active in this area, although not exclusively concerned with *adult* mathematics education, include the International Study Group on Ethnomathematics (ISGEm), Political Dimensions of Mathematics Education (PDME), Mathematics Education and Society (MEAS) and the Critical Mathematics Educators Group (CMEG).

Although not specifically limited to adults learning mathematics, the American Mathematical Association of Two-Year Colleges (AMATYC) in the US, is a network for practitioners which arose from the continual pressure on two-year and community colleges to be the venue for most of the remediation and preparatory work in mathematics and other areas. (The four-year colleges and most universities do in fact have such programmes.) AMATYC has published a set of standards for introductory mathematics which cover curriculum, assessment, and pedagogy, and also makes recommendations for use of technology, professional development, learning facilities, and programme evaluation (see Cohen, 1995). In the US, there are also conferences on Adult Mathematical Literacy, and the Adult Numeracy

Network (ANN) works to put adult numeracy practitioners in touch with each other and with developments in the field (e.g. Gal & Schmitt, 1994). Many countries host adult literacy and basic education conferences where adult numeracy issues are raised.

The four-yearly International Congress on Mathematical Education (ICME) meetings are increasingly promoting adult education. For example there was a discussion group on mathematics learning centres at the meeting held in Budapest in 1988 (Hirst & Hirst 1988), and in 1996 in Seville there was a Working Group, *Adults Returning to Mathematics Education*, (FitzSimons, 1997). For the Tokyo meeting in 2000 there are planned working groups for action on *Mathematics Education in Two-Year Colleges and Other Tertiary Institutions* as well as *Adult and Lifelong Education in Mathematics*. There is a continuing topic group on vocational mathematics education which encompasses school as well as adult education.

An Undergraduate Mathematics Symposium (Delta '97) was conducted for the first time in Queensland. Originally aimed at discussions on the Harvard-type Reform Calculus, it drew a much wider coverage of undergraduate mathematics, and statistics, including bridging mathematics. Based on a meeting in Singapore in 1998 there is planned an International Commission on Mathematics Instruction (ICMI) publication on undergraduate mathematics for the year 2000 ICME conference.

UNESCO has taken a continuing interest in the needs of adult education, stressing the importance of lifelong learning as an integral part of its philosophy (e.g. Delors, 1996; Faure et al., 1972). It published a Final Report of the Conference on Adult Numeracy held at Marly-sur-Roi, near Paris in 1993. Jointly sponsored by UNESCO and the University of Pennsylvania, USA, the International Literacy Institute (ILI) opened in September 1994 at the University of Pennsylvania. ILI mainly focuses on developing countries and includes some activity in the area of adult numeracy/mathematics. Also UNESCO's Fifth International Conference on Adult Education, 'Adult Learning: A Key for the Twenty-First Century', held 14-18 July, 1997 in Hamburg, Germany, included in its *Agenda for the Future of Adult Learning*: 'Ensuring the universal right to literacy and basic education'. For a critical evaluation of this conference, see Forrester (1998).

Before the research fora evolved, the dispersion of information, particularly research, about mathematics bridging programmes and their culture was rather limited. There were no specific journals on bridging developmental mathematics, and researchers had difficulty having their work published in established mathematics education journals because they were unable to present statistically significant results (Wepner, 1986). This was due to the volatility and fluidity of student attendance patterns, and the spontaneous way in which assistance is provided, with interchangeable learning modes and media.

Mathematics education research for adults often remains linked in with other research fields. Journal publications are likely to be found in fields such as ABE, VET, lifelong learning, as well as mathematics education research. Knowing the most common descriptors is essential although, as mentioned above, searching for 'remedial', for example, will result in limited information, whereas once the US terminology of 'developmental' is known, much more is available, albeit intertwined with literacy and learning assistance issues. The time-consuming and frustrating worldwide searching of the (English-speaking) marginal literature by (Godden 1992), prompted the presentation of an annotated bibliography (Godden 1994).

CONCLUSION

As practitioners and researchers enter the field of adults learning mathematics they need to understand what has gone before in order to cement their own existing knowledge base and to contribute to that which is publicly shared, from the micro through to the macro levels. Apart from access to relevant materials, this requires time and money in addition to the goodwill of the researcher. In this chapter we have reviewed a selection of the literature on adult learners of mathematics, from entry to undergraduate levels, in practical, social, and political contexts. Underpreparedness for further study as well as mathematical illiteracy can and should be combated, especially when there are renewed calls for lifelong learning and the empowerment of all peoples of the world (e.g. Delors, 1996).

Wedege, Benn, and Maasz (1999) have progressed a meta-discussion about the nature of this new research domain, cultivated between adult education and mathematics education. They question whether it is situated within or exceeds the limits of the didactics of mathematics, taken as the scientific discipline related to research and development work in mathematics education. One of the conclusions reached is that the domain is currently under-theorised and needs to extend in both directions, drawing upon as many relevant disciplines as possible to assist in its growth.

ACKNOWLEDGEMENT

The authors would like to thank Diana Coben and John O'Donoghue and the anonymous reviewers for their thoughtful comments and suggestions although we accept responsibility for the chapter as a whole.

REFERENCES

Achtenhagen, F. (1994). 'Vocational education and training'. (P. Mann Trans.). In *Education 49/50*. Tübingen, FDR: Institute for Scientific Co-operation, 19-39.

Agar, D. L. & Knopfmacher, N. (1995). 'The Learning and Study Skills Inventory: A South African application'. *Higher Education, 30*, 115-126.

Aiken (1979). 'Attitudes towards mathematics and science in Iranian middle schools'. *School Science and Mathematics, 79*, 229-234.

Apple, M. W. (1992). 'Do the Standards go far enough? Power, policy, and practice in mathematics education'. *Journal for Research in Mathematics Education, 23*(5), 412-431.

Australian Association of Mathematics Teachers (AAMT). (1997). *Final report of the Rich Interpretation of Using Mathematical Ideas and Techniques Key Competency Project*. Adelaide, SA: Author.

Bagnall, R. (1994). 'Pluralising continuing education and training in a postmodern world: Whither competence?' *Australian & New Zealand Journal of Vocational Education Research*, 2(2), 18-39.

Balacheff, N. (1993). 'Artificial intelligence and real teaching'. In C. Keitel & K. Ruthven (Eds.), *Learning from computers: Mathematics education and technology*. Berlin: Springer Verlag, 131-158.

Barling, C. & Jones:(1991, September). *Bridging the gap. An intervention strategy for improving the mathematical competencies of students in first year Applied Science and Engineering*. Final report to the sponsor: The Victorian Education Foundation.

Barnes, M. (1990). 'Bridging the gap: The role of mathematics learning centres'. In P. L. Jones (Ed.), *Bridging mathematics: An international perspective* . Melbourne, Vic.: Swinburne Institute of Technology, 101-109.

Barnes, M. (1994). 'Interaction between theory and practice in bridging mathematics'. In *4th Australian Bridging Mathematics Network Conference Proceedings* (Vol. 1). Sydney: University of Sydney, 1-10.

Beilby, M. (1990). 'Bridging mathematics: The United Kingdom perspective'. In P. L. Jones (Ed.), *Bridging mathematics: An international perspective* . Melbourne, Vic.: Swinburne Institute of Technology 87-100.

Benn, R. (1997). *Adults count too: Mathematics for empowerment*. Leicester, UK: National Institute of Adult Continuing Education (NIACE).

Berenson, S. B., Best, M. A., Stiff, L. V. & Wasik, J. L. (1990). 'Levels of thinking and success in college developmental algebra'. *Focus on Learning Problems in Mathematics, 12*(1), 3-13.

Bers, T. H. 1987. *Evaluating remedial education programmes*. Association for Institutional Research, Tallahassee. ED282492.

Billett, S. (1998). 'Transfer and social practice'. *Australian & New Zealand Journal of Vocational Education Research, 6*(1), 1-25.

Bishop, A. J. (1988). *Mathematical enculturation*. Dordrecht: Kluwer.

Blackburn, K. T. (1984). 'The path from Algebra I to Geometry to Algebra II to Developmental Studies'. *Reflections, 32*, 9-12.

Boers, M. A. M. & Jones:L. (1992). 'The graphics calculator in tertiary mathematics'. In B. Southwell, B. Perry & K. Owens (Eds.), *Space - The first and final frontier: Proceedings of the Fifteenth Annual Conference of the Mathematics Education Research Group of Australasia (MERGA)*. Kingswood, NSW: Mathematics Education Research Group of Australasia (MERGA), 155-164.

Boers, M. & Jones:(1994). 'Students' use of graphics calculators under examination conditions' *International Journal of Mathematical Education in Science and Technology, 25*(4), 491-516.

Boylan, H. R & Bonham, B. S. (1994). 'Seven myths about developmental education'. *Research and Teaching in Developmental Education, 10*(2) 5-12.

Boylan, H. R, Bliss, L. B. & Bonham, B. S. (1997). 'Programme components and their relationship to student performance'. *Journal of Developmental Education. 20*(3), 2-8.

Brown, A. (1998). 'Designing effective learning programs for the development of a broad occupational competence.' In W.M. Nijhof & J.N. Streumer (Eds), *Key qualifications in work and education.* Dordrecht: Kluwer Academic Publishers, 165-186.

Brown, D. E. (1975). *Planning an Effective Math Lab.* ED146963

Buckingham, E. A. (1997). *Specific and generic numeracies of the workplace: How is numeracy learnt and used by workers in production industries, and what learning/working environments promote this?* Burwood, Vic.: Centre for Studies in Mathematics, Science, and Environmental Education, Deakin University.

Burton, L. (1987). 'From failure to success: Changing the experience of adult learners of mathematics'. *Educational Studies in Mathematics, 18*(3), 305-316.

Buxton, L. G. (1981). *Do you panic about maths? Coping with maths anxiety.* London: Heinemann.

Cantwell, R & Beamish, P. (1994). *Executive strategy control in secondary and tertiary populations: contrasting understandings of self-regulation.* Unpublished paper presented at the Annual Conference of the Australian Association for Research in Education (AARE), Educational Research: Innovation and Practice, University of Newcastle, Australia, 27 Nov - 1 Dec.

Capps, J. (1984). *Individual Instruction Programmes & Learning Centers.* NJ: Somerset County College. ED246967.

Clarke, D. & Helme, S. (1993, July). *Context as construct.* Paper presented at the 16th Annual Conference of the Mathematics Education Research Group of Australasia, Brisbane.

Coady, C. & Pegg, J. (1991). 'An investigation of five first-year tertiary students' understandings of basic algebraic concepts'. *Australian Senior Mathematics Journal, 5*(2), 111-120.

Coben, D. (1997). 'Mathematics or common sense? Some reflections on research into adults' mathematics life histories'. In G.E. FitzSimons (Ed.), *Adults returning to study mathematics: Papers from Working Group 18, 8th International Congress on Mathematical Education, ICME 8.* Adelaide: Australian Association of Mathematics Teachers, 37-48.

Coben, D. (comp.) (1995) *Adults Learning Maths – A Research Forum: Papers Presented at The Inaugural Conference of ALM 1994 (ALM-1).* London: Goldsmiths College, University of London, in association with ALM.

Coben, D. & Atere-Roberts, E. (1996). *Carefree calculations for healthcare students.* London: Macmillan.

Cockcroft, W. H. (Chairman). (1982). *Mathematics counts: Report of the Committee of Inquiry into the Teaching of Mathematics in Schools.* London: Her Majesty's Stationery Office.

Cohen, D. (Ed.) (1995). *Crossroads in mathematics: Standards for introductory college mathematics before calculus.* Memphis, TN: American Mathematical Association of Two-Year Colleges (AMATYC).

Coffey, J. C. 1983. *Remedial education in California's public colleges and universities: Campus perspectives on a serious problem.* CA. Postsecondary Education Commission. ED230227.

Cope, B. & Kalantzis, M. (1998). 'Multiliteracies: Meeting the communications challenge in TAFE'. *The Australian TAFE Teacher, 32*(2), 28-29.

Cranton, P. A. (1992). *Working with adult learners.* Toronto: Wall & Emerson.

Crawford, K, Gordon, S., Nicholas, J. & Prosser, M. (1994). 'Conceptions of mathematics and how it is learned: The perspectives of students entering university'. *Learning and Instruction, 4,* 331-345.

Crawford-Nutt, D. (1987). 'Statistics is a problem to social science degree students with problem backgrounds - being female, older, and shaky at maths'. In A. H. Miller & G. Sachse-Akerlind (Eds.), *The learner in higher education: A forgotten species. Proceedings of the 12th annual HERDSA conference.* Sydney, NSW: Higher Education Research & Development Society of Australasia, 341-347.

Cumming, J. J. (1995, June). *Defining contextualized assessment: Authenticity, anchoring, simulation, abstraction, representation, camouflage.* Paper presented at the Conference of the International Association for Educational Assessment, Montreal, Canada.

Cumming, J. J. (in press). 'Towards a theoretical base for assessment in adult numeracy'. In J. Izard (Ed.), *Assessment practices in the mathematical sciences.* Melbourne, Vic.: Australian Council for Educational Research.

Davis, G. E. (1996). 'What is the difference between remembering someone posting a letter and remembering the square root of 2?' In L. Puig & A. Gutiérrez (Eds.), *Proceedings of the 20th Conference of the International Group for the Psychology of Mathematics Education, Vol. 2.* Valencia: Universitat de València, 265-272.

Delors, J. (Chair)(1996). *Learning: The treasure within.* Report to UNESCO of the International Commission on Education for the Twenty-first Century. Paris: United Nations Scientific, Cultural and Scientific Organization (UNESCO).

Dossel, S. (1993) 'Maths anxiety'. *The Australian Mathematics Teacher, 49*(1), 4-8.

Dowling:(1998). *The sociology of mathematics education: Mathematical myths/ pedagogic texts.* London: Falmer Press.

Ellsworth, E. (1989). 'Why doesn't this feel empowering? Working through the repressive myths of critical pedagogy'. *Harvard Educational Review, 59*(3), 297-324.

Elsy, A. (1995). 'Do patients count? Learning mathematics in a special hospital'. In *ALM-2: Mathematics with a human face. Proceedings of the Second Annual Conference of Adults Learning Mathematics - A Research Forum.* London: Goldsmiths College, University of London, 112-115.

Ernest:(1995).'Images of mathematics, values and gender: A philosophical perspective'. In *ALM-2: Mathematics with a human face. Proceedings of the Second Annual Conference of Adults Learning Mathematics - A Research Forum.* London: Goldsmiths College, University of London, 1-15.

Evans, J. (1995). In B. Grevholm & G. Hanna (Eds.), *Gender and mathematics education, an ICMI study.* Lund: Lund University Press, 233-242.

Evans, J. (2000). 'Building bridges: Reflections on the problem of transfer of learning in mathematics'. *Educational Studies in Mathematics, 30,* 1-3.

Evans, J. & Thorstad, I. (1995). 'Mathematics and numeracy in the practice of critical citizenship'. In: *ALM-1: Proceedings of the Inaugural Conference of Adults Learning Mathematics - A Research Forum.* London: Goldsmiths College, University of London, 64-70.

Fagin, M. C. (1971). 'Analysis of the performance of adult women in Missouri on three general examinations of the college level examination program'. *Adult Education Journal, 21*(3), 148-165.

Faure, E., Herrera, F., Kaddoura, A-R., Lopes, H., Petrovsky, A. V., Rahnema, M. & Champion Ward, F. (1972). *Learning to be: The world of education today and tomorrow.* Paris: UNESCO.

FitzSimons, G. E. (1993, March). *Constructivism and the adult learner: Jane's story.* Paper presented at the Constructivism: The Intersection of Disciplines Symposium, Deakin University, Geelong.

FitzSimons, G. E. (1993a).' Constructivism and the adult learner: Marieanne's story'. In B. Atweh, C. Kanes, M. Carss, & G. Booker (Eds.), *Contexts in mathematics education: Proceedings of the 16th Annual Conference of the Mathematics Education Research Group of Australasia (MERGA).* Brisbane, Qld: Mathematics Education Research Group of Australasia, 247-252.

FitzSimons, G. E. (1994a). 'TAFE students: The affective domain and mathematics.' In G. Bell, B. Wright, N. Leeson & J. Geake (Eds.), *Challenges in mathematics education: Constraints on construction: Proceedings of the 17th Annual Conference of the Mathematics Education Research Group of Australasia (MERGA).* Lismore, NSW: Mathematics Education Research Group of Australasia, 233-241.

FitzSimons, G. E. (1994b). *Teaching mathematics to adults returning to study.* Geelong: Deakin University Press.

FitzSimons, G. E. (1995, July). *The inter-relationship of the history and pedagogy of mathematics for adults returning to study.* Paper presented at the International Study Group for the Relations of History and Pedagogy of Mathematics, Cairns.

FitzSimons, G. E. (Ed.) (1997). *Adults returning to study mathematics: Papers from Working Group 18, 8th International Congress on Mathematical Education, ICME 8.* Adelaide, SA: Australian Association of Mathematics Teachers.

FitzSimons, G. E. (1998). *Economic change and new learning demands: A case study from the pharmaceutical industry.* Paper presented at CEET conference, Rapid Economic Change and Lifelong Learning. WWW: http://edx1.educ.monash.edu.au/centres/CEET/

FitzSimons, G. E., Jungwirth, H., Maaß, J., & Schloeglmann, W. (1996). 'Adults and mathematics (Adult numeracy)'. In A. J. Bishop, K. Clements, C. Keitel, J. Kilpatrick, & C. Laborde (Eds.), *International handbook of mathematics education.* Dordrecht: Kluwer, 755-784.

Forrester, K. (1998). 'Adult learning: 'A key for the twenty-first century': Reflections on the UNESCO fifth international conference 1997'. *International Journal of Lifelong Education,* 17(6), 423-434.

Foyster, J. (1988). *Maths beyond the classroom.* Canberra: Curriculum Development Centre.

Foyster, J. (1990). 'Beyond the mathematics classroom: Numeracy on the job'. In S. Willis (Ed.), *Being numerate: What counts?.* Melbourne: Australian Council for Educational Research,119-137.

Frankenstein, M. (1989). *Relearning mathematics: A different third R – Radical maths.* London: Free Association Books.

Frankenstein, M. (1996). 'Critical mathematical literacy: Teaching through real real-life math world problems'. In T. Kjærgård, A. Kvamme, & N. Lindén (Eds.), *Numeracy, race, gender, and class: Proceedings of the third international conference on the Political Dimensions of Mathematics Education (PDME III).* Landås, Norway: Caspar Forlag 59,76.

Fredrick, D., Mishler, C., & Hogan, T. P. (1984). 'College freshmen mathematics abilities: Adults versus younger students'. *School science and mathematics, 84*(4), 327-336.

Freire:(1976). *Education: The practice of freedom* (M. Bergman Ramos, Trans.). London: Writers and Readers.

Gal, I. & Schmitt, M. J. (Eds.) (1994). *Conference on Adult Mathematical Literacy: Proceedings*. Philadelphia, PA: National Center on Adult Literacy, University of Pennsylvania.

Gal, I. (1997). 'On developing statistically literate adults'. In G. E. FitzSimons (Ed.), *Adults returning to study mathematics: Papers from Working Group 18, 8th International Congress on Mathematical Education, ICME 8*. Adelaide, SA: Australian Association of Mathematics Teachers,49-53.

Gal, I. & Schuh, A. (1994). *Who counts in adult literacy programmes? A national survey of numeracy education*. NCAL Technical report TR 94-09. Philadelphia, PA: National Center on Adult Literacy, University of Pennsylvania.

Galbraith: (1990). 'Bridging mathematics: Some recurring themes'. In P. L. Jones (Ed.), *Bridging mathematics: An international perspective*. Melbourne, Vic: Swinburne Institute of Technology, 141-143.

Gates, P. (ed.) (1998) Mathematics Education and Society. *Proceedings of the First International Mathematics Education and Society Conference (MEAS1) 6-11 September 1998*. Nottingham: Centre for the Study of Mathematics Education, Nottingham University.

Gillies, R. (1991, July). *Activities in nursing mathematics*. Paper presented at Inaugural Conference of NSW Bridging Mathematics Group, Charles Sturt University - Mitchell, Bathurst, NSW.

Gillies, R. (1994). 'Drug calculations for nurses: more than a formula and a calculator?' In *4th Australian Bridging Mathematics Network Conference Proceedings* (Vol. 1). Sydney: University of Sydney, 56-66).

Ginsburg, L. & Gal, I. (1997). 'Uncovering the knowledge adult learners bring to class'. In G. E. FitzSimons (Ed.), *Adults returning to study mathematics: Papers from Working Group 18, 8th International Congress on Mathematical Education, ICME 8*. Adelaide, SA: Australian Association of Mathematics Teachers, 55-61.

Godden, G. L. (1992). *Synthesis of research on facilities provided by tertiary institutions for mathematically underprepared students*. Unpublished Masters thesis, University of New England, Armidale, Australia.

Godden, G. (1994). 'A guide to tertiary bridging mathematics research to mid-1992; including an annotated bibliography'. In *4th Australian Bridging Mathematics Network Conference: Proceedings (Vol. 1)*. Sydney, NSW: University of Sydney, 67-91.

Godden, G. & Coady, C. (1997). 'Mature-Age Students in Service Statistics'. In G. E. FitzSimons (Ed.), *Adults returning to study mathematics: Papers from Working Group 18, 8th International Congress on Mathematical Education, ICME 8*. Adelaide, SA: Australian Association of Mathematics Teachers, 63-70.

Godden, G. & Pegg, J. (1993a). 'Identified problems impeding effective evaluation of tertiary bridging mathematics programs'. In B. Atweh, C. Kanes, M. Carss, & G. Booker (Eds.), *Contexts in mathematics education*. Brisbane, Qld: Mathematics Education Research Group of Australasia, 297-302.

Godden, G. & Pegg, J. (1993b). 'Confronting image issues which restrict the effectiveness of bridging mathematics programs.' In *3rd Australian Bridging Mathematics Network Conference Proceedings*. Brisbane, Qld: Queensland University of Technology.

Gordon, S. (1992). 'Task Definition: Have We Got It Right?' *Australian Senior Mathematics Journal*, 6(1), 53-55.

Gordon, S. (1993). 'Mature students learning statistics: The activity perspective.' *Mathematics Education Research Journal, 5*(1), 34-49.

Gordon, S. (1994). 'Understanding the reluctant learner of statistics: Some examples from my practice'. In *4th Australian Bridging Mathematics Network Conference Proceedings* (Vol. 1). Sydney: University of Sydney, 11-18.

Gordon, S. (1995). 'A theoretical approach to understanding learners of statistics.' *Journal of Statistics Education, 3*(3).

Gordon, S. & Nicholas, J. (1992). 'An investigation of students' attitudes to and beliefs about mathematics and statistics'. *Australian Senior Mathematics Journal 6*(2), 103-107.

Gowen, S. G (1992). *The politics of workplace literacy: A case study.* New York: Teachers College, Columbia University.

Griffin, H. (1994). 'Bridging mathematics and sub-culture.' In *4th Australian Bridging Mathematics Network Conference Proceedings* (Vol. 1). Sydney, NSW: University of Sydney, 92-97.

Groenestijn, M. van (1997). 'Numeracy education to illiterate and semi-literate adults in Adult Basic Education.' In *ALM-3: Proceedings of the Third Annual Conference of Adults Learning Mathematics - A Research Forum.* London: Goldsmiths College, University of London, 144-148.

Groenestijn, M. van (1998). 'Constructive numeracy teaching as a gateway to independent learning.' In *ALM-4: Proceedings of the Fourth Annual Conference of Adults Learning Mathematics - A Research Forum* . London: Goldsmiths College, University of London, 224-231.

Guedes, E. M. & Zandonadi, R. M. (1998). 'Rediscovering mathematics by adult worker students'. In *ALM-3: Proceedings of the Third Annual Conference of Adults Learning Mathematics - A Research Forum.* London: Goldsmiths College, University of London, 247-248.

Halliday, C. (1997). 'Maths refresher: A prison perspective.' In M. Thomas (Ed.), *Proceedings of the Seventh Annual Australasian Bridging Maths Network Conference.* Auckland: University of Auckland, 79-85.

Harris, M. (1987). 'An example of traditional women's work as a mathematics resource', *For the Learning of Mathematics, 7*(3), 26-28.

Harris, M. (1991). 'Looking for the maths in work.' In M. Harris (Ed.), *Schools, mathematics and work.* Basingstoke, UK: Falmer Press, 132-144.

Harris, M. (1995). *Common threads: Women maths and work.* London: Trentham.

Harvey, D. (1989). *The condition of postmodernity: An enquiry into the origins of cultural change.* Oxford, UK: Basil Blackwell.

Hashway, R. M., Duke, L. I., & Farmer, V. F. (1993). 'The reading habits of adult learners.' *Reading Improvement, 30*(1) Spring, 21-25.

Hembree, R. (1990). 'The nature, effects, and relief of mathematics anxiety.' *Journal for Research in Mathematics Education, 21*(1), 33-46.

Hirst, A., & Hirst, K. (Eds.). (1988). *Proceedings of the Sixth International Congress on Mathematical Education.* Malev, Hungary: International Commission on Mathematical Instruction.

Horne, M. (1998). 'Linking parents and school mathematics.' In N. Ellerton (Ed.), *Issues in mathematics education: A contemporary perspective.* Perth, WA: Mathematics, Science and Technology Education Centre, Edith Cowan University, 115-135.

Hubbard, R. (1994). 'Some reasons why mathematics is so hard to learn and some things we can do to make it easier'. Keynote address in *4th Australian Bridging Mathematics Network Conference Proceedings* (Vol. 1). Sydney, NSW: University of Sydney, 19-27.

Hubbard, R. (1986). 'The secondary/tertiary interface: A view from a tertiary casualty ward.' In K. V. Swinson (Ed.), *Mathematics teaching: Challenges for change. (Proceedings of*

Australian Association of Mathematics Teachers Eleventh Biennial Conference). Brisbane, Qld.: Australian Association of Mathematics Teachers, 284-290.

Johnson, S., & Elliot, S. (1998) 'Independent versus autonomous adult learning in mathematics?' In *ALM-4: Proceedings of the Fourth Annual Conference of Adults Learning Mathematics — A Research Forum.* London: Goldsmiths College, University of London, 123-134.

Jones, P.L. (Ed.) (1990). *Bridging mathematics: An international perspective.* Hawthorn, Vic.: Swinburne Institute of Technology.

Jungwirth, H. (1993). 'Reflections on the foundations of research on women and mathematics.' In S. Restivo, J. P. van Bendegem, & R. Fischer (Eds.), *Math worlds: Philosophical and social studies of mathematics and mathematics education.* New York: State University of New York Press, 134-149.

Kanes, C. (1997a). 'An investigation of artifact mediation and task organisation involving numerical workplace knowledge.' In *Good thinking - Good practice: Research perspectives on learning and work. Proceedings of the 5th Annual International Conference on Post-Compulsory Education and Training* (Vol. 1). Brisbane, Qld.: Centre for Learning and Work Research, Griffith University, 79-91.

Kanes, C. (1997b). 'Towards an understanding of numerical knowledge in the workplace.' In F. Biddulph & K. Carr (Eds.), *People in mathematics education* (Vol. 1). University of Waikato, NZ: Mathematics Education Research Group of Australasia.

Kasworm, C. E. (1990). 'Adult undergraduates in higher education: A review of past research perspectives.' *Review of Educational Research, 60*(3), 345-372.

Keitel, C., Kotzmann, E. & Skovsmose, O. (1993). 'Beyond the tunnel vision: Analysing the relationships between mathematics, society and technology.' In C. Keitel & K. Ruthven (Eds.), *Learning from computers: Mathematics education and technology.* Berlin: Springer Verlag, 243-279.

Kinsler, K. & Robinson, A. (1990). 'Research in developmental education.' In R. M. Hashway (Ed.), *Handbook of developmental education.* New York: Praeger, 335-355.

Kjaergaard, T., Kvamme, A. & Linden, N. (eds) (1996) *Numeracy, Race, Gender and Class: Proceedings of the Third International Conference of Political Dimensions of Mathematics Education (PDME) III,* Bergen, Norway. Landaas, Norway: Caspar Publishing Company.

Klein, M. (1998). 'New knowledge/new teachers/new times: How processes of subjectification undermine the implementation of investigatory approaches to teaching mathematics.' In C. Kanes, M. Goos, & E. Warren (Eds.), *Teaching mathematics in new times* (Vol. 1). Griffith University, Brisbane: Mathematics Education Research Group of Australasia, 295-302.

Knijnik, G. (1997). Mathematics Education and the Struggle for Land in Brazil. In G. E. FitzSimons (Ed.), *Adults returning to study mathematics: Papers from Working Group 18, 8th International Congress on Mathematical Education, ICME 8.* Adelaide, SA: Australian Association of Mathematics Teachers, 87-91.

Knowles, M. S. (1990). *The adult learner: A neglected species* (4th ed.). Houston, TX: Gulf Publishing Company.

Kogan, M. & Tuijnman, A.C. (1995). *Education research and development: Trends, issues and challenges.* Paris: OECD.

Kurz, G. 1990. 'Bridging courses in mathematics: The German perspective.' In P. L. Jones (Ed.), *Bridging mathematics: An international perspective.* Hawthorn, Vic.: Swinburne Institute of Technology, 47-86.

Lave, J. (1988). *Cognition in practice: Mind, mathematics and culture in every day life.* Cambridge: Cambridge University Press.

Lave, J. & Wenger, E. (1991). *Situated learning: Legitimate peripheral participation.* Cambridge: Cambridge University Press.

Leder, G. (1991). 'Is teaching learning?' *The Australian Mathematics Teacher, 47*(1), 4-7.

Leder, G. C. (1993). 'Constructivism: Theory for practice? The case of mathematics.' *Higher Education Research & Development, 12*(1), 5-20.

Lehmann, C. H. (1987, April). *The adult mathematics learner: Attitudes, expectations, attributions.* Paper presented at the Annual Meeting of the American Educational Research Association (Washington, DC). ED 283 680

Lerman, S. (1998). 'The intension/intention of teaching mathematics.' In C. Kanes, M. Goos, & E. Warren (Eds.), *Teaching mathematics in new times* (Vol. 1). Griffith University, Brisbane, Qld.: Mathematics Education Research Group of Australasia, 29-44.

Lord, S. (1991). 'Women, maths and workplace education.' In P. O'Connor (Ed.), *Pitfalls and possibilities: Women and workplace basic education.* Redfern, NSW: NSW Adult Literacy Council, 67-71.

Lunneborg, P. W., Olch, D. R., & de Wolf, V. (1974). 'Prediction of college performance in older students.' *Journal of Counselling Psychology, 21*(3), 215-221.

Maaß, J. (1998). 'Technology transfer - A useful metaphor for university level mathematics courses for engineers and scientists.' Keynote address. In *ALM-4. Proceedings of the Fourth Annual Conference of Adults Learning Mathematics - A Research Forum.* London: Goldsmiths College, University of London, 58-62.

Marginson, S. (1997). *Markets in education.* St. Leonards, NSW: Allen & Unwin.

Martin, B. (1988/1997). 'Mathematics and social interests.' In A. B. Powell, & M. Frankenstein (Eds.), *Ethnomathematics: Challenging eurocentrism in mathematics education.* Albany, NY: State University of New York, 155-171. (Reprinted from *Search, 19*(4), 1988, 209-214)

Masingila, J. (1993). 'Learning from mathematics practice in out-of-school situations.' *For the Learning of Mathematics, 13*(2), 18-22.

McCorkindale, M. (1987). 'Telementoring project: Long-distance training for developmental educators: Maricopa Community Colleges.' In D. C. Scott (Ed.), *Community College Programmes for Underprepared Students.* Los Angeles, CA: League for Innovation in the Community College. ED294626.

McRae, A. (1995). 'Assessing students in numeracy programs.' *Numeracy in Focus, 1,* 15-19.

Miller-Reilly, B. J. (1997). 'Reactions of Adults to an Investigative Mathematics Course.' In G. E. FitzSimons (Ed.), *Adults returning to study mathematics: Papers from Working Group 18, 8th International Congress on Mathematical Education, ICME 8.* Adelaide, SA: Australian Association of Mathematics Teachers, 101-117.

Mohney, C. & Anderson, W. (1988). 'The effect of life events and relationships on adult women's decisions to enrol in college.' *Journal of Counselling and Development, 66,* 271-274.

Mullinix, B. B. & Comings, J. P. (1994). 'Exploring what counts: A summary report of research into ABE math in Massachusetts.' In I. Gal & M. J. Schmitt (Eds.) *Conference on Adult Mathematical Literacy: Proceedings.* Philadelphia, PA: National Center on Adult Literacy, University of Pennsylvania, 73-81.

Narode, R. B. (1989). *A constructivist programme for college remedial mathematics: Design, implementation, and evaluation.* Dissertation. Amherst, MA: University of Massachusetts. ED309988.

Nesbit, T. (1995). *Teaching mathematics to adults.* Paper presented at the Annual Meeting of the American Educational Research Association San Francisco California, April. (ERIC Report).

Newman, A., Lewis, W., & Beverstock, C. (1994, June). Prison literacy: Implications for programme and assessment (extracted from Executive Summary of NCAL Technical Report TR93-01), *NCAL Connections*. Philadelphia, PA: National Center on Adult Literacy, University of, 1, 7-8.

Nicholas, J. (1994). 'Mathematics Learning Centre: why we do the things we do.' *In 4th Australian Bridging Mathematics Network Conference Proceedings* (Vol. 1). Sydney, NSW: University of Sydney, 108-111.

Nordstrom, B. H. (1989). *Non-traditional students: Adults in transition*. Flagstaff, AZ: Northern Arizona University.

Noss, R., Hoyles, C. & Pozzi, S. (in press). Working knowledge: Mathematics in use. In A. Bessot & J. Ridgway (Eds.), *Education for mathematics in the workplace*. Dordrecht: Kluwer Academic Press.

O'Connor, P. (1994). 'Workplaces as sites of learning.' In P. O'Connor (Ed.), *Thinking Work: Vol. 1. Theoretical perspectives on workers' literacies*. Sydney: Adult Literacy and Basic Skills Action Coalition, 257-295.

O'Donoghue, J. (1997). 'An assessment-driven open learning system for adults learning mathematics.' In G. E. FitzSimons (Ed.), *Adults returning to study mathematics: Papers from Working Group 18, 8th International Congress on Mathematical Education, ICME 8*. Adelaide, SA: Australian Association of Mathematics Teachers, 119-128.

Onstenk, J. (1998). 'New structures and new contents in Dutch vocational education.' In. W.J. Nijhof & J.N. Streumer (Eds.), *Key qualifications in work and education*. Dordrecht: Kluwer Academic Publishers, 117-132.

Patterson, D., & Sallee, T. (1986). 'Successful remedial mathematics programmes: Why they work.' In M. R. Wardrop, & R. F. Wardrop (Eds.), The Teaching of Mathematics, *American Mathematical Monthly, 93*(9), 724-727.

Pickard, P. & Cock, S. (1997). 'Flexible mathematics at university.' In *ALM-3: Proceedings of the Third Annual Conference of Adults Learning Mathematics - A Research Forum*. London: Goldsmiths College, University of London, 123-134.

Pitney, D. W. (1991). *Interactive video mathematics: An investigation of four key processes in an interactive video-based pre-calculus system of practice and review*. Unpublished PhD thesis, University of Western Australia, Perth, Australia.

Popkewitz, T. S. (1988). 'Institutional issues in the study of school mathematics: Curriculum research.' *Educational Studies in Mathematics, 19*, 221-249.

Popkewitz, T. S. (1997). 'The production of reason and power: Curriculum history and intellectual traditions.' *Journal of Curriculum Studies, 29*(2), 131-164.

Powell, A. B. & Frankenstein, M. (eds) (1997) *Ethnomathematics: Challenging Eurocentrism in Mathematics Education*. Albany, NY: State University of New York Press.

Pozzi, S., Noss, R. & Hoyles, C. (1998). 'Tools in practice, mathematics in use'. *Educational Studies in Mathematics, 36*(2), 105-122.

Ross, E. P. & Roe, B. D. (1986). 'The case for basic skills programmes in higher education.' Fastback 238. *Phi Delta Kappa*. ED273166.

Rubenson, K. (1995, May). 'Lifelong learning: Between Utopia and economic imperatives' . Papers presented at Adult Education Research in Nordic Countries conference, Linköping University, Göteborg, Sweden. (Republished as: Livslångt Lärande: Mellan utopioch Ekonomi. In P-E Ellström, et al. (Eds), *Livslångt Lärande* (1996). Lund: Studentlitteratur, 48-72.

Seddon, T. (1994). *Context and beyond: Reframing the theory and practice of education*. London: Falmer Press.

Sewall, T. J. (1984*). Academic skills of the returning adult student. Report of a pilot study.* Green Bay, WI: University of Wisconsin.

Shaw, P. F. (1993). *A remedial mathematics course for adults studying statistics: changes that it may be able to effect.* Unpublished Masters thesis, Macquarie University, North Ryde, Australia.

Skemp, R. (1976/1978). 'Relational understanding and instrumental understanding.' *Arithmetic Teacher, November.* [Reprinted from *Mathematics Teaching, December* 1976.]

Skovsmose, O. (1996). *Meaning in mathematics education.* BACOMET Research Report No. 4: Meaning and Communication in Mathematics Education.

Smart, J. C., & Pascarella, E. T. (1987). 'Influences on the intention to reenter higher education.' *Journal of Higher Education, 58*(3), 306-322.

Spanard, J. A. (1990). 'Beyond intent: Reentering college to complete the degree.' *Review of Educational Research, 60*(3), 309-344.

Stonehocker, L. (1985). *Institutional Response to Student Skills Needs at Grande Prairie Regional College, Alberta.* ED257489.

Strässer, R (1998). Mathematics for work: A didactical perspective. In C. Alsina, J.M. Alvarez, B. Hodgson, C. Laborde & A. Pérez (Eds), *8th International Congress on Mathematics Education: Selected lectures.* Sevilla: S.A.E.M. 'THALES', 427-441.

Strässer, R., Barr, G., Evans, J., and Wolf, A. (1989/1991). 'Skills versus understanding.' In M. Harris (Ed.), (1991), *Schools, mathematics and work.* Basingstoke, UK: Falmer, 158-169. (Reprinted from *Zentralblatt für Didaktik der Mathematik 21*(6), 197-202)

Suddick, D. E., & Collins, B. A. (1984, September). *A longitudinal cross validation of the English usage and algebra basic skills testing remediation paradigm for older, masters' level students.* Paper presented at the Annual Meeting of the Midwestern Educational Research Association, Chicago.

Suddick, D. E. & Collins, B. A. (1986, April). *A longitudinal cross validation of a basic skills testing remediation paradigm for older, reentry college juniors.* Paper presented at the 67th Annual Meeting of the American Educational Research Association, San Francisco.

Surman, P. (1993). 'Empowering students - empowering teachers: Lessons for mainstream tertiary teachers of mathematics from bridging mathematics.' In *3rd Australian Bridging Mathematics Network Conference Proceedings.* Brisbane: Queensland University of Technology, 31-41.

Surman, P., & Galligan, L. (1993, October). *Addressing metacognitive aspects of learning of disadvantaged adults preparing for post-secondary study in the distance mode.* Paper presented at the National Equity and Access Conference, Newcastle.

Swindell, R. (1995). 'Demolishing the traditional participation barriers confronting older adults.' In *Barriers and boundaries in adult, vocational and post-compulsory education and training: Goals, values, knowledge, structures, participation and outcomes, Conference Papers* (Vol. 2). Brisbane, Qld.: Centre for Skill Formation Research and Development, Griffith University.

Taffe, J. (1984). 'Bridging the mathematics gap.' In I. R. Dunn (Ed*.), Research and development in higher education* (Vol. 5), Papers presented at 8th Annual conference of the Higher Education Research and Development Society of Australasia. Sydney, NSW: HERDSA, 163-168.

Taylor, J. A. (1994). 'Attitudes to mathematics of adult students.' In *4th Australian Bridging Mathematics Network Conference Proceedings* (Vol. I). Sydney: University of Sydney, 182-187.

Taylor, J. A. (1995). 'Attitude to mathematics of adults returning to tertiary study in the distance mode.' In R. P. Hunting, G. E. FitzSimons:C. Clarkson, & A. J. Bishop (Eds.),

Regional collaboration in mathematics education 1995. Melbourne: Monash University, 685-694.

Taylor, J. A. (1997). 'Factorial validity of the Aiken Attitude to Mathematics Scales for adult pre-tertiary students.' *Educational and Psychological Measurement, 57*(1), 125-130.

Taylor, J. & Mander, D. (1997, November). *A foundation course in General Mathematics: An experiment in flexible learning for on and off campus students.* Paper presented at Delta 1997: What can we do to improve learning?: A symposium on modern undergraduate mathematics, Brisbane.

Tobias, S. (1978/1993). *Overcoming math anxiety.* New York, NY: Norton.

Tobias, S. (1987). *Succeed with math: Every student's guide to conquering math anxiety.* New York, NY: The College Board.

Tobias, S. (1990). *They're not dumb, they're different: Stalking the second tier.* Tucson, AZ: Research Corporation.

Tomlinson, L. M. (1989). *Postsecondary Development Programmes: A Traditional Agenda with New Imperatives. Report No. 3.* School of Education and Human Development, The George Washington Uni., Washington DC

Tout, D. & Marr, B. (1997). 'Changing practice: Adult Numeracy Professional Development.' In G. E. FitzSimons (Ed.), *Adults returning to study mathematics: Papers from Working Group 18, 8th International Congress on Mathematical Education, ICME 8.* Adelaide, SA: Australian Association of Mathematics Teachers, 141-153.

Van Aardt, A. M., & van Wyk, C. K. (1991). 'Individual learning and study skills of first-year mathematics students and its influence on mathematics achievement.' In *Proceedings of the 6th Conference of the South African Association for Academic Development.* Johannesburg: University of Witwatersrand, 326-343.

Van Groenestijn, M. & Coben, D. (comps) (1999) *Mathematics as Part of Lifelong Learning. Proceedings of the Fifth International Conference of Adults Learning Maths - A Research Forum,(ALM-5)* held at Utrecht, The Netherlands, 1-2-3 July 1998.

Vanhille, B. & D'Halluin, C. (1997) 'A flexible training system for adults returning to mathematics.' In G. E. FitzSimons (Ed.), *Adults returning to study mathematics: Papers from Working Group 18, 8th International Congress on Mathematical Education, ICME 8* . Adelaide, SA: Australian Association of Mathematics Teachers, 155-164.

Walkerdine, V. (1994). 'Reasoning in a post-modern age.' In P. Ernest (Ed.), *Mathematics, education and philosophy: An international perspective.* London: Falmer Press, 61-75.

Wall, A. D., Sersland, C. J., & Hoban, G. (1996). 'Adult learner's self-efficacy, readiness for self-directed learning, and gender: Implication for math performance.' In H. B. Long (Ed.), Current developments in self-directed learning. Norman, OK: Classic Book Distributors, 107-125.

Ward, P. (1997). 'The provision of mathematical education for people with special needs in the National Training and Development Institute.' In G. E. FitzSimons (Ed.), *Adults returning to study mathematics: Papers from Working Group 18, 8th International Congress on Mathematical Education, ICME 8* (pp. 165-175). Adelaide, SA: Australian Association of Mathematics Teachers, 165-175.

Watkins, A. J. P. (1997). 'Adult students returning to study mathematics for an engineering degree.' In G. E. FitzSimons (Ed.), *Adults returning to study mathematics: Papers from the 8th International Congress on Mathematical Education (ICME 8) Working Group18.* Adelaide, SA: Australian Association of Mathematics Teachers, 177-189.

Wedege, T. (1995). 'Technological competence and mathematics.' In *Mathematics with a human face. In D. Coben and M. Groenstijn (Comps),* Proceedings of the second international conference of Adults Learning Mathematics - A Research Forum. London: Goldsmiths College, University of London, 53-59.

Wedege, T. (1997). 'Profile in mathematics of adults returning to education: Can a basis be created for a relevant learning process?' In G. E. FitzSimons (Ed.), *Adults returning to study mathematics: Papers from Working Group 18, 8th International Congress on Mathematical Education, ICME 8.* Adelaide, SA: Australian Association of Mathematics Teachers, 191-201.

Wedege, T. (1998). 'Adults knowing and learning mathematics.' In S. Tøsse, B. Bergstedt, A. Puurula, & P. Falkencrone (Eds.), *Corporate and nonformal learning. Adult education research in Nordic countries.* Trondheim: Tapir Forlag, 177-197.

Wedege, T. (1999). 'To know - or not to know - mathematics, that is a question of context.' *Educational Studies in Mathematics*, 39(1-3), 205-227.

Wedege, T., Benn, R., & Maasz, J. (in press). ''Adults learning mathematics' as a community of practice and research.' In D. Coben & M. van Groenestijn (Comps.), *Proceedings of the fifth international conference of Adults Learning Mathematics (ALM-5), 54-63.*

Wepner, G. (1986). 'Mathematics & Remediation. What is the Real Problem.' *Mathematics and Computer Education, 20*(2) 103-106.

Withnall, A. (1995). *Older Adults' Needs and Usage of Numerical Skills in Everyday Life.* Lancaster, England: Lancaster University. ED383879.

Wolf, A., Silver, R. & Kelson, M. (1990). *Learning in Context: Patterns of Skill Transfer and Their Training Implications.* R & D Monograph No. 43. Sheffield: Department of Employment.

Wolfgang, M. E. & Dowling, W. D. (1981). 'Differences in motivation of adult and younger undergraduates.' *Journal of Higher Education, 52*(6), 640-648.

Wood, L. N., & Perrett, G. (1997). *Advanced mathematical discourse.* Sydney, NSW: University of Technology, Sydney.

Yasukawa, K., Johnston, B. & Yates, W. (1995). 'Numeracy as a critical constructivist awareness of Maths -Case studies from Engineering and Adult Basic Education.' In R. P. Hunting, G. E. FitzSimons:C. Clarkson, & A. J. Bishop (Eds.), *Regional collaboration in mathematics education 1995.* Melbourne: Monash University, 815-825.

Zevenbergen, R. (1996). The situated numeracy of pool builders. *Critical Forum, 4*(2), 34-46.

Section I: Perspectives on Research on Adults Learning Mathematics

Introduction

Diana Coben
School of Continuing Education, University of Nottingham, UK

What do we know, what do we need to know, and how should we go about researching adults learning mathematics? These are the questions addressed in various ways by the authors of chapters in the opening section of this book. These chapters, which are outlined in Chapter 1, are offered as examples of some of the many different perspectives on research into adults learning mathematics. They focus particularly on theoretical and methodological issues and draw on various theoretical frameworks. They are not intended to be representative of the field as a whole. Indeed, it is hard to imagine at this juncture how one might represent 'the field as a whole', since to do so would imply a consensus about the constitution of the research domain where none exists. Such a consensus takes time to emerge and the review by Gail Godden and Gail FitzSimons reveals that the field is, if not quite in its infancy, still in the first flush of youth. Much of the research activity reviewed dates from the mid-1990s, a time when various initiatives, including the founding of Adults Learning Mathematics - A Research Forum (ALM), aimed to develop research and/or practice in the field. Moreover, the field itself is ill-defined - or wide open, depending on one's point of view. This aspect of the research domain raises a question which is explored briefly here as a prelude to the chapters following: what is the nature of 'adults learning mathematics' as a research domain?

A debate on this question was initiated by Tine Wedege (1998) at the fourth international conference of ALM (ALM-4) and continued at ALM-5 (Wedege, Benn & Maaß, 1999). In her account of the debate at ALM-5, Wedege argues that the definition of mathematics is a central task in the

47

D. Coben et al. (eds.), Perspectives on Adults Learning Mathematics, 47–51.
© 2000 *Kluwer Academic Publishers. Printed in the Netherlands.*

construction of a 'problematique' of adults learning mathematics because "when mathematics is defined to include numeracy we have moved out of the mathematics teaching in school and into society and adults lived life". (1999:56). She also concludes that practice and research in adults learning mathematics are *"situated in the border area between sociology, adult education and mathematics education"* (italics in original)(1999:57). Finally, she distinguishes between two different approaches: "an objective perspective (society's requirements of numeracy) and a subjective perspective (adults' individual need for numeracy)" (Wedege, in Wedege, Benn & Maaß, 1999:58).

Roseanne Benn also regards the concept of mathematics as key. In her book, *Adults Count Too* (Benn 1997:27) she examines whether mathematics is "rational thought evolving according to its own inner logic or an irreducibly social and cultural phenomenon, open to rational and irrational influences", a distinction also characterised as between 'absolutist' and 'fallibilist' views of mathematics, the latter following Lakatos (1976). She acknowledges the continuing power and influence of the absolutist view but argues that the way towards a more egalitarian society is that of the fallibilist social constructivists (Benn, 1997: 39).

In her contribution to the debate at ALM-5, Benn proposes the analogy of a 'moorland' rather than a 'bounded field' of adults learning mathematics because of "its connotation of informal, uneven edges, public ownership, open access". Drawing on Foucault's construction of academic disciplines as notions which control and bound our world, she asks: does the investigation of adults learning mathematics need to sit inside established boundaries in order to gain status and power? Is it more advantageous to be on the periphery of a powerful centre (such as mainstream mathematics education) or risk being at the centre of a new but (or therefore) powerless centre? (Benn, in Wedege, Benn & Maaß, 1999).

Benn's tentative conceptualisation is reproduced below (Figure 1) and shows adults learning mathematics "drawing most heavily on adult education, mathematics education and mathematics but also being influenced by theories from philosophy, sociology, psychology, history, literacy and education".

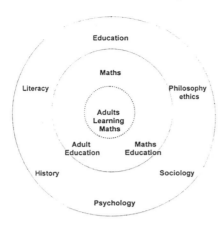

Figure 1. Benn's 'Concentric Circles' in Wedege, Benn & Maaß, 1999.

Benn's conceptualisation of concentric rings offers a way of thinking about research in adults learning mathematics in relation to neighbouring disciplines. But are the 'neighbours' correctly positioned and is the picture complete? The 'outer ring' is distant from the central 'moorland', a positioning not borne out by Juan Carlos Llorente's or Adrian Simpson's and Janet Duffin's research (described in this section). For example, Llorente utilises psychological theory to explore a research question spanning psychology, epistemology and mathematics ('how do uneducated adults constitute knowledge of proportionality?') and he does so for educational purposes (in order to inform the teaching of adults with little formal education). Also, I use political and anthropological theory in my chapter in this section, neither of which appear on Benn's diagram. Moreover, Benn's conceptualisation treats as 'givens' the research domains of mathematics education and adult education, each of which is problematic in its own right. In the case of mathematics education this is evidenced by the title of the International Congress on Mathematics Instruction (ICMI) study, *Mathematics Education as a Research Domain: A Search for Identity* (Sierpinska & Kilpatrick, 1998). Similarly, adult education is an exceptionally diverse and under-theorised field (see Tight, 1996; Usher & Bryant, 1989) and the authors of a study of citation patterns point out that adult education has not yet generated significant "'invisible colleges' of scholars pursuing common debates and themes" (Field et al., 1991:20).

Perhaps no two-dimensional representation could do justice to the complexity of the field (or moorland). It may be appropriate instead to consider the nature of academic disciplines *per se*. A useful source in this respect is Tony Becher, who, in his cogent study of 'Academic Tribes and Territories' (1989:33) cites Dill's (1982) view that "knowledge communities are defined and reinforced by the 'nurturance of myth, the identification of unifying symbols, the cannonisation of exemplars, and the formation of guilds'" (Dill, quoted in Becher, 1989:33). In these terms, adults learning mathematics appears too young a formation to have acquired its own 'myths', identified its 'unifying symbols' or 'cannonised its exemplars', although ALM and other organisations in the field might perhaps be described as 'guilds'.

More concretely, Becher characterises knowledge forms and knowledge communities as having "four basic sets of properties: hard/soft and pure/applied in the cognitive realm; convergent/divergent and urban/rural in the social" (Becher, 1989:153). In these terms, adults learning mathematics is cognate with 'soft pure knowledge', meaning that it has "unclear boundaries, problems which are broad in scope and loose in definition, a relatively unspecific theoretical structure, a concern with the qualitative and particular, and a reiterative pattern of enquiry" (Becher, 1989:153). It is also a 'divergent rural' knowledge community in Becher's terms. It is 'divergent' because it lacks intellectual control and a stable elite and tolerates a measure of intellectual deviance, thereby risking, according to Becher, "degenerating into self-destructive disputation", and 'rural' since researchers span a broad area, across which problems are thinly scattered and within which they are not sharply distinguished (Becher, 1989:154). But Becher also points out that academic disciplines may vary in different places and change over time - the latter point being particularly relevant to an emergent area of research.

However, adults learning mathematics was a field of practice before it became a research domain; it remains an extremely diverse and challenging field of practice. It is the inter-relations between research and practice that are important here. As Benn notes, research looks to practice, in this if no other discipline, for its grassroots. Without the link to practice it would become sterile. Practice not bedded in research is vulnerable both to accusations of narrowness and parochial thinking but also to the low status that un-researched disciplines are accorded in our society. (Benn, in Wedege, Benn & Maaß, 1999). She goes on to say that "While the teaching is sound and dedicated, as a discipline [adults learning mathematics] is still under-theorised and this is to its detriment" (Benn, in Wedege, Benn & Maaß, 1999:62).

The attempt to define the research domain of adults learning mathematics might be of no more than academic interest were it not for the fact that how we think about the field delimits what we consider researchable and, if left unclear, can lead to confusion and misunderstandings. For the purposes of this book, therefore, it is important to be clear about what we mean by 'adults learning mathematics' as a research domain, however soft, pure, rural and divergent, in Becher's terms. So, to sum up: here adults learning mathematics is regarded as an emerging research domain, interdisciplinary within the social sciences (as is its 'parent' field, education) and spanning the sub-fields of mathematics education and adult education. 'Mathematics' is taken to mean mathematics learned and taught at any level, including the most basic and, in Wedege's terms, it includes 'numeracy', or mathematics in the social context.

REFERENCES

Becher, T. (1989) *Academic Tribes and Territories - Intellectual Enquiry and the Cultures of Disciplines.* Milton Keynes: Open University Press/Society for Research into Higher Education

Benn, R. (1997) *Adults Count Too: Mathematics for Empowerment.* Leicester: NIACE

Dill, D.D. (1982) 'The management of academic culture'. *Higher Education,* 11, 303-20

Field, J., Lovell, T. & Weller, P. (1991) *Research Quality in Continuing Education: A Study of Citations Patterns.* Coventry: University of Warwick Research Paper in Continuing Education, No. 3

Lakatos, I. (1976) *Proofs and Refutations: The Logic of Mathematical Discovery.* Cambridge: Cambridge University Press

Sierpinska, A. & Kilpatrick, J. (Eds) (1998) *Mathematics Education as a Research Domain: A Search for Identity.* Dordrecht, The Netherlands: Kluwer Academic Publishers

Tight, M. (1996) *Key Concepts in Adult Education and Training.* London and New York: Routledge

Usher, R.S. & Bryant, I. (1989) *Adult Education as Theory, Practice and Research: The Captive Triangle.* London: Routledge

Wedege, T. (1998) 'Could there be a specific problematique for research in adult mathematics education'. In D. Coben & J. O'Donoghue (Comps.) *Adults Learning Maths-4: Proceedings of ALM-4, the Fourth International Conference of Adults Learning Maths - A Research Forum* held at University of Limerick, Ireland, July 4-6 1997. London: Goldsmiths College, University of London in association with Adults Learning Maths - A Research Forum (ALM), 210-17

Wedege, T., Benn, R. & Maaß, J. (1999) '"Adults Learning Mathematics" as a community of research and practice'. In M. van Groenestijn & D. Coben (Comps) *Mathematics as Part of Lifelong Learning. Proceedings of ALM-5, the Fifth International Conference of Adults Learning Maths - A Research Forum* held in Utrecht, The Netherlands, July 1-3 1998. London: Goldsmiths College, University of London in association with Adults Learning Maths - A Research Forum (ALM).

Chapter 3

Mathematics or Common Sense?
Researching 'Invisible' Mathematics through Adults' Mathematics Life Histories

Diana Coben
School of Continuing Education, University of Nottingham, UK

INTRODUCTION

This chapter reflects on research I undertook with Gillian Thumpston at Goldsmiths College, University of London, in which we interviewed adults about the mathematics in their lives, both past and present, in order to create a series of what we called 'mathematics life histories'[1]. We used the term 'mathematics life histories' to describe adults' accounts of their mathematical experiences throughout life - both those that are explicitly mathematical (such as being taught subtraction at school, or working out a budget as an adult) as well as those in which mathematics is implicit (such as knitting or judging distances when driving). Originally developed by oral historians and by educationalists, especially in the field of language and literacy (see Hoar *et al.* eds, 1994), mathematics life history research is a new and exciting area (see Bloomfield & Clews, 1995; Thumpston & Coben, 1995; Briggs, 1994). We hope our work might contribute to the development of greater understanding in the hitherto neglected area of adults learning mathematics[2]. Our aim was to learn more about the place and meaning of mathematics in adults' lives, to open up the area for further research, and to begin to develop some themes and ideas which might lead to the construction of original interpretative frameworks.

In the pilot stage of our research (from January to September 1994) we interviewed neighbours, friends and family members - any adult who came forward and expressed an interest. We tried out various approaches and

D. Coben et al. (eds.), Perspectives on Adults Learning Mathematics, 53–66.
© 2000 *Kluwer Academic Publishers. Printed in the Netherlands.*

refined our interview technique. Our interviewees at this stage were a very diverse group in educational terms, ranging from one who had left school at 13 after a minimal mathematical education, to people with mathematics degrees or many years of experience in work in which mathematics plays a major part, such as engineering.

In phase two, from September 1994 to July 1995, we concentrated on adult students (for this purpose we defined an adult as anyone over 20) at Goldsmiths, studying any of the range of liberal arts and social sciences subjects offered by the College. Our research subjects at this stage were educationally more homogeneous insofar as they were all studying for, or preparing to study for a degree, although not necessarily one involving mathematics. All our interviewees were self-selected volunteers, contacted either through word-of-mouth or through newspaper and poster announcements in the College.

In both phases of the research we used qualitative non-observational research techniques (McKernan, 1991) involving semi-structured interviews (Spradley, 1979; Denzin, 1978; Schatzman & Strauss, 1973) which we recorded on audio tape. This technique enabled us to maintain points of comparison between interviews while engaging in open-ended, in-depth, one-to-one conversations lasting about one hour each. After the interview, we transcribed the tape, sent the transcript to the interviewee and asked him or her to reflect on the interview and amend or augment the transcript.

EMERGENT THEMES

Some themes emerged from our research, which we designated as follows:

- **the brick wall** - the point (usually in childhood) at which mathematics ceased to make sense; for some people it was long division, for others fractions or algebra, while others never hit the brick wall. For those who did, the impact was often traumatic and long-lasting.

- **the 'significant other'** - someone perceived by the interviewee as a major influence on his or her mathematics life history. The influence might be positive or negative, past or present, persisting sometimes for many years after the event. Significant others include, for example: a parent who tried to help with mathematics homework; a teacher who abused her authority and the power of the subject; a partner who undermined the interviewee's confidence in her mathematical abilities.

- **the door** - marked 'Mathematics', locked or unlocked, through which one has to go to enter or progress within a chosen line of work or study. This image was often used, reflecting the frequency with which mathematics tests are used to filter entry into training and employment.

• **invisible mathematics** - the mathematics one can do, which one does not think of as mathematics - also known as common sense.

In the rest of this chapter I shall focus on the last of these themes.

INVISIBLE MATHEMATICS

The mathematics one can do but which one does not recognise as mathematics, we term 'invisible mathematics', after Paulus Gerdes (1986) and Mary Harris (1995; this volume). This 'invisible mathematics' is intriguing in that it opens up fascinating questions about the nature of mathematical knowledge and understanding; it is also worrying in that rendering mathematics invisible may have potentially harmful - or at least, limiting - effects on the individuals concerned and perhaps, more widely, on perceptions of mathematics in society in general. Firstly, for the individuals concerned, 'mathematics' is rendered unattainable, always out of reach - it becomes, by definition, that which they cannot do. Secondly, the individual's negative self-image as someone who is unable to do mathematics may impact on his or her confidence as a learner, since mathematical ability is widely considered to be related to - even an index of - general intellectual ability. Thirdly, knowledge, understanding and skills which are not recognised as mathematical may be more difficult to transfer to different situations than those which are so recognised, although this is debatable (see Evans, this volume). Fourthly, in society at large, the image of mathematics as difficult, only for the select few, is maintained rather than challenged.

Having come to recognise her own 'invisible mathematics' as an adult, this is how one of our interviewees, Eileen, (39 years old and studying for a psychology degree) put it:

> If somebody says 'I can't do maths' I think what they are saying is 'I can't do that part of it', they are not saying 'I can't add up or take away, I can't work out how much my mortgage is going to be, or I can't work out how much I've got left'. What they are saying is 'I can't do that part of it' but that's what they call maths and I realise that was what I was doing.

Similarly, some people do not appear to recognise what they can do as mathematics unless it is in the form of a standard algorithm or formula. 'Proper mathematics', for most of our interviewees, seemed to consist mainly of arithmetic - indeed, not only arithmetic, but standard algorithms in arithmetic. This is compounded by the widely-held view that there is only one standard algorithm for each operation - usually the one the person was taught in school. For example, one man talked about a problem he had of marking out an athletics field for young children, reducing the standard adult track and throwing pitch markings. He had converted the running track but was having difficulty with the curved markings for the throwing events. How could he find the correct formula that would allow him to mark the pitch? He knew he could do it by using rope and pegs - but as he would not be able to write down the calculation in a suitably 'mathematical' form, he felt that this was not 'doing mathematics'.

Such narrow conceptions of mathematical legitimacy prompt speculation about the relationship between adults' mathematical practices and the ways in which mathematics has been taught to them as children. Perhaps this man's reluctance to experiment with a practical method reflected an emphasis in his mathematics education on factual recall and skills practice rather than investigation.

Of course, the fact that something has been taught does not necessarily mean that it has been learned (or that it is remembered). Conversely, what has been learned may not have been formally taught. By the time they are adults, many people seem to be operating with a mixture of mathematics remembered (or half-forgotten) from school, together with concepts and methods they have developed in adult life and which they may not recognise as mathematical. It is a mixture of visible and invisible mathematics and the mixture does not always cohere. Accordingly, adults' mathematical knowledge often appears fragmented, rather like the knowledge of a city acquired by people who travel mostly by underground railway and do not know how the stations relate to each other on the surface (an image which raises interesting questions about which is more 'real', the surface or the underground?). When connections are made they may come as a revelation. For example, Eileen recalled her experience of studying for her General Certificate of Secondary Education (GCSE) in mathematics as an adult:

> I remember being totally surprised that when I went on the GCSE maths course I could work with shapes, circles, triangles and squares, because I thought I didn't know what the angles of a triangle came to, and I guessed on this test paper and I got it right - so I must have known and I just didn't think I knew.

So how does invisible mathematics relate to common sense? Another of our interviewees, May, a woman of 79, expressed it like this: talking about doing do-it-yourself jobs around the house she said:

You measure, put up shelves, you measure distance, size, and the brackets, where they go - that all involves general maths. To me, though, that's just common sense. [...] You don't think of [it] as being maths.

Let's look more closely at the concept of 'common sense', drawing on the formulation first discussed at the *Political Dimensions of Mathematics Education III* (PDME-III) conference (Coben & Thumpston, 1996). In this formulation, common sense is considered in terms of what it is perceived to be, as opposed to what it is perceived not to be, and whether this perception is generally regarded as positive, negative or neutral.

Common Sense

common sense as:	*regarded as:*	*as opposed to:*
general intelligence, 'native wit' 'nous'	positive	stupidity
rationality 'making sense'	positive	incoherence, nonsense
being down-to-earth	positive (particularly in USA)	out of touch with reality
something that 'feels right', that 'fits'	positive	out of place, awkward
being mature, experienced, 'knowing your way around'	positive	uninitiated, ignorant, gauche
the sense which you have made your own	positive	untested 'second-hand' ideas
well-worked out, thought-through	positive	wildly 'off-beam'
dependable, reliable	positive	shaky, uncertain
being practical, 'hands on'	neutral-positive	theoretical
'second nature', instinct, intuition	neutral-positive	that which has to be learned

'the sense you were born with' habitual	neutral-positive	special, unusual
something everyone has - or should have	neutral	something idiosyncratic
'sense' which is 'common' to the majority	neutral-negative (Manzoni)	'good sense' = knowing the truth
the jumble of unthought-out ideas that we all carry around with us	neutral-negative (Gramsci)	'good sense' = critical, open, Marxism
self-evident, hardly worth mentioning, 'just common sense'	dismissive-neutral	serious knowledge
taken for granted	negative	critical

As the list above indicates, common sense is multi-faceted, with positive, negative and neutral connotations. One of the most interesting meanings listed above was developed by Antonio Gramsci in his prison notebooks (1971), written during his 11 years as a prisoner of Mussolini's fascist government. His source is the nineteenth century Italian novelist, Manzoni, in his novel *The Betrothed*. In the novel, a group of people is wrongly blamed for an outbreak of plague; while many people (of 'good sense') realise that the accusation is false, out of fear of the 'common sense' of the majority they do nothing to prevent the victimisation of the scapegoats. Writing under the constraints of censorship, Gramsci developed Manzoni's distinction, using 'good sense' partly as a code term for his own brand of critical, open, Marxism, and 'common sense' to mean the jumble of unthought-out ideas that we all carry around with us and which he saw as consisting of myriad historical and cultural traces. The task for Gramsci is to create 'good sense' out of 'common sense' through an educative politics - that is, not just political education but education through engagement in political activity - which Gramsci saw in very wide terms, including theatre, art and all forms of culture.

I find Gramsci's distinction an apt analogy for adults learning mathematics: they (we) are trying to create 'good sense' out of 'common sense' in mathematics. I also find Gramsci's broad conception of culture and politics wonderfully fruitful when considering mathematics (a field of knowledge which is often regarded as culture-free) as a cultural phenomenon (see Ernest, 1989:200-2; Bishop, 1991:29-41). Moreover, Gramsci's concept of common sense as something to be transcended rather than rejected, implies an educative process rooted in, and respectful of, people's lived experience, and it is the nature of people's experience in relation to mathematics that Gillian Thumpston and I sought to explore in our mathematics life history research. As the anthropologist Clifford Geertz puts it, "Common sense is not what the mind cleared of cant spontaneously apprehends; it is what the mind filled with presuppositions [...] concludes" (Geertz, 1993:84).

There are problems in the linking of mathematical meaning with common sense, not least because important aspects of mathematics are counter-intuitive. Such questions as: how can π 'go on for ever'? why does 'a minus times a minus make a plus'? what are negative numbers? cannot be answered very easily, if at all, in common sense terms.

Nevertheless, we believe that paying attention to common sense may help us to understand better the difficulties that so many adults have with mathematics, particularly those which seem out of proportion with the mathematical abilities they may display in aspects of their lives. For example, William, an unemployed labourer who left school at 13, described how he kept his accounts and how he had worked in harness-making, in terms which made it clear he understood the mathematics involved, despite his professed fear of mathematics.

Mathematics is not a singular subject, it has its sub-disciplines, and our research indicates that people may find some of these more congenial than others. In the case of Leonard, a retired bank worker who had spent many years calculating 'by hand' before the advent of the electronic calculator and computer, he liked arithmetic (apart from decimals and percentages), but disliked

> the science of maths - trigonometry and all that... algebra, I never took to that [...]
> logarithms - what is all that for? [...] 'to the power of something', that's another
> thing... square roots, in everyday life you don't do them.

We are interested in the way that, for some of the people we interviewed, liking, familiarity and usefulness seem to combine to turn some aspects of mathematics into common sense, while other areas remained inaccessible. Eileen's example seems to show that recognising the mathematics embedded in what one thinks of as common sense can make a significant breakthrough towards seeing oneself as mathematically capable. This is not to argue that mathematics and common sense are one and the same; rather it is to say that a recognition of the mathematics embedded in their common sense may help some people to develop mathematically in adulthood beyond the point they have already reached. But common sense is not only embedded *within* mathematics, a recognition of the tension between mathematics and common sense is surely also essential - how else can counter-intuitive elements of mathematics ever become accepted as part of one's mathematical 'good sense'?

In his lecture on mathematics and common sense at the eighth International Congress on Mathematical Education (ICME-8), Professor Geoffrey Howson stressed the need to demonstrate that, unlike common sense, mathematics relies on construction, organisation and sharing of concepts. Mathematics is therefore more than common sense and mathematics teaching needs to develop common sense to "bring it up" to mathematics (Howson, 1998). But is the quantitative, incremental metaphor appropriate here? I am not sure that it is, and this raises a corresponding question about Gramsci's 'common sense'/'good sense' dichotomy[4]. A horticultural metaphor may be more appropriate: for Gramsci, common sense is the overgrown weed-infested area containing the seeds from which good sense may be cultivated. Gramsci clearly ranks 'good sense' above the weeds of 'common sense', just as Howson ranks 'common sense' lower than mathematics. This ranking of good sense/mathematics over common sense may appear anti-democratic (although of course it depends what one means by that notoriously elastic concept: democracy). In mathematical terms, it seems to downgrade popular knowledge and informal techniques and understandings, just at a time when their importance is beginning to be recognised (see for example, Llorente, this volume; Llorente, 1996; Powell & Frankenstein eds 1997; Knijnik, this volume; Nunes, Schliemann & Carraher, 1993; Powell & Frankenstein, 1997). On the basis of our life histories research I am not convinced that adults' mathematical common sense, the mathematics which remains stubbornly 'invisible', is any less meaningful and valuable than the systematised public mathematics of the academy.

Certainly, Gramsci did not see common sense and good sense as equally valuable or desirable: he tried and ultimately failed to transform the common sense of his place and time into what he saw as good sense. But the seriousness of his interest in common sense is one of the things that I find most compelling in Gramsci. He respects and analyses common sense, recognising its importance and its resilience and seeking to understand it: in this he provides a model for educators and researchers seeking to understand adults' mathematical practices.

Furthermore, for Gramsci, both common sense and good sense are dynamic concepts, in keeping with his theory of hegemony. Hegemony is characterised by a blend of force and consent; power is articulated through a complex of historically-specific forces and counter-forces; any settlement is inevitably provisional. Accordingly, any victory of good sense over common sense is temporary, holding only for as long as good sense is able to renew itself, partly through its relationship with common sense. Good sense is constantly being developed or deteriorating, as is common sense, and the relationship between the two is constantly developing or deteriorating also. Therefore, while conceptually the two elements are distinct and one is superior to the other, in practice they are intermingled and the task of the educator/political activist (the gardener) is to distinguish good sense and encourage its growth. But it is not a question of weeding out common sense, although some elements of common sense may be judged to be pernicious. To extend the horticultural metaphor: the gardener may seek to modify the plants themselves in order to develop new varieties - new forms of good sense.

However, the fact remains that such judgements are based on a ranking of good sense above common sense. How does this stand up in terms of mathematics? I think it stands up well if one takes a view of mathematical knowledge as itself dynamic and changing, with new knowledge regarded as provisional; it stands up less well if one takes a traditional view of mathematics as a set of absolute and unchanging truths.

Geertz's (1993) analysis of common sense may be useful here. He characterises common sense as "natural, practical, thin, immethodical, accessible" (Geertz, 1993:85). By 'naturalness' he means the quality of common sense that

represents matters [...] as being what they are in the simple nature of the case. An air of 'of courseness' a sense of 'it figures' is cast over things [...]. They are depicted as inherent in the situation, intrinsic aspects of reality, the way things go. (Geertz, 1993:85)

Naturalness certainly seems to be a feature of common sense for many people. In relation to mathematics, it is perhaps the naturalness of common sense that renders the mathematics it encompasses invisible.

Common sense also has the quality of 'practicalness', in Geertz's terms, since it entails being sagacious, prudent, level headed (Geertz, 1993:87). These are qualities which people seem to associate with common sense - and also with mathematics. Particularly when describing operations and transactions with money, even people who describe themselves as 'hopeless at mathematics', reveal a sureness that belies their professed inadequacy. For example, Maria, a woman of 63 who admitted she was "not a great lover of the subject" (mathematics), said she always checked her bank statements because she had to be very careful:

I have money in the building society and a lot of that has to come out in a couple of months because I'm going on holiday, so I have to calculate how much to take out and how much to leave in. But I am very good with money I must admit, one thing I am good at.

Being 'good with money' entails the exercise of mathematical skills, as she implicitly acknowledges with the use of the word 'calculate'. But more importantly, it entails exercising sound judgement, making decisions based on a clear-sighted view of the situation in which one finds oneself.

Money was also the key to mathematical common sense for Alan, a self-employed man who prided himself on his financial acumen: he said that when he was younger he "just figured maths was all geometry and algebra" and did not care for it. Now, at 40, he enjoyed the very different mathematics involved in his work - it made sense to him in a way that school mathematics never did - I think this is because he can see the 'practicalness' of it, in Geertz's terms:

I really like business in conjunction with finance - I love money!! Profit and loss... I enjoy doing it - I'm not an expert, lots to learn. I understand it when I do accounts. [...] I love company accounts better than anything.

Another man, Joe, 33, who described mathematics as "a brick wall" nevertheless said

You won't believe this, but I do get pleasure from this - when it is relevant - for solving real problems, when I know what I'm doing and everything is correct [...]. I get irritable when it is not real and I don't know how to tackle it.

Thinness, Geertz's next quality of common sense, is rather more elusive:

Thinness is like modesty in cheese, rather hard to formulate in more explicit terms. 'Simpleness' or even 'literalness' might serve as well or better [...]. The world is what the wide-awake, uncomplicated person takes it to be. (Geertz, 1993:89)

It is the 'thinness' of common sense - its openness and fragility - that renders it vulnerable to attack from reason. Perhaps because of this, it is often held as beyond argument, a matter of faith; consequently, though 'thin', it may prove remarkably resilient. It may be, also, that the 'thinness' of common sense is borne out as much in what people do not say in the interviews as in what they do say. For example, the man for whom mathematics is a 'brick wall' made no mention of the mathematics involved in his photography course, nor of that in his job in telecommunications. It is as if he were saying that if he can do it, it cannot be mathematics. Is he perhaps maintaining his common sense view of his life - as mathematically uncomplicated - at the expense of a fuller recognition of the mathematics he does? Perhaps the 'thinness' of mathematical common sense matches the invisibility of mathematics for him.

Common sense is also, for Geertz, 'immethodical', by which he means that it is "shamelessly and unapologetically *ad hoc* [...] a sort of *pot pourri* of disparate notions" (Geertz, 1993:91). Of all the qualities of common sense that Geertz identifies, 'immethodicalness' is perhaps the most problematic in relation to mathematics, which is, on the face of it, the least *ad hoc* of all disciplines. But if mathematics is considered as a set of practices - which is what we are doing in our mathematics life histories research - we are trying to identify and understand the mathematics practices in people's lives - a different picture emerges. Certainly, in our research, examples abound of the *ad hoc* nature of common sense techniques involving aspects of mathematics. For example, in answer to a question about whether she uses knitting patterns, May, the 79 year old woman quoted above, said:

Sometimes I make up my own. When I say I make up my own, I make it up as I go along, I do that. Sometimes I make patterns in the actual pattern itself. I mean design, not the shape, I might adapt one from another, you know, partly because I've made things for the children which is from a grown-up pattern and I think 'That would be rather nice around the edge' so I change it and adapt it to fit. [...] To me, it's common sense, I suppose if you think about it, it does involve mathematics.

Finally, common sense is 'accessible'; by 'accessibleness', Geertz means that:

any person with faculties reasonably intact can grasp common-sense conclusions, and indeed, once they are unequivocally enough stated, will not only grasp but embrace them. But, for all that, there are no acknowledged specialists in common sense. Everyone thinks he is an expert. (Geertz, 1993:91)

The 'accessibleness' of common sense works both ways in relation to mathematics practices - on the one hand the assumption that at least some aspects of mathematics are 'just common sense', accessible to everyone, makes it shaming to admit incompetence or lack of understanding; on the other hand, the accessibility of common sense mathematics might be expected to remove some of the mystique surrounding mathematics, although our research suggests that the mystique remains, because the definition of mathematics is adjusted to exclude common sense explanations and techniques.

CONCLUSION

So where does this leave us? Certainly we are left with more questions than answers, but perhaps some provisional answers may be given. Is common sense essential for the development of mathematical good sense in Gramsci's terms? Is it, as the writers of one paper at a recent conference on mathematics education and common sense stated: "a form of awareness that can be educated" (Mason & Monteiro in Keitel *et al.*, 1996:97)? Does Geertz' analysis of common sense as "natural, practical, thin, immethodical, accessible" offer useful insights for adult mathematics educators? I have argued that the answer to these questions is 'yes'. Further research may shed more light on the place and meaning of mathematics in adults' lives and perhaps help to render 'invisible' mathematics more visible to us all.

ACKNOWLEDGEMENT

This is an edited version of a paper which first appeared as 'Mathematics or Common Sense? Some Reflections on Research into Adults' Mathematics Life Histories' in Gail E. FitzSimons (ed.) (1997) *Adults Returning to Study Mathematics: Papers from Working Group 18, 8th International Congress on Mathematical Education ICME 8*. Adelaide, SA: Australian Association of Mathematics Teachers, 37-48. It is reprinted with permission from the Australian Association of Mathematics Teachers.

NOTES

1. This paper draws on research undertaken with Gillian Thumpston at Goldsmiths College, University of London. We have written about this research in a series of conference papers (see References, below).
2. *Adults Learning Mathematics - A Research Forum* (ALM) is an international forum founded in 1994 to promote research in this field. Membership is open to individuals and institutions. For details, please contact: Professor John O'Donoghue, ALM Chair, Department of Mathematics and Statistics, University of Limerick, Limerick, Rep. Ireland; email: john.odonoghue@ul.ie
3. Gramsci's ideas in relation to the education of adults are discussed in my book, *Radical Heroes: Gramsci, Freire and the Politics of Adult Education,* published in 1998 in New York and London by Garland Publishing Inc./Taylor and Francis.

4. I am grateful to Dr Gelsa Knijnik of Universidade do Vale do Sinos, Brazil, for some fruitful discussions on this point.

REFERENCES

Bishop, A. (1991) 'Mathematics education in its cultural context'. In M. Harris (Ed.) *Schools, Mathematics and Work*. Basingstoke: Falmer Press, 29-41.

Bloomfield, A. & Clews, J. (1995) 'Mathematical Voyages: The factors which influence students' involvement in mathematics'. In D. Coben (Comp) *Proceedings of the Inaugural Conference of Adults Learning Maths - A Research Forum (ALM-1)*. London: Goldsmiths College, University of London in conjunction with ALM, 34-5

Briggs, M. (1994) 'Automathematics biographies' . In *Life Histories and Learning: Language, the Self and Education* Conference Papers, University of Sussex, Brighton 19-21 September 1994, 24-28

Coben, D. & Atere-Roberts, E. (1996) *Carefree Calculations for Healthcare Students*. London: Macmillan

Coben, D. & Thumpston, G. (1995) 'Researching Mathematics Life Histories: A Case Study'. In D. Coben (Comp) *Mathematics with a Human Face, Proceedings of the Second Conference of Adults Learning: Maths - A Research Forum (ALM-2)*. London: Goldsmiths, University of London in conjunction with ALM, 40-45

Coben, D. & Thumpston, G. (1996) 'Common Sense, Good Sense and Invisible Mathematics'. In T. Kjærgård, A. Kvamme, N. Lindén (Eds) *PDME III Proceedings: Numeracy, Gender, Class, Race*. eds. *Numeracy, Race, Gender and Class*, Proceedings of the Third International Conference of Political Dimensions of Mathematics Education (PDME) III, Bergen, Norway, July 24-27 1995. Landås, Norway: Caspar, 284-298

Denzin, N. (1978) *The Research Act: A Theoretical Introduction to Sociological Methods* 2nd ed. New York: McGraw-Hill

Ernest, P. (Ed.) (1989) *Mathematics Teaching: the state of the art*. London: Falmer Press

Geertz, C. (1993) *Local Knowledge: further essays in interpretive anthropology*. London: Fontana

Gramsci, A. (1971) *Selections from the Prison Notebooks* edited and translated by Q. Hoare and G. Nowell-Smith. London: Lawrence and Wishart

Harris, M. (1995) *Common Threads: Women Maths and Work*, London: Trentham

Harris, M. (Ed.) (1991) *Schools, Mathematics and Work*. Basingstoke: Falmer Press

Hoar, M., Thomson, A., & West, L. (Eds) (1994) *'Life Histories and Learning: Language, the Self and Education'* Conference Papers, September 1994, University of Sussex, Brighton, 19-21

Howson, G. (1998) 'Mathematics and Common Sense'. In Alsina, C., Alvarez, J.M., Hodgson, B., Laborde, C. and Pérez, A. (Eds) *8th International Congress on Mathematical Education. Selected Lectures*. Seville, Spain: S.A.E.M. 'THALES', 257-69

Keitel, C., Gellert, U., Jablonka, E. & Müller, M. (Eds) (1996) *Mathematics Education and Common Sense: the challenge of social change and technological development*, Proceedings of the 47th meeting of the International Commission for the Study and Improvement of Mathematics Teaching (ICSIMT/CIEAEM) in Berlin, 23-29 July 1995

Llorente, J. C. (1996) 'Problem Solving and Constitution of Knowledge at Work', *Research Bulletin 92*. Helsinki, Finland: Department of Education, University of Helsinki

McKernan, J. (1991) *Curriculum Action Research: A Handbook of Methods and Resources for the Reflective Practitioner*. New York: St. Martin's Press

Mason, J. & Monteiro, B. (1996) 'Conflicts Between Common Sense and Experience and Concomitant Shifts in Attention' in Keitel *et al.* (Eds) *Mathematics Education and Common Sense: the challenge of social change and technological development,* Proceedings of the 47th meeting of the International Commission for the Study and Improvement of Mathematics Teaching (ICSIMT/CIEAEM) in Berlin, 23-29 July 1995, 97-101

Nunes, T., Schliemann, A.D. & Carraher, D.W. (1993) *Street Mathematics and School Mathematics.* Cambridge: Cambridge University Press

Powell, A.B. & Frankenstein, M. (eds) (1997) *Ethnomathematics: Challenging Eurocentrism in Mathematics Education.* Albany, NY: State University of New York Press

Schatzman, L. & Strauss, A. (1973) *Field Research: Strategies for a Natural Sociology.* New Jersey: Prentice Hall

Spradley, J.P. (1979) *The Ethnographic Interview.* New York: Holt Rinehart and Winston

Thumpston, G. & Coben, D., (1995) 'Getting personal: research into adults' maths life histories'. In D. Coben (Comp) *Proceedings of the Inaugural Conference of Adults Learning Maths - A Research Forum (ALM-1).* London: Goldsmiths College, University of London, 30-33

Chapter 4

Researching Adults' Knowledge Through Piagetian Clinical Exploration - the case of domestic work.

Juan Carlos Llorente
CONICET - Argentina and University of Helsinki

INTRODUCTION

Piaget's work was confined to developmental explanations of childhood. Consequently clinical-critical exploration was developed and criticized within the same frame. I support the idea that the Piagetian central thesis and methodology give a good basis from which to study learning processes at any stage of human development. Adult learning can be studied and understood in terms of genetic epistemology and psychology.

First, I will address the theoretical and methodological possibilities of the Piagetian tradition in adult education by outlining its historical evolution. Second, I will refer to the use I have made of it in exploring domestic work (e.g. preparing jam).

I will present examples using data collected in Argentina to illuminate both the use of mathematical knowledge in task-oriented situations at work and the methodological approach used to capture it.

PIAGETIAN CLINICAL-CRITICAL EXPLORATION

In Piagetian studies generally the use of clinical exploration is presented as a function of the results attained and rarely do we find a characterization of this research perspective except in relation to the specific research task at hand. There is very little explicit literature dealing with the core of the

67

D. Coben et al. (eds.), Perspectives on Adults Learning Mathematics, 67–81.
© 2000 *Kluwer Academic Publishers. Printed in the Netherlands.*

Piagetian methodological approach. I shall present some of the main features of the method in order to analyse the use I have made of it.

Piaget started with a number of studies using clinical interrogation for formulating as well as verifying hypotheses. The new data obtained by Piaget constituted at that moment a gold mine for psychology and this was possible because of the clinical method. This potential and originality place Piagetian method among the best in psychological research. The clinical method is a key instrument for studying the complex formation of cognition (Vygotsky, 1982:31-32). From the first studies conducted by Piaget, the method has been applied with modifications enriching the research approach for studying cognition[1].

This method has undergone a number of changes in the course of the investigations carried out by Piaget and his collaborators. Initially, Piaget conceived of the interaction which occurs in the acquisition of knowledge in terms of interindividual relationships and viewed intellectual growth in terms of progressive decentration of the child's point of view. In order to explore their reasoning, he talked with children and tried to follow the often intricate patterns of their thoughts, taking as a model the 'clinical method' in which the psychiatrist tries to discover the roots of a patient's beliefs and to explore the nature of his pathological imagination (Inhelder, Sinclair & Bovet, 1974:19)

This analogy with psychiatric interviews was present in Piagetian studies in the beginning (1929). Though it is true that Piagetian methodological approach kept on developing based on this general analogy with psychiatric dialogues, its particular features came about little by little. These modifications were related to the objectives of the research. When Piaget started observing his own children he made natural observations combined with observations in contrived situations, but soon he turned to a combination of clinical method with experimentation for studying the concepts of conservation. Therefore, it is necessary to understand the historical transformations regarding the unity of the method through its diversity. That is, we can find many different variations of this methodological approach, but all share the main characteristics which constitute the core of the method.

The core of the method consists of the elaboration of hypotheses and their verification through the clinical interview or dialogue. The discourse includes instant checking of hypotheses (Perret-Clemont, 1980). This means a constant interaction between questions and answers but with specific focus on the answers of the subjects. Materials to organize the task are often used, e.g. from simple clay pallets to sophisticated coloured toys. However they are not a precondition in psychogenetic studies. In order to be able to constantly formulate hypotheses during the interview along with the movement question-answer-new-question the interviewer needs acute theoretical awareness. Otherwise there would be a failure to take advantage of the novelties given by the subjects. (Inhelder, Sinclair & Bovet, 1984)

Theoretical awareness[2] on the part of the interviewer, which may seem trivial, is related to essential aspects of the clinical exploration. If we reduce the critical exploration to a simple instrument of data collection the theoretical awareness needed to formulate and check hypotheses during the ongoing interview would have no place. In fact, if it were so, it would be just a technique for collecting empirical data where two clearly identifiable moments come about: (1) data collecting (2) hypotheses (Castorina, Lenzi & Fernandez, 1984:114). On the contrary, the clinical-critical exploration constitutes a method characterized by a single process which comprises both aspects - data collecting and hypotheses - as complementary and interdependent.

The analysis and interpretation of responses relies partly on what is called *vérification sur le vif.* This fundamental feature of the critical exploration method requires that the experimenter constantly formulate hypotheses about the children's reactions from the cognitive point of view, and then devise ways of immediately checking these suppositions in the experimental situation. (Inhelder, Sinclair & Bovet, 1974:22)

In this paragraph the authors refer to experimental situations. It must be noticed that a clinical interview does not necessarily involve an experimental task. It is possible to conduct the interview using the subjects' answers and ideas as sources for checking and formulating hypotheses without presenting any experimental task. The point in any case is to focus on the arguments and justifications given by the subject and not solely on the 'correct' or 'incorrect' answers. Clinical interviews have been combined with different research instruments.

In France, studies on the role of different types of social interactions in development (Perret-Clermont, 1980:1-36) have used a dual clinical and experimental approach. The clinical method was used to get access to fundamental cognitive organizations and the quantitative experimental method to make comparisons. With a different research interest, Schliemann (1988:69-85) has combined naturalistic observations with clinical interviews. The research focused on the differences in strategies of problem-solving between adults with formal schooling and adults without. In this study the interviewer presented a problem situation to the subjects during the interview. In Brazil, approaching the notion of space in adults without schooling, Colinvaux and Dibar Ure (1989:172-200) have used clinical interviews, which were conducted in groups. This way of using the Piagetian interview differs from the traditional studies as these interviews were always conducted individually.

Up to now I have tried to focus on the main features of the Piagetian method and to point out different uses of it. I will continue sketching the way I have used and developed the clinical-critical exploration for the purposes of the present inquiry. Figure 1 shows the two research procedures I have considered as methodological sources of inquiry by summarizing their distinctive features. Figure 2 shows the combination I have made of them to construct my own research instrument.

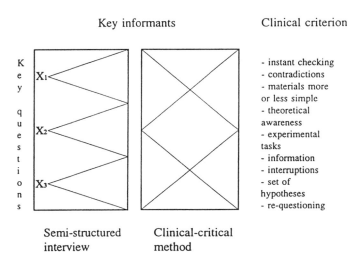

Figure 1. Two research procedures

I will start by juxtaposing two alternatives, a semi-structured interview and the clinical-critical method (Figure 1). These two procedures are strictly speaking not comparable. The semi-structured interview is mainly a technique for collecting data in qualitative research. Instead, the clinical-critical approach is a full-blown research method as I have presented before. Figure 1 shows that the semi-structured interview allows the interviewer to go to a greater or lesser extent beyond the key questions (X_n in Figure 1). S/he may open each key question when s/he considers it timely or otherwise proper. However the interview has always a predefined structure, the key questions, which will eventually be asked of every subject of the sample. In principle a semi-structured interview does not allow the interviewer to alter the key questions or topics predefined. The researcher's freedom follows the structure of the interview and thus is adjusted to it.

When applying clinical interviews the dialogue develops differently. There is no pre-established order for the questions. The direction of the interview is led by the emerging dialectic between interviewer-interviewee, questions-answers and formulation of hypotheses-verification of hypotheses. With clinical interviews the researcher tries to extract arguments and justifications from the subjects in order to unpack the closed answers given by the subjects. This is done in the ongoing interview. The interviewee's answers are the source of information for the researcher by which s/he guides the interview.

In this study I have combined both procedures, semi-structured interview and clinical interview. I have not applied them separately but in a single interview or research instrument. Instead of questions for structuring the interview, I defined key topics or thematic blocks and for each one a set of possible questions. When I applied this interview scheme I went through the predefined thematic blocks but unpacked them by questioning according to the clinical criterion.

The term clinical critierion[3] refers to the general characteristics of Piagetian method and to the instrumental techniques for interviewing which are the core of the method. The term is useful to differentiate the classical clinical interviews put forward by Piaget from other ways of using the method. Figure 2 shows the combination I have used to construct my own research instrument.

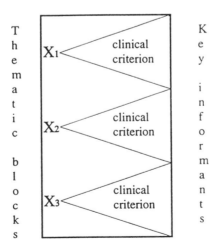

Figure 2. Research Instrument semi-structured interview with clinical criterion

The combination shown by Figure 2 matches to the third stage of the research process. It constitutes the application of the latest form of the research instrument to the final sample. The key blocks were evolving alongside the exploratory interviews. The first interviews were conducted giving priority to the clinical criterion. There was no predefined structure for interviewing. The successive interviews gained some structure based on the information obtained from both the interviewees and the key informants.

In the final stage the interview had a structure to follow. The structure was given by the thematic blocks rather than key questions. But the structure was not based on a set of hypotheses independent of the data. Instead, the structure of the interview was all the time empirically anchored due to the exploratory process developed. The dialectic process between concept-driven research and the light thrown by the data resulted in a structure every time. This way of defining the structure of the interview differs from the usual design and application of a semi-structured interview. In addition, the clinical criterion used to explore the thematic blocks produces qualitative information according to the research focus.

APPLYING THE INTERVIEW

Housewives and domestic helps

The housewives and domestic helps studied were interviewed in their homes or in their workplace. Within their everyday activities, I asked them to describe the procedures for preparing preserves and for knitting. For the first work task, although they could choose whatever preserves they wanted to talk about, they spontaneously decided to tell me about the preparation of jam. What varied from case to case was the type of fruit used, e.g. pears, apples, quince. I have chosen simply to analyze the preparation of jam. In any case, there was no substantial variation observed in the procedures and knowledge for preparing jam with different fruits. On the contrary, they reinforced and brought out the same evidence.

Before conducting the final interviews, I looked into the proportions for different jams and the characteristics e.g. the quantity of sugar per kilo of fruit, water, the simmering time, and the like. I attempted to obtain general information about the knowledge involved in the interviewees' everyday activities. The interviews were then conducted using clinical criteria (see Llorente 1996, Chapter 4) trying to problematize the procedure for the subjects during the description, allowing them to show how much they knew.

Fourteen women were interviewed who had school experience ranging from none to four years during their childhood[4]. Following is a case which may serve to analyze the knowledge involved in preparing apple jam.

Case: Preparing jam

Mónica is 27 years old. She attended school as a child until the 2nd grade. She works as domestic help and lives in a rural area. The interview was conducted in her house.

I: Let's see, how do you prepare apple jam?

Mónica: Well, I peel the apples, Granny Smiths, they are the green ones. After that I just cut them in pieces and pass them through the meat grinder. Then I put them on the wood stove because the gas is consumed very quickly, and then I let it simmer slowly. And when it has simmered, more or less, two or three hours, I put the sugar into it.

I: How much apple do you use?

Mónica: Well, some three kilos of apples.

I: And for that many kilos of apples, how much sugar do you use?

Mónica: One and a half kilos if they are green, if they are red, one kilo, because the green ones are always more acid.

Mónica was interviewed in her house and her description relates to preparing jam for her family rather than for an employer. This distinction is important because of the availability of different equipment depending on whether she is preparing the jam for her own use or for her employer. In each case the strategy and the meaning of the situations is different. It is difficult to imagine that Mónica would find a wood-burning stove in her employer's house to prepare jam. Furthermore, the preparation of jam in both situations acquires different economic meanings. In other words, when preparing it for herself she prefers to use a wood-burning stove instead gas, both because of the scarcity of gas and its expensiveness in rural areas, and because of the possibility of replacing gas with a wood-burning stove.

Consequently, when referring to the simmering time, she makes an approximate estimation, i.e. two to three hours. However, the absence of exactness for measuring the simmering time may be due to the difficulty of maintaining a constant temperature on a wood-burning stove.

A distinction was made between two varieties of fruits, i.e. green and red apples, to define the quantity of sugar to be used. She applied different proportions in each case. Thus, the distinction she makes between the two apples is not just a question of colour but of chemical constitution. What

Mónica refers to is the acidity-sweetness relationship considering the properties of the materials she uses in each case. Further, she relates these properties to the amount of fruit and the amount of sugar required to perform the task. The next paragraph of Mónica´s interview shows how she deals with proportions when the interviewer changes the quantities of fruits.

> I: You said that you use 3 kilos of green apples and one kilo and a half of sugar.
>
> Mónica: Yes.
>
> I: And what if you use more apples, for example five kilos of apples?
>
> Mónica: For example, for 5 kilos of apples, you should add about two to two and a half kilos of sugar.
>
> I: If you'd like to make less jam, how would you do it?
>
> Mónica: Less jam...less apples and less sugar, too. One kilo of apples would need half a kilo of sugar.
>
> I: With 3 kilos of apples and one and a half kilos of sugar, how much jam do you get?
>
> Mónica: Well, when I made it I got eight jars.
>
> I: Eight jars of how much?
>
> Mónica: That I don't know, whether they are half kilo jars or whatever. I don't know. I got eight jars, big and small ones.
>
> I: And if you were to use one-kilo jars?
>
> Mónica: There´d be less. There might be two to three jars.
>
> I: And if you'd put it in half-kilo jars?
>
> Mónica: Well, there might be 4, 4 or 5.

We could see in this paragraph that Mónica had no difficulties whatsoever in answering correctly when one of the terms of the proportion was changed. However, I am not aware of the procedure used by Mónica for giving the correct answer. I presume that she could not use a **scalar solution**[5] because she was asked about 5 kilos of fruit instead of 6. That is, she could not find the correct answer by carrying out parallel transformations on the variables, thus keeping the ratio (3 kilos of fruit - 1.5 kilos of sugar) constant.

Instead, I think that she found the answer through applying a **functional solution,** that is, by finding the fruit-sugar unit ratio (1 kilo of fruit - 0.5 kilos of sugar) and using it to calculate the desired value. What should be noticed is that the answer was given orally, without the support of paper and pencil. The same occurs when she is asked about diminishing the quantity of fruit. She applies proportionality in giving the answer.

Then I switched the questions in the interview to change the variables in question. That is, instead of considering the fruit-sugar relationship, I asked Mónica about the fruit-jam (unprocessed-processed) relationship. She used the jars to refer to the jam produced instead of expressing it directly in kilos. This must be interpreted as the jar being her reference for measuring the jam. However, though she could not fix the relation kilos-jars, she could still answer correctly, applying a scalar solution when I fixed the size of the jars to one or half a kilo.

The next paragraph of the interview shows us how Mónica dealt with physical-chemical transformations and equipment.

> I: How do you know when the jam is ready?
>
> Mónica: By the colour and the form it has. Because it becomes light brown in colour and it doesn't have juice any more, the water from the apples, when they are simmering. It gets dry.
>
> I: About how long do you simmer it?
>
> Mónica: Well, sometimes for five hours.
>
> I: What happens if you simmer it for less time?
>
> Mónica: It doesn't turn out well. It depends, because if you cook the apples cut into pieces, it takes more time until it is all mashed. Now, if you grind them, if you pass them through the machine, you know, it takes less time.

The relations between colour, form (as she expresses the density of the jam) and the simmering time involve chemical processes and transformations during the elaboration. The process of dehydration, occurring in the apples when put in contact with the heat, is observed by Mónica. She presents the relation between the time of simmering and the way the fruit is cut. Then she refers to a piece of equipment. That is, she compares the difference between using or not using the machine for grinding the fruits. I point this out because the piece of equipment, in this case, leads Mónica to anticipate different simmering times. So, another variable is added to obtain the proper fruit dehydration. Thus, whether she expresses and figures out the situation, she shows some physical-chemical knowledge. That is, she makes explicit cause and effect deductions in relating different variables.

Comments on Monica's case

In the case of Mónica we could observe the different variables she explicitly takes into account for preparing apple jam: the amount of apples, the properties of the apples, the amount of sugar, the simmering time, and so forth. In relation to the apples, she establishes differences according to the variety, green or red and she puts that difference in relation to the amount of sugar. As to the simmering time, she relates it to how the apples are cut and then to the colour and density of the jam.

In addition to Mónica's description of the variables she takes into account and the relations she establishes between them - which reveals a structuring of the data - we can observe her knowledge of weight measures, the number system as well as the physical-chemical dehydrating process.

It might be possible to imagine that all the quantities Mónica used for preparing jam might simply be the application of a cooking recipe. However, when she was asked for quantities other than those she had initially presented, she revealed, not only the notion of proportionality, but also the capacity to reorganize the data from the recipe she might have learnt. Preparing jam is for Mónica a routinized activity but however she was able to put it in words and explain step by step the different alternatives available. Can we say then that routinized activities are simply mechanical ones? The case we have gone through at least shows a very interesting structuring activity by the subject which as such cannot be reduced to mechanical nor to context-bound actions.

KNOWLEDGE AND CONTEXT

From some positions, a status that transforms knowledge into a simple practical knowledge or knowledge in action is granted to the knowledge used in task-oriented working situations. As empirical knowledge, cognitive processes are governed by technical rules (Mezirow, 1981: 3-4). Though from this position it is accepted that instrumental actions always include some organizing activity on the part of the subject, the activity is limited in this learning domain to predictions about observable events which can be proved correct or incorrect. In other words, everyday thinking is viewed as governed by efficiency rather than the full and systematic consideration of alternatives (Rogoff, 1984). Thus, it is explained that knowledge utilized for practical problem solving in everyday situations would be tacit knowledge, that is, knowledge available in the relevant setting rather than by relying on explicit propositions. In the same way, Mezirow refers to knowledge as being deduced from rules of value systems and from rules of investigation.

In turn, I would contend that everyday thinking, or what is termed instrumental learning, is governed by both efficiency and a systematic consideration of alternatives. Therefore, I consider that efficiency would be linked to the contextual constraints. The analysis of the processes of knowledge constitution in the workplace gives a good opportunity to examine this issue.

On the other hand knowledge in work-related tasks is seen through the subjects´organizing activity of the situations as interfaced in a particular social setting. Thus, I stress the constructive activity of the subjects and the assimilating progressive character of everyday knowledge.

In any case, everyday knowledge interpreted as instrumental learning, may rapidly be transformed into contextualized knowledge. That is, knowledge then becomes bound to the content and the situation from which it was deduced or acquired. In this respect, such a determinism leaves fairly little room for the subject´s activity. As this study focuses on illiterate adults this aspect is extremely relevant. I have discussed (Llorente 1996, Chapter 5) the incongruences I see in adult education, particularly in *Educación Popular* in this aspect. Educational practices aim at fostering adults' developmental autonomy but often treat them in educational settings as if they were lacking experience in curricular contents. In some cases this occurs as a consequence of openly assuming an empiricist position on learning. In others, this contradiction appears just as result of the inability to design educational practices based on subjects' experiences.

Studies focused on reversibility and transfer in the schema of proportionality and developed in everyday contexts (Nunes & Shliemann 1993, 107-26), present a different perspective for considering everyday knowledge. They proved that the concept of proportionality, learnt in everyday practices, can be applied in new situations. Thus, this result contradicts the hypothesis that everyday knowledge may be so entangled with situational relations that it cannot be applied in other situations or social settings.

These results clearly contradict the idea that street mathematics is the product of concrete thinking and that it generalizes poorly. Both flexibility and transfer were more clearly demonstrated for everyday practices than for school-taught proportions algorithm.(...) It seems that everyday procedures, which are likely to be already available to students before they are taught the algorithm, compete with the algorithm. The conflict stems from the fact that the everyday knowledge uses calculation procedures in which variables are kept separated. (Nunes & Shliemann 1993:126)

I have presented a case where it is possible to observe some logical-mathematical and physical-chemical knowledge that adults with little education possess and use. The exploratory character of the present study permits me, in this context only, to stress some evidence. Finally, I would like to point out that this case shows both particular knowledge learnt and utilized in out-of-school settings, and a systematic display of steps and interrelationships between the intervening variables to develop work-related tasks.

LIMITATIONS OF THE APPROACH

The critical exploration has been criticized (Castorina, Lenzi & Fernandez, 1984: 84; Vygotsky, 1971: 52-3; Llorente, 1996) as a subjectivist method due to the extreme freedom given to the researcher or experimenter. In my view, this kind of criticism fails to recognize that freedom is limited by the central theses of the theory. The researcher is necessarily committed to a system of conceptual interpretation.

In genetic psychology beyond and above the hypotheses checked through the clinical method, there is a theoretical commitment to work with some methods and not others. This theoretical engagement presupposes that there are forms of knowledge or systems of actions which are not observable. It is not possible to get access to those unobservable mechanisms just by posing isolated questions. The answers - containing the subject hypotheses, changes and continuities - constitute a whole which must be understood as such. A single answer can only be understood in close relation to the whole.

In this study the use of clinical method is linked with both the theory or conceptual system of interpretation and the object of study. Matching theoretical concepts with empirical data during the interview is a difficult task to achieve. This probably is the most risky point of the clinical method which may lead to the gathering of rather anecdotal data without much profitable information.

Finally, another aspect I would like to point out has to do with the theoretical limitations of Piagetian approach. Clinical exploration is mainly centred on the investigated subject and his/her actions and not really on the conditions and motives of them. A struggle is needed to capture the subject's activity as a whole, as a system that socio-historically evolves. To capture an activity system, Piagetian interview is not enough as such. Other research instruments should be brought into analysis to reach a deeper understanding of the systems of communications, interactions and performances in social settings.

NOTES

1   Piagetian theory is commonly presented as a twofold approach where the epistemological approach and the stages of development approach are identified as different approaches. I disagree with this interpretation because of Piaget's lengthy explanations of the development of stages. For a summarized but extended review of Piaget-oriented research see Modgil, 1974.

2   In my view theoretical awareness refers to the presence of the central theses of the theory when interviewing, i.e. interactionism, constructivism and equilibration. This is the only way for the instant checking which is a crucial aspect of the method.

3   I use the term 'clinical criterion' in the same way that the term *sentido clínico* or *espíritu Piagetiano* is used in Spanish. The clinical interrogation is not to register questions and answers. The interviewer lets the subjects speak and tries to get the fleeing thoughts by following them.

4.   A detailed characterisation of the sample is presented in Llorente (1996:123-5, 252-6).

5.   For a distinction in the strategies used for solving proportion problems see: "Reversibility and Transfer in the Schema of Proportionality", in Nunes 1993. *Street Mathematics and School Mathematics.* (103-126).

REFERENCES

Bright, B. (1989) *Theory and Practice in the Study of Adult Education. The Epistemological Debate*. London: Routledge

Castorina. J., Lenzi, A. & Fernandez, S. (1984) *Psicología Genética: aspectos metodológicos e implicaciones pedagógicas*. Buenos Aires: Editorial Miño and Dávila.

Colinvaux & Divar Ure (1989) 'Trabajando con Adultos no alfabetizados: La construcción de la noción de espacio'. In J. Castorina, *et al. Problemas de Psicología Genética*. Buenos Aires: Editorial Miño and Dávila

Gruver, H. & Vonèche, J. (1977) *The Essential Piaget*. London: Routledge and Kegan Paul

Inhelder. B., Sinclair, H. & Bovet, M. (1974) *Learning and Development of Cognition*, translated by S. Wedgwood from *Apprentissage et Structures de La Connaissance*. London: Routledge and Kegan Paul

Jacob, E. (1992) 'Culture, Context and Cognition'. In X. Le Compte, X. Millroy & X. Preissle, *Handbook of Qualitative Research in Education*. London: Academic Press Inc.

Kitchener, R. (1986) *Piaget's Theory of Knowledge. Genetic Epistemology and Scientific Reason*. New Haven and London: Yale University Press.

Lenzi. A. (1989) 'La teoría Psicogenética de Piaget y sus consecuencias para la enseñanza y el aprendizaje'. (Unpublished work presented to the concourse of Titular Professor, Cátedra de Psicología y Epistemología Genética.). Facultad de Psicología, Universidad de Buenos Aires.

Llorente, J. (1991) *Los saberes cotidianos de Adultos Analfabetos*. Universidad Nacional del Comahue, Secretaría de Investigación, Argentina.

Llorente, J. (1996) *Constitution of Knowledge and Problem Solving*. Research Bulletin 92. University of Helsinki, Department of Education. In M. Villar, *Adultos in Situación escolar: Una aproximación a su realidad*. Research Report. Secretaria de Investigación. Universidad Nacional del Comahue, Argentina.

Modgil, S. (1974) *Piagetian Research: a handbook of recent research*. Great Britain: NFER Publishing Company Ltd.

Perret Clermont, A. (1980) *Social interactions and cognitive development in children*. London: Academic Press.

Perret Clermont, A. & Nicolet, M. (1992) *Interactuar y Conocer. Desafíos y regulaciones sociales en el desarrollo cognitivo*. Translated by E. Langlois from *Interagir et connaître. Enjeux et régulations sociales dans le développement cognitif*. Buenos Aires:Editorial Miño and Dávila

Piaget, J. (1970/1985) *Psicología y Epistemología*, translated by Francisco Fernandez Buey from *Psychology et épistémologie*. Barcelona, España: Editorial Planeta de Agostini

Piaget, J. (1977) *The Grasp of Consciousness: action and concept in the young child*. London: Routledge and Kegan Paul.

Piaget, J. (1978b) *Success and Understanding*, translated by A. Pomerans. from *Réussir et comprendre*. Cambridge, MA: Harvard University Press.

Piaget, J. & Garcia, R. (1982) *Psicogénesis e Historia de las Ciencias*. Mexico: Editorial Siglo XXI

Piaget, J. (1985) *The Equilibration of Cognitive Structures. The Central Problem of Intellectual Development*, translated by T. Brown from *L' équilibration des structures cognitives.*: The University of Chicago Press

Schliemann, A. (1988) 'Escolarização Formal versus Experiencia Práctica na Resolução de Problemas'. In *Na Vida Dez Na Escola Zero*. Brazil: Cortez Editora, 69-85

Tennant, M. (1993) 'Adult Development' in M. Thorpe, R. Edwards & A. Hanson, (Eds), *Culture and Processes of Adult Learning*. London: Routledge, 118-38

Usher, R. (1989) 'Locating adult education in the practical'. In B. Bright (Ed.), *Theory and Practice in the Study of Adult Education. The epistemological debate*. London: Routledge, 65-93

Vygotsky, L. (1982) *Pensamiento y Lenguanje. El problema del lenguaje y el pensamiento del niño en la teoría de Piaget*, translated by J. Bravo. Moscú: Editorial Pedagógica

Chapter 5

Understanding their Thinking: the tension between the Cognitive and the Affective

Janet Duffin & Adrian Simpson
Department of Mathematics, University of Hull, UK / Mathematics Education Research Centre, Institute of Education, University of Warwick, UK

ATTITUDES TO MATHEMATICS

Those who work with adults learning mathematics have probably had the experience of feeling that some of the difficulties students can reveal about their earlier learning of mathematics might be better understood if we could 'get inside' their personal thinking about the mathematical processes which cause them difficulty.

At a reunion of former pupils taught by one of us, a discussion arose in which they proceeded to offer spontaneous judgements on themselves about their mathematical ability. They appeared to be highly intelligent and articulate women, yet their comments about themselves were typified by:

- Numbers always foxed me
- I was thick
- I must have been the world's worst at mathematics
- I'm mathematically dyslexic

These comments highlight attitudes that must be commonplace amongst adult learners and familiar to those working in the realm of teaching mathematics to adults. Indeed, such attitudes appear to arise across a wide spectrum of mathematical ability. Cooper (1990) reports very similar attitudes even amongst those who have completed mathematics degrees. He found that students reported having enjoyed mathematics at school, but their descriptions of their attitudes to university mathematics mirror those above,

D. Coben et al. (eds.), Perspectives on Adults Learning Mathematics, 83–99.
© 2000 *Kluwer Academic Publishers. Printed in the Netherlands.*

giving a sense of themselves as unintelligent despite having what others would consider to be an excellent mathematics background. Cooper called this movement, from enjoyment to dislike, 'cooling out'.

We must try to find ways of countering such attitudes to enable our students to achieve confidence in mathematics at whatever level. Our concern is that these attitudes are intimately bound up with the understanding of mathematics which has been built through the learner's previous experiences of the subject. The way of thinking a learner has built up affects their attitude to mathematics, while the attitude they have affects how they approach new ways of thinking. It is the duality of the affective and the cognitive aspects of learning that is at the heart of our current thinking about adults learning mathematics.

COMING TO A THEORY OF LEARNING

In addressing this duality we have been working together on a theory of learning to act as a framework for researching how others learn. This framework has been built on an exploration of the learning which we see in our own classrooms, a sharing of each other's personal ways of learning and an attempt to explain our observations of others by considering what internal influences there might have been on their actions.

Mason (1987: 207) discusses the ways in which researchers work and suggests

> Some of us proceed by contemplating and studying other people [from outside], or... ourselves as if from outside; others proceed by contemplating and studying ourselves from inside.

In building our theory we are trying to study and contemplate others 'as if from the inside', thus completing the symmetry of these observations. When working with learners who have longer learning histories, the relationship between what we see from outside and what might be happening inside may be more complex. This way of working appears to be of particular importance in the area of adults learning mathematics.

Most theories of learning seem to concentrate on the stage of learning as observed from the outside, but, by contrast, what we are trying to do is build up a theory about the learning process from the viewpoint of the learner. That is, we are trying to classify the experiences of learners during the learning process using the perspective of the learner's previous experiences.

THE THEORY

The theory we have built is an attempt to explain our observations of learners. We do so by classifying learners' experiences - and their responses to those experiences - into three distinct categories: natural, conflicting and alien.

In our theory, a *natural* experience is one which 'fits' the way the learner already thinks, it feels comfortable and can be easily assimilated into what is already known. In contrast, an *alien* experience is one which does not fit and appears not to connect with anything we have learned before. A *conflicting* experience is one which appears to contradict earlier experience and forces us to think further.

Learners may respond in different ways to each of these experiences. Natural experiences strengthen our current way of thinking and extend its scope. A conflicting experience can destroy or limit the current way of thinking but can result in a merging of the familiar with the new experience to form a more connected way of thinking. Responses to an alien experience can be to ignore it (perhaps temporarily), to avoid it by going back to something which is more familiar (natural) or to absorb it as a completely separate and discrete experience (Duffin & Simpson, 1993).

For example, a well-known 'bug' in the learning of a standard subtraction algorithm is to take the smaller digit from the larger, irrespective of whether or not the digit is in the subtrahend (Davis, 1984). Early experience with a standard subtraction algorithm may involve the learner in working only with problems in which this smaller digit is always in the number to be subtracted (as the teacher may, sensibly, be trying to avoid introducing the issue of 'borrowing' at this stage). In doing so, however, the teacher is providing an environment in which experiences are *natural* for this 'buggy' algorithm, in the sense that they fit with this existing way of working and will reinforce it.

In later questions, the learner may encounter smaller digits in the minuend. In one example (detailed in Duffin and Simpson, 1993), a young learner with precisely this 'bug' writes, under the standard layout for the subtraction 526-249, the 'answer' 323, and beside it 'but the real answer is 277'. In this situation, the learner has the standard algorithm as something *alien*, separate from his own method of calculating the 'real' answer and ignores the discrepancy.

In contrast, if the learner had noticed the discrepancy as a *conflict*, he may have tried to restructure his way of working to cope with the new situation in which smaller digits may appear in the decimal representation of either number. Such constructive resolution of a conflict (similar to Piaget's *accommodation*) is how the learner's understanding may be extended.

Using our theory, and our way of working, to influence our responses to those we teach brought a new dimension to the way we perceived student mistakes and misconceptions. Instead of merely seeing them as things to be 'put right', we saw that, to the learner concerned, such mistakes may appear to be perfectly natural because they are in accord with what has already been built up from previous experiences. In that case the work of the teacher takes on a new dimension: trying to understand, 'as if from inside', what brought them to this 'mistake'.

In the longer term this can enable learners to see 'mistakes' as something to welcome, because they can lead to a better understanding and a more connected way of thinking, rather than seeing them and their consequences as 'anti-goals' (in the sense of Skemp, 1979): outcomes to be avoided at all costs.

DIFFERENT KINDS OF LEARNERS

As we have continued to work together we have discovered that our chosen ways of learning mathematics are very different: one of us prefers to seek connections with a new experience in order to aid understanding of it; the other prefers to learn each piece of mathematics as a distinct entity and only to make connections at a later stage.

From our two distinct ways of learning we began to classify learners as basically either natural or alien learners though we also recognise that, without conflict and the resolution of conflict, neither kind of learner will be able to advance as far as would otherwise be possible. So we also distinguish two further types of learner: natural/conflicting and alien/conflicting. It is, however, important to recognise that these are not discreet classifications but that there is a continuum of types with individuals perhaps learning in different ways in different situations.

For both natural and alien learners it is through the constructive resolution of conflict, described above, that their understanding is extended. However, there are many alien learners who never come to the point of unifying their knowledge through conflict. Some learners who become teachers do not appear themselves to have made the connections that come from resolving conflict, or have not apparently come to see the value of such connections. In consequence, these teachers are not in the habit of encouraging their students to use conflict to further their learning.

However, there may be students in any class who welcome the experience of alien learning and who have the potential to achieve the connections required for understanding through conflict at some later stage. Such students, therefore, may find the experience of being taught by a teacher who uses natural/conflicting ways of teaching a frustrating one, as may a student who seeks connections in learning but whose teacher teaches in an alien or alien/conflicting way. This means that, in every classroom, there is the potential for a mismatch between the fundamental ways in which both teachers and learners want to operate. Perry (1970) refers to the problems in which different types of learner (perhaps with different preferences for learning through natural, conflicting or alien experiences) intermingle, as 'different worlds in the same classroom'

In addition to differences amongst individual learners, it is clear from this that there are different styles of teaching. Askew et. al. (1997) identify categories of teacher who we suggest provide different balances of natural, conflicting and alien experiences for their learners. These categories are characterised (Wiliam et al. 1998:11-14) by:

> Discovery: "tends to treat all methods of calculation as equally acceptable – what is important is that the answer is obtained by some method that is understood by the pupil. ... Such teachers place great emphasis on 'readiness' – and generally interpret students' misconceptions as evidence that they are not 'ready' to learn ideas."

> Transmission: "tend to view mathematics as the acquisition of procedures and routines. There is an emphasis on standard routines ... efficiency of calculation is given more emphasis than effectiveness."

> Connectionist: "emphasise the links between different topics. ... [their teaching] builds on students' existing strategies but with a responsibility on the teacher to intervene to improve the efficiency of students' naive strategies".

These descriptions suggest a transmission teacher might provide an environment in which alien experiences are common. The discovery teacher, in the terms given above, would seem to provide an environment in which existing ways of working should be strengthened by giving examples for which the learner is ready: a natural environment. The connectionist teacher appears to intervene with potential conflicts for the students to reorganise ways of working into more efficient methods.

The report suggests that the last, more flexible type of teacher is more successful. We postulate that this may be because they can model and respond to the different ways their different pupils learn.

In adult classes, the opportunity for mismatches in the classroom may be increased by the more complex nature of the internal mental structures that the learners have built over longer periods. The nature of the learner's response to such a mismatch is different from that in the school environment: in schools the teacher is seen as the authority and challenges to it are significant threats to the teacher-pupil role-pair (which Skemp, 1979, notes is an 'imposed' role-pair). In the majority of adult situations, role-pairs are 'elective' - the learner chooses to attend a class and an unresolved mismatch can cause the learner to choose not to attend just as easily.

THINKING ABOUT UNDERSTANDING

To enable people to be flexible teachers and avoid threatening the elective nature of the role-pair caused by mismatch, it is important, then, that they understand the nature of how adults learn mathematics and, most important, understand how they might understand mathematics.

In many cases the interest of the adults learning mathematics community is in people who have, in their own view at least, previously failed to learn mathematics and are now returning to study with the partial understandings they have built (as well as the 'emotional baggage' they will have built up with the previous 'failure', which we discuss later).

The central assumption in this is that learners build new understandings or modify old ones on the basis of their existing understanding. For the time being, we will consider only this aspect, separating the nature of understanding from the emotional resonances that accompany learning.

We wish to treat 'understanding' as a 'scientific' term, just as Sierpinska (1994) does. It was important for us that 'understanding' didn't become another 'wakalixes' word[1]. That is, we want to pin down its meaning as precisely as we can within our theory of learning and without denying the valuable 'everyday' meanings with which the term is associated. This attempt to pin down the meaning within a given theoretical framework has a long and distinguished history within mathematics education and, of course, as different people work within their own theoretical frameworks, they come to different definitions. The strong echoes of many of these (such as Skemp, 1976, Hiebert & Carpenter, 1992 and Sierpinska, 1994) can be heard in our definition and we have even found some resonance with ideas from those who, we feel, take a quite different line (such as Gagné, 1990)

Our work on understanding grew naturally from our development of the theory of natural, conflicting and alien learning experiences. Our discussions centred on the language used within the theory of natural, conflicting and alien and our initial definition was "understanding is the awareness of connections between internal mental structures".

Having come to this definition, we explored with colleagues what we came to call 'internal characteristics' (an individual's own feelings about things they understand) and 'external manifestations' (actions of the learner from which we might reasonably infer understanding) (Duffin & Simpson,

1997a). These included 'feeling comfortable' and 'feeling able to forget the detail, knowing I can reconstruct it whenever I need it' as internal characteristics and 'being able to explain' and 'being able to recognise in other contexts' as external manifestations.

Later our attention was caught by a fundamental question raised by Sierpinska (1990), "is understanding an act, an emotional experience, an intellectual process or a way of knowing?". Our initial definition seemed to suggest that the learner's understanding is a mental state. But thinking about this aspect of the nature of understanding led us to realise that there is a gap between the static internal characteristics and the dynamic external manifestations. We realised that we could give an interpretation to some of the possible aspects of understanding in Sierpinska's question. We interpret an act of understanding as the use of internal mental connections to solve a problem. It is the act of using those connections to solve a problem that might manifest itself as an action for a teacher to interpret. Similarly, we can see a long-term process involved in understanding - that is the process of building the internal mental connections in the first place (and, of course, modifying them in the light of new natural, conflicting and alien experiences). We realised that our initial definition formed an intermediate stage between building and enacting.

So we came to a three-part definition of 'understanding' to fit with our theoretical perspective:

- Building understanding - the formation of connections between internal mental structures
- Having understanding - the state a learner is in by virtue of the connections they have at any particular time
- Enacting understanding - the use of these connections to solve a problem or construct a response to a question

Within these parts we can still see the fundamental idea of a network of connections that is at the heart of Skemp's (1979) work and is explicit in the definition of Hiebert and Carpenter (1992). It also addresses one of the problems Byers (1980) notes: whether understanding is given in absolute, 'yes-or-no' terms. By concentrating on connections, we can think of someone having more or less understanding in two senses: more connections to a given concept, or connections to further connected concepts. This adopts the 'breadth and depth' notion of Nickerson (1985).

If, again, we temporarily ignore the affective aspect of their previous experience, adults learning mathematics have already built much understanding. They have some connections, perhaps a few deep ones, perhaps a few broad ones, but many do not have sufficient to feel they have the internal characteristics of understanding (like comfort and confidence) or exhibit the external manifestations from which we might infer a significant understanding (like explaining and deriving consequences).

TWO STORIES ABOUT UNDERSTANDING

Two incidents from our own experience, which occurred spontaneously some time after we came to our first definition, have shown how this more recent interpretation of the word 'understanding' has enabled us to examine such incidents more fruitfully.

The second of these incidents shows a learner enacting his understanding to reconstruct something he had forgotten. The first is much more complex because it shows a learner who has forgotten what we claim had been an alien learning experience, but who has some understanding of a relevant mathematical concept which interferes with her attempt to reproduce the procedure which constituted this alien experience.

The first incident occurred in the numeracy classes run by one of us for university students who believe they lack the basic number skills required for future employment. Some of these students bear a marked resemblance in their attitudes to mathematics to those described at the beginning of this chapter.

Early in the course there is an investigation of student methods for subtraction, as learned at school, largely in order to discuss the two standard written methods taught throughout this century. This opens up the opportunity to discuss these before looking at the self-devised mental methods most have developed, usually secretly, as their personal alternatives to the school written methods. Most feel that their personal methods are 'not the right way to do it'.

Two students were discussing what they were doing. One said "Why have you put that 2 there?" to which the other replied "Well, I have to put 1 there and 1 there but, for this, 1 will not be enough so I have to put a 2 there and there". She went on to say "I wish she'd let us do it in our heads".

This snippet of conversation was intriguing, compelling investigation. This was what she had done for 532-286:

$$
\begin{array}{r}
5\ {}^{2}3\ {}^{1}2 \\
2^{2}\ {}_{1}8\ \ 6 \\
\hline
5\ \ 2
\end{array}
$$

The first impression here is of a learner in complete confusion. She appears to be trying to reproduce the 'equal addition' method of subtraction but with the inexplicable introduction of a 2 in the tens and hundreds columns. She appears, moreover, to have remembered only one element in the procedure, that of putting a 1 at the top of the column she is working in and a corresponding 1 in the next column. She recognises that this is intended to help her to perform a subtraction that is, in terms of this procedure, impossible: 6 from 2 in the units column. She fails to remember that, while in the units column the 1 stands for ten, it stands for one in the tens column because, here, she thinks she is trying to subtract 18 from 3, requiring her to introduce a 2 in the tens and hundreds columns. It is at this stage that she realises that she cannot complete the subtraction because she cannot take 22 from 5.

In operating this strategy she is attempting to enact her understanding that 'when you put a number in front of another one, it increases that number by ten times the one you put in front' but she fails to do so because she neglects to appreciate that the 1 (or 2) in front of digits in different columns have different effects. Her failure to remember the procedure means that she has to try to reconstruct it but, without 'having' understanding of that procedure which she can enact to help sort out the meaning of the digits, she fails to do so. There is a clear interference between her own correct thinking about place value and the alien nature of the subtraction procedure she is trying to reproduce.

What is interesting, though unfortunately not investigated at the time, is that her later statement indicates she could do the calculation in her head and the method for this was probably something she had devised for herself. She seemed to be confident that she would have been able to do it in her head.

This certainly prompts the question about the efficacy of teaching procedures without ensuring that there is an understanding about how and why they work, especially for those learners whose memory is not reliable so that they are unlikely to be able to recall something they are no longer currently practising.

In contrast the other incident demonstrated the power of understanding in enabling a learner to reconstruct something they may have forgotten through disuse. We were discussing the first incident in the departmental coffee room when a colleague suddenly joined in, saying "I was so proud of myself the other day, I managed to remember all the trig. formulae I learned at school". He later amended this to saying that he had actually remembered one significant fact about them from which he had been able to reconstruct them all. His story illustrates that he 'had' understanding and could enact it by calling on a relevant fact to help him to reconstruct all that he had forgotten. The incident demonstrates the power of understanding to enable people to overcome the handicap of forgetting in contrast to the difficulties that can arise where failure to remember plunges them into predicaments from which they cannot extricate themselves.

REPRODUCING OR RECONSTRUCTING: THE ROLE OF ENACTING UNDERSTANDING

In these two incidents we see a very clear split between a failed attempt to reproduce an algorithm and a successful attempt to reconstruct a connected sequence of formulae from one remembered fact. It is in this distinction - between reproducing an answer or solution strategy and using one's connections to rebuild one - that the heart of the problem of understanding lies.

One of the roles of the teacher is to model the understanding of the pupil so that they can provide appropriate future experiences to enable the learner to build the further, deeper connections that constitute enhanced understanding. Someone who has few connections within their internal mental structures (who 'has' little understanding in our terms) is in no position to reconstruct - they only have access to reproducing. Indeed, they only have that provided that their memory serves them well and that other understandings (such as the student's sensible interpretation of the role of 'carried' digits in our first incident) do not interfere.

However, the act of reproducing is considerably less onerous than reconstructing. Thus, even learners who, in our sense, 'have' considerable understanding are unlikely to enact that understanding by reconstructing a solution if they are able to rely on their memory. So on top of the problem of distinguishing between a reproduced answer and a reconstructed one, the teacher has a problem of identifying those students who are reproducing an answer because they are unable to reconstruct one from those who are reproducing a solution because it is easier than reconstructing. This diagnostic ability is of particular importance to teachers of adults learning mathematics.

An obvious suggestion is that such teachers should provide situations in which enacting understanding is the only real option - that is, where there is no real prospect of reproducing an answer. A request to explain why some method works; a question set in an unusual context or a situation in which the learner is asked to derive a consequence all make it much more likely that a learner will not be able to rely on their memory for an answer, but will need to use the connections that constitute their 'having' understanding to build a new solution.

ADULTS LEARNING MATHEMATICS

The suggestions that follow from our theory of learning and definition of 'understanding' are designed to be applicable across all learners. They come from an analysis of how the mind responds to new experiences by reorganising its internal mental structures and so should be generally applicable. However, we predicated most of the last few sections on the separation of this cognitive aspect of learning from the affective, the emotional aspects of learning. It is in this separation, convenient for the purposes of analysis, that many of the problems of the application of our theory (and, in particular, the application to adults learning mathematics) lie.

Genuine explorations of the link between the affective and cognitive aspects of learning are quite rare within mathematics education. One researcher, however, has put the nature of emotional responses to situations at the heart of his theory of 'intelligence, learning and action'. This is Richard Skemp who introduced the notion of goals and anti-goals (Skemp, 1979). A goal is a state the learner wishes to be in and, through their actions, tries to approach. An anti-goal is a state the learner wishes to avoid and, through their actions, tries to move away from. Skemp's theory is built on the notion of what he called a director system (delta-one) whose role it is to move the learner towards a goal and to monitor that movement. In addition he posits a 'meta-director system' (delta-two) whose role it is to make delta-one systems more effective in their goal-seeking behaviour. From this rather simple, and decidedly mechanistic beginning Skemp addresses a number of areas of learning. Two areas are of most importance in our discussion of how adults learn mathematics: emotional aspects and the teacher-learner role pair.

Skemp notes that we can associate various emotions with the movement towards or away from goals and anti-goals, as well as with the learner's perception of their potential to cause desired movement. These are shown in the table below. This linking of emotions to goal states has been likened to a dynamical system, with the goals and anti-goals playing the parts of attractors and repellers (Tall, 1977).

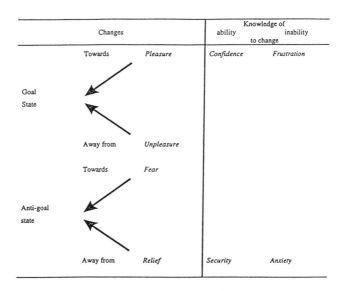

Figure 1. Reproduced, with permission from David Fulton Publishers, from *Intelligence, Learning and Action* by R.R. Skemp (1979).

Many of the words which Skemp uses (particularly, perhaps, the negative ones) are ones with which teachers of adults learning mathematics will be familiar. In particular the quartet of confidence/frustration and security/anxiety are emotional responses we associate with adults learning mathematics. These areas are the ones which are governed by the learner's perception of their own ability to move towards a goal or away from an anti-goal. They are the results of longer term exposure to the learning of mathematics. We might see these as the 'emotional experiences' which Sierpinska (1990) postulates as one of the possible meanings of the word 'understanding'. Indeed, many adult learners may have come to view the whole of mathematics as an anti-goal: something to be avoided to gain relief. When they are faced with a mathematical situation they cannot avoid they can be overcome with fear: one colleague recalls a mature student on a primary teacher training course who was so afraid of mathematics she had to leave the room and be physically sick when she was reintroduced to division of fractions.

One aspect that Skemp does not directly address, but which is clearly of importance for those working with such profoundly affected learners, is how goal and anti-goal states come into being or how an anti-goal state can be reconstructed as a goal state for a learner. A number of people writing in the field of adults learning mathematics note that helping the learner to feel confident is important (Benn, 1997; Safford, 1995). It is clear from Skemp's analysis that this involves a transition from seeing mathematics as an anti-goal to be avoided towards a goal to be reached. The assessment of these goals and anti-goals is a function of the learner's delta-two system. That is, it is a function of the reflective and self-monitoring part of the learner's mind: their meta-cognitive ability. It requires the learner to explore the nature of their previous learning of mathematics, that caused the anti-goal nature of the subject for them, and to consider the valuable role that mathematics might play in their lives. This latter form of reflection is tied up with the purpose of mathematics for a learner.

In the design of a support service for mathematics across a university (Duffin & Simpson, 1996) we distinguished between the teaching of mathematics for the purposes of supporting the learning of another subject and mathematics as a life skill. In both of these, the utility of mathematics can be emphasised, but in the latter the aim is to ensure that learners can draw on their existing mental methods, their often very sophisticated abilities to form arguments within their own subjects and their increased ability to reflect and monitor their own learning. In doing this, the teacher can build upon existing understandings which the learners have built, strengthen them through constructive conflict and use this new, stronger understanding as the basis for mathematics as a goal which learners feel they can move towards - thus giving them confidence in their mathematics.

This change in the nature of teaching can, of itself, cause problems for adults learning mathematics. Learners build up an expectation about how a class is meant to be conducted and the roles played by the teacher and the learner. When this is challenged, it can cause considerable distress (Brousseau & Otte (1991), call it 'breaking the didactic contract'). In particular, learners who have come to see the learning of mathematics as an alien activity (even if they are not, themselves, alien learners) can find that teaching sessions based on explorations of their existing understandings and the formation of connections between different ways of thinking are unacceptable. In such situations it is not unusual for students to ask 'just tell me how to do it' or to request some form of drill and practice teaching. Even if they are aware that such teaching methods have failed them in the past, they may see previous failure as something wrong with them rather than something caused by a mismatch in the classroom.

This causes a difficult problem for the teacher in the classroom: on the one hand the learners may be expecting an 'alien' teacher and may have difficulty if that 'didactic contract' is broken while, on the other hand, the learners are likely to find no value in a repeat of the alien teaching which has failed them in the past. One possible solution to this difficulty may lie in a second consequence that comes from Skemp's analysis of learning: the nature of the teacher-learner role-pair.

In schools, the role-pair is imposed: pupils are expected to go to school and that expectation is backed by the power of law. Inevitably, then, the role-pair contains an element of imbalance within it - the goals of learning are externally imposed (and may not match with the internal goals of the learner). In the situation where adults return to learning mathematics the role-pair is normally elective - there is less imbalance between the partners. It is in the nature of learning that the learner is trying to gain some skill or understanding in some area where they do not already have great skill or understanding and the role of the teacher is to support them in the zone between what they are able to do with their current understandings and what they are able to do with the teacher's help (the so-called 'Zone of Proximal Development', Vygotsky (1978).

Within an imposed role-pair in schools, pupils trust the teacher to provide appropriate content. This often manifests itself in adults learning mathematics by, as Benn (1997:56) puts it:

> The learner who wants to sit at the feet of the master and receive predigested wisdom. ... such learners may have built up an expectation of learning that is not about understanding but about trusting in the teacher and doing what they are told.

In the elective role-pairs of an adult class there needs to be a different form of trust: the learner trusts the tutor to provide an appropriate pedagogical environment. We distinguish between these two types of trust with the phrases 'content trust' and 'pedagogic trust'.

Being in the zone of proximal development is necessarily accompanied by feelings of insecurity on the part of the learner, but in an elective role pair, the learner gives their pedagogic trust to the teacher to help them through it. If that trust is ill-founded or, worse, abused, the learner retains the right to annul the role-pair relationship. However, while they have that trust, the teacher has the right to use it - they can ask the learner to try a new way of learning and accept a break in the didactic contract; they can ask people to reveal their mental methods or to reflect back on their learning of mathematics as a child. They can do this as long as they feel that such a use of trust will genuinely help the learner in the transition from mathematics as an anti-goal to mathematics as a goal which they can approach with confidence.

CONCLUSION

The purpose of research and of theory building in education should be to improve the learning which takes place. Such research need not perform this task directly: the path from theory building to classroom practice may pass through many 'methodological neighbourhoods' (Duffin & Simpson, 1997b). However, in exploring our theory in synthesis with the work of Skemp, amongst others, we can discern the basic tension in the problems of adults learning mathematics: a tension between the cognitive and the affective.

Adults who return to the learning of mathematics do so for a variety of reasons, but often it is to gain a qualification in it: a qualification they failed to obtain at the first attempt (and perhaps at other subsequent attempts). The fact of that failure is often, of itself, sufficient to have made mathematical situations anti-goals for the learners involved and this brings with it emotional indicators which can prevent an otherwise intelligent adult from attempting any form of mathematical task. The development of the anti-goal nature of mathematics has come from their learning in school and, perhaps, from a mismatch between the learner's way of thinking and the teacher's style. The perception of the mismatch from the learner's point of view is of their own failure: leading to the self-image in relation to mathematics embodied in the comments which began this chapter.

On the other hand, away from threatening situations, adults are more able to perform the higher level, meta-cognitive tasks which enable them to make rational decisions about their own learning and understanding. Their more developed reflective abilities (delta-two systems) make them more able to enact their understanding - use (and monitor the use of) the connections between internal mental structures they have built to enable them to solve difficult problems.

The release of the tension between these two aspects must lie in the nature of the teaching of adults learning mathematics. The advantage for the teacher when a learner comes to them as an adult is in the changed nature of the teacher-learner role pair: the elective role pair allows the relationship to be one of partnership. In this partnership the learner can give their pedagogic trust to the teacher and the teacher can help them see that there are things they can do and understand. This can begin to relieve some of the anxiety and frustration: emotions associated with moving away from goals and towards anti-goals. During this time the teacher has an opportunity to draw on the learner's increased ability to examine their own thinking and model the understanding the learner has by trying to look at them 'as if from inside'. From this model they can consider what kind of subsequent natural, conflicting or alien experiences might help to build a strong understanding of mathematics that is the basis of confidence.

NOTES

1. Feynman (1985) recalls with horror reviewing a textbook which asked pupils to think about what makes a wind-up toy, a person on a bicycle or a motor car go, only to find the answer 'energy makes it go' to each question: "Now that doesn't mean anything. Suppose it's 'Wakalixes.' That's the general principle: 'Wakalixes makes it go.' There's no knowledge coming in ... it's just a word".

REFERENCES

Askew, M., Brown, M., Rhodes, V., Johnson, D & Wiliam, D. (1997) *Effective Teachers of Numeracy*, London: King's College.

Benn, R. (1997) *Adults Count Too: mathematics for empowerment*, Leicester: National Institute of Adult Continuing Education.

Brousseau, G. & Otte, M. (1991) 'The fragility of knowledge'. In A.J. Bishop, S. Mellin-Olsen & J. van Dormolen (Eds.) *Mathematical Knowledge: Its Growth through Teaching*, Dordrecht: Kluwer.

Byers, V. (1980) 'What does it mean to understand mathematics?' *International Journal of Mathematical Education in Science and Technology*, 11(1), 1-10.

Cooper, B. (1990) 'PGCE student and investigational approaches in secondary maths', *Research Papers in Education*, 5(2), 127-151.

Davis, R.B. (1984) *Learning Mathematics: the cognitive science approach to mathematics education*, London: Croom Helm.

Duffin, J.M. & Simpson, A.P. (1993) 'Natural, conflicting and alien'. *Journal of Mathematical Behavior*, 12(4), 313-328.

Duffin, J.M. & Simpson, A.P. (1996) 'Mathematics across the university: facing the problem' *Journal of Further and Higher Education*, 20(2), 116-124.

Duffin, J.M. & Simpson, A.P. (1997a) 'Towards a new theory of understanding'. In E. Pehkonen (Ed.) *Proceedings of the 21st Conference of the International Group for the Psychology of Mathematics Education*, Vol 4. Helsinki: University of Helsinki, 166-173.

Duffin, J.M. & Simpson, A.P. (1997b) 'When does a way of working become a methodology?'. In E. Pehkonen (Ed.) *Proceedings of the 21st Conference of the International Group for the Psychology of Mathematics Education*, Vol 2. Helsinki: University of Helsinki, 233-240

Feynman, R. (1985) *Surely you're joking, Mr. Feynman!*, London: Norton.

Gagné, R.M. (1970) *The Conditions of Learning*, New York: Holt, Rinehart and Winston.

Hiebert, J. & Carpenter, T.P. (1992) 'Learning and teaching with understanding'. In D. Grouws (Ed.) *Handbook of Research on Mathematics Teaching and Learning*, New York: Macmillan. 65-97.

Mason, J.H. (1987) 'Representing representing'. In C. Janvier (Ed.) *Problems of Representation in the Teaching and Learning of Mathematics*, Hillsdale: Erlbaum.

Nickerson, R.S. (1985) 'Understanding understanding'. *American Journal of Education*, 93(2), 201-239.

Perry, W.G. (1970) *Forms of Intellectual and Ethical Development in the College Years*, New York: Holt, Rinehart and Winston.

Safford, K. (1995) 'Algebra for adult students: the students' voices'. In D. Coben (Ed.) *Mathematics with a Human Face, Proceedings of the second international conference of Adults Learning Maths - A Research Forum (ALM-2)*. London: Goldsmiths College, University of London in association with ALM, 88-91.

Sierpinska, A. (1990) 'Some remarks on understanding in mathematics'. *For the Learning of Mathematics*, 10(3), 24-36.

Sierpinska, A. (1994) *Understanding in Mathematics*, London: Falmer.

Skemp, R.R. (1976) 'Relational understanding and instrumental understanding'. *Mathematics Teaching*, 77, 20-26.

Skemp, R.R. (1979) *Intelligence, Learning and Action*, Chichester: Wiley.

Tall, D.O. (1977) 'Conflicts and catastrophes in the learning of mathematics'. *Mathematical Education for Teaching*, 2(4), 2-18.

Vygotsky, L.S. (1978). *Mind in Society: The Development of Higher Psychological Processes*. Cambridge, MA: Harvard University Press.

Wiliam, D., Askew, A., Rhodes, V., Brown, M. and Johnson, D. (1998) 'Discover, Transmit or Connect: approaches to teaching numeracy in primary schools'. *Equals*, 4(2), 9-15.

Section II: Adults, Mathematics, Culture and Society

Introduction

John O'Donoghue
University of Limerick, Limerick, Ireland

Every human endeavour including education, mathematics and mathematics education has a social and cultural context. Every society differs in its social, cultural and political organization and in the ways it challenges its members educationally and otherwise. The lived experience and aspirations of citizens in technologically advanced countries are different from their counterparts in so-called Third World countries which are heavily dependent on agriculture. It is also true to say the nature and reality of society have a significant influence on how educational goals are defined. For example, mathematics educators have urged reforms of school mathematics in their own countries that align it more closely with the needs of adults living and working in a modern technological society (Cockcroft, 1982; NCTM, 1989). Others, conscious of the fact that most of the world's peoples live in rural or village communities, advocate approaches to school mathematics in these societies which take account of the reality of rural or nomadic life and relate to the indigenous mathematics embedded in their respective cultures (Broomes, 1993; Ale, 1993; Crawford, 1993).

While educational priorities differ world-wide, nevertheless, there is evident a growing emphasis on the education of adults. We acknowledge that the reality of adults' lives in society is lived in multiple roles as parent, worker, citizen, student, to name but some of these roles, and recognise each role places educational demands on individuals and society. The multi-dimensional nature of adults' lives and society creates a complex web of interactions that affects individuals through the opportunities they have and the choices they make. Mathematics is perceived as playing a significant role in people's life's chances (Benn, 1997). Universally, mathematics is accorded a significant place in adults' education. This state of affairs is not

D. Coben et al. (eds.), Perspectives on Adults Learning Mathematics, 101–107.
© 2000 *Kluwer Academic Publishers. Printed in the Netherlands.*

unproblematic. Adults with prior experience of formal mathematics often express negative feelings towards mathematics including fear, anxiety, inadequacy and even guilt (Cockcroft, 1982: par 20-22). These issues and others shape practice and research in adults learning mathematics.

Different writers offer us different perspectives on adults learning mathematics by problematizing different aspects of the triad adults, mathematics and society and their inter-relationships. For example, it is commonplace now to question the certainty of mathematics. This position finds expression in mainstream mathematics education as proponents argue the case for a fallibilist versus absolutist view of mathematics (Ernest, 1991). Many mathematics educators now start with the premise that mathematical knowledge is a social construct and explore the consequences of this position for mathematics education (Lerman, 1993) or adults' mathematics education (Benn, 1997).

The everyday lives and activities of adults in society were largely neglected by mathematics education researchers as sites for mathematical knowledge development and use. Normal, everyday activities of adults were treated as transparent and unproblematic by mathematics educators. There are some notable exceptions to this rule. The Cockcroft Commission investigated the mathematical needs of adult life and based its recommendations on specially commissioned reports and surveys including surveys of the level of mathematical skills in the general population (Sewell, 1981). Others such as Carraher, Carraher and Schlieman (1985) showed that school children acquire mathematical knowledge outside school in cultural activities such as street-selling. The work of Lave and her colleagues emphasized the crucial role of context in learning and using mathematics. Lave's (1988) theory of situated cognition has added a new dimension and impetus to mathematics education research in recent years. These developments would seem to have much to offer practitioners and researchers whose primary concern is adults learning mathematics.

Many forms of mathematics exist in society side by side with academic mathematics. These forms of mathematics are embedded in cultural activities such as street-selling and house-building and are described as ethnomathematics (D'Ambrosio, 1994). These out-of-school practices may help to shed light on ways of improving school mathematics teaching and learning (Nunes, 1992). Recently, Schliemann (1999) reported on new insights into transfer of skills based on her work with schooled and unschooled bookies. These new developments sit uneasily beside Lave's work since she questions the very idea of transfer and promotes the ascendancy of contextual learning. Returning to ethnomathematics; it seems that an ethnomathematics approach to mathematics education in native cultures might offer the prospect of achieving a school mathematics curriculum that respects local culture and integrates new mathematical knowledge and skills for the betterment of these communities.

The mathematical needs of individuals are treated in different ways in different societies. Important issues arising from practice and research in adults learning mathematics are finding expression in the academic debate on numeracy. The literature reflects different concerns and perspectives resulting in various conceptions of numeracy ranging from very narrowly focused functional models (Adult Literacy and Basic Skills Unit, 1993) to more challenging definitions represented by informed numeracy (Willis, 1990), critical numeracy (Chapman & Lee, 1990) and mathematical literacy (National Research Council, 1989). The perception that the mathematical and literacy needs of an information society are greater than any other experienced, is a significant feature of this debate (NRC, 1989). Greater exposure to information in the media and society generally has put the spotlight on communication skills and sense-making abilities of adults, and this in turn has caused mathematics educators to add a communication and statistical dimension to numeracy (e.g. Cockcroft, 1982; Evans, 1992).

This section is concerned with adults learning mathematics for a variety of reasons in a variety of social contexts and offers multiple perspectives on adults, mathematics and society and their interrelationships.

Sadly in many developed countries the legacy of school mathematics is widespread innumeracy in the adult population. Two recent reports confirmed the low levels of adult numeracy in the UK. (Basic Skills Agency, 1997; Bynner & Parsons, 1997). This lack of even basic mathematical competence is exacerbated by negative attitudes of adults towards mathematics and school mathematics in particular. Roseanne Benn addresses these issues for a specific segment of the adult population in the UK namely those adults who return to study through the national Access programme for higher education. Access courses, she explains, are targeted at groups which are traditionally under-represented in higher education in the UK comprising women, ethnic minorities, unemployed adults, and learners from working class backgrounds.

Benn contrasts two incompatible views of mathematics, absolutist and fallibilist views. She attributes the failures of school mathematics to the absolutist approach. She argues that the ill effects of the absolutist approach are compounded for disadvantaged groups in society by a Eurocentric bias that is elitist, racist and sexist. The absolutist approach is based on the certainty and neutrality of mathematics and leads to a pedagogy that is unsuitable for many learners. Benn (1997) posits an alternative approach and pedagogy based on the fallibilist view that mathematics is a social construct. She argues that such approaches are more inclusive and resonate with the needs of adults returners. She cites her experiences with adult returners learning mathematics on a variety of Access programmes including teacher training (B.Ed.) programmes, in support of her position but this is reinforced by results from a national survey of Access programmes conducted by herself and colleagues at the University of Exeter. The main finding is that approaches based on a fallibilist view of mathematics lead to an increase in student motivation for students on Access courses which in turn leads to an increase in success. These arguments are a forerunner for Benn's (1997) extended critique of these and other issues related to adults learning mathematics in her book *Adults count too: mathematics for empowerment.*

In her chapter, Knijnik discusses aspects of her educational work for the Landless People's Movement (MST), a national movement for social justice for peasants in Brazil. Her mathematics education work for this social movement is informed by an ethnomathematics perspective, and is analysed by the author from the dual perspectives of participant and researcher. As participant she contributes directly to the mathematics education of the landless peasants using the ethnomathematics method. As researcher she reflects and theorizes on the basis of empirical data her projects provide, and in this way she contributes to the academic debate on the possibilities of the ethnomathematics method.

As a consequence of her work, her own conceptualization of the ethnomathematics approach has evolved over time incorporating new emphases and elements. In particular, Knijnik re-appraises the issue of power relations when native knowledge and new technologies interact. Thus a techno-culture dimension which was absent from her previous work, is introduced into the ethnomathematics perspective. Her current work integrates key pedagogical principles from the MST Education Programme and her ethnomathematics method and these are elaborated in a project at an MST settlement school for children, youths and adults at Itapuí. Here the school curriculum was shaped by the real practical needs of the community which in this case revolved around productive activities associated with crop husbandry. In this context it made sense that such issues as debt profile and production planning for specific crops e.g. rice, should be dealt with in school thus ensuring a two-way exchange between the school and the community. On the one hand the school curriculum was built around community problems, and on the other knowledge and benefits flowed from school directly into the community. Knijink concludes that ethnomathematics is most relevant when it confronts social, cultural and political issues in the political struggle for social justice.

Iddo Gal claims that the educational goal of developing informed citizens and workers for an information-laden society demands new competencies of adults. He makes a case for statistical literacy as a necessary constituent of adult numeracy and goes on to characterize this new conception as having four *cognitive* components and one *dispositional*. He limits his universe of discourse here to two types of contexts, *reporting* and *listening* contexts, and focuses on the latter. In these listening contexts the challenge for adults is to understand and critically examine messages in the media which have statistical content. Gal goes on to address the educational task of developing knowledge, skills and attitudes that allow adult learners to make sense of such messages. Not surprisingly he looks to good practice in statistical education for guidance and uses this and his own research to build a pedagogical framework for developing statistical literacy. Gal acknowledges his conception of statistical literacy is related to basic skills but clearly moves beyond these to critical and interpretive skills which can hardly be classified as basic. Gal concludes by arguing that statistical literacy is not a necessary by-product of statistics teaching, and consequently, effort must be directed specifically and explicitly to nurturing critical and interpretive skills.

Dhamma Colwell, in her chapter, reports on her research with adults in natural settings. She problematizes adults' use of mathematics in their everyday lives and focuses on adult problem solving in a wide range of everyday activities. Her observations of three groups of adults - a focus group of women, a firm of gardeners and some upholsterers - provide the data for analysis and reflection. Her work with upholsters and gardeners is reported elsewhere (Colwell, 1998). Here she reports on her research with a group of well-educated women. She recorded the women's stories and conversations on audio-tape and transcribed them for subsequent analysis using a grounded theory approach. Her conclusions are interesting and surprising.

Based on her analysis of the data, Colwell developed a four-stage model of problem solving. Surprisingly, this model displays a logical structure which is affected by the feelings and emotions of the problem solver. At this stage, Colwell is not prepared to say whether this logical structure is a feature of the constructed accounts of the problem solving activity or of the activity itself. In a wider context, she claims her results are consistent with Lave's theory of situated cognition and Saxe's four-parameter model of culture and cognition which she adapted by adding a fifth parameter *affectivity*, to account for the role of feelings in problem solving.

These chapters show researchers applying different perspectives to adults' mathematics education. What is definite in mainstream mathematics education is problematized in the context of adults learning mathematics in society e.g. mathematics and society. Fresh approaches promise worthwhile insights which may improve practice in the field of adults learning mathematics as this work shows.

REFERENCES

Adult Literacy and Basic Skills Unit. (1993). *Basic skills support in Colleges.* London: ALBSU.

Ale, S.O. (1993). 'Mathematics in Rural Societies'. In C. Keitel, P.Damerow, A. Bishop & P. Gerdes, *Mathematics, Education and Society.* Paris: UNESCO. (Science and Technology Education, Document Series No. 35), 35-38.

Basic Skills Agency. (1997). *International Numeracy Survey: a comparison of basic skills of adults 16-60 in seven countries.* London: The Basic Skills Agency.

Benn, R. (1997). *Adults count too: mathematics for empowerment.* Leicester: National Institute of Adult Continuing Education (England and Wales).

Broomes, D. (1993). 'The Mathematical Demands of a Rural Economy'. In C.Keitel, P. Damerow, A. Bishop & P. Gerdes (Eds), *Mathematics, Education and Society.* Paris: UNESCO. (Science and Technology Education, Document Series No. 35), 19-21.

Bynner, J. & S. Parsons. (1997) *Does numeracy matter? Evidence from the national Child Development Study on the impact of poor numeracy on adult life.* London: The Basic Skills Agency.

Carraher, T.N., Carraher, D.W. & Schliemann, A.D. (1985) 'Mathematics in the streets and in schools'. *British Journal of Developmental Psychology.* 3, 21-29.

Chapman, A & A. Lee. (1990). 'Rethinking literacy and numeracy'. *Australian Journal of Education.* 34 (3), 277-289.

Cockcroft, W.H. (Chairman). (1982). *Mathematics Counts: Report of the Committee of Inquiry into the Teaching of Mathematics in Schools.* London: Her Majesty's Stationery Office.

Colwell, D (1998) 'An exploration of situated cognition in two professional crafts: upholstery and gardening'. In D. Coben & J. O'Donoghue (Comps), *Adults Learning Mathematics - 4, Proceedings of the fourth international conference of Adults Learning Mathematics - A Research Forum* (ALM-4). London: Goldsmiths College, 199 - 209.

Crawford, K. (1993). ' Knowing What Versus Knowing How: The need for a change in emphasis for minority Group education in Mathematics'. In C. Keitel, P. Damerow, A. Bishop & P. Gerdes (Eds), *Mathematics, Education and Society.* Paris: UNESCO. (Science and Technology Education, Document Series No. 35), 22-24.

D'Ambrosio, U. (1993). 'Ethnomathematics, the Nature of mathematics and mathematics education'. In, P. Ernest (Ed) *Mathematics, Education and Philosophy: An international perspective,* London: Falmer, 230-242.

Ernest, P. (1991). *The Philosophy of Mathematics Education.* Basingstoke: Falmer.

Evans, J. (1992). 'Mathematics for Adults - Community research and 'Barefoot Statisticians''. In M. Nickson & S. Lerman (Eds), *The Social Context of Mathematics: theory and practice.* London: South Bank Press, 202-216.

Lave, J. (1988). *Cognition in practice: mind, mathematics and culture in everyday life.* Cambridge: Cambridge University Press.

Lerman, S. (1993). 'A Social view of mathematics - Implications for mathematics education'. In C. Keitel, P. Damerow, A. Bishop & P. Gerdes (Eds), *Mathematics, Education and Society.* Paris: UNESCO. (Science and Technology Education, Document Series No. 35), 42-44.

National Council of Teachers of Mathematics. (1989) *Curriculum and evaluation standards for school mathematics.* Reston, VA: NCTM.

National Research Council (1989) *Everybody Counts: A report to the nation on the future of mathematics education.* Washington D.C.: National Academy Press.

Nunes, T (1992). 'Ethnomathematics and everyday cognition'. In D.A. Grouws (Ed), *Handbook of Research on Mathematics Teaching and Learning.* New York: Macmillan Publishing Company, 557-574.

Sewell, B. (1981). *Use of mathematics by Adults in Everyday Life.* Leicester: ACACE.

Schlieman, A. D. (1999). 'Everyday mathematics and adults mathematics education'. In D. Coben & M. van Groenestijn (Comps), *Proceedings of the Fifth International Conference of Adults Learning Mathematics (ALM-5).* London: Goldsmiths College.

Willis, S. (1990). 'Numeracy and Society: the shifting ground'. In S. Willis (Ed). *Being numerate: what counts?.* Hawthorn, Victoria: Australian Council for Educational Research, 1-23.

Chapter 6

Mathematics: Certainty in an Uncertain World?

Roseanne Benn
Unviersity of Exeter, UK

I wanted certainty in the kind of way in which people want religious faith. I thought that certainty was more likely to be found in mathematics than elsewhere. But I discovered that many mathematical demonstrations, which my teachers expected me to accept, were full of fallacies.... Having constructed an elephant upon which the mathematical world could rest, I found the elephant tottering, and proceeded to construct a tortoise to keep the elephant from falling. But the tortoise was no more secure than the elephant, and after some twenty years of very arduous toil, I came to the conclusion that there was nothing more that I could do...(Russell 1956:54-55)

INTRODUCTION

This chapter looks at two incompatible views of mathematics. Is it a body of infallible and objective truth, a 'peek into the mind of God' or a human construct with all the fallibility that this would imply? It is then argued that these differing views lead to different approaches to the teaching and learning of mathematics and the implications and outcomes of these different approaches are explored. Finally the discussion is viewed through the lens of a large national survey of adult returners and their experiences of mathematics and the conclusion drawn that the absolutist approach has failed large numbers in our society whilst approaches based on more constructivist thinking would seem to be more successful.

D. Coben et al. (eds.), Perspectives on Adults Learning Mathematics, 109–118.
© 2000 *Kluwer Academic Publishers. Printed in the Netherlands.*

CERTAINTY AND NEUTRALITY

For over two thousand years, mathematics has been dominated by the belief that it is a body of infallible and objective truth, far removed from the affairs and values of humanity (Ernest, 1991). This body of truth is seen as existing in its own right independently of whether anyone believes or even knows about it. Bloor (1973) argues that this belief in the independent existence of mathematical truth implies that mathematics is a realm, a bounded territory. Knowledge and the use of mathematics then requires two stages, access to the realm and then activity within it. The first stage is fallible. Hence discussion of the process of selection and education and the influences which promote or inhibit access to mathematical skills is possible. However what happens within mathematics itself is regarded as closed to discussion. This is seen as predetermined and certain. Therefore a mathematical calculation is the tracing out of what is already there, the calculation exists 'in advance'. It was this belief in the certainty of mathematics which allowed Kant (1783) to write:

> We can say with confidence that certain pure a priori synthetical cognitions, pure mathematics and pure physics, are actual and given; for both contain propositions which are thoroughly recognised as absolutely certain...and yet as independent of experience.

In more recent times there have been serious critiques of this belief in the certainty of mathematics, the belief that fundamentally mathematics exists apart from the human beings that do mathematics and that Pi is in the sky. However, as argued by Davis (1986), the reception given to opponents of this belief still ranges from coolness to indifference. We argue that this belief is not only deep in the psyche of mathematicians but also of learners and teachers and its influence still distorts mathematics education.

MATHEMATICS AS A SOCIAL CONSTRUCT

The certainty of mathematics has been under question. A growing number of mathematicians and philosophers are arguing that mathematics is fallible, changing and the product of human inventiveness (Ernest, 1991). Others (Bloor, 1973; Wittgenstein, 1956) argue that rather than a calculation corresponding to an absolute truth, this truth is located in utility and the enduring character of social practice.

And of course there is such a thing as right and wrong...but what is the reality that 'right' accords with here? Presumably a convention, or a use, and perhaps our practical requirements (Wittgenstein, 1956).

They argue that mathematics is not a body of truth existing outside human experience. It is a construct or an invention rather than a discovery, a collection of norms and hence social in nature.

Sociologists and mathematicians such as Ashley and Betebenner (1993) argue that philosophers have tried but failed to show how modern mathematics and science either pictured the world as it was or used a perfectly consistent, neutral meta-language. They suggest that mathematics did not develop in a cultural or social vacuum but rather that it reflects and magnifies cultural transformations. Bertrand Russell outlined his conversion to this view in the opening quote of this chapter. Hersh (1986) echoes Russell's regret at the loss of certainty but still argues against the attempt to root mathematics in some non-human reality and for the acceptance of the nature of mathematics as a certain kind of human mental activity. He suggests that the result would be a loss of some age-old hopes but a clearer understanding of what we are doing and why.

This attack on the certainty of mathematics led to the questioning of its neutrality. If mathematics is certain, if it reflects the God-like power of innate, transcendent human reason, if it is a body of absolute truth, and if the answers are already written, then it is independent of society. It must be neutral. However if mathematics is a social construct, an invention not a discovery, then it carries a social responsibility.

A EUROCENTRIC BIAS

A proponent of this view, Joseph (1987:22-23) suggests that the present structure of mathematics education is Eurocentric, being based upon four historiographic pillars:-

1.   the general disinclination to locate mathematics in a materialistic base and thus to link its development with economic, political, and cultural changes;
2.   the confinement of mathematical pursuits to an elite few who are believed to possess the requisite qualities or gifts denied the vast majority of humanity;
3.   the widespread acceptance of the view that mathematical discovery can only follow from a rigorous application of a form of deductive axiomatic logic believed to be a unique product of Greek

mathematics; hence, intuitive or empirical methods are dismissed as
having little mathematical relevance;

4. the belief that the presentation of mathematical results must conform to the
formal and didactic style devised by the Greeks over 2,000 years ago and that,
as a corollary, the validations of new additions to mathematical knowledge can
only be taken by a small, self selecting coterie whose control over the
acquisition and dissemination of such knowledge has a highly Eurocentric
character.

Many writers (Joseph, 1987; Anderson, 1990; Bishop, 1990) argue that
the Eurocentric bias of mathematics infuses the subject with an elitist, racist
and sexist bias. They argue that the belief in the certainty and neutrality of
mathematics and science deprives these subjects of any cultural or social
context. Hence mathematics and the natural sciences place no value upon the
historical, cultural or political milieu within which they are located. Indeed
mathematicians such as Pythagoras, Euclid, Cauchy, Riemann, Fourier, and
Newton are cited as the source of western mathematics without any further
reference to the times within which they lived or to the influences upon their
work. They are abstracted from time and space and presented as if they and
their work are timeless, complete and the absolute truth. This separation
from culture and relevance makes mathematics inaccessible to those already
alienated from society by educational disadvantage and by gender, race and
class.

So we have outlined two incompatible views of mathematics. One is
premised on certainty, neutrality, the peek into the mind of God. The other
sees mathematics as a social construct and hence open to change, progress
and development and as an unfinished project. These differing views lead to
a fundamentally different approach to mathematics teaching and learning
and hence different attitudes of students to learning mathematics.

TEACHING AND LEARNING

Nearly two decades after the Cockcroft Report (1982) the British
education system still fails to provide a substantial proportion of the
population with even basic mathematical skills (Basic Skills Agency, 1997).
Even worse, it leaves many with an abiding dislike of the subject. We will
now examine mathematics education in the context of the belief in the
certainty and neutrality of mathematics for part of the explanation of this
failure.

The concept of mathematics as a body of infallible and objective truth,
whilst questioned by many mathematicians and philosophers, appears to be

still widely held by society, teachers and students. Ernest's (1991) analysis of both the Cockcroft Report (1982) and a report by Her Majesty's Inspectorate which looked into the nature of mathematics teaching in Britain (1985), concludes that the mathematical approach taken in schools in Britain assumes an absolutist view of mathematics.

This perception that mathematics is a certain and neutral subject clearly has a number of consequences for the teaching of the subject. Abstracted from any socio-political context, mathematics can be taught within the strictures of its own boundaries thus retaining for the pupils its mysticism and ritualistic nature. Certainly much work has been done since the introduction of mathematics into the mass education system to increase understanding of mathematics. However, just as certainly the history of mathematics is one of failure on a large scale for the students of mathematics. The Cockcroft Report (1982:56) notes that at the time the report was written 'about...one-third of the year group, leave school without any mathematical qualifications in 'O' level or CSE'.

It seems that despite calls for over one hundred years for an approach to mathematics that interests and stimulates children at school, mathematics is still a subject that confuses and alienates. A school inspector wrote in 1989 that she was horrified to find that at both primary and secondary level 'nobody seemed to enjoy mathematics; not even the teachers' (Cross, 1990:4)

Writers such as Rogers (1969), Dewey (1964) and Knowles (1980) argue that learners are self-directed beings who learn best when they perceive the relevance of knowledge to their lives, and when learning is related to problem solving. If mathematics is perceived as a fixed and unvarying body of truth independent of social concerns, then it is difficult to see any room for negotiation or where life experiences can be used in the learning process. If mathematics is neutral it has little to contribute to the learner's knowledge of themselves or their immediate world. All this contributes to a lack of motivation and hence a tendency to failure.

As Thom (1973:202-3) writes:

> In practice a mathematician's thought is never a formalised one...one accedes to absolute rigour only by eliminating meaning; absolute rigour is only possible in, and by, such destitution of meaning. But if one must choose between rigour and meaning, I shall unhesitatingly choose the latter.

AN ALTERNATIVE APPROACH

The Cockcroft Report (1982:71) suggested that there are three elements in mathematics teaching - facts and skills, conceptual structures, and general strategies and appreciation. The last is of interest to this chapter. General strategies are defined as procedures which guide the choice of which skills to use and which knowledge to draw on. Crucially they enable a problem to be approached with confidence and with the expectation that a solution will be possible. Associated with these strategies are an awareness of the nature of mathematics and certain attitudes towards it. An alternative approach to mathematics teaching can be developed by adopting an alternative view of the nature of mathematics. What follows are two examples of viewing mathematics, not as a certain, abstract, neutral discipline but as a human invention, a world of ideas created not by God but by human beings.

Anderson (1990) horrified at the high failure rate in mathematics by non-whites in his classes, outlined a non-Eurocentric approach to mathematics teaching that by jettisoning the absolutist approach endeavours to ensure the relevance of mathematics for all. The early sessions are discussions on the historical, cultural, and socio-political implications of mathematics. At all stages an emphasis is placed on the role of other races and cultures in the development of the subject. The importance of mathematics to real people in real life is drawn out by regular class discussions of current issues in the social and natural sciences, the development of technology and job market skills. The emphasis is on the quality of mathematics knowledge rather than the quantity, thus reducing the time pressure. Anderson claims that this approach leads to students having a more positive, self-assured attitude about themselves successfully doing mathematics.

The Department of Adult and Continuing Education at the University of Exeter instigated a research project to see whether mathematics acts as a barrier to access to higher education to adult returners. On the basis of data gathered from a national survey of Access courses (full details of the methodology and results can be found in Benn & Burton, 1993), it became clear that, as with Anderson's work, Access mathematics tutors were succeeding with groups who had low levels of general education and very low levels of earlier achievement and confidence in mathematics.

Access courses are targeted at those groups traditionally under-represented in higher education namely women, ethnic minorities, unemployed and those from working class backgrounds. For these groups to succeed, their attitudes and approaches to mathematics need to be fundamentally changed. Many of the students on Access courses displayed low confidence levels and high anxiety levels. Access courses which capitalise on the adult experience of the students and their motivation; offer learning experiences which build confidence and a positive self image; encourage students to change their perspective on the learning and teaching of mathematics; and present mathematics as an active, enquiry-based subject enable students to change their image of mathematics and their own relationship to it (Burton, 1987).

Learners on Access courses are introduced to a mathematics that takes into account the personal, interpretative and relativistic approach which other subjects allow. The freedom to explore mathematics gives meaning where meaning had been lost in earlier experiences. Without this freedom students are likely to reject mathematics that are presented to them in a non-personal and mechanistic way. Burton (1987: 307) argues that:

> Mathematics, for the students who joined...Access course[s], not only had a mystique which included the expectation that it was ritualistic and arbitrary, but they also had considerable experience of their own inability to understand.

This is supported in the Exeter survey by student comments such as 'I found maths pretty tough and sometimes mysterious'. Access students are encouraged to approach mathematics in a manner more closely resembling that of mathematicians than learners in school, that is, to encounter mathematics as a discipline that requires investigation, conjecture and activity, as a social construct rather than an immutable law of nature.

Low levels of mathematics achievement seem to be a shared experience for Access students. With approximately 35% of the Exeter sample reporting that they had left school with no mathematical qualifications and a further 49% with less than O level equivalence, this amounted to a significant 84% of the cohort with low or no mathematics qualification, many showing a negative attitude to school mathematics. The overall context within which an Access student's attitude to mathematics must be set is a very strong motivation to get into higher education. Over 80% agreed that, whatever the requirement for entry, they would have attempted to get it. But another important factor to emerge amongst at least some of the group who had been on Access courses for about six months was a positive attitude to mathematics itself and a growing sense of confidence. Almost half the students agreed that they enjoyed mathematics, with over half feeling reasonably confident in tackling mathematical problems. Again half perceived no problems in understanding mathematics. Although the subject brought 30% out in a cold sweat, it did not have that effect on a sizeable 60%. This showed approximately half the cohort enjoying mathematics and feeling confident with no major difficulties or fears. There was an undecided or wavering group of 10%-20%, with 20%-30% with negative feelings in this area.

Student comments are typically 'an excellent maths tutor at....has made maths enjoyable for me'. At the same time, tutors were saying 'A lot of my time is spent convincing them that they 'do maths' and praising every small success' and mathematics teachers should be 'be as different as it is humanly possible from the stereotyped maths teacher!'.

The considerable and commendable success in both overcoming fears of mathematics and the high success rate on Access mathematics can be attributed to the motivation of students and the approach taken by tutors. The need to see mathematics as a construct which involves interpersonal and human skills was illustrated by the student responses to questions on preferred learning situations. Students are passing Access mathematics and achieving levels of mathematics which seem to surprise themselves. As these students put it:

Once I was on the Access BEd course I found that the different style of teaching refreshing, and I now enjoy maths. I am now doing well.

I've just realised why I was taught algebra.

Just a drastic change in teaching techniques ... demonstrated my enthusiasm to learn maths.

This new found confidence in mathematics has wider effects. As one tutor noted:

by making progress with a subject they had thought they were unable to do, they gained an enormous sense of achievement and increased confidence which informed their whole approach to study.

Access students need to see the subject not as one more absolute, unyielding barrier but as social construct, a tool pliable to their bidding. This is done by breaking down the concept of mathematics as a body of infallible and objective truth and giving ownership and control of the subject to the students. Access mathematics tutors reported that the main elements of their teaching is encouragement and understanding; that tutors need to be patient and remove the often difficult and disabling pressures of time, and that Access mathematics needs to be taught in context and have a relevancy to real life and other parts of the course. They note that the involvement of students and tutors in free discussion and dialogue in a supportive atmosphere helps students develop confidence.

Initial contact with mathematics staff was seen as important, with clear and friendly pre-course counselling essential. If possible pre-course assistance and/or workshops should be available. Students should be given an honest indication of the work involved. It is reassuring for students if "maths phobia" and the reasons for it are discussed early in the course. The methodological approaches recommended are open access workshops, flexible learning tutorial packs, self-help groups and a modular approach, with one-to-one support most frequently mentioned even in these financially constrained days.

There is an urgent need to build confidence by showing that it is acceptable to be wrong and by placing the emphasis on methods rather than answers; to develop a positive attitude to mathematics by encouraging students to take ownership of mathematics by "messing around" with, exploring and enjoying numbers. The survey showed that students were coming onto the Access courses very worried by the mathematics component, but the techniques outlined gave them a sense of confidence and control.

CONCLUSION

This chapter has discussed two incompatible views of mathematics: that of a body of infallible and objective truth rooted in the belief in the essential certainty and neutrality of the subject, and that of mathematics as a social construct.

The danger of regarding mathematics as a God-given, absolute subject is that it may, and arguably has in many cases, lead to an absolutist pedagogy which ensures that mathematics remains a collection of rules and facts to be remembered, a subject that has a mystique which makes it accessible only to a chosen few. It remains a subject that seems to have very little relevance to life outside of the classroom, but where success or failure has implications for a person's self or moral worth.

This pedagogical approach has had limited success when the whole body of students in Britain is considered. Its failure is even more marked with groups that consistently underachieve in our education system, groups such as ethnic minorities, the working class and girls or women. As has been illustrated earlier, practitioners in the field who are teaching these groups have developed alternative approaches. They set mathematics in a historical, cultural and socio-political environment and they ensure a more relevant syllabus set in the context of every-day life. They ensure mathematics is seen like other disciplines as a negotiated journey, a quest and a voyage of discovery.

The main result is an increase in student motivation with subsequent increase in success. This practice, though perhaps pragmatic rather than theoretical in origin, reflects the view of some philosophers that mathematics, far from being a body of truth, is in fact a collection of norms. Far from a peek into the mind of God, it is not even supported by a tortoise.

And, most interestingly, this practice appears to work.   For further discussion on this and other issues involved in adults learning mathematics see: Benn, R. (1997) *Adults count too: mathematics for empowerment*, Leicester: NIACE

REFERENCES

Anderson, S. E. (1990) 'Worldmath Curriculum: Fighting Eurocentism in Mathematics'. *Journal of Negro Education, 59* (3), 349-359.

Ashley, D. & Betebenner, D. (1993) *Mathematics, Post-Modernism, and the Loss of Certainty*. Paper presented to the British Sociological Association Annual Conference. University of Essex.

Basic Skills Agency (1997) *International Numeracy Survey: a comparision of the basic skills of adults 16-60 in seven countries*. London: The Basic Skills Agency

Benn, R & Burton, R. (1994) 'Access Mathematics: A Bridge over troubled waters'. *Journal of Access Studies, 9(*1).

Bishop, A.J. (1990) 'Western mathematics: the secret weapon of cultural imperialism'. *Race and Class, 32(*2), 180-190.

Bloor, D. (1973) 'Wittgenstein and Mannheim on the Sociology of Mathematics'. *Studies in the History and Philosophy of Science, 4(*2), 173 - 191.

Burton, L. (1987) 'From failure to success: changing the experience of adult learners of mathematics'. *Educational Studies in Mathematics 18*, 305-316.

Cockcroft, W. H. (Chairman of the Committee of Inquiry into the Teaching of Mathematics in Schools) (1982), *Mathematics Counts*, London: HMSO.

Cross, K. (1990) 'Sharing Perspectives: People Learning Mathematics'. *Mathematics Teaching, 130.*

Davis, P. J. (1986) 'Fidelity in Mathematical Discourse: Is One and One Really Two?'. In Tymoczko, T.(Ed.), *New Directions in the Philosophy of Mathematics*, Boston: Birkhauser, 163-175.

Dewey, J. (1964) *Democracy and Education*, London: Macmillan.

Ernest, P. (1991) *The Philosophy of Mathematics Education*, London: Falmer Press.

Her Majesty's Inspectorate (1985) *Mathematics from 5 to 16,* London: HMSO

Hersh, R.(1986) 'Some Proposals for Reviving the Philosophy of Mathematics'. In Tymoczko, T.(Ed.) *New Directions in the Philosophy of Mathematics*, Boston: Birkhauser, 9-28.

Joseph, G.G. (1987) 'Foundations of Eurocentrism in Mathematics'. *Race and Class, 28(3)*, 13-28.

Kant, I. (1783) Prolegomena to any future Metaphysics.

Knowles, M. (1980) (2nd Ed) *The Modern Practice of Adult Education from Pedagogy to Andragogy.* Chicago: Association Press.

Rogers, C. R. (1969) *Freedom to Learn*, Ohio: Merrill Publishing Company.

Russell, B. (1956) *Portraits From Memory and Other Essays* , New York: Simon & Schuster.

Thom, R. (1973) 'Modern Mathematics: does it exist?' . In A.G. Howson (Ed), *Developments in Mathematical Education*, Cambridge: Cambridge University Press, 194-209.

Wittgenstein, L. (1956) *Remarks on the Foundations of Mathematics*, Oxford: Blackwell.

Chapter 7

Ethnomathematics and Political Struggles

Gelsa Knijnik
Universidade do Vale do Rio dos Sinos, Brazil

INTRODUCTION

Youth and Adult Education is one of the most important social issues in Brazil, since 14.7% of the country's population over 15 years of age is illiterate (i.e., unable to read or write a simple letter), and the average schooling period is 5.3 years long. In the rural areas these rates become even higher (IBGE, 1996). It is against this background that youth and adult mathematics education emerges.

In this chapter, originally published in *ZDM* journal (Knijnik, 1998a), I present and analyse elements of a research study in the field of mathematics education which I have been developing in the South of Brazil since 1991, with the Movimento Sem-Terra, MST (in English, Landless People's Movement). This is a nationally organized movement involving approximately 160 000 families. At the centre of their struggle is the implementation of a land reform which will contribute to the democratization of wealth in a country with the largest concentration of land ownership in the world. One of the dimensions of this struggle for social justice is precisely education, where MST has made an original contribution to the trajectory in which Brazil is internationally renowned, thanks mainly to the ideas of Paulo Freire, beginning in the sixties.

MST today represents the new, both as regards forms of popular organization and in terms of education. Further, the organizational dimension of the struggle for land could be said to be so amalgamated to education which is carried out in this process of struggle that both reinforce each other mutually. It was the very impasses that arose in the struggle for land that indicated the need to set education as one of the priorities. Thus, we

D. Coben et al. (eds.), Perspectives on Adults Learning Mathematics, 119–133.

are now facing a social movement which, while struggling for land reform, a structural struggle, takes on as one of its priorities the education of its members. It is an education which takes place during the struggle, to strengthen the very struggle, mainly involving the challenge of showing that collective production in the settlements is a feasible solution from the economic standpoint, producing new social and cultural conditions.

Considering the lack of attention that has been given to questions of education by the Brazilian government agencies, it is far from surprising that a social movement involving thousands of youths and adults who are still illiterate, and children that are outside the schooling process, takes onto itself the task of education. Even more than this: aware that the education currently provided in Brazil does not fulfil the concrete needs of life in the camps and settlements[1], MST is pressured to seek pedagogical alternatives which will attempt to overcome the limitations of traditional teaching, both for those who have not yet had access to education, and for those who, while still in school, do not have their intellectual needs fulfilled and their culture valued.

One of the relevant aspects of the educational proposal of MST (expressed as one of its pedagogical principles) refers specifically to the question of valuing popular culture. Here are continuities with the positions advocated by Freire since his first studies: the ways in which people produce meanings, understand the world, live their daily life, are considered as relevant, even central elements of the educational process. In this sense the positions presented in the official documents of the education sector of MST converge towards Freirean theorizations. However, there is no exacerbated relativism, no naive approach to the potential of such popular knowledge in the pedagogical process. Herein, the interrelations between popular and academic knowledge are qualified, allowing the adults, youths and children who participate in it to concurrently understand their own culture more profoundly, and also to have access to contemporary scientific and technological production.

Even in such a 'hard' area as mathematics, there has been an attempt to provide education which will be able to deal with the permanent tension between local and more general knowledge. In this sense there is a tendency to guide the work towards the perspective of ethnomathematics, as I have discussed in other studies (Knijnik, 1996, 1997b). I refer to a tendency to indicate that the process is slow, with advances and withdrawals, considering the difficulties found in teacher training, material conditions at the schools, and resistances encountered in the school community, to mention just a few of the limiting factors found in the processes of formal education linked to MST. When the question is considered in terms of education performed at the camps that do not even have a school, these limiting factors become even greater. The pedagogical projects that I have been developing from the ethnomathematics perspective seek to contribute to the implementation of the MST education proposal, at the same time as they constitute empirical material to take a deeper look at what I have been discussing about the theory of ethnomathematics.

THEORETICAL ROOTS

Ethnomathematics[2] is a relatively recent area of mathematics education, beginning with the contributions of the Brazilian educator Ubiratan D'Ambrosio (1990, 1997). Its constitution as a field of knowledge covers a broad, heterogeneous spectrum of approaches, among them mine, based on the pedagogical work I have been constructing with MST. When I did my first research projects at MST (Knijnik, 1996, 1997c) I enunciated it as: the investigation of the traditions, practices and mathematical concepts of a subordinated social group (subordinated as to the volume and composition of the cultural, economic and social capital) and the pedagogical work which was developed in order for the group to be able to interpret and decode its knowledge; to acquire the knowledge produced by academic mathematics and to establish comparisons between its knowledge and academic knowledge, thus being able to analyze the power relations involved in the use of these two kinds of knowledge.

This concept, opposing an ethnocentric view with which the popular cultures have often been treated, seeks to articulate the relativistic and legitimistic perspectives in examining the mathematics practices of the socially subordinated groups. In fact, as I have put forward in other texts (Knijnik, 1997a), I have sought to incorporate the interpretation and decoding of native knowledge in pedagogical work, stressing its internal coherence, trying to describe it from a point of view which is not external to the context in which it is produced, so that the values, codes which give it meaning, and in turn, give meaning to such mathematics, can be described within their own logic. In this sense, what I have been developing within the ethnomathematics field is aligned with a relativistic perspective of popular cultures. However, I have been watchful to avoid exacerbated relativism which would end up by producing what Grignon (Grignon & Passeron, 1992), properly called "ghettoization of the subordinated groups". In the case of MST, a social movement in permanent interaction with the dominant groups, this ghettoization process would occur if the pedagogical process were limited to the recovery of native knowledge, leading to a possible glorification of this knowledge, with the consequent reinforcement of social inequalities. This type of operation, i.e. incorporation of the legitimistic perspective in pedagogical work, must be avoided. It is a question of examining the cultural differences not only from the anthropological standpoint, but also of seeking to understand them sociologically, in what differences constitute inequalities. It is in this sense that pedagogical work, as proposed in my above conceptualization, examines the power relations produced in the confrontation between popular culture, here understood as the native mathematics knowledge, and the socially legitimated culture, here understood as academic mathematics[3].

Summarizing, these theorizations were present at the conceptualization of the ethnomathematics approach I had been using up until recently to perform my mathematics education work at MST. This conceptualization was increasingly broadened when, from 1996 onwards, I began a new research project at MST. In this research, the centrality of the discussion of power relations remained, but now they are analyzed in the pedagogical work where different native knowledge interacts at the same time as it confronts technical knowledge, in a process which does not take the former only as a point of departure for the acquisition of the latter. Thus, new elements begin to be integrated in what I call the ethnomathematics approach. The first of these regards power relations. Previously, power relations were examined from the external standpoint, i.e., when popular knowledge interacted with academic knowledge, in an operation which sought to articulate the relativistic and legitimistic perspectives. Now I examine the power relations also from the internal standpoint, seeking to problematise what Skovsmose and Vithal properly pointed to as one of the fragilities of ethnomathematics production. The authors said:

> The ethnomathematical practice, generated by a particular cultural group, is not only the result of interactions with the natural and social environment but also subjected to interactions with the power relations both among and within cultural groups. Ethnomathematical studies shown how this has been played out between the Eurocentrism of academic mathematics and the mathematics of identifiable cultural groups, but have not equally applied this analysis to an analogous situation that occurs within an identified cultural group. (Skovsmose & Vithal, 1997:11)

It is these power relations which will now become the subject of analysis in my formulation of the ethnomathematics approach. The latter takes over a second element previously absent as an object of study: the analysis of power relations instituted in the interaction of native knowledge with the use of technologies. More precisely, it is to examine the repercussions of a work in education which at the same time as it looks carefully at the social practices that do not involve the use of 'new' technologies - such as those connected to what I have been calling Popular Mathematics (Knijnik, 1997a, 1997c) - incorporates in its analyses those that are produced by the appropriation of contemporary technological resources[4]. The introduction of the techno-culture dimension - as mentioned by Skovsmose and Vithal (1997) - in the ethnomathematics perspective, had as sources of inspiration two matrices which, although coming from very different 'places', ended up by reinforcing each other.

The first matrix is located on the level of the academic debate about ethnomathematics. Authors such as Skovsmose and Vithal (1997) argue about the 'ghettoization' operation that is implemented by ethnomathematics when the latter is restricted solely to the studies of 'native' knowledge of the different cultural groups, and that in this sense, ethnomathematics would come to constitute an approach that above all reinforces social inequalities. Ethnomathematics, according to this argument, deals with the connections between culture and mathematics, between 'daily practices' and school curriculum, circumscribing these connections to an exclusively 'local' culture, and to a daily life which is understood exclusively as an experience acquired in material, immediate, present concreteness, narrowly configured by this 'local' dimension

The second matrix which inspires the incorporation of the techno-culture dimension in what I call an ethnomathematics approach, appeared in 1996 when the project Lumiar (in English, 'Threshold') was established - a joint effort of MST and the Institute of Colonization and Land Reform, a government agency. From this occasion on, new social actors began to participate in settlement life, with the implementation of specialized technical assistance to the peasant families, a process whose educational dimensions are also included in the sphere of schooling for the youth and children. The presence of technical knowledge in communities which had so far been producing in an artisanal manner, without any technical guidance, is leading to repercussions in different dimensions of life in the settlements. What are these repercussions? What is the ecological, economic and social impact of the introduction of these 'new' technologies? What are their effects in terms of power relations? How will the 'encounter' (or 'disencounter') of this world which had previously been characterized by popular knowledge, be when it encounters the world of science and technology? How do the settlement schools participate in this process? What effects will this participation have on the school curriculum? On this scene - which until then had been marked exclusively by popular knowledge which now confronts technology and technical knowledge - these questions are very fruitful from the theoretical standpoint, broadening the ethnomathematics approach which I have sought to construct.

This approach is closely connected to the field of cultural studies, first of all due to the fact that the work I am performing with the MST and the theoretical analysis I am developing based on this work are cultural and political interventions. As Lawrence Grossberg (1996:90) says:

> Cultural studies is obviously a set of approaches that attempt to understand and intervene in the relations of culture and power; but the particular relationship between theory and context in cultural studies is equally central to its definition. Cultural studies neither applies theory as if answers could be known in advance nor is empirism without theory. (...) Furthermore, cultural studies is committed to contestation, both as a fact of reality (although not necessarily in every instant) and as a strategic practice in itself.

The ethnomathematics approach, as I am formulating it for now, has points of intersection with the field of cultural studies also because I have taken for analysis daily school life in a community constituted by peasants who are members of a social movement, taking as a premise that this group is not a homogeneous whole. Thus "more than treating minority groups as homogeneous entities, we emphasize the contradictory interests, needs and wishes which inform their political, cultural and educational behavior" (McCarthy & Cricholow, 1993:xix). Finally, the above mentioned ethnomathematics approach is connected to the field of cultural studies insofar as I take as subject of investigation a process in which I myself am involved, and concurrently make an effort to produce a distance which will allow me to analyse practices in which I myself participate.

The debate on ethnomathematics has gained international visibility. There are growing demands to inquire and problematize it. Not in search of the 'true' truth, the last instance where will be decided what, after all, is 'good' and 'evil' in the field of ethnomathematics. What is at stake is the academic debate which will point out its possibilities and limitations. In order to implement this, it is necessary to built concrete pedagogical experiences - which will offer us empirical material for reflection - and new theorizations which will make it possible to feed the discussion. The next section of this essay proposes to contribute toward this.

EMPIRICAL RESEARCH

The projects I have been developing with MST have constituted empirical research material. Collecting this material has involved methodological procedures which seek to compatibilise ethnographic techniques such as direct and participant observation, interviews and field diary with a specific pedagogical process in the field of mathematics, guided by the ethnomathematics perspective. The project to which this article refers is underway at a school in the settlement of Itapuí, 43 km from the capital of the southernmost state of Brazil.

The school has approximately 150 students, distributed in 9 classes, from pre-school to 8th grade. After a period in which the faculty was restructured - as a consequence of the school community 'squat' in the School District Office and a statewide teachers' strike - currently there are 11 teachers at the school. Among them are members of MST and female and male teachers 'from outside', a nomenclature used by the group to describe those who, although they do not belong to the Movement, teach at settlement schools. Although it is a state public institution, and its curriculum and administration are therefore directly connected to the guidelines of the State Department of Education, there is a relative autonomy in the direction of pedagogical work performed there, strongly influenced by the educational proposal of the education sector of MST[5].

This proposal which is being constructed for a social movement from the same movement, has contributed significantly, in many ways, to the trajectory of education of the socially subordinated groups in the country (Knijnik, 1998b). The MST elaboration process is supported by a set of pedagogical principles, three of which are particularly relevant to the current project: 'Reality as a base of production of knowledge', 'Organic connection between educational processes and economic processes' and 'Organic connection between education and culture'. The discussion regarding the relevance of the rescue of popular knowledge, which has often resulted in the pedagogical cliche 'beginning with reality' lies currently on another level in the official MST documents, as the following argument well shows:

> What we must not lose sight of is the higher goal of all this and which regards not a simple rescue of the so-called popular culture but mainly producing a new culture a 'culture of change which takes the past as a reference, the present as the experience which can at the same time be fulfilling in itself and is also an anticipation of the future, our Utopian project, our horizon. (MST, 1996:19)

Here the current understanding of the concept of 'reality' and 'culture' becomes clearly explicit also within the sphere of MST. The pedagogical principle of 'reality as a base' includes the concept that techno-culture must necessarily be the subject of studies in pedagogical work, either as a reflection and learning of the immediately present reality, or announcing a future which is being constructed. Obviously there is tension between this present that is loaded with the past, and a future which must be 'hurried up', since, as a peasant said when referring to the need for technological advances: "There is historical urgency".

This "urgency" has been dealt with at unequal rates in Brazil. In fact, the pedagogical principles of MST have so far constituted guidelines for the work developed in its schools, guidelines which have been very heterogeneously incorporated in the different educational instances of the Movement, rather configuring a pedagogical trend than a closed set of principles proper. Since it is necessary to follow up the proposal for education in the most distant points of the country, at the same time as qualification is achieved, actions are being implemented involving universities and the education collectives of MST. The implementation of the project I describe and analyze below constitutes one of these actions.

THE DEBT PROFILE AND PRODUCTION PLANNING

In the last few years, there has been growing concern in MST with the young people, since it is found that many of them are seeking cultural and work alternatives in the cities, thus moving away from the specific struggles of the Movement. In fact, this 'second generation' of Landless People - the children of those who lived in tents for years and years in the camps and since childhood learned the harshness of struggles - now that their material needs are reasonably fulfilled, pressure for new possibilities of work and leisure. The media seduces them with the charms of the city and dreams of consumption and the traditional school, rooted in urban culture, remaining silent about the rural life, reinforces this feeling that the only way out is to migrate to the city. It is in this context that MST has sought to implement new projects involving the settlement youths, in a process that produces new forms of living and signifying the rural culture and the struggle for land.

It was these social, cultural and political needs that inspired the project which began at the Itapuí settlement with 7th graders, involving from its conception the joint action of peasants, students, teachers and specialists (agronomists and veterinarians), of the Lumiar project, in constructing pedagogical work in the field of mathematics, focused on productive activities in the settlement. These activities are organized by groups of peasants who, collectively, carry out all stages of production, from planning to commercialization.

Initially the students - guided by the agronomist and the teachers - analyzed the previous projects and bank loan contracts of each group of settlers, to configure the profile of each debt. This was the first opportunity this youth had had of looking at official documents which, in order to analyse their complexity, required understanding the dynamics of financial mathematics and previously unknown mathematical tools, such as compound interest. The profile of the debt, produced by analyzing the contracts, was presented at meetings with each group of settlers. For the peasants - many of whom were illiterate and most of whom with at most 4 year schooling - this was the first time they had access not only to the final amount to be paid to the bank, but to the details (albeit simplified) that produced this result.

The meetings to discuss the debt profile supplied the elements required for each group to be able to plan the production they would develop, having as parameter their ability to pay. Difficult situations occurred where it was found that there was no way to pay past debts. One group, for instance, seeing what the young people pointed out, decided to get rid of the truck they were using to transport their crops; another group questioned the advantages and feasibility of requesting a new loan to pay the harvest (even if it were given at relatively low rates of interest), since, as one settler explained "it is better to be free of debt, since an ox free of its yoke finds it easier to lick itself".

The participation of the youth in these meetings had a effect on life in the settlement. The first effect refers to the participation of women who had been absent from collective discussion in the group and now began to take part. A second repercussion concerns the qualification of planning settlement production. In fact, the pedagogical work which was constructed - from the initial analyses of contracts to their discussion with the community - at the same time as it allowed situated learning (in the sense of Lave, 1988) of new mathematical tools, favoured a more qualified discussion of financial aspects of settlement activity. This qualification had as its central element the incorporation of techno-culture in pedagogical work. Techno-culture is here defined as the use of calculators and more sophisticated planning processes, which had been previously unknown to the young people. This educational approach also allowed new decisions to be taken about production, integrating the youth in the work world of their families. As a girl said, referring to her father, "I have never talked with him about this. It is only now that I have taken an interest in what is happening to us". This interest was valued by the adults who are aware of how important it is that the new generation participate more actively in the productive process. This participation is directly related the education given in the settlement schools, particularly as regards the dimension of its mathematics education.

TRADITIONS AND 'TRANSLATIONS' IN RICE-PLANTING

The first stage of the project focusing on the discussion of the debt profile of each group in the settlement triggered other stages. Each of them involved the problematization of the production of a specific crop which was analyzed in multiple dimensions. During the analytic process pedagogical work was constructed from an ethnomathematics perspective. This is what happened for instance, beginning at a joint meeting of the agronomist students and teachers with the settlers of the 'Rice Group'. This group consists of peasants coming from a region far from the one where they are established today, (in which soybeans, maize and bean crops predominate) and of former employees of the farm which after expropriation by the State gave rise to the Itapuí settlement. The characteristics of the soil render it appropriate for rice crops, which are in fact its main agricultural activity. Thus, in the group there are women and men for whom rice production is part of their life trajectories and those for whom it is a foreign element with which they still have difficulty in dealing. As Seu Arnoldo explained: "I am from elsewhere, I have been here for ten years but I have not yet caught up with the pace". The presence of the Lumiar project agronomist in the settlement and the pedagogical work which is being developed seeks to understand this "pace" to which the peasant refers, attempting to speed it up by technical qualification.

During the first meeting organised with the group of settlers in order to plan the rice crop (in which students and teachers participated), one of the questions initially raised concerned the amount of land which would be planted. In fact this information would define the remainder of the plan. One settler suggested that 30 *quadras* could be planted, another showed the possibility of planting "up to one *colônia*". When they heard these terms, one of the students interrupted the discussion to ask how many *quadras* there were in a *colônia*[6]. The settler answered. "Look, I deal in *quadras*, they in *colônia*". The dialogue continued.

> Agronomist: One *quadra* is 1.7 ha, i.e. 17424 metres.
> Seu Hélio (settler): That is saying it in metres, in *braças* it is 3600 *braças*.
> Márcio (student): What is *braça*, Seu Hélio?
> Seu Hélio: One *braça* is 2 meters and 20 ... is a *braça* see? Let's say: *cuba* here, *cuba* there ... 60 *braças* like this, the four strips here: see, 60 there, here, 60, 60, 60, 60, to see how it makes a *quadra*, we will have exactly the 3,600.[7]

Initially, it appeared that the answers given by the agronomist and the settler were enough for the youth. But when they returned to the classroom the explanations proved unsatisfactory and required more detailed study. The discussion began with what the specialist said, explaining that in the rice plantation, peasants deal mainly with the *quadra*: there are also those who use *'colônia'* as a measure, but he does everything in hectares in order "to keep things straight in my mind", since the bank loan contracts are in hectares. Several questions thus arose. What kind of "translation" occurs when *quadra* is expressed in hectares instead of *braças*? How is *colônia* translated into *quadra*? And how do both connect to hectare? How can one establish bridges and shifts between these knowledges? What are the effects, in terms of power relations, of these 'translation' processes which occur in the Rice Group and in the community?

The pedagogical work sought to problematize these questions. It was not a matter of performing 'translations' which would be limited to numerical equivalences, reducing the study to the demonstration that if a *braça* is 2.2 metres, then 60 *braças* are 132 metres, and therefore a *quadra* is 17424 square meters, i.e.(1.724 ha.). An approach which limited itself to this kind of operation would precisely be reducing the work to the formal academic mathematics in which, as Walkerdine argues, "the practice operates by means of suppression of all aspects of multiple signification" (Walkerdine 1988:96). Following this author, I emphasize that "the position which I have adopted is that the object world cannot be known outside the relations of signification in which objects are inscribed" (Walkerdine, 1988:119).

At the Itapuí settlement, such relations of meaning are produced in a process where different cultural traditions meet and confront each other, recalling what Stuart Hall well described as an oscillatory movement between tradition and "translation". For the author the concept of "translation"[8]:

> describes those identity formations which cross and intersect natural borders constituted by people who were dispersed forever from their native land. These people retain strong ties to their places of origin and their traditions but without the illusion of a return to the past. They are obliged to negotiate with the new cultures in which they live, without simply being assimilated by them and without completely losing their identities. They carry with them the traits of the cultures, traditions, languages and specific histories which marked them. (Hall, 1997:96)

Among these traits are the use of specific surface measures, expressed also based on specific units whose meanings are culturally constructed. The history of imposing a standard of specific surface measures was not the result of a consensus produced by the supremacy of their precision, nor by arguments of universalisation. On the contrary, there are examples of popular revolts such as the one which became known as the 'Kilo Revolt' which took place in Brazil in 1871 (Souto Maior, 1978). This revolt, which had as one of its causes the imposition in the country of the French metric system, shows the rebellion of colonized groups and some of their forms of resistance. This part of the history of popular struggles in Brazil, usually not mentioned in the school curriculum, was present in the work developed at Itapuí, allowing the construction of bridges between the history (of mathematics) and the perspective of ethnomathematics. The past and the present were understood as culture,

> the site of the struggle to define how life is lived and experienced, a struggle carried out in the discursive forms available to us. Cultural practices articulate the meanings of particular social practices and events, they define the ways we make sense of them, how they are experienced and lived. (Grossberg, 1996:158)

The past and present cultural practices were examined in the dimensions of conflict, of the struggle to impose meanings, in a dynamics in which unofficial knowledge, vocalized by peasants coming from different regions of the state, whose life experiences are marked by different traditions, were recovered and confronted amongst themselves and in their traditions - *quadra, braça,* hectare and *colônia* - were also translated.

FINAL REMARKS

The project begun in 1996 in the Itapuí settlement, under an ethnomathematics perspective, has pointed to several questions which could possibly be relevant in other social contexts. Peasants, students, teachers and technicians are experiencing the construction of an educational process in which local and more global knowledge interact, where native and technical knowledge are confronted and incorporated, in a dynamics where the school is not turned inwards, with its back to the community of which it is part. On the contrary, pedagogical work has overflowed the school limits, extrapolated its borders, producing the double movement of making community life penetrate the school at the same time as knowledge produced during this process pours out from the school space. What was at stake, in carrying out this two-way movement was the construction of ethnomathematical work which would not be limited strictly to the school space, and would end up by constituting, above all, a perspective that would only reinforce the hegemonic ways of learning and teaching mathematics marked by the Western, white, urban male culture (Knijnik, 1996). Such a perspective runs counter to the arguments presented by Nick Taylor (1993) in his criticism of ethnomathematics, based on Valerie Walkerdine's theorizations. In fact, Taylor identifies the "dilemma of ethnomathematics" precisely in the focus used by the author in approaching the discussion on context and transference. Criticizing her he says:

(...) The end goal in working from a specific bit of local knowledge - one metaphorical manifestation - to the underlying metonymic principle (Walkerdine, 1982), is formal mathematics. It is hard to square this mathematics as a central repressive mechanism of modernity (Taylor, 1991). It is hard to reconcile the connection she draws between the metaphorical and metonymic elements of knowledge, with her postulation of a disjuncture between 'problems of practical and material necessity versus problems of symbolic control' (Walkerdine, 1990:52). (Taylor, 1993:132)

The approach used in the pedagogical work developed in the Itapuí settlement focused on problems of practical and material needs. They were not transmuted into symbolic control problems, indicating other possibilities in the field of ethnomathematics, especially in mathematics education, which is carried out with social movements such as MST. The connection between the struggle for land and the perspective of ethnomathematics is mediated by the dimension of the social, the cultural and the political. Ethnomathematics finds its most relevant expression when it exposes its social engagement, when it treats cultural questions as non-exotic and rooted elements, when it shows its commitment to political struggles widespread throughout the world.

ACKNOWLEDGEMENT

This chapter is an edited version of Gelsa Knijnik's article, 'Ethnomathematics and Political Struggles' in *ZDM*, 98/5, pp186-92, reproduced by kind permission of ZDM.

NOTES

1   Camps are places where the MST families stay, after squatting on a previously selected unproductive large estate. Land squats are usually violently repressed by the police forces, sometimes resulting in deaths. Squats have constituted one of the strategies used by MST to pressure the State into carrying out land reform. The stay in the camps is used to prepare for the next stage of the struggle: settlement. In this new stage, female and male peasants receive the official, definitive possession of the land from the State.

2   In referring to ethnomathematics, in this initial approach to the topic, I explain it through what is today already considered their classic 'conceptualization': "(...) 'ethno' refers to identifiable cultural groups, as for instance national-tribal societies, unions and professional groups, children in a certain age group, etc. And includes cultural memory, codes, symbols, myths and specific ways of reasoning and inferring. Just as mathematics is also seen in a broader manner which includes counting, measuring, reckoning, classifying, ordering, inferring and modelling" (D'Ambrosio, 1990:17-18). It should be stressed that

the use of the classic term 'conceptualization' does not mean to constitute an element which will fix the meaning of ethnomathematics. If I did so I would be opposing a non-essentialist concept of knowledge which I accept, in which there is no sense in asking about 'what is, once and for all, ethnomathematics', and it is also not appropriate to ask about the 'essence' of mathematics.

3 Following authors such as Grignon and Passeron (1992) I have stressed that the articulation between relativist and legitimist perspectives of culture is not a simple operation. However, not doing so is also problematic.

4 Here I would like to emphasize a key argument presented by Arthur Powell and Hartmut Koehler, when they read the draft version of this paper. They both argued the importance of stressing that 'old' ways of producing, mainly centred in manual work, are also technologies. This sort of approach puts clearly our understanding that traditional communities did and still do produce technologies and, at the same time, reinforce the importance of avoiding the glorification of 'new' technologies, examining critically their ecological, economic and social impact.

5 The documents published by the education sector of MST, in particular the *Cadernos de Educação*, present a detailed description of the above mentioned proposal. An analysis of the proposal is found in Knijnik 1996, 1997b.

6 The expression *colônia* is used with different meaning in the Brazilian rural areas. In this situation the settler was using it to signify 2.5 hectares.

7 Seu Hélio was saying that one *quadra* is the equivalent of the area of a square of 60 *braça* on each side, i.e. a square of 3600 'square *braça'*. The use of measures such as *braças* in the Brazilian rural environment has been examined by authors like Guida Abreu (1989) and Helena Oliveira (1997). The latter study also analyzes the introduction of the French metric system in Brazil from the historical point of view, and has been used in pedagogical work in the settlement of Itapuí.

8 Stuart Hall (Morley & Chen,1996:393) argues that he uses "translation" in quotation marks to emphasize that it is "a continuous process of re-articulation and re-contextualization, without any notion of primary origin".

REFERENCES

Abreu, G. M. & Carraher, D. W. (1989) 'The mathematics of Brazilian sugar cane farmers' in *Mathematics, Education and Society*. (Document Series; 35) Paris: UNESCO, 60-70

D'Ambrosio, U. (1990) *Etnomatemática*. São Paulo: Atica

D'Ambrosio, U. (1997) *Educação Matemática: da teoria à prática*. São Paulo: Papirus

Grignon, C.& Passeron, J.C. (1992) *Lo culto y lo popular*. Madrid: La Piqueta

Grossberg, L. (1996) 'History, politics and postmodernism: Stuart Hall and cultural studies'. In D. Morley, K-H. Chen & S. Hall (Eds), *Critical Dialogues in Cultural Studies*.London: Routledge, 151-73

Hall, S. (1997) *A questão da Identidade Cultural*. Texto traduzido por Tomaz Tadeu da Silva e Guacira Louro. Texto digitado

IBGE, the Brazilian Institute of Geography and Statistics (1996)

Knijnik, G. (1996) *Exclusão e Resistência Educação Matemática e Legitimidade Cultural*. Porto Alegre, Brazil: Artes Médicas

Knijnik, G. (1997a) 'Popular knowledge and academic knowledge in the Brazilian peasants' struggle for land'. *Educational Action Research Journal*, 5, (3)

Knijnik, G. (1997b) 'A contribuição do MST pare a Educação Popular o novo na luta pela terra' in João Pedro Stedile, *O MST e a luta pela Reforma Agrária*. Petrópolis: Vozes

Knijnik, G. (1997c) 'Culture, Mathematics and the Landless of Southern Brazil'. In A. Powell & M. Frankenstein (Eds), *Ethnomathematics: Challenging Eurocentrism in Mathematics Education*. New York: SUNY Press

Knijnik, G. (1998a) 'Ethnomathematics and Political Struggles'. *Zentralblätt für Didaktik der Mathematik*, 98/5, 186-92

Knijnik, G. (1998b) 'Ethnomathematics and the Brazilian Landless People's Movement's Pedagogical Principles'. Paper presented at the First International Congress on Ethnomathematics, University of Granada, Granada, Spain, September 2-5, 1998

Lave, J. (1988) *Cognition in Practice: mind, mathematics and culture in everyday life*. New York: Cambridge University Press

Lucas de Oliveira, H. (1997) *Educação Rural e Etnomatemática*. Monografia do Curso do Especialização. UFRGS. Texto Digitado

McCarthy, C. & Cricholow, W. (Eds) (1993) *Race, Identity and Representation in Education*. New York: Routledge

Morley, D. & Chen, K. (1996) *Stuart Hall: Critical dialogues in cultural studies*. London: Routledge

MST (1996) *Cadernos de Educação do Movimento Sem-Terra*, n°8

Projeto LUMIAR (1997) *Instituto Nacional da Colonização e Reforma Agrária*. Texto Digitado

Skovsmose, O. & Vithal, R. (1997) *The End of Innocence: a critique of 'ethnomathematics'*. Copenhagen: The Royal Danish School of Educational Studies, Department of Mathematics, Physics, Chemistry and Informatics. Texto Digitado

Souto Major, A. (1978) *Quebra-quilos: lutas sociais no outono do império*. São Paulo: Nacional

Taylor, N. (1993) 'Desire, repression and ethnomathematics'. In Cyril Julie & Desi Angelis (Eds) *Political Dimensions of Mathematics Education 2: curriculum reconstruction for society in transition*. Johannesburg: Maskew Miller Longman, 130-7

Walkerdine, V. (1988) *The Mastery of Reason*. London: Routledge

Walkerdine, V. (1990) 'Subjectivity, discourse and practice in mathematics education'. In R. Noss, A. Brown, P. Drake *et al.* (Eds) *Political Dimensions of Mathematics Education: action & critique*, Proceedings of the First International Conference. London: Department of Mathematics, Statistics and Computing, Institute of Education. University of London.

Chapter 8

Statistical Literacy: Conceptual and Instructional issues

Iddo Gal
University of Haifa, Israel

FRAMING THE PROBLEM

One key declared goal of education programs at all levels is preparing learners to become more informed citizens and workers who can effectively function in an information-laden society. Towards that end, instruction in literacy and mathematics is usually provided, in part because adults will need to interact daily with quantitative situations, including many where quantitative information is embedded in text. This paper focuses on one critical but often neglected aspect of mathematics (numeracy) education, that of developing statistical literacy.

The term "statistical literacy" does not have an agreed-upon meaning. In public discourse, when "literacy" is combined with any term referring to a specific knowledge domain (e.g. "computer literacy") it conjures up an image of the *minimal subset* of "basic skills" expected *of all* learners or citizens, as opposed to a more advanced set of skills and knowledge that only some people may achieve. In this sense, statistical literacy may be understood by some to denote a minimal knowledge of basic statistical concepts, tools, and procedures, possibly including some interpretive skills.

In this chapter "statistical literacy" describes people's ability to interpret and critically evaluate statistical information and data-based arguments appearing in diverse media channels (e.g. newspaper articles, TV and radio news and programs, publications of political groups, advertisements) and their ability to discuss their opinions regarding such statistical information. This conception is related to a "minimal skills" conception, yet emphasizes sense-making and communicative capacities, more than formal statistical

135

D. Coben et al. (eds.), Perspectives on Adults Learning Mathematics, 135–150.
© 2000 *Kluwer Academic Publishers. Printed in the Netherlands.*

knowledge, assuming that most adults are *consumers* rather than producers of statistical information.

Statistical literacy is needed if adults are to be fully aware of trends and phenomena of social and personal importance, such as crime, population growth, spread of diseases, industrial production, educational achievement, employment, and so forth, or to enable informed participation in public debate or action regarding national or community issues (Wallman, 1993). Similar needs arise in many workplaces, given increasing demands for quality and employee self-management (Carnevale, Gainer & Meltzer, 1990; Packer, 1997).

Despite the importance of statistical literacy and its role in adults' general numeracy (Gal, 1997), almost no in-depth discussions regarding statistical literacy and the educational processes needed to develop it have been published. This chapter aims to contribute to a needed dialogue among practitioners, educational planners, and researchers in order to promote statistical literacy. The chapter is organized in three parts. First, key contexts where statistical literacy is needed and can be developed are described. Next, key components of statistical literacy are outlined. Finally, some instructional dilemmas and implications for teaching and research are discussed.

TYPES OF INTERPRETIVE CONTEXTS

A discussion of statistical literacy should first consider the contexts in which such "literacy" may both develop and be called for. We start by discussing the classroom or teaching context, since students should learn and know something about statistical and probabilistic concepts and procedures as a prerequisite for making sense of statistical messages.

Introducing statistical ideas

Various sources exist that discuss goals and approaches to instruction in introductory statistics at different levels of instruction (e.g. Friel, Russell & Mokros, 1990; Moore, 1992; Gal & Garfield, 1997; Lajoie, 1998). Such sources usually make quite similar recommendations, though the range of topics to be covered and the sequencing of topics and activities may vary depending on student, teacher, and context factors. An approach often suggested for almost any level of instruction is that teachers spend some time on basic concepts and procedures, and also take students on at least one complete cycle of a statistical investigation, where students engage all these phases:

- Formulate a question or hypothesis of interest to the students
- Plan the study (e.g. overall approach, sampling, how to measure target variables)
- Collect data and organize it
- Display, explore, and analyze data
- Interpret findings (in light of the question)
- Discuss conclusions and implications.

The expectation is that by interweaving focused instruction with actual experiences in all phases of a statistical inquiry, students will gradually understand key goals, decisions, and dilemmas associated with designing a data-based study, become familiar with issues involved in making sense of data, and realize that statistical findings can be used to answer many questions and to support or reject hypotheses, depending on the quality and credibility of available information.

To be sure, the chosen learning process must also develop learners' awareness of the "big ideas" that underlie all statistical thinking, such as: there is variation in the world and it has to be estimated in various ways by statistical methods; there is often a need to study samples instead of populations and to infer from samples to populations; errors are likely in measurement and inference, and there is a need to estimate errors; there is a need to reduce large amounts of raw data by noting trends and main features (see Moore, 1990; Gal & Garfield, 1997).

Interpretive contexts

The specific nature of interpretive skills will depend on the context(s) in which they are needed. Gal (1998) distinguishes two such contexts:

Reporting contexts emerge when learners are "data producers" and take part in all phases of a data-based study as described above. They have to interpret their own data/results in order to prepare a report, and discuss with others their findings, conclusions, implications, etc.

Listening (reading) contexts emerge when learners are "data consumers" and are encountered either (a) in the classroom, where learners have to listen to (or read) a report from other learners, or (b) in or outside the classroom, where people have to make sense of and possibly react to messages that contain statistical elements.

Listening contexts, especially those outside the classroom, are our main concern here when we speak about statistical literacy. In such contexts, people do not engage in generating any data or in making any computations. Their familiarity with the data-generation process (e.g. study design, sampling plan, questionnaires, etc), or with the procedures used to analyze the data, depend on the details and clarity of the information given by the message producer. Yet, they do have to comprehend the meaning of messages they are presented with, and be both interested and able to critically examine the reasonableness of such messages or claims, or to reflect about different implications of findings being reported.

To illustrate some of the many ways in which statistical concepts and findings and statistics-related issues appear in the media, consider the following excerpts. These are taken from newspapers, which provide a prime example for a listening/reading context where statistical content is embedded in text.

...The study found that women of average weight in the U.S. had a 50 per cent higher chance of heart attack than did women weighing 15 per cent below average. (Hobart Mercury, Australia, February 10, 1995, cited in Watson, 1997: 109).

Judges count out Census sampling:...at issue is far more than the accuracy of sampling in the Census held every 10 years: Billions of dollars in federal funds are allocated on the basis of how many people live in each state and city, and shifts in population can lead to the redrawing of House districts. A boost in the count of minorities would normally help Democrats. (Philadelphia Inquirer, August 25, 1998)

Poll backs limits on drinking by teens: The survey of more than 7000 adults... which has a margin of error of 2 percentage points, found that... More than half favoured restrictions on alcohol advertising... More than 60% would ban TV ads for beer and wine. (USA Today, October 5, 1998)

The human race held this year many more sexual intercourses than last year; the world average was 112 per person this year, compared to 109 last year. This, according to a comprehensive survey initiated and funded, for the second year, by Durex, a manufacturer of prophylactics. The survey was held in 14 countries that according to experts represent all the world citizens... (Yediot Aharonot, Israel, October 28, 1997).

The demands in listening contexts may differ from those in reporting contexts with regard to several related facets. (The reader is advised to apply points made below to the excerpts above).

1.   Literacy and background knowledge demands of the messages involved: In the classroom, adult students will most likely use language that is quite simple, due to their still developing linguistic and statistical skills. In the real world, listeners will have to make sense of messages of different degrees of complexity, created by journalists, officials, or others with diverse (and possibly advanced) linguistic and numeracy skills. Space limitations may make messages terse, choppy, or lacking in essential information.

2. ***Range of statistical topics involved:*** Messages in the media or other real-world contexts will cover a much broader range of statistical or probabilistic concepts, findings, and problems, compared to what learners usually bring up on their own in the classroom. For example, the design of controlled experiments, sampling techniques, correlations, trends over time, or risk assessment, are only some of the subjects that beginning learners of statistics are not likely to choose as a classroom project.

3. ***Degree of familiarity with sources for variation and measurement error:*** In listening contexts people are less aware of flaws in doing research or problems with collecting credible data when the given study is about an unfamiliar topic.

4. ***Degree of need for critical evaluation of the source of a message:*** When an adult has to think critically about the validity of a message presented by a source such as a journalist, a politician, or an advertiser, there may be a greater need to suspect the message producer is trying to advance his or her agenda, than is the case in classroom reporting.

Despite these differences, in both reporting and listening context the actors (learners) will be involved in the interpretation, creation, communication, or defence of *opinions* (for example, about the implications of a graph, the adequacy of a certain sample, or the validity of an argument). The development of students' ability to generate sensible and justifiable opinions should thus become a target area for instruction (Gal, 1998).

BUILDING BLOCKS OF INTERPRETIVE PROCESSES

What knowledge bases and other enabling processes should be in place so that people can come up with reasonable and, if needed, critical interpretations of messages encountered in statistical tasks? It is argued here that adults' ability to effectively manage interpretive statistical tasks involves both a *cognitive component* (comprised of three elements: statistical knowledge bases, literacy skills, and a list of critical questions) as well as a *dispositional component*. (Gal (1997) introduces the idea of management of quantitative situations).These four building blocks are described below separately, but are interdependent in operation and development.

Statistical knowledge bases

A prerequisite for comprehension and interpretation of statistical messages is that students possess knowledge of basic statistical and probabilistic concepts and procedures. Obviously, what constitutes "basic" will depend on the students' level and context of learning. It is important to note that almost all authors who are concerned about the ability of adults or of school graduates to function in a statistics-rich society do *not* discuss what knowledge is needed to be statistically literate *per se*, but usually argue that all school (or college) graduates should master a wide range of statistical topics, assuming this will ensure learners' ability to engage both in interpretive as well as in other statistical tasks as adults.

A recent example can be found in a comprehensive chapter by Scheaffer, Watkins and Landwehr (1998), titled, "What every high-school graduate should know about statistics." Based on their extensive prior work in the area of teaching statistics, and on reviewing various curriculum frameworks, these authors describe numerous areas as essential to include in a study of statistical topics towards a high-school diploma:

- Number sense
- Understanding variables
- Interpreting tables and graphs
- Aspects of planning a survey or experiment, including what constitutes a good sample, methods of data collection and questionnaire design, etc.
- Data analysis processes, such as detecting patterns in univariate or two-way frequency data, summarizing key features with summary statistics, etc.
- Relationships between probability and statistics (e.g. in determining characteristics of random samples, background for significance testing)
- Inferential reasoning (including confidence intervals, testing hypotheses, etc.).

Clearly, few if any adult education programs cover such an agenda, due to time constraints but also given teachers' lack of relevant knowledge and training. Watson (1997) is one of the very few sources that refer, albeit briefly, to the basic knowledge and skills needed specifically for statistical literacy. She suggests that these include percentage, median, mean, specific probabilities, odds, graphing, measures of spread, and exploratory data analysis.

It is proposed here that six different but related mathematical and statistical knowledge bases are needed for statistical literacy. These were identified on the basis of reviewing (a) writing by mathematics and statistics educators (examples are Moore, 1990; and chapters in Steen, 1997; Gal & Garfield, 1997; Lajoie, 1998), and (b) sources discussing mathematics and statistics in the news (such as, Huff, 1954; Hooke, 1983; Crossen, 1994; Paulus, 1995; Kolata, 1998). Given space limitations, these knowledge bases are described in broad strokes only; they are presented to suggest what kinds of "things" adults need to know and develop in a lifelong perspective, rather than determine what students are supposed to formally study at any specific educational stage. It is recognized that adult learners may bring with them diverse prior knowledge acquired both formally and informally, and that people engage in multiple learning episodes throughout their lives. Also, these knowledge bases are described in absolute terms but have to be interpreted in light of people's specific life contexts, keeping in mind that people's numeracy (Gal, 1997) is not a fixed entity but a relative and dynamic set of skills and interrelated processes.

*1. **Possess mathematical foundations**:* Adults should possess not only number sense (pertaining both to numbers and probabilities), but also knowledge of proportionality concepts, especially of percent, which is a key concept used when reporting statistical results in the media. They need to be familiar with principles of reading graphs and tables and ability to integrate information from their different parts. Advanced arithmetical knowledge and multi-step problem-solving are needed mainly for learning data-analysis techniques, but are somewhat less important for functioning in listening contexts *per se*. That said, broader mathematical knowledge is essential overall, since statistical arguments may appear together with other mathematical issues that are not statistical in nature (Paulus, 1995).

*2. **Know why data is needed and where it comes from**:* Understand key "big ideas" behind statistical investigations in general, and have some technical knowledge of approaches to the design of different studies (survey, experiment, Census, exploratory), and the logic behind these, including some sampling and measurement methods and dilemmas. Understand the influence of sampling processes and sample size or composition on representativeness and ability to generalize or infer to a population.

*3. **Know how data are processed and analyzed**:* Know that the same data can be analyzed or displayed in multiple ways (e.g. by using different measures of central tendency, different graphs, etc.), and that different methods may lead to similar results but may also yield a different and at times conflicting view of the phenomena under investigation. Be aware that errors are unavoidable but that they can be controlled at various stages of a research and be estimated statistically.

*4. **Know how statistical conclusions are reached**:* Be aware of the need to base claims or conclusions on credible empirical evidence. Know that observed differences, associations, or trends may exist but may not necessarily be large or stable enough to be meaningful or important. Realize that results of studies may fluctuate over episodes of data collection, but that such issues should diminish when studies are well-designed. Know that there are ways to determine the significance of a difference between groups, or of an association between variables, for example, by comparing summary statistics.

*5. **Understand basic notions of probability and risk**:* Understand basic notions of probability and chance, and be familiar with the many ways in which they may be reported, such as percents, odds, or verbal estimates (see Wallsten, Fillenbaum & Cox, 1986). Understand that statements of chance may come from diverse sources, both formal and subjective, with different degrees of credibility. Realize that judgements of chance may fluctuate when additional data is available.

*6. **Know about typical flaws in executing studies, analyzing data, or interpreting results:*** Be familiar with key "things that can go wrong" during the lifecycle of a study. Be aware of typical errors that researchers, public officials, and others make when reaching conclusions or conveying findings to the public, such as confusing correlation with causality, making small differences loom large, ignoring significance of observed differences, and so on.

This list, offered here in outline form, can be modified or expanded, depending on the level of the student and on the desired sophistication of statistical literacy. For practical reasons, this list is restricted here to domains that can reasonably be addressed (and in turn assessed) as part of ongoing educational processes. That said, we must keep in mind that numerous other knowledge elements that contribute to statistical literacy can be described but are beyond the scope of this paper. Some involve more literacy-related issues, such as having a sense for what good journalistic writing looks like (e.g. objective writing, presentation of two-sided arguments; provision of background information to orient readers to the context of a story, etc). Others involve broader cognitive and metacognitive capacities that can support statistically literate behaviour, such as having a propensity for logical reasoning, curiosity, and open-minded thinking.

Literacy skills

The development of statistical literacy requires that people can comprehend text and the meaning and implications of the statistical information in it, in the context of the topic to which the reported statistical information pertains (Watson, 1997). The statistical portion of a message may sometimes not be large; comprehension of surrounding or knowledge of background information will be needed to enable a reader or listener to place the statistical part in a wider context. In addition, learners should also be able to present, orally or in writing, clear and well-articulated opinions, that is, ones that contain enough information about the reasoning or evidence on which they are based so as to enable another listener to judge their reasonableness. Thus, statistical literacy and general literacy are intertwined.

Curriculum frameworks in mathematics now emphasize the need to develop all learners' communication skills (e.g. NCTM, 1989; Curry, Schmidt & Waldron, 1996). Such calls are also being echoed in statistics education circles (e.g. Samsa, & Oddone, 1994). However, as several authors have pointed out (e.g. Laborde, 1990), learning mathematical topics requires various types and degrees of interaction with learners' literacy skills. Applied to learning statistics, such interaction may involve, for instance:

- Learning new words or word clusters (e.g. median, standard deviation, statistically significant, margin of error) that have only a mathematical usage and meaning or where the cluster has a meaning different from those of its components.

- Realizing that meanings of mathematical, statistical, or probabilistic terms used in a classroom context (e.g. random, table, association, average, sample, representative, error) may be different or more precise than those used in everyday speech.

- Being aware that some quantitative information might be conveyed by terms or embedded in displays even if no numbers or formal statistical terms are used, for example, information about degrees of uncertainty, trends or changes over time, and more.

- Realizing the need to apply a range of reading comprehension strategies to extract meaning from diverse texts which touch on statistical or probabilistic issues, from tersely-written mathematics or statistics textbooks, to journalistic texts, and so on.

Such and related demands may affect learning, comprehension, and resulting real-world performance, not only of adults who are bilingual or otherwise have a weak mastery of English (Cocking & Mestre, 1988), but also of people who have a relatively good command of the language. The results pertaining to Document Literacy, one of three facets of literacy assessed by the recent International Adult Literacy Survey (IALS), are interesting in this regard (Organisation for Economic Co-operation and Development & Human Resources Development Canada, 1997). The IALS employed functional, realistic tasks to assess literacy in large samples of adults in several industrialized countries, such as the U.S., U.K., Canada, Sweden, Germany and others. Literacy was viewed as the ability to understand and employ printed and written information in daily activities, in order to function in society, to achieve one's goals, and to develop one's knowledge and potential. Document Literacy was defined as the knowledge and skills required to locate and use information contained in various formats, including job applications, payroll forms, transportation schedules, maps, tables, and graphics.

Statistical literacy as described in this paper is related to Document Literacy (Kirsch & Mosenthal, 1990).The IALS Document Literacy scale included numerous statistics-related tasks, for instance making sense of graphs such as those that routinely appear in newspapers, interpreting statements with percents, or integrating information across graphs and tables. Such tasks require that adults not only locate specific information in given texts or displays, but cycle through various parts of diverse texts or displays, make inferences, or apply other reading comprehension strategies, quite often in the presence of irrelevant or distracting information. IALS results indicated that, roughly speaking, between one-third and two-thirds of all adults in most of the countries studied had difficulty with many Document Literacy tasks. While details of the IALS results are too complex to be described here, they do serve to demonstrate the many interdependencies between literacy and statistical knowledge and highlight the complexity of the notion of statistical literacy.

Critical questions

We would like adults not only to be able to comprehend graphical displays or statements and texts with embedded statistical terms or data-based claims (i.e. simply understand what is being said or shown), but also have "in their head" a list of critical questions which relate to things to worry about regarding that which is being communicated or displayed to them. Such a critical list should be a direct outgrowth of adults' possession of the statistical knowledge bases outlined above, at least in a rudimentary form.

When faced with an interpretive statistical task, we imagine people running through this mental list and asking for each item, "Is this question relevant for the situation/ message/task I face right now?" Examples for possible questions include (but are not limited to):

1. Where did the data (on which this statement is based) come from? What kind of study was it? Is this kind of study reasonable in this context?
2. Was a sample used? How was it sampled? Is the sample large enough? Did the sample include people/things which are representative of the population? Overall, could this sample reasonably lead to valid inferences about the target population?
3. How reliable or accurate were the measures used to generate the reported data?
4. What is the shape of the underlying distribution of raw data (on which this summary statistic is based)? Does it matter how it is shaped?
5. Are the reported statistics appropriate for this kind of data, for example, was an average used to summarize ordinal data; is a mode a reasonable summary? Could outliers cause a summary statistic to misrepresent the true picture?
6. Is a given graph drawn appropriately, or does it distort trends in the data?
7. How was this probabilistic statement calculated, and are there enough credible data to justify such an estimate of likelihood?
8. Overall, are the claims made here sensible? Are they supported by the data? (e.g. confusing correlation with causation)
9. Should additional information or procedures be made available to enable me to evaluate the sensibility of these arguments? Is something missing?
10. Are there alternative interpretations for the meaning of the findings, different explanations for what caused them, or additional or different implications?

Answers people generate to such and related questions can support the process of evaluating statistical messages and lead to the creation of more informed opinions. This list can of course be modified and expanded, depending on the level and functional needs of the learners and on the context and goals of instruction. For example, it can expand beyond basic statistical issues to cover statements of probability and risk, statistical significance, or more advanced or job-specific statistical topics, such as those related to statistical process control or quality management processes.

Dispositions and beliefs

It is not enough that students have access to relevant knowledge bases or are aware of critical questions they *could* apply to a message at hand. To actually act in a statistically literate way, certain dispositions and beliefs need to be in place. First, and most importantly, learners should develop a propensity to spontaneously invoke, *without* external cues, the list of worry questions, and invest the mental effort needed to ask penetrating questions and try to answer them. Otherwise, they might learn to accept without questioning objectionable arguments, and may develop an incorrect world view.

Further, learners should uphold the belief that there may be alternative interpretations or implications to any finding which is based on statistical processes (e.g. a sample may be non-representative, an intervening variable affected the results of the study). They should feel comfortable with the role of being a critical evaluator of statistical claims, and accept that it is legitimate to have doubts and concerns about any aspect of the study or the interpretation of its results, and to raise questions about statistical information being communicated to them, even if they have not learned much formal statistics.

While we want students to develop a critical stance, we also want them to develop an appreciation for the power of statistical processes, and accept that the use of systematic data-gathering procedures, be they surveys, controlled experiments, or exploratory studies, often leads to conclusions that are better than those obtained by relying on anecdotal data or subjective experiences.

DISCUSSION AND IMPLICATIONS

Statistical literacy is part of both people's numeracy and literacy (Gal, 1999). A recent white paper of the European Commission argued that in a society in which the individual will have to understand complex situations and vast quantities of varied information, "there is a risk of a rift appearing between those who are able to interpret, those who can only use, and those who can do neither" (European Commission, 1996:8). Yet, even though statistical literacy is an important area and included in the rhetoric of public officials and educators at all levels, especially those involved in numeracy education, it is hardly represented in existing textbooks or training materials for adult educators, and gets little attention in standard assessments.

The question is then - how should students' interpretive skills and statistical literacy be developed? Many teachers most likely will argue that learning to "do" statistics promotes achievement of statistical literacy. Many adult educators, however, visit only briefly the topic of statistics. They may teach their students, for instance, about bar graphs, how to calculate an average, or what a median means. This is important as a first step towards statistical literacy, but unfortunately, such topics are all too often taught in an isolated manner, without explicit connection to the way the underlying concepts appear in adults' everyday lives. Fragmented teaching is not likely to contribute much to students' understanding of statistical concepts (Shaughnessy, 1992), or to their ability to make sense of statistical messages.

Students' statistical and mathematical knowledge bases, as described above, are a necessary component of statistical literacy, yet some of them are not at the heart of existing curricula in statistics. It is argued here that teachers must therefore also work *directly* towards statistical literacy, and emphasize broader aspects of research design and origins of data, interpretation issues, critical questions, and supporting dispositions and reasoning processes as described earlier. The development of statistical literacy requires work on broader interpretive questions that put into action concepts as well as critical perspectives learned before, in the context of authentic tasks. Texts of relevance to learners' lives can be found in local newspapers or TV broadcasts, leaflets distributed by political candidates, advertisements, health education brochures from medical organizations, and so on. Many resources for statistics education can be used to obtain examples for media-related classroom projects and ideas for class discussions, from the seminal Quantitative Literacy series (e.g. Landwehr, Swift & Watkins, 1987), to the newspaper excerpts and accompanying discussion questions distributed regularly on the internet by the Chance Course (at: www.dartmouth.edu/~chance).

To support the development of adult learners' statistical vocabulary and communication skills, including those needed for modern workplaces, better integration of numeracy-related and literacy activities is required. Many suggestions made towards developing communication aspects in mathematical classes can be adapted, such as having students keep journals of their work, prepare oral or written reports from statistical projects, make short presentations, or design their own math stories (Hicks & Wadlington, 1999).

Motivational barriers are likely to be an issue, as statistical work often ends with findings whose interpretation, meaning and quality are a matter of opinion. In contrast, much of school-type mathematics is often viewed by many adult learners, and sometimes by their teachers, as involving procedural learning and solutions that can be categorized as right or wrong. Students as well as teachers should realize that the "rules of the game" are different when it comes to thinking about statistical issues, and that they should take an active role in forming opinions and in explaining the reasoning behind them (Gal, 1998).

Extension of numeracy education to include an emphasis on statistics in general and on development of statistical literacy in particular may be also hampered by teachers' lack of knowledge, or concern about need to devote more time to topics that appear more central. However, work on statistical topics offers unique opportunities to enhance quantitative reasoning and important communication skills that mathematics educators have been struggling for years to advance, but with limited success. At a time when statistical knowledge, in both formal and informal forms, is increasingly being considered essential for effective citizenship and as a part of required workforce preparation, adult education systems should open a dialogue and seek strategies that can support the development of statistical literacy and thus help fulfil the promise of informed citizenship for all.

ACKNOWLEDGEMENTS

Some ideas in this paper are an outgrowth of brief discussions that started at a working conference on Assessment Issues in Statistics Education, co-chaired by Iddo Gal and Joan Garfield and held at the University of Pennsylvania in 1994 with partial support from the National Science Foundation and from the National Center on Adult Literacy at the University of Pennsylvania, Philadelphia. I would like to especially thank the colleagues in the working group I facilitated, on Assessment of Interpretive Skills: Andrew Ahlgren, Gail Burrill, James Landwehr, Wendy Rich, and Andy Begg.

REFERENCES

Carnevale, A. P., Gainer, L. J., & Meltzer, A. S. (1990). *Workplace basics: The essential skills employers want*. San Francisco: Jossey-Bass.

Cocking, R. R. & Mestre, J. P. (Eds.) (1988). *Linguistic and cultural influences on learning mathematics*. Hillsdale, NJ: Lawrence Erlbaum.

Crossen, C. (1994). *Tainted truth: The manipulation of fact in America*. New York: Simon & Schuster.

Curry, D., Schmitt, M. J. & Waldron, W. (1996). *A Framework for adult numeracy standards: The mathematical skills and abilities adults need to be equipped for the future*. Final report from the System Reform Planning Project of the Adult Numeracy Network. Washington, DC: National Institute for Literacy.

European Commission (1996). *White paper on education and training: Teaching and learning—towards the learning society*. Luxembourg: Office for official publications of the European Commission.

Friel, S. N., Russell, S. & Mokros, J. R. (1990). *Used Numbers: Statistics: middles, means, and in-betweens*. Palo Alto, CA: Dale Seymour Publications.

Gal, I. (1997). 'Numeracy: reflections on imperatives of a forgotten goal'. In L. A. Steen (Ed.), *Quantitative literacy*. Washington, DC: College Board, 36-44.

Gal, I. (1998). 'Assessing statistical knowledge as it relates to students' interpretation of data'. In S. Lajoie (Ed.), *Reflections on statistics: Learning, teaching, and assessment in grades K-12*. Mahwah, NJ: Lawrence Erlbaum, 275-295

Gal, I. (1999). 'The numeracy challenge'. In I. Gal (Ed.), *Developing adult numeracy: From theory to practice.* Cresskill, NJ: Hampton Press, 1-25.

Gal, I. & Garfield, J. (1997). 'Curricular goals and assessment challenges in statistics education'. In I. Gal & J. B. Garfield (Eds.), *The assessment challenge in statistics education.* Amsterdam, The Netherlands: IOS Press, 1-13.

Gal, I. & Garfield, J. (Eds.) (1997). *The assessment challenge in statistics education.* Amsterdam, the Netherlands: IOS Press, 1-13.

Hicks, K. & Wadlington, B. (1999). 'Making life balance: Writing original math projects with adults'. In I. Gal (Ed.), *Developing adult numeracy: From theory to practice.* Cresskill, NJ: Hampton Press, 145-160.

Hooke, R. (1983). *How to tell the liars from the statisticians.* New York: Marcel Dekker.

Huff, D. (1954). *How to lie with statistics.* New York: W. W. Norton.

Kirsch, I. & Mosenthal, P. (1990). 'Understanding the news'. In L. A. Steen (Ed.), *Reading research quarterly, 22*(2), 83-99.

Kolata, G. (1997). 'Understanding the news'. In L. A. Steen (Ed.), *Why numbers count: quantitative literacy for tomorrow's America.* New York: The College Board, 23-29.

Laborde, C. (1990). 'Language and mathematics'. In P. Nesher & J. Kilpatrick (Eds.), *Mathematics and cognition.* New York: Cambridge University Press, 53-69.

Lajoie, S. P. (Ed.) (1998). *Reflections on statistics: learning, teaching, and assessment in grades K-12.* Mahwah, NJ: Lawrence Erlbaum, 63-88.

Landwehr, J. M., Swift, J. & Watkins, A. E. (1987). *Exploring surveys and information from samples.* (Quantitative literacy series). Palo Alto, CA: Dale Seymour publications.

Moore, D. S. (1990). 'Uncertainty'. In L. A. Steen (Ed.), *On the shoulders of giants: New approaches to numeracy.* Mathematical Sciences Education Board. Washington, DC: National Academy Press, 95-137.

Moore, D. S. (1992). 'Teaching statistics as a respectable subject'. In F. & S. Gordon (Eds.), *Statistics for the twenty-first century.* Washington, DC: The Mathematical Association of America, 14-25.

National Council of Teachers of Mathematics (NCTM) (1989). *Curriculum and evaluation standards for school mathematics.* Reston, VA: Author.

Organisation for Economic Co-operation and Development (OECD) and Human Resources Development Canada (1997). *Literacy for the knowledge society: Further results from the International Adult Literacy Survey.* Paris and Ottawa: OECD and Statistics Canada.

Packer, A. (1997). 'Mathematical Competencies that employers expect'. In L. A. Steen (Ed.), *Why numbers count: quantitative literacy for tomorrow's America.* New York: The College Board. 137-154.

Paulus, J. A. (1996). *A mathematician reads the newspaper.* New York: Anchor books/Doubleday.

Samsa, G. & Oddone, E. Z. (1994). 'Integrating scientific writing into a statistics curriculum: A course of statistically based scientific writing'. *The American Statistician, 48*(2), 117-119.

Scheaffer, R. L., Watkins, A. E. & Landwehr, J. M. (1998). 'What every high-school graduate should know about statistics'. In S. O. Lajoie (Ed.), *Reflections on statistics: learning, teaching and assessment in grades K-12.* Mahwah, New Jersey: Lawrence Erlbaum, 3-31.

Shaughnessy, M. J. (1992). 'Research in probability and statistics: Reflections and directions'. In D. A. Grouws, (Ed.), *Handbook of research on mathematics teaching and learning.* NY: Macmillan, 465-494.

Steen, L. A. (Ed.) (1997). *Why numbers count: quantitative literacy for tomorrow's America.* New York: The College Board, 137-154.

Wallman, K. K. (1993). 'Enhancing statistical literacy: Enriching our society'. *Journal of the American Statistical Association, 88,* 1-8.

Wallsten, T. S., Fillenbaum, S. & Cox, J. A. (1986). 'Base rate effects on the interpretations of probability and frequency expressions'. *Journal of Memory and Language, 25,* 571-587.

Watson, J. (1997). 'Assessing statistical literacy through the use of media surveys'. In I. Gal & J. Garfield, (Eds.), *The assessment challenge in statistics education.* Voorburg, The Netherlands: IOS Press.

Chapter 9

The roles of feelings and logic and their interaction in the solution of everyday problems

Dhamma Colwell
King's College, London, UK

INTRODUCTION

What mathematics do adults use in their everyday lives, how is it done and what are the contexts in which is used? To investigate these questions I set up a focus group of women and asked them to talk about their everyday activities which involved mathematics or numbers. I also observed a firm of gardeners and some upholsterers at work and talked to them about the mathematics they use.

In this paper, I shall be considering data from the focus group. I first briefly describe how the group runs and how I analysed the data. I found a logical structure in the participants' accounts of solving problems and I discuss whether this is actually part of the problem-solving process, or a feature of construction of *post hoc* accounts. I show that the four parameters of culture which Saxe (1991) proposes as being inseparable from cognition are an integral part of each stage of problem-solving in the participants' accounts. Next I demonstrate that affectivity is a fifth parameter in my data. Finally I raise some questions which I intend to explore further with the focus group and in observations of people at work and conversations with them.

The names used in this paper are pseudonyms chosen by the participants in the study.

D. Coben et al. (eds.), Perspectives on Adults Learning Mathematics, 151–164.

DATA COLLECTION AND ANALYSIS

The data for this part of the study were collected from discussions in a focus group of women about the mathematics they use in everyday life. The participants are well-educated people: professional women and mature university students, only one of whom has studied mathematics beyond GCSE level (the examination most children take at age 16 in England and Wales). I have discussed the constitution of the group more fully elsewhere (1998a).

I asked the participants to tell stories about their everyday experiences of using mathematics and numbers. When they ran out of spontaneous stories I gave them a series of questions on individual cards which they could read through and choose any they would like to answer. The questions were about numbers, time and money, measurement and estimation, shape and spatial orientation. They were worded in a way which would invite the participants to consider specific instances when these concepts had been called into play in their everyday lives, and to encourage them to describe the whole context of the event. An example of the questions is, 'When you were coming here today, how did you decide what time to leave home?'

I asked the questions in this way because I am particularly interested in the socio-cultural contexts in which people use mathematics, as in Lave's theory of situated cognition. Rather than understanding knowledge as something individuals possess, she sees that,

> ... a more appropriate unit of analysis is the whole person in action, acting with the settings of that activity. This shifts the boundaries of activity well outside the skull and beyond the hypothetical economic actor, to persons engaged with the world for a variety of "reasons" ... (Lave, 1988:17-18)

I recorded the conversations in the group on audio-tape and transcribed the tapes. I coded the data systematically using Lincoln and Guba's (1985) system for developing grounded theory: I labelled words, phrases and sentences with names that described the content. I then physically cut up the transcript with a scalpel and grouped the pieces of paper in envelopes according to their labels. When a piece of text fitted more than one label, I copied it so that it could be put into all the appropriate envelopes. I then went through each envelope to check whether the pieces of text were in accord with each other and with the label. Finally I made a list of the labels and tried to organise them into a schema (see Appendix).

Examples of the labels are: 'calculation', 'tool, 'affectivity, 'identifying a problem'. In choosing these names for pieces of text, I was influenced by what my interests are in the data: firstly, what mathematics people use in everyday life; secondly, how they do the mathematics; and thirdly, the socio-cultural contexts in which the mathematics is used.

THE LOGICAL STRUCTURE IN THE
ACCOUNTS OF PROBLEM-SOLVING

The participants gave accounts of a wide range of everyday activities such as travelling, cooking, crafts, dancing, shopping, video-recording, remembering telephone and personal identification numbers. The analysis revealed a logical structure to their accounts of the solution of problems in four stages: the identification of a problem; deciding how to set about solving the problem; what actually happened; and a review of how far the problem had been solved. In order to solve one problem, many contributory problems may have had to be solved. Also, at the review stage, if the solution has not worked, it might be necessary to go back to any of the previous stages: to reformulate the problem; to make another decision about what to do; or to try again to carry out the original decision.

I developed the model of problem-solving shown in Figure 1 directly from this analysis of the data. The accounts that the participants in the focus group gave of a wide variety of activities all fit this model of logical problem-solving. Participants did not necessarily have fully developed overall plans for solving complex problems when they began. They may have identified one or more sub-goals which needed to be achieved first, before proceeding to make further decisions.

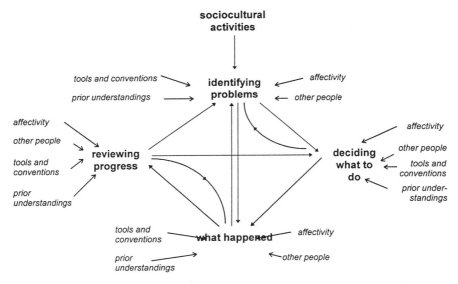

Figure 1. The logical structure in accounts of the solving of everyday problems

Decisions do not have to be made on each occasion. When habitual activities are undertaken, it is more appropriate to use the term 'achievement of goals' than 'solving a problem': there is no problem. But this still fits the model: the goal is identified and actions are performed to achieve the goal. The outcome may only be reviewed if there is a change of circumstance.

I am using the term 'logical' because following this four-stage process requires an understanding of cause and effect, '*if* I do this *then* this will happen', and its corollaries, '*if* I want this to happen *then* I must do this', and 'this has happened *because of* that.' Nunes, Schliemann and Carraher describe an investigation by Cheng and Holyoak who found that participants could solve similar logical problems where the contexts were meaningful for them, but found them much more difficult when the problems were non-contextual (Nunes, Schliemann & Carraher, 1993). However, the real world is far more complex than the psychology laboratory: problems do not arise, and are not solved, in isolation: they are part of the complex web of social relationships and our whole environment. We use our past experiences to predict what will probably happen, but we have to constantly modify our predictions in the light of what actually happens.

I will demonstrate how my model works in detail by an example. Figure 2 shows how the model in Figure 1 applies to part of this example.

Sheda's account of getting up, getting ready, and coming to the group.

Sheda gave an account of how she got herself to the focus group that morning. She identified two sub-goals she needed to achieve first, getting up and feeding her son, and she made some decisions. "Last night I said, 'OK, I have to get up at 8 o'clock' because my son, who is a year old, gets up at 8 o'clock. I allocated an hour for his feed. 'I will finish feeding him at 9 o'clock.'" A second sub-goal was to get herself ready, so she made a plan for this, "'Then maybe an hour will be enough for me to get ready.'" This would give her time to get to the group by 11 o'clock.

But things did not go according to plan. Sheda reviewed the situation, "First of all I had broken sleep, because [the baby] was a bit unsettled last night. So I woke up a couple of times, then I couldn't get up at 8 o'clock. I woke up at half past eight. I went into the living room to look at the clock on the wall. It was half past eight. I said 'Oh' Still I was a bit tired."

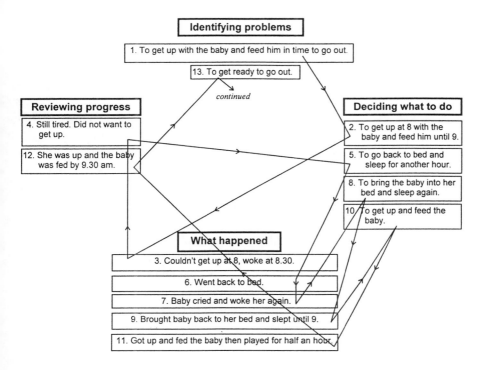

Figure 2. The stages in Sheda's account of solving the problem of getting ready to go out

She had a new goal of getting more sleep, so she made another decision. "I say 'Let me go back to bed and sleep for another half an hour.'" But that did not work out either. "Hussain got up and started crying." Sheda made a fourth decision. "I took him out of his cot and put him beside me in the big bed." She got half way to getting her extra hour's sleep, "Finally I get out of bed at 9 o'clock."

She then continued with her original plan. "Then I start feeding Hussain his milk and his breakfast. I think I finish it at half past nine." Then she did something she had not previously decided to do. "For another half hour I play with him." Then she continued with her original plan of getting herself ready to go out, "I have my breakfast."

A new sub-goal emerged, to leave the baby with her husband. To achieve this she first had to wake him (another sub-goal). "... at 10 o'clock ... he was still in bed and he wanted to continue. He said, 'Oh, I'm tired.'" Sheda made a decision and carried it out. "I took Hussain and both of us walked to his room, and we say 'OK, get up. Hussain, wake up your dad, it's time Mum should leave.'" This plan eventually worked: "He managed to get up at half past ten."

At a quarter to 11, when she tried to carry out her plan of leaving the house, the baby stopped her. "But Hussain cried when he saw me leaving. He wanted to be picked up and he wanted me to walk with him." So she revised her plan, played with Hussain for ten minutes and then left the house. "I left home at 7 or 8 to 11." She was now on her way to the group. She had decided to walk to Archway to catch the bus. At this point she reviewed her progress again, "I thought, 'Oh. I'll be late.'"

Then her plan went wrong again. "The bus didn't come. I waited for about 5 minutes." So she reviewed the situation again, "Then I thought, as it was Sunday maybe it won't come soon, so I said, 'Oh, I shouldn't wait any longer.'" She made another decision, "I walked. Always I was checking behind to see if it was coming so that I could run to it at the next stop. But I didn't see one." At the group she reviewed her decision, "It took me about 35 minutes from home, so good exercise. I was quite right that I didn't wait, because I wouldn't be here. I would wait for bus."

As she was giving her account to the group, she reviewed the whole situation, "That's why I was late, things didn't happen the way I plan it."

Sheda started off with a clearly identified overall goal: to get to the group at 11 o'clock. She recounted piecemeal the decisions she made which identified the main sub-goals she needed to achieve in order to reach this main goal: to get her baby up at 8 o'clock and feed him by 9 o'clock, to get herself ready by 10 o'clock, to get her husband up so that she could leave the baby with him, to walk to Archway and catch a bus to the group venue. She had calculated the time she needed for each sub-task. She reviewed what had actually happened from when she woke up late, and at each stage of the proceedings, and reformulated her goals and how to achieve them as she went along.

Sometimes she does not separate her statement of the decision she has made and the description of how she carried it out, "I walked. Always I was checking behind to see if (the bus) was coming so that I could run to it at the next stop." She is recounting what she did, and the decision to do it is implied. If she had not decided to walk she would have waited at the bus stop until the bus came. She may have made the decision to keep looking behind her either before she started walking or while she was walking.

Some of the sub-goals only emerged during the process of achieving her main goal, for example to get her husband out of bed. Others, though formulated at the outset, were modified during the process, for example getting up at nine instead of eight.

The participants' accounts of their activities all fit this model of identifying problems or goals, of making decisions about what to do, of carrying out those decisions and then reviewing how far the goal has been reached or the problem solved. However, it is the participants' accounts of their past experiences which reveal this logical structure, rather than the experiences themselves. The question arises of whether the logical structure might be part of a reconstruction of a past experience, which happens during the formulation of the experience into the account. In telling a story about what has happened to us, do we unconsciously make it fit a logical framework which is part of our culture, the way we give accounts of ourselves? In the focus group, I only have access to accounts of previous experiences, not the experiences themselves. I am therefore being cautious about assigning the logical structure to the participants' solving of problems, and only saying that it appears in their retrospective accounts.

CULTURAL FACTORS IN SOLVING PROBLEMS

As well as revealing an essentially logical structure, the participants' accounts also accord with Saxe's (1991) four-parameter model of culture and cognition, where he demonstrates that problems emerge out of cultural activities and are solved by people interacting in social relationships, with artifacts and conventions, and by drawing on their prior understandings. He suggests that culture and cognition cannot be separated: these cultural parameters are both constructed by people as a result of their thinking and they are used by people in their problem-solving processes.

These parameters appear at each stage of the process of problem-solving in the participants' accounts. The problems or goals which the participants described emerged from the socio-cultural activities in which they were engaged. The participants interacted in social relationships, used artifacts and conventions, and drew on their prior understandings, during the identification of problems and goals, deciding what to do, carrying out the decision, and reviewing the results. I have used Saxe's parameters in Figure 1, but I have called what he terms 'social interactions' 'other people', and what he terms 'artifacts', 'tools'.

For example, in Sheda's account of getting up and getting ready to go out, her relationship with her baby is central to the whole process: her first consideration is his health and happiness in deciding what she has to do, in carrying out the decision, in reviewing her progress and in modifying her decision and the way she carried it out. She used her previous experience of feeding him and getting herself ready to go out to estimate how long these activities should take, and she used the convention of clock time and the tools of the clock and calculating in hours to work out what time she should get up and to monitor her progress as she went along.

I shall be considering the roles of social interaction, artifacts and conventions and prior understandings in other papers. In this, I shall focus on the role of feelings.

THE ROLE OF FEELINGS IN PROBLEM-SOLVING

There is an additional factor which does not appear in Saxe's model: affectivity. In the participants' accounts I found that they used many emotive words and talked a lot about their feelings. These were factors at every stage of the problem-solving process. The rest of this paper will focus on affectivity in problem-solving and its relationship to the logical process.

The role of feelings seems to fall into three categories: self-identity and choice; relationships; and feelings about mathematics, including the avoidance of calculation and the use of formal tools.

Self identity and choice

Choice is a strong strand of Western culture: people feel they have a right to make choices about things which affect them. For example, the participants in the group had strong feelings about being early or late. Some of them did not like being early, for example, Claire said, "I hate arriving anywhere early. I go for being on time, but I don't like being early." Others took the opposite view, like Eileen who said, "I prefer to be a bit early." Only Jean said she is not consistently early or late, "Sometimes I'm very early, sometimes I'm horribly late. I tend to sort of go with the flow." But she describes being late as horrible, indicating a strong emotion.

These feelings about punctuality affect the way the participants make decisions about time for their activities. For example, Eileen said, "If it will take half an hour, I allow three quarters of an hour. I need to get up at eight, so I'll get up at half past seven."

The participants were aware that their attitudes to punctuality often either made them late or meant that they were wasting time. Eileen said, "I allow too much time: I get to lectures half an hour early. I end up waiting for people for ages. I'll end up faffing round because I've got so much time on my hands, which I could be using better, if I organised myself better and realised I was leaving too much time." Claire said, "I never allow for the fact that I might not be able to find my shoes or my keys." However it seemed as if these patterns of behaviour were ones people did not want to change: they were describing situations which had occurred many times. Jean said, "There's not a lot I intend to do about it. It's something that I accept what I do." It seems as if each person had a view about their own punctuality which was an element of their self-identity.

Relationships

Social relationships are an important factor in problem-solving in everyday life, as Saxe (1991) showed. How people feel about the important relationships in their lives also affects how they resolve problems that emerge as part of their day-to-day relationships, such as managing their time and money with their partner.

Ruth talked about her feelings about the financial side of her relationship with her partner. "He used to make jokes when I was working part-time that he was keeping me, which I didn't like, despite the fact that I've kept him before when he was on the dole." Even though she said, "It's not really serious", she seemed to feel this was an attack on her identity as a woman who can support herself, as well as being unfair.

Until recently Ruth and her partner had not kept accounts together. "We lived together 10 years without structuring who paid what." But buying a flat changed the way they managed their money together,

> ... since we moved into this flat that we bought, I've started putting the big things on a spreadsheet, like the bills. Because he believes he pays a lot more than me. I wanted to prove to him that although he does pay more it's not a vast amount. I pay the gas, he pays the electricity. I pay the phone, he pays the water. Now my little computer has it in black and white: I do pay hundreds and hundreds of pounds every year, despite his beliefs to the contrary.

Ruth's position in the relationship as nearly financially equal is important enough for her to go to the trouble of creating the spreadsheet of their expenditure. She did not do this to help her manage her money, but to demonstrate her position to her partner.

On the other hand, Ruth is adamant that she does not want to be meticulous about everyday spending. She was horrified by the behaviour of some friends of hers,

> ... a couple who have just moved in together, keep a note of everything so that they can balance it out, so one person didn't pay more than the other and all that. I couldn't do that, not for anything in the world. Can't bear to do that sort of thing somehow, it's horrible isn't it? I wouldn't like to keep a record of, we went out for dinner and I paid for that. It's too much really.

Ruth's relationship with her partner and the way they manage their money are deeply intertwined: their management of their money defines their positions relative to each other, and their feelings about their relationship structures the way they manage their money.

Feelings about mathematics: the avoidance of calculation and formal tools

Although the participants in the group did describe using tools such as clocks, money and spreadsheets, there was a lot of evidence of the avoidance of other formal mathematical tools such as timetables and measures, and of exact calculations. The participants employed strategies to solve some of their everyday problems which did not require the use of such tools. Cathy recounted her procedure for catching trains from Harrow,

> There's two trains going into central London. There's the fast train and the slow train and I never know which it is going to be. I know there's a train every ten

minutes or so. I have to allow for the fact that it's going to be the slow train which takes an extra 15 minutes. Quite often I might catch the fast one. I allow an hour to get into the centre of London and quite often I'm there half an hour early. But if I didn't plan that, I could be late.

So Cathy's method of getting to London at a certain time is to calculate what time she needs to leave Harrow if she is travelling by slow train and to arrive at the station at that time.

Then she said, "I should look at the timetable and work out when (the fast train) is, but that's a bit too organised." She is displaying a reluctance to use a mathematical tool, the timetable, and to be 'organised', to behave in the most efficient way. She prefers to arrive at the station with enough time to get on whichever train comes along and still be early enough for her appointments.

But she said she 'should' look at the timetable: she is expressing a moral imperative to behave efficiently, which she is choosing not to obey. I suspect that this may be a response to her perception of me as a mathematical person, representing mathematics teachers in her past, who in turn represent the view of the wider society's institutions: that people *should* behave efficiently. It is one of the rationales for providing universal formal mathematics education: to equip future citizens with skills which are supposed to enable them to function efficiently in a post-industrial society.

But the well-educated adults in my group choose not to read timetables, not to calculate their money exactly, not to measure things exactly and not to calculate exact times, in many of the situations they described. When they did do calculations, they often did not use the standard methods taught in schools. Rhiannon tried to divide the three hour span of an examination into

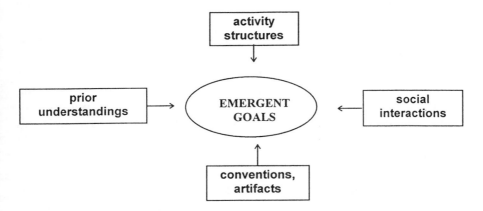

Figure 3. Saxe's four-parameter model

equal time periods for four questions by using an informal method,

> I worked it out using a circle. I drew a circle to represent a clock-face at the top of the page. I kind of imagined 40 minutes for each question first of all. Then I traced from the top, the 12 o'clock point, to 40 minutes, and made a mark for one. [She indicated this with her finger.] Then let's see, another 40 minutes would be 20 past, so I made another mark. Then another 40 minutes would be up to the hour. So that's two hours for three questions. Another hour for the other, so that was wrong. It was this kind of not very exact testing out of how much time.

She did not complete her calculation, 'At this point I abandoned (it). I decided I better start (answering the examination questions). She had worked out enough to know that she could spend 40 minutes on each question and have some time left over. She did not feel it was necessary to complete the calculation.

DISCUSSION

The cultural factors identified by Saxe, social relationships, artifacts and conventions, and prior understandings, are an integral part of every stage of the problem-solving process. Affectivity is an additional important factor at every stage in my data. The focus group seemed to be a particularly fruitful way of collecting such data. My data also demonstrate that people's accounts of the way they solve problems that emerge from their everyday activities have a logical structure: they employ the law of cause and effect. This might appear to be a contradiction: that people solve problems logically but that their feelings are factors which contribute to the logical process. But people are giving value to their feelings in making decisions, both in what they choose to do and how they choose to do it.

The question of whether people put the logical construction on their activities afterwards when they are giving an account, or whether the logical structure is present throughout the problem-solving process, requires further investigation. I am planning to inquire into this in the focus group by asking the participants to consider it themselves. In the other part of my research project, where I am observing people at work and therefore have access to problem-solving in process (Colwell, 1998b), I intend to follow the whole restructuring of a garden and upholstering of a piece of furniture. I will discuss with the workers their perspective on their progress as they proceed. They will still be formulating accounts of what they are doing, but these will be as the problems are being solved, not afterwards, so the accounts should be closer to the workers' thinking process.

Another area which I think would be worth focusing on is the point at which people decide to review their progress during the process of solving a problem, especially when the activity is an unfamiliar one, or when things go wrong. What makes them stop what they are doing and consider whether they are likely to achieve their goal if they continue? I am planning to investigate this by asking both the participants of the group and the workers.

SUMMARY

In this paper I have described how the accounts women gave of events in their lives had a logical structure. I have considered whether this might be a result of the participants making post-hoc reconstructions of these events and I discussed how I could investigate this question further. I have demonstrated that my data concur with Lave's (1988:17-18) theory of situated cognition and with Saxe's (1991:17) model of culture and cognition. But, in addition to Saxe's four parameters, affectivity appears as a very strong strand in the data: what people do and how they do it is affected by their self-identity and consciousness of choice, by their feelings about their relationships with other people, and by their feelings about mathematics, which often causes them to avoid calculation and the use of formal mathematical tools.

APPENDIX

Everyday mathematics group coding list
    identification of goals
        affectivity (preference)
        description of goals
    planning the process of achieving the goal
            conceptualisation of the result
                visualisation
                tools
            obtaining information
                remembering previous experience/knowledge
                    cultural patterns
                    intuitive/subconscious
                from elsewhere
                measurement
                    standard units

                                                            tools
                                            traditional or natural units
                                                            tools
                                        estimation without tools
                                        calculation
                                                    methods
                                        making comparisons
                                        representation
                            affectivity
            execution of task
                process
                learning
                            process of learning
                                        by observation of other people
                                        from instruction
                                        practice
                resources/tools
                affectivity
            reviewing the execution of the task/achievement of goal
                affective issues
                            perception of ability
                            habits
                            relationships
                                        others' reactions

REFERENCES

Colwell. D., (1998a) 'Towards a theory of adults using mathematics: time in everyday life'. In A. Watson, (Ed). *Situated cognition and the learning of mathematics* . Oxford: Centre for Mathematics Education Research, University of Oxford Department of Educational Studies, 45-58.

Colwell. D (1998b) 'An exploration of situated cognition in two professional crafts: upholstery and gardening'. In D. Coben & J. O'Donoghue (Comps), *Adults Learning Maths-4*. Proceedings of ALM-4, the Fourth International Conference of Adults Learning Maths - A Research Forum. London: Goldsmiths College, University of London, in association with Adults Learning Maths - A Research Forum, 199-209.

Lave, J. (1988). *Cognition in practice: mind, mathematics and culture in everyday life*. Cambridge: Cambridge University Press.

Lincoln, Y. S., & Guba, B. G.. (1985), *Naturalistic Inquiry*. London: Sage Publications Inc.

Nunes, T.. Schliemann, A. D.. & Carraher, D. W., (1993), *Street Mathematics and School Mathematics*. Cambridge: Cambridge University Press.

Saxe, G. B., (1991), *Culture and Cognitive Development - studies in mathematical understanding*. Hillsdale, New Jersey: Lawrence Erlbaum Associates.

Section III: Adults, Mathematics and Work

Introduction

Gail E. FitzSimons
Monash University/Swinburne University of Technology, Victoria, Australia

VOCATIONAL EDUCATION AND TRAINING

Vocational education and training has existed for as long as the novice, or newcomer, has sought to appropriate and even surpass the skills of the old-timer, to use Lave and Wenger's (1991) terminology. The concept of apprenticeship has existed in Europe for many centuries. Formalised institutional provision for adults, associated since the last century with mechanics institutes in England and its colonies has, this century, seen the burgeoning of organised vocational education and training. The impetus given to the concept of lifelong learning in the 1970s by reports of bodies such as UNESCO (Faure et al., 1972), was revitalised in the 1990s (e.g., UNESCO, 1996) as nations sought to establish, maintain and enhance economic advantage through the development of a more highly skilled labour force.

The Australian Qualifications Framework, for example, encompasses occupations ranging from operators, through tradespersons and technicians, to paraprofessionals. Other terms for qualifications more familiar to Europeans might be: *craft* (for trade and equivalent); *master-craft* (for post-trade supervisory type); and *technician* (for technicians and paraprofessionals) (Maglen & Hopkins, 1998). There is a blurring of the boundaries at the upper levels where some qualifications are recognised by universities to give advanced standing to people wishing to undertake degree courses. Even the term 'vocational education and training' is contested, as illustrated by one academic who included within its realm his university's

D. Coben et al. (eds.), Perspectives on Adults Learning Mathematics, 165–170.
© 2000 *Kluwer Academic Publishers. Printed in the Netherlands.*

provision of "law, medicine, dentistry, optometry, veterinary science and pharmacy" (Maglen, 1996:9).

Within the education sphere, vocational education and training has generally been accorded a lower status than academic education. In Australia Terri Seddon (1992/1993, 1994) traced the history of the subordination of technical education, one antecedent of the present vocational education and training system - the other being the mechanics institutes and mining schools. Since the 1920s there has been an academic - non-academic dualism, which Seddon termed the *liberal meritocratic educational settlement*, and described as a product of structural and discursive changes within the larger Australian society. This dualism polarised education and training along class, race, and gender lines. Education was linked to academic credentials and preparation for professional employment, the province of universities and private schools; whereas training was linked to apprenticeships and skilled employment, the province of the predominantly white male industrial labour movement and employers. Both education and training were thus privileged as distinct enclaves of educational practice, but at the post-compulsory level the academic institutions were absolutely dominant. Seddon asserted that a utilitarian curriculum has been perpetuated in both sectors, polarising rigour and relevance, abstract and practical knowledge, in order to maximise occupational gatekeeping. However the subordination of technical to academic education and the institutionalisation of failure as the entry requirement to training undermined the settlement. Recent decades have witnessed a training reform agenda explainable, in part, according to Seddon as an attempt by its proponents to regain control of the post-compulsory years from the academics.

MATHEMATICS FOR WORK

The history of mathematics (or numeracy) used in the work environment indicates that 'Applied' Mathematics has generally been regarded as inferior to its more detached academic counterpart nowadays known as 'Pure' Mathematics (e.g. Jahnke, 1994; Kline, 1980). In many cases its worth was and still is disparaged or ignored, even to the point of being invisible to its users (see Coben, this volume). However, as Gibbons et al. (1994) argue, the adequacy of traditional knowledge producing institutions is being called into question with the emergence of a new mode of knowledge production. They identify the traditional kind of knowledge as 'Mode 1,' characterised by disciplinarity and homogeneity, as hierarchical and tending to preservation of form. The second, 'Mode 2,' characterised by transdisciplinarity and heterogeneity, is heterarchical and transient. Whereas the problems of Mode

1 "are set and solved in a context governed by the, largely academic, interests of a specific community" (p.3) those of Mode 2 are set in the context of application. Mode 2 is more socially accountable and reflexive, according to Gibbons et al.. The mathematics used in the workplace is arguably aligned with Mode 2, as it emanates from a broad range of considerations. This has important implications for vocational education and training, which are addressed in their discussion of mathematical modelling by Keitel, Kotzmann, and Skovsmose (1993).

In this section, Mary Harris in her chapter *Women, Mathematics and Work* describes the evolution of mathematics education from an English perspective. Mathematics education has always been controlled by sectional interests, from the Church to the élite and powerful in the civil society, and harnessed to their own perceptions of personal and social good. This hegemonic interest worked to the detriment of women and the lower classes, by excluding or restricting their participation in the full range of mathematics offered to those more privileged. This was achieved partly through restricted access to education and partly through curricula designed to reflect and reproduce social differences.

An example of the dialectic relationship between curriculum and social forces is provided by Fred Inglis (1985). Arguing that social disintegration arising from the industrial revolution impacted on the curriculum for lower classes, he traced the genesis of home economics, included under the 1904 *Regulations for Secondary Schools* which codified time to be spent on instruction. He asserted that housewifery for girls, together with manual work and physical exercises for boys, was a consequence of the nation's realisation of the destruction of social fabric where, within a period of eighty years, "the urban poorest no longer knew how to bake bread or make butter or brew beer, even if they could have found the ingredients" (Inglis, 1985:36).

Harris argues that, throughout history, people with responsibility for running households and rearing children, animals, and plants, must have had to be numerate to survive, even if they were classed as illiterate. She also argues that, although much of women's work throughout the ages has been invisible, the most consistent subject of a girl's education was work with cloth: its production and the manufacture of clothing. However the advent of capitalism, with the gendering of work, transformed tasks that had been developed into art-forms into means of social control while imposing idealisations of femininity. Harris argues that whenever it was recognised that work in clothing and textiles implied a knowledge of mathematics, it was trivialised or ignored. Thus, until the challenges of feminists and others in the 1970s, compulsory schooling engendered low intellectual expectations for girls, accompanied by feelings of low self-esteem and self-confidence, according to Harris - thus reflecting a dual system of education. Harris's chapter concludes with a discussion of some important work which has taken place in recent decades, from the field of anthropological mathematics, on the mathematics that women use outside of school.

Unskilled[1] and semi-skilled workers the world over are among those who, individually and collectively, have not been well served by formal mathematics education. Tine Wedege's chapter is focused on the mathematical needs of unskilled and semi-skilled workers in Denmark. She makes a distinction between competencies and qualifications - a distinction which is blurred in many English-speaking countries - arguing from research which indicates that the former are subjective, personal qualities, not able to be assessed. Within the workplace, Wedege makes an analytical distinction between three types of qualification: professional, general, and social. Utilising a four-dimensional model to analyse numeracy in the workplace, she presents evidence of the incorporation of numeracy as a math-containing competence relevant in the technological workplace, reflecting the needs of the workplace as well as the individual's perspectives. Following Skovsmose's theoretical work concerning mathematics and democracy, Wedege defines technological competence in the workplace, based on the above qualifications. Her work, stressing the contextualised nature of numeracy in the workplace and emphasising a broader view of qualifications than is currently recognised in most education and training systems, has important implications for the teaching of mathematics in vocational education and training.

The chapter by Gail FitzSimons, from Australia, differentiates between the so-called Key Competencies, which were supposed to frame the intended curricula, and their implementation in the form of competency-based education and training (CBT) curriculum documents. Billett (1998) illuminates this distinction, tracing the social genesis of vocational practice in an interlinked knowledge system. He asserts that the former belong in the realm of socio-historic knowledge of guiding principles and procedures, whereas the latter are at a different level, reflecting the socio-cultural practice of industry. These are further transformed within the community of practice of the vocational classroom - which is functionally distinct from the community of practice of the work site. Finally, Billett claims that the individual's construction of socially derived knowledge, at the microgenetic level is further influenced by their ontogenetic development, including their personal history and participation in a range of overlapping communities. FitzSimons's review of the literature on workplace studies related to mathematics underlines the distance between essentialist, behaviourist, CBT vocational mathematics curricula and the kinds of knowledges which may be required in the technological workplace. She also argues that little attention has been paid to the professional development of teachers in a sector which has been almost totally isolated from the local and international mathematics education community. From a research perspective, the issues associated with teaching and learning at the micro level, within the institution as well as the workplace, have been largely neglected by policy makers, their funding bodies, and the university sector as a whole. This is especially the case for mathematics which has no industry support-base in an industry-driven system. The question arises as to why, in a country such as Australia, the status of mathematics is so lowly in a sector which prides itself on responding to the needs of industry in an era of globalisation and high technology.

Taken as a whole, these three papers represent a range of perspectives on adults, mathematics and work from an international perspective. An underlying theme is that of knowledge interests. Whose interests have been served in the past, and whose interests are we, as educators of adults in the workplace, paid and unpaid, fully employed, under-employed and unemployed, intending to serve?

NOTES

1 The term 'unskilled' is not intended in the pejorative sense. It is recognised that any worker, no matter how mundane and repetitive the task may seem to the onlooker, has skills in task management to ensure that the process runs effectively (or indeed at times, ineffectively).

REFERENCES

Billett, S. (1998). 'Transfer and social practice'. *Australian & New Zealand Journal of Vocational Education Research*, 6(1), 1-25.

Faure, E., Herrera, F., Kaddoura, A-R., Lopes, H., Petrovsky, A. V., Rahnema, M., & Champion Ward, F. (1972). *Learning to be: The world of education today and tomorrow*. Paris: UNESCO.

Gibbons, M., Limoges, C., Nowotny, H., Schwartzman, S., Scott, P., & Trow, M. (1994). *The new production of knowledge: The dynamics of science and research in contemporary societies*. London: Sage Publications.

Inglis, F. (1985). *The management of ignorance*. Oxford: Basil Blackwell.

Jahnke, H. N. (1994). 'Cultural influences on mathematics teaching: The ambiguous role of applications in nineteenth-century Germany'. In R. Biehler, R. W. Scholz, R. Strasser, & B. Winkelmann (Eds), *Didactics of mathematics as a scientific discipline*. Dordrecht: Kluwer, 415-429.

Keitel, C., Kotzmann, E., & Skovsmose, O. (1993). 'Beyond the tunnel vision: Analysing the relationships between mathematics, society and technology'. In C. Keitel & K. Ruthven

(Eds.), *Learning from computers: Mathematics education and technology*. Berlin: Springer Verlag, 243-279.

Kline, M. (1980). *Mathematics: The loss of certainty*. New York: Oxford University Press.

Lave, J., & Wenger, E. (1991). *Situated learning: Legitimate peripheral participation*. Cambridge: Cambridge University Press.

Maglen, L. (1996). *VET and the university*. Inaugural professorial lecture. Melbourne: The University of Melbourne.

Maglen, L., & Hopkins, S. (1998). *Linking VET to productivity differences: An evaluation of the Prais Program and its implications for Australia*. Working Paper No. 18. Melbourne, Vic.: Centre for the Economics of Education and Training, Monash University.

Seddon, T. (1992/93).'An historical reckoning: Education & training reform'. *Education Links*, 44, 5-9.

Seddon, T. (1994*). Context and beyond: Reframing the theory and practice of education*. London: Falmer Press.

United Nations Educational, Scientific and Cultural Organization (UNESCO) 1996. *Learning: The treasure within*. Report to UNESCO of the International Commission on Education for the Twenty-first Century. Paris: Author.

Chapter 10

Women, Mathematics and Work

Mary Harris
Institute of Education, University of London, UK

INTRODUCTION

The three categories, women, mathematics and work are, by tradition, mutually exclusive. Throughout the world, and in spite of women's contributions to all economies, the words *women's work* still bring to most minds the domestic activities of a home or its immediate environment: cooking and cleaning; the rearing of children, plants and animals; and something to do with cloth, either making it, or making or mending garments and other household goods made from it. Throughout the world most women do work which is mainly done by women. Holland (1991) notes that the category women's work in fact refers to two types of sexual division: most work in the home is seen as women's and most work in the labour market is seen as men's. Women's domestic work has never counted as real work. It is not very difficult. It is just something that women do. It is laughable to think of it as having intellectual content.

Mathematics is the polar opposite. In common perception, mathematics is a highly cerebral activity, far removed from the practical realities of daily life and over the heads of most people. With a few rare and eccentric exceptions, it has always been done by men. Certainly generations of women have been brought up, indeed taught to believe that women cannot do mathematics (Harris, 1997). Mathematics is seen as something different from practical daily arithmetic, although paradoxically, in daily conversation when the word 'mathematics' is used, people usually start talking about arithmetic. When some arithmetic is needed in a workplace and where it causes no problems, it is perceived as just common sense, indeed it is a commonplace of research in workplace mathematics to find people who use

171

D. Coben et al. (eds.), Perspectives on Adults Learning Mathematics, 171–190.
© 2000 *Kluwer Academic Publishers. Printed in the Netherlands.*

number with confidence, but remain convinced that they cannot do mathematics (for example Wolf, 1984; Harris, 1991b).

Yet practical work has always involved the working use of a variety of mathematical concepts and women have always used mathematical ideas in their domestic work. The reasons that this mathematics has never 'counted' are more to do with the history of education and other forms of social organisation and control, than with any individual's cerebral activity.

The task undertaken here is to address these two widely and long maintained stereotypes, that mathematics is a highly intellectual masculine study, and that feminine work has no intellectual content, by reviewing briefly some of the historical factors that have given rise to them, and by challenging both in discussing some of the mathematical thinking that necessarily goes on when women do their traditional and characteristic work with cloth. Finally the task is to explore the possibility of accrediting this mathematics. The aim is to remove or at least dent some of the barriers of self doubt and imposed control that have kept generations of women from access to one of the most powerful tools of their culture.

MATHEMATICS EDUCATION IN ENGLAND

For nearly the whole of the 2000 years of its existence, European education was a minority activity of the Christian Church. It was from within the Church that knowledge was defined, and it was the Church that controlled access to that knowledge. The philosophies of the early Church were derived from those of the Hellenism and Judaism of the Mediterranean rim, with the addition its own Messianic message. From the Hellenistic tradition was taken the 'stage theory' of Liberal Arts education leading towards the achievement of Virtue, and from the Judaic tradition was taken, amongst other things, the idea of the synagogue as a place of teaching. Christianity was always a teaching religion, though its formal education began for the purposes of servicing its own internal needs for literacy.

The curriculum that eventually emerged in Britain after the collapse of the Roman Empire, was a Romanised and much bowdlerised version of the classical Greek Liberal Arts. The content of this changed over the centuries but its structure for a significant part of the time consisted of the trivium of grammar, rhetoric and logic, followed by the higher level quadrivium of arithmetic, geometry, astronomy and music, the mathematics of the day. The highest level, the classical goal of the pursuit of Virtue was replaced by the Christian view of the ultimate truth, direct revelation from God through study of the Scriptures. Liberal education was deliberately detached from the world outside; it was conducted in places set aside for quiet contemplation and, as the private activity of a small élite under the aegis of the highest authority in the land, it had high social status in itself. Within it, mathematics was the highest point of the human intellect, below direct revelation.

In contrast to the Liberal Arts stood the Mechanical Arts, what we might loosely call Vocational Studies. One authoritative version, that of the twelfth century Hugh of St Victor, described a Mechanical Arts trivium of armaments, commerce and textiles with a quadrivium of agriculture, hunting, medicine and the theatrical arts. Unlike the Liberal Arts however, the Mechanical Arts could not lead to true wisdom because they were adulterated with matters of nature; they were too close to the affairs of life. The social distinction of Liberal over Mechanical, of academic and professional over vocational, of intellectual over practical, was a philosophical one that defined education itself, from the beginning.

At least two other sorts of mathematical activity went on in the seats of learning however. The liturgy of the church centred on the lunar feast of Easter, whose date had to be calculated. In days when the earth was known not only to be flat, but the centre of the universe, this was a vastly complicated, indeed necessarily abstruse business, and far too difficult for most people. This art of Computus was separate from the quadrivium which in any case was concerned with Pythagorean and Platonic philosophy. Secondly, all the monasteries were large land owners, and there is no way that anybody could house, clothe and feed a monastery full of monks (or nuns) through unrefrigerated summers and deadly winters, run a large estate and manage a feudal farming community without being numerate, whatever methods were used and however they were recorded. This practical activity, far removed from the Liberal Arts of the cloisters that it sustained, and not even a Mechanical Art, was of lower social status than both. We get a glimpse of what such practical managers thought of their academic betters, from Chaucer's description of the Manciple, a domestic Bursar, in the fourteenth century Canterbury Tales.

> The Manciple came from the Inner Temple;
> All caterers might follow his example
> In buying victuals; he was never rash
> Whether he bought on credit or paid cash.
> He used to watch the market most precisely
> And got in first, and so he did quite nicely.
> Now isn't it a marvel of God's grace
> Than an illiterate fellow can outpace
> The wisdom of a heap of learned men?
> (Chaucer, Coghill translation, 1977:18)

The translation is of course in modern English but it shows clearly, firstly that the Manciple was functionally highly numerate, and secondly, and in passing, that he was illiterate. It is salutary to be reminded in these days of education through the spoken and written word, that being numerate does not require being literate as a prior condition.

As Howson points out (1982), the history of mathematics education has been punctuated by attempts of mathematics educators who have tried to bring closer together what we might call the mathematical activity of Master and Manciple. The thirteenth century Roger Bacon; Vives, the tutor that Henry VIII hired for his daughter Mary; the Elizabethan mathematical practitioners; and the eighteenth century dissenting academies, all preached and practised a closer relationship. These, the schools of the armed forces and the places where academics and practical men (sic) worked together to some practical end were where realistic mathematics education developed, that is outside the remote, abstract and esoteric studies of the Universities.

From the beginning mathematics education, like all education, was a masculine business because it was of and for the Church and the Church was male. Mathematics itself received further gendered reinforcement, too, by the thirteenth century reaffirmation of the Pythagorean tradition (Wertheim, 1997), a world view in which mathematics held the key to both physical and spiritual reality. For Pythagoras, numbers as timeless abstractions were gods, and the study of relationships between numbers was by its nature religious activity. The number 1 was the supreme male principle and immaterial deity, the number 2 the supreme female principle associated with the material world, but since all numbers belonged to the psychic realm, mathematics as a whole was masculine. It was possible for women to study mathematics but if they did so they had to abandon their femininity, a characteristic pursued to this day in the cartoon idea of the female mathematician. There were periods of course when we hear of highly educated women, the formidable St Hilda for example; indeed ninth century clerics endorsed the idea of educating such honorary men, because the study of the bible made women more virile, literally more like a man and thus more holy (Anderson and Zinsser, 1988).

By the Victorian era and the beginnings of a late and reluctant State education for the masses, the nearly two thousand year social distinctions between the minority, élite, Liberal education, mathematics, and the practically oriented mathematics education of men who needed to use it, became incorporated into separate curricula that reflected their social differences as intellectual differences, at a time in history when society was heavily hierarchical. Social stratification was fundamentally important to Victorian society. It was believed to be natural and God-given, and necessary for economic prosperity, and it was supported by the science of the day not the least that of Charles Darwin whose model of explanation for the new and teeming forms of life in newly revealed lands, was a concept of evolution aimed at explaining the hierarchy.

The children of the aristocracy generally followed a classical Liberal education, often with tutors before they went to those exclusive private schools called Public from the days when they moved outside the monastery walls. There they undertook the classical study of Euclid before proceeding to the classical university education required of the rulers of the Empire. For the children of the working class, that is six sevenths of the total population, there was an entirely separate system not intended to be the fore-runner of any other education, but the minimum of sound but cheap training that would make them into good workers. There was still some doubt at first as to whether working class children should be taught any arithmetic at all for fear that the mental exercise might give them the means to question their station in life. There were no State schools as such until the end of the nineteenth century, though the State did manipulate the curriculum of the existing, mainly Church schools from the 1830s, through a system of grants. That curriculum consisted of the 3Rs with rote taught and frequently tested arithmetic, and needlework for the girls.

The Victorian era of a mere hundred years ago, the one in which our modern education system was worked out, (and which it still resembles), produced a number of Commissions and Reports on various aspects of education and society. The Taunton Commission of the 1860s looked at middle class education and stratified mathematics within that class, in an attempt to build socially appropriate layers in the philosophical void between the classical Euclid of the Liberal education of the upper classes, and the training of basic arithmetic for the working classes.

Taunton divided the endowed middle class schools into three grades, each oriented towards a different level of employment and supported by a different sort of mathematics curriculum. That for the first grade, for the sons of men with considerable incomes independent of their own exertions, or professional men, and men in business whose profits put them on the same level . . . indeed all who having received a cultivated education themselves are anxious that their sons should not fall below them studied classical mathematics suited to the classical curriculum. For the mercantile classes of the second grade the curriculum stressed practical arithmetic and the rudiments of mathematics beyond it. For the third grade sons of tenant farmers, small tradesmen and superior artisans there was very good arithmetic (Cooper, 1985). Girls of any class were not considered.

The Universities, notably Cambridge, clung to the dying embers of the quadrivium imposing the continuing study of Euclid on the upper classes. No less than 73 new editions were published in the 1840s (Price, 1994) as adherence to the Liberal tradition as mental and moral training of a social élite was maintained and exported to the colonies. Colonial aristocracies, for example in Melbourne subjected Australian upper class youth to hundreds of hours of committing to memory pages of a geometry two millennia old, in the interests of maintaining parity with a 'home' where Cambridge maintained its dead hand on curriculum advance to modern reality into the twentieth century (Clements, 1989).

The social divisions of 2000 years were thus built into the school curriculum, and a hierarchically ordered mathematics and its poor relation arithmetic, came formally to mark social distinctions, more clearly than any other subject. Mathematics and social class defined each other, and the level of both determined the type of employment that followed. By the early decades of the twentieth century, mathematics had also become the major constituent of intelligence testing, confirming some of those methods and interpretations founded on a belief in a direct relationship between intellect and social class. Mathematics was and still is one of the most powerful stratifying tools society has.

This hierarchical view of mathematics education, was continued well into the present century by the School Board, the State governing body of education. Both the Board's values and its personnel were thoroughly Victorian in outlook and they maintained that ethos until the Board was replaced by a Ministry of Education, only at the end of the second world war. Echoes of the Taunton hierarchy still exist not only in Britain but in countries whose education it has influenced, and the question of whether or not new schools for élites should be built in democratic societies is still in current debate.

PERCEPTIONS OF MATHEMATICS AND MATHEMATICS EDUCATION

One of the legacies of this roughly sketched history is a number of different perceptions of what mathematics and mathematics education are about. These depend on the standpoint in the social and economic status of the person or people who hold the perception, and assumed relationships between social class and intellectual ability are still often implicit. Most histories of mathematics do not record much of the numerate goings-on of the world outside formal education, for they are mostly written within and for the Liberal tradition. The mathematics used in agriculture, trade and commerce during the fifteen hundred or so years when mathematics was a university matter, has to be sought in their own histories and their artifacts (e.g. Gimpel, 1988). Neither can social histories of literacy inform us on how numerate people were. Chaucer's Manciple was illiterate but that did not stop him being effectively numerate. It depends of course on how numeracy is defined, but it cannot be assumed from the modern teaching of numeracy, though, because it appears that numeracy depends upon literacy and its assessment by the written means of the Liberal tradition. The *examining* of numeracy may, but that is a bureaucratic, not an educational matter.

Nobody who effectively builds a house, manages a market stall or runs a farm however small, is innumerate. It is ridiculous to think of a farmer who does not know how many chickens she has and how many eggs she expects, how much milk she is getting from how many cows or goats, and how much winter fodder will have to be laid in for them. Nobody ploughs a furrow without some clear idea of how long it will take, how many furrows can be ploughed in a day and what crop yield is hoped for, whether or not the farmer writes it down. Nobody spins for a livelihood without knowing how much thread she will produce from how many fleeces and how much more she will have to spin before she has enough to send to the weaver.

WOMEN IN SOCIETY

The Church was not simply male: it was openly and aggressively misogynist and the effects of its preaching and practice are still deeply embedded in many aspects of our society. The question of whether or not women should be priests is still a matter of raw debate.

The very nature of monotheisms is power relations, for a single god rules over all. All patriarchal monotheisms are built on the idea of men and women as complementary opposites. Under such a system, if men are superior then logically women have to be inferior. When God is male, then the opposite that is female, embodies the characteristics that contrast with the masculine virtues (Miles, 1993). It was essential for a young Church fighting against the still widely practised, gynocentric Old Religion, to establish male supremacy. Fear, resentment and denigration of women were already a strong force in the cultures from which Christianity grew and they were built into the powerful myth of Eve. Eve, the embodiment of what was wrong with women, was wrong on several counts: she was disobedient; she pursued knowledge; and she seduced Adam, causing him to lose self control. This wilfulness, this ambition, this power had to be repressed in the strongest possible terms. Christianity invented woman as an instrument of the devil.

But even Jesus had a mother and for a young Church in an age that had no knowledge of anatomy and was obsessed by the animal messiness of childbirth, the only way they could provide a clean mother for Jesus, was to decide, in solemn convocation, that Mary was a virgin even after the event.

In the teaching of the Church, in the words of Eileen Power, the position of woman was continually shunted between pit and throne. Workers, male and female alike went to their churches on Sundays and listened while preachers told them in one breath that woman was the gate of hell and that Mary was Queen of Heaven (Power, 1975).

There is no need to set up conspiracy theories when misogyny is preached from every pulpit in the land.

Diatribes against women were a conspicuous feature of the centuries in which the foundations of the universities were laid, and uncontrolled sexual and often scatological language was still being heard in arguments against educating women at all, in the years when our modern system of education was being built. In the late 1880s it was still possible to refer to women in the Saturday Review as "defeminated, hermaphrodite, mongrel and a species of vermin" (Delamont, 1978:179). In the 1920s and 30s, during the energetic campaigns of the National Association of Schoolmasters against the increasing number of women teachers, the language of complaint reveals the same fears as those of the early Church. Women teachers were accused of having a castrating effect on the nascent virility of boys, of nipping out the budding shoots of young manhood (Dyhouse, 1987).

Every major change of society, that we mark by periodic labels of history, has been accompanied by fresh justifications for controlling women and reaffirmations both of their inferiority and of their inherent threats to men. It was the incessant abuse that roused the fifteenth century Christine de Pisan to set up her own research study of women's abilities, and to publish the results (see Anderson & Zinsser, 1988:xiii). The Renaissance Humanist pursuit of male perfection elaborated on the feminine virtues required to support the ideal. Women were to stay at home to provide the domestic base from which the new man of affairs could conduct his business. The long tradition of women working alongside men in field, farm, workshop and building site, was increasingly frowned upon as a new advisory literature on the role of women burgeoned with the advent of printing. From the Reformation onwards there was a crescendo of pressure on women to stick to the domestics. By the time of the first national curriculum of the 1870s a domestic future for the mass of girls was the only one that was considered.

WOMEN AND WORK

As we have noted, women have always worked, that is they have always contributed to economies, in addition to their domestic work. The Industrial Age and Victorian ideals may have changed traditional patterns of employment, but women always worked, because they had to. Their domestic work counted for nought and their most obvious economic activity, however necessarily numerate, also remained mostly invisible because it was included in the work of a male head of household. Much of women's economic work was bye-lines, a second reason for its not featuring in economic history. Even when they were working alongside men on the farm or in the workshop, women undertook the additional work of selling products of both, and making foods and textiles surplus for family needs, to be sold. Managing a household, small or large, in which everything has to be made is full of problem solving activity both strategic and numerate. Christine de Pisan writing for a literate audience, was also writing for a numerate one. Why else would she suggest budget headings for women running households?

From the same era also comes a complaint about women who were perhaps too numerate in their trading activities for one disgruntled author:

> . . . if a woman be at it, she in her stinginess useth much more machination and deceit than a man; for never alloweth she the profit of a single crumb to escape her, nor faileth to hold her neighbour to paying his price. All who beseech her do lose but their time, for nothing doth she by courtesy, as anyone who drinketh in her house knoweth full well. (quoted by Power, 1975:69)

Renaissance changes in attitudes to women also include an assumption of numeracy. One of many sixteenth century advice books declares that it is the wife's duty:

> to go to market, to sell butter, cheese, milk, eggs, chickens, capons, hens, pigs, geese and all manner of corn. And also to buy all manner of necessary things belonging to the household, and to make a true reckoning and account to her husband what she had received and what she hath paid. (quoted by Miles, 1993:159)

WOMEN'S EDUCATION

However numerate in practice, there were few places where girls could obtain any formal education until the late nineteenth century. In mediaeval times there were nunneries but they varied in what education they could provide and they were always less well endowed than the monasteries. The usual prime reason for a girl being there was not to receive an education but because her parents could not afford a dowry. Most of the nunneries that remained by the time of the Reformation were then abolished, and the rise of the grammar schools, which fed the universities, and from which girls were barred, took place at about the same time.

Most of the teaching of girls took place at mother's knee, that very under-researched educational resource. Better-off girls could obtain an education in households that permitted them to share it with their brothers or where, like the daughters of Henry VIII they were given an appropriate humanist education for leadership. But the celebrated Vives who set out the case for teaching mathematics as the subject that encouraged sharpness of mind, was hardly egalitarian. His treatise on the education of women represents them more as people suffering from clinical depression (even given a modern reading of *sad* as *sober*) than of displaying any such sharpness. Women required the constant guiding hand of a man against the danger of any such thing. For Vives, maidens should be full of prayer and piety, humbleness and obedience; wives should be full of great sadness of behaviour and arrangement; and widows must not remarry but stay at home praying, going out only with some good and sad woman (Hufton, 1995).

The most consistent subject of a girl's education throughout the centuries was work with cloth. All girls learned how to make cloth and clothes for themselves and their families, and there was always a market for any surplus. In the Middle Ages, both women and men worked in the professional embroidery workshops that exported all over Europe the highly respected art of English embroidery known as *Opus Anglicanum*. But as economies became more sophisticated and capitalism developed, jobs became gendered. Women's embroidery stopped being art and became domestic craft at precisely the same time that art became a high status, masculine activity.

Much of the Church's teaching to and about women was on the subject of the right sort of submissive femininity. Roszika Parker (1984) traces the story of how embroidery became feminised and how that femininity became increasingly negative, empty and brainless. By collecting all the terms she uses to describe the downward spiralling views of femininity that embroidery came to represent over the years, and arranging them in alphabetical order, a picture emerges of women who were expected to be:

> chaste, delicate, dependent, devoted, docile, domestic, dutiful, frail, frivolous, humble, innocent, meek, modest, moral, obedient, patient, pure, sedentary, seductive, selfless, shameful, silent, spiritual, still, subjugated, subservient, subordinated, trivial, vain and virtuous. (Harris, 1997:13)

By the early Victorian era, and its elaborate fashions, all hand sewn until the arrival of sewing machines, needlework was still a marketable, and very exploited skill. But as a means of social control and of imposing idealisations of femininity, it was second to none. In the eyes of those concerned with the condition of the poor in nineteenth century England, the patched garments of working class families came to represent their efforts to make decent homes in appalling conditions, to raise themselves above dire poverty into decent domesticity (Davin, 1996). It was widely believed that if poor girls could be taught to sew properly then they would become better wives, mothers and home makers, indeed better women. The State's first contribution to the education of working class children that the Church was already providing, was in the form of grants for premises, for which conditions were imposed. The only curriculum subject mentioned was the mandatory teaching of needlework for girls, and this requirement stood alongside such other essentials as adequate premises and paying the teachers (Sutton, 1967).

The curriculum of boys and girls was thus immediately differentiated from the beginning of State education: for all children there was the 3Rs, but for girls there was 3Rs and 1N, and the N brought with it all the characteristics of femininity that Parker (1984) describes. There were obvious time table implications because clearly the boys had to be doing something while the girls were sewing. Typically what they did was more arithmetic. The boys not only studied more arithmetic, but to a higher level. It was acceptable for the majority of Victorian curriculum planners and the School Board that girls should do less and at a lower level, indeed these low expectations were written into curriculum administration, into instructions to Inspectors and into teacher training.

The use of the education system for feeding children into different levels of the economy armed with the appropriate mathematics, as discussed for example in the middle class Taunton report, applied only to boys. For a girl, the purpose of education was entirely different; it was not for a job but for a role in life, that of domestic supporter of males either in their own home as sister, daughter, wife or mother (or of course any combination of the four) or in someone else's home as servant. The education of girls was always seen as something different, an afterthought, a problem, separated from education itself in the category of girls' education. The distinction still shows in phrases like *girl-friendly mathematics*, modification of some implied real mathematics that would make it palatable for girls.

But in spite of widespread beliefs based on contemporary theories of physiology that girls were physically incapable of learning mathematics, there was evidence, even in the early days of state education, of girls' equal attainment with boys in school arithmetic (Harris, 1997). Occasionally too it was recognised, indeed undeniable, that girls' compulsory sewing involved a certain amount of mathematics: garments after all are a form of three dimensional geometry aimed at fitting particular sizes and shapes of people;

table cloths and curtains are made to fit tables and windows. But even when recognised, such mathematics was immediately negated by disclaimers that what girls really needed was only enough domestic arithmetic for budgeting or by dismissing abilities to cut accurate rectangles to scale, for example, as not requiring any particular skill (Harris, 1997:51,59). When not negated, necessary mathematical language was babyfied for example by describing geometric shapes as 'funny angular outlines' (Harris, 1997:55).

Demands for the domestic education of girls accompanied by lack of recognition of any intellectual content to it, remained state policy in spite of increasing opposition to its domination of the curriculum. The revolution in girls' education that took place at the end of the nineteenth century, and that saw girls allowed to sit the same arithmetic examination as boys for the first time, was a middle class one that affected only a small minority of the nation's girls for whom the domestic imperative remained. The implicit contrast, between the intellectual activity of mathematics and the subservience of female education to the male will, remained. Every economic, social or political crisis since the beginnings of State Education that saw advances in mathematics education itself, was accompanied by demands on schools for greater domesticity for girls aimed at better mothering, as women were belaboured for all the nation's ills; for the servant problem, for the lack of enough physically fit recruits for the Boer War, for racial degeneration in an increasingly contended empire, for high mortality rates and low birth rates and today, for some of the more unsubstantiated ills of one-parent families.

Low intellectual expectation, low self-esteem, low self-confidence were all built in to the schooling of the mass of girls from the beginning both by the presence of too much sewing and other domestic subjects, and by the inability to recognise that what girls did could have any intellectual content, even when it was blindingly obvious. This state of affairs was maintained by practice, by policy and by default, until challenged by feminist mathematics educators of the 1970s.

Since the 1970s however a great deal of work has been done in the field of girls and mathematics and there is now a large literature (Leder, 1992 for example). Most of the research is concerned with school mathematics however. There is little indeed on the mathematics that women use in their lives outside school, though new literature is developing on the mathematics implicit in some professional practices including nursing (Hoyles, Noss & Pozzi, 1999). What little there is on mathematics implicit in women's domestic work tends to come from the field of anthropological mathematics (Gerdes, 1995 for example) discussed briefly below.

COMMON THREADS

In the late 1980s, a project called Maths in Work (Harris, 1991a) was set up with the aim of developing closer relationships between the less academic levels of school mathematics and the mathematical reality of working life outside schools. By chance the work ran at the time when American feminist research had already fired world-wide interest and research into reasons why girls appeared to achieve comparatively less well in mathematics than boys. A mounting description of widespread gendering in all aspects of mathematics and girls' learning accompanied it. Mathematics textbooks were shown mainly to address boys and to marginalise girls (e.g. Northam, 1982). Teaching methods were shown to be competitive, male oriented and to include particularly aggressive forms of masculinity (Burton, 1986; Willis, 1989). Theories of learning mathematics and their resulting expectations on girls were also shown to be highly gendered (Walkerdine, 1989). Theories of moral development were found to be premised on wholly male samples, pathologising the reactions of females (Gilligan, 1982). Theories of occupational choice for school leavers were similarly biased (Chisholm, 1987). All aspects of girls' lives appeared to be subject to expectations that demeaned them as active, thinking beings. Even a task as apparently humble as knitting turned out to be subject to disparaging differentiation. A recent Archbishop of Canterbury had his sons taught to knit because such a repetitive activity permits the mind to reflect on life (Rutt, 1987). Freud, in a separate discourse however, had already established that the same activity induced in women the daydreaming that induces in them dispositional hypnoid states that render them prone to hysteria (Parker, 1984).

In the Inner London Education Authority, which set up the Maths in Work Project, as in other education authorities with a high proportion of immigrant children, it was shown that a disproportional number of children from particular ethnic minority groups were achieving less well than their host peers. One outcome of the investigation into the anomalies was the discovery of the range and bias and insensitivity in primary mathematics materials (Mosley, 1985). The times therefore were receptive for a challenge to both the stereotypes that are the object of this discussion, that of exclusively masculine mathematical ability and that of the mindless femininity of needlework.

In most countries, most people wear clothes most of the time and most clothes are made by women. Very few garments and textiles can be made without the use of some mathematics, so an exhibition of examples of textiles work of women was devised, in which each item was described not in terms of its aesthetic but in terms of the mathematics concepts necessarily involved in its making. A Fair Isle sweater for example cannot be made both to fit a person and to sustain the traditional continuous bands of translated geometric designs that form its fabric, without a working understanding of the mathematical idea of ratio, some use of symmetry, some measurement and some arithmetic including the use of factors. Knitting itself is a binary system of plain and purl stitches and an Aran sweater is a sophisticated use of the system that incorporates a number of symmetrical designs into a fabric that also has to conform to particular dimensions. Kilim rugs woven in Turkey are a sophisticated play on symmetry. Traditional baskets from Botswana are made in spiral formation with coils of constant diameter, and designs worked into the structure in three dimensional symmetry. An examination of hand knitted socks reveals a large number of solutions to the problem of lagging the right angled bend of a cylinder in a continuous and even layer that permits full movement of the ankle.

The exhibition, called *Common Threads* in a deliberate play on words, had a wide and immediate impact in mathematics education both on a two-year tour of England and subsequently, as the result of demand, on a four-year tour of 23 countries under the auspices of the British Council which took it over and redesigned it for touring. The educational effects of the tour have been described in detail elsewhere (Harris, 1997), but the clearest outcome has been to establish, visibly and incontrovertibly that the stereotypical activity that more than any other, and over many centuries defines feminine lack of intellect, is in fact highly mathematical. Not only is mathematics very far from being an exclusively male activity: the very activity that stereotypes women as brainless, is apparently full of it. A number of educational implications arise from this. One of the questions that was most widely asked in all the locations of the tours was: "Since there is so much mathematics in women's textiles work, how can it be accredited?"

WOMEN AND WORKING MATHEMATICS

Since the whole business of mathematics and its teaching is so highly gendered, it is only to be expected that its examination and accreditation are part of the same gendered process.

Examinations were first introduced into public life in England as a fair means of countering nepotism in entry to the Civil service and armed forces; they were tools of social engineering. In the Victorian era when the education system was set up, the theories of Darwin on the survival of the fittest, were intended to provide a scientific explanation of the accepted hierarchical nature of society. Examinations provided a method of indicating which people were fitter than others. They became the ideal person-measuring instrument of an hierarchical, masculine, literary, Liberal education tradition and its control over the education of the masses. The right for girls to enter public mathematics examinations was one of the first major victories of middle-class reformers of middle-class girls' education. As the power and extent of written examinations increased however, so did questions about their uses and abuses, their fairness and the sometimes differential results for boys and girls. In the late 1940s and 1950s controversy round the 11+ examination that controlled entrance to academic grammar schools, revealed that the test, far from selecting all pupils expected to benefit from a grammar school education, were in fact being used bureaucratically as a selective filter to fill places that were available. In many cases, girls outperformed boys in the actual examination but several education authorities required higher marks from girls than from boys under policies that equalised the number of school places (Thom, 1987).

Other negative effects of examinations on girls are discussed in recent research. Smart (1996) summarises gains made by girls up to the late 1980s following the introduction of the assessment of course work which shows what pupils can do, in contrast to traditional pencil and paper tests which undermine confidence by stressing what they do not. Coursework gives recognition to mathematics done in contexts where it makes sense, and has been shown to particularly favour girls. More recently Boaler (1997) has confirmed through systematic qualitative and quantitative research, how girls do better in teaching which develops understanding, and does not depend on the memory trained by traditional rote methods. Such gains have been eroded however by political decisions to return to more traditional, more formal testing methods that are known to favour boys. Inevitably this will mean a return to testing and to detachment again of the learning of mathematics from the circumstances in which it makes sense to use its sophistications.

Other movements in mathematics education research however, provide rationales in which the contexts of learning mathematics can continue to be researched. In addition to the literatures of ethnomathematics (e.g. Gerdes, 1997) and the identification of mathematics in professional practice (Hoyles et al., 1999) cited above, there is a accumulating literature on situated cognition (following the work of Lave, 1988) and an increasing literature in adult numeracy (e.g. Coben & O'Donoghue, 1997), a field that does not have to be subject to the same political, historical or administrative constraints on schools.

Gerdes (1997) defines ethnomathematics as the cultural anthropology of mathematics and mathematics education. It has arisen as a relatively new field of interest by the recognition within mathematics and outside it (Ernest, 1991) that if mathematics is a human construction, and not an exclusive, arcane activity descended from the gods, then it can no longer be seen as value and culture free. From this perspective, the academic mathematics of the liberal education tradition that still ultimately controls the assessment of vocational mathematics through various pencil and paper forms, is seen as only one sort of mathematics and mathematics education, those of a particular culture of an particular era. The way is open for alternatives.

Ethnomathematics recognises for example the geometrical forms worked by Southern African women into their weaving, decorated pottery, grass brooms, bead ornaments, tattooing and body painting, and mural decoration (Gerdes, 1995) and tries to introduce and develop them in school mathematics teaching (e.g. Soares, 1996). So far as accrediting existing mathematics embedded in women's work goes however, most published work currently being reviewed in an ongoing programme, seems to be concerned with teaching more mathematics, rather than with detailed analysis and recognition of what is already going on.

A small project, *Craftmaths*, funded by the Millennium Commission in the UK is currently exploring the possibility of revealing, developing and accrediting developing mathematics in patchwork and quilting courses taught within the National Federation of Women's Institutes. This is an organisation of some 250 000 members in England, Wales, Isle of Man and Channel Islands, with its own developing education programme, and its own adult education college, Denman. Preliminary participant observer studies (Harris, 1994) of three textiles courses taught at Denman College (knitting, machine patchwork, and curtain cushion and blind making), have revealed a range of arithmetical activity on which the practical work depended. All the mathematical skills are well within the range of existing numeracy accreditation. Yet, while course members clearly used mathematics as they worked, they frequently denied it during feedback, to the extent of denying what they themselves had been heard to say (Harris, 1994). Such self-negation confirms the finding of Wolf (1984) and Harris (1991b) above, and appears as a feature of craft publications written for women and reminiscent of the nineteenth century denial or trivialisation of the mathematics without which they cannot do patchwork. Publications that unselfconsciously celebrate the mathematical potential of patchwork are exceptions, and are written by and for quilters who are already mathematically literate. For example McDowell (1994) defines and uses mathematical symmetry in the design of patchwork including the seventeen wallpaper patterns of group theory in the design of patchwork blocks. Another (Venters & Ellison, 1999) reverses the traditional order in the title *Mathematical Quilts*, with the subtitle *No Sewing Required*. These publications however are unusual. There is also a mathematical literature on computer generation of quilting designs which tends not to consider the practicalities of sewing.

There are several strands to the research within the Craftmaths Project. It draws on the experience of mathematics education research and practice (e.g. Murray, 1979; Hawkin, 1990; Lolley & Ross, 1990; and Paechter, 1990) as well as the practical experience of Women's Institute patchwork tutors and students. At the same time it recognises the phenomenon of denial, against a research background that has already demonstrated differences between the effectiveness of 'home-grown' mathematical methods in revealing understandings of mathematical principles and the fact that they do not generalise to more formal education in mathematics (e.g. Lave, 1988; Carraher, 1991).

Implications of such research go beyond the confines of one particular project in one women's organisation in England and Wales. Questions of gendering in school mathematics education and in the quite separate literature on women's development are now seriously addressed in many parts of the world. In many countries the low recruitment and retainment rates of girls in schools is recognised as insensitivities and biases in the education system (Nayar, 1995; Obura, 1991; Goel & Burton, 1996; Harris, 1998). During the tours of the Common Threads exhibition it was possible for the author to work with a number of women's development groups, concerned with teaching both textiles skills and numeracy (Harris, 1997). In several of these, it was noted that the assessment undertaken by women on some textiles courses were of traditional pencil and paper manipulations of figures, developed in the nineteenth century UK tradition and bearing little relationship to the women's own considerable experience of working with cloth, or of their own cultural traditions and symbols in handling mathematical ideas associated with cloth working. Development programmes themselves can also be highly gendered (Mosse, 1993). For many years women have been handicapped by development work that, accepting traditional stereotypes, has assumed that they are or should be recipients of it, not economically active contributors to it. Many development projects teach numeracy using the old fashioned methods of a foreign, literary culture and a different ethnomathematics, both of which are irrelevant to the needs and aspirations of the women themselves, but may be required under the conditions of an aid programme (Harris, 1997).

As we have noted above, the idea that numeracy depends on prior literacy is a conceit, a function of the Liberal education tradition and its control over the vocational education of social classes and their activities which it has always seen as hierarchically inferior. Challenges to this view have been a long time coming, but Freirean approaches originally applied to literacy teaching are now beginning to appear in, for example, the work of the REFLECT programme (Rampal et al., 1998) of the charity ActionAid (Archer & Cottingham, 1996) which gives recognition to existing numerate skills of illiterate people. Accreditation of such existing practical skills, their development through home-made forms of recording and their translation into forms that can allow women in particular to step from where they are already working onto recognised ladders of empowerment, can now be explored.

Mathematics is a very powerful subject, holding a unique place in economics, education and society (Harris, 1999). It is the means of presenting facts and figures, on which policies and planning are researched, organised, analysed, justified and reported. Mathematics is the gateway to jobs that can be done indoors and sitting down, a significant step up from work that is done outdoors and standing up. It provides the language for wages, allowances and pensions. It is the tool of science, the provider of models, the arbiter of progress, the measure of success. Armed with a mathematics qualification, however lowly, a person has a choice of how she wishes to use it, to boost self-esteem trained out by millennia of prejudice, to understand economic procedures and processes that keep her in a state of deprivation, or to gain access to a fundamental part of education that has always excluded her.

REFERENCES

Anderson, Bonnie & Zinsser, Judith (1988) *A History of Their Own: Women in Europe from Prehistory to the Present* (Vol I). Harmondsworth: Penguin.

Archer, David & Cottingham, Sara (1996). *Action Research Report on REFLECT, Regenerated Freirean Literacy through Community Techniques.* London: Overseas Development Administration.

Boaler, Jo (1997) *Experiencing School Mathematics, Teaching Styles, Sex and Setting.* Buckingham & Philadelphia: Open University Press.

Burton, Leone (1986) *Girls into Maths Can Go.* London: Holt, Rinehart and Winston.

Carraher, David (1991) 'Mathematics in and out of School. A Selective Review of Studies from Brazil'. In Mary Harris (Ed) *Schools Mathematics and Work.* London & Philadelphia: Falmer Press, 169-202.

Chaucer, Geoffrey (1971 revision of 1951 translation) *Canterbury Tales.* Modern English version by Neville Coghill. London: Penguin Books.

Chisholm, Lynne (1987) *Gender and Vocation Working Paper No 1, New Series.* London: University of London Institute of Education.

Clements, M. A. (Ken) (1989) *Mathematics for the Minority: Some Historical Perspectives of School Mathematics in Victoria.* Geelong: Deakin University.

Coben, Diana & O'Donoghue, John (1997) *Adults Learning Mathematics - 4. Proceedings of the Fourth International Conference of Adults Learning Mathematics - A Research Forum.* London: Goldsmiths College.

Cooper, B (1985) *Renegotiating School Mathematics.* Lewes: Falmer Press.

Davin, Anna (1996) *Growing up Poor. School and Street in London 1830 - 1914.* London: Rivers Oram Press.

Delamont, Sara (1978) 'Domestic Ideology and Women's Education'. In Sara Delamont & Lorna Duffin (Eds) *The Nineteenth Century Woman: Her Cultural and Physical World*. London: Croom Helm, 164-188.

Dyhouse, Carol (1987). 'Miss Buss and Miss Beale. Gender and Authority in the History of Education'. In Felicity Hunt (Ed*)* *Lessons for Life. The Schooling of Girls and Women 1850 - 1950*. Oxford: Basil Blackwell, 22-38.

Ernest, Paul (1991) *The Philosophy of Mathematics Education*. London & New York: Falmer Press.

Gerdes, Paulus (1995) *Women and Geometry in Southern Africa*. Mozambique: Ethnomathematics Research Project, Universidade Pedagógica Moçambique.

Gerdes, Paulus (1997) 'A Survey of Current Work in Ethnomathematics'. In Arthur B Powell & Marilyn Frankenstein. *Ethnomathematics: Challenging Eurocentrism in Mathematics Education*. New York: State University of New York Press, 331-371.

Gilligan, Carol (1982) *In a Different Voice. Psychological Theory and Women's Development*. Cambridge Mass. & London: Harvard University Press.

Gimpel, H (1988) *The Mediaeval Machine. The Industrial Revolution of the Middle Ages*. Aldershot: Wildwood House.

Goel, Ved & Burton, Leone (1996) *Mathematics as a Barrier to Learning of Science and Technology by Girls*. Report of a Conference held at Amedabad, India 11 -12 January 1996. London: Commonwealth Secretariat.

Harris, Mary (1991a) *Schools Mathematics and Work*. London & Philadelphia: Falmer Press.

Harris, Mary (1991b) 'Postscript: The Maths in Work Project'. In Mary Harris (Ed) *Schools Mathematics and Work*. London & Philadelphia: Falmer Press, 284-291.

Harris, Mary (1994) *Mathematics in Denman Textile Courses*. Three reports for Denman College, National Federation of Women's Institutes. Unpublished.

Harris, Mary (1997) *Common Threads. Women Mathematics and Work*. Stoke-on-Trent. Trentham Books.

Harris, Mary (1998) *Gender Sensitivity in Primary School Mathematics in India*. London: Commonwealth Secretariat.

Harris, Mary (1999) 'Women and Working Mathematics. Ignoring a Majority?' In Fiona Leach & Angela Little (Eds) *Education, Culture and Economics: Dilemmas for Development*. New York: Garland, 315-326.

Hawkin, Wendy (1990) 'Patchwork:Tessellation'. In Mary Harris (Ed) *Textiles in Mathematics Teaching*. London: Maths in Work Project, University of London Institute of Education, 10.

Holland, Janet (1991) 'The Gendering of Work'. In: Mary Harris (Ed) *Schools Mathematics and Work*. London & Philadelphia: Falmer Press, 230-252.

Howson, Geoffrey (1982) *A History of Mathematics Education in England*. Cambridge: Cambridge University Press.

Hoyles, Celia. Noss, Richard & Pozzi, Stefano (1999) Mathematising in Practice. In Celia Hoyles, Candia Morgan & Geoffrey Woodhouse (Eds) *Rethinking the Mathematics Curriculum*. London: Falmer Press, 48 - 62.

Hufton, Olwen (1995) *The Prospect Before Her: A History of Women in Western Europe Vol 1500 - 1800*. London: Harper Collins.

Lave, Jean (1988) *Cognition in Practice. Mind, Mathematics and Culture in Everyday Life*. Cambridge: Cambridge University Press.

Lolley, Marylynne & Ross, Kirsten (1990). 'The Patchwork Quilt Project: Geometry of Polygons'. In Mary Harris (Ed) *Textiles in Mathematics Teaching*. London: Maths in Work Project, University of London Institute of Education, 18-20.

McDowell, Ruth B (1994) *Symmetry. A Design System for Quiltmakers*. Lafayette, California: C & T Publishing.

Miles, Rosalind (1993) *The Women's History of the World*. London: Harper Collins.

Mosley, Fran (1985) *Everyone Counts. Looking for Bias and Insensitivity in Primary Mathematics Materials*. London: Inner London Education Authority.

Mosse, Julia Cleves (1993) *Half the World, Half a Chance. An Introduction to Gender and Development*. Oxford: Oxfam.

Murray, Jenny (1979). *Square, Patterns and Quilts. Exploration in Shape using Designs in Squares from American Patchwork Quilts*. Derby: Association of Teachers of Mathematics.

Nayar, Usha (1995) 'Gender Issues in Primary Education'. *Indian Education Review 30(1)*, 220 - 245.

Northam, Jean (1982) '*Girls and Boys in Primary Maths Books*'. *Education, 10* (1), Spring, 11 - 14.

Obura, Anna P (1991) *Changing Images. Portrayal of Girls and Women in Kenyan Textbooks*. Nairobi: ACTS Press.

Paechter, Carrie (1990) 'Patchwork'. In Mary Harris (Ed) *Textiles in Mathematics Teaching*. London: University of London Institute of Education, Maths in Work Project, 14.

Parker, Rozsika (1984) *The Subversive Stitch. Embroidery and the Making of the Feminine*. London: The Womens Press.

Power, Eileen (1975) (Edited by M M Postan) *Mediaeval Women*. Cambridge: Cambridge University Press.

Price, Michael. A (1994) *Mathematics for the Multitude: A History of the Mathematical Association*. Leicester: The Mathematical Association.

Rampal, Anita. Ramanujam, R & Saraswati, L. S (1998) *Numeracy Counts*. Mussourie: National Literacy Resource Centre.

Rutt, Richard (1987). *A History of Hand Knitting*. London: Batsford.

Smart, Teresa (1996) 'Gender and Mathematics in England and Wales'. In Gila Hanna (Ed) *Towards Gender Equity in Mathematics*. Dordrecht: Kluwer, 215-237.

Soares, Daniel Bernardo (1996) 'The Incorporation of the Geometry of Traditional Housebuilding in Mathematics Education in Mozambique'. In Tore Kjærgård, Aasmund Kvamme, & Nora Lindén (Eds.), *Numeracy, race, gender, and class: Proceedings of the third international conference on the Political Dimensions of Mathematics Education (PDME III)*. Landås, Norway: Caspar Forlag, 242-244.

Sutton, Gordon (1967) *Artisan or Artist? A History of the Teaching of Arts and Crafts in English Schools*. Oxford: Pergamon Press.

Thom, Deborah (1987) 'Better a Teacher Than a Hairdresser? "A Mad Passion for Equality" or, Keeping Molly and Betty down'. In Felicity Hunt (Ed) *Lessons for Life. The Schooling of Girls and Women 1850 - 1950*. Oxford: Basil Blackwell, 124-145.

Venters, Diana & Ellison, Elaine Krajenke (1999). *Mathematical Quilts: No Sewing Required*. Berkeley: Key Curriculum Press.

Walkerdine, Valerie (comp) & the Girls & Maths Unit (1989) *Counting Girls Out*. London: Virago.

Wertheim, Margaret (1977) *Pythagoras Trousers: God, Physics and the Gender Wars*. London: Fourth Estate.

Willis, Sue (1989) *'Real Girls don't do Maths'. Gender and the Construction of Privilege*. Geelong: Deakin University Press.

Wolf, Alison (1984) *Practical Mathematics at Work. Learning through YTS*. Sheffield: Manpower Services Commission.

Chapter 11

Technology, Competences and Mathematics

Tine Wedege
IMFUFA, Roskilde University, Denmark

INTRODUCTION

In the labour market, technological development is considered by most people as more or less the same as evolution. The development of technology and the pace at which it takes place are experienced as being unavoidable, something we are helplessly confronted with. In this context mathematics may become personified and perceived as power: "Mathematics is not democratic. Mathematics is evil. It has caused unemployment in my trade." This statement by a former graphic designer illustrates at one and the same time a feeling of impotence in the face of technological progress, and a perception of mathematics as power.

In the late 1960s, "Power to the people" was introduced as a political slogan. Now the slogan has reappeared in the 1990s, but in a different context with a different meaning. Leading industrialists recommend upgrading competitiveness through empowering employees. General qualifications such as languages, mathematics, responsibility, and flexibility are in demand within labour market sectors which use new techniques in production and have flatter management structures and wider job constructions than the Taylorist model with its narrow routine job functions and hierarchical management structure. The 'new' work is organised in autonomous groups or production groups where semi-skilled workers assume planning functions that previously were management tasks. It might be said that it has been realised in practice that technology includes more than machinery.

I shall define *technology* on the labour market as consisting of three elements - technique, qualifications, and work organization - and their

D. Coben et al. (eds.), Perspectives on Adults Learning Mathematics, 191–207.
© 2000 *Kluwer Academic Publishers. Printed in the Netherlands.*

dynamic interrelation. *Technique* is used in the broader sense to include not only tools, machines and technical equipment, but also cultural techniques (such as language, mathematics and time), and techniques for deliberate structuring of the working process (as for instance in Taylor's 'scientific management' and ISO 9000 quality certification). *Work organization* is used to designate the way in which tasks and functions, responsibility and authority are structured in the workplace. I define *qualifications* as the knowledge, skills and properties that are relevant to technique and work organisation as well as to their interaction in a work function. I make an analytical distinction between two types of qualification:

- *specific professional qualifications* (technical-professional knowledge and skills);
- *general qualifications* (general and professional knowledge and abilities such as functional mathematical knowledge).

A third type of qualification is defined as a quality in these two types of qualifications:

- *social qualifications* (personal traits/attitudes such as precision, solidarity, flexibility and the ability to cooperate).

In the definition of qualification I speak of *relevant* knowledge, skills and properties rather than of *necessary* knowledge and so on (see Wedege, 1995a; 1999). This makes it possible to perceive qualifications from two different points of view: subjective and objective, that is, from the point of view of individual workers as well as from the point of view of the labour market (Olesen, 1996). For further discussion of the concept of qualification, see Wedege (1995a & 1999).

The concept of qualification offers a framework for didactic reflection on the relation between education and work. In Denmark the political and economic prioritisation of Formal Adult Education and Adult Vocational Training is primarily an answer to the qualification demand of the labour market, and mathematics teaching and learning in the two educational sectors contribute, each in their own way, to the qualification[2] of unskilled and semi-skilled workers. In Denmark, as in many English-speaking countries, it seems that the human capital paradigm has replaced that of social and personal development in adult education over the last two decades (see FitzSimons, this volume).

Adult Vocational Training activities have as their general objective to provide, maintain and improve the vocational qualifications of the participants in accordance with the needs of enterprises, the labour market and individual persons, in line with technological and social development.

But there are some difficulties in 'translating' qualification analyses into adult mathematics education which have to do with the context-determination of mathematical competences. Firstly, the general categories of qualifications (such as numeracy) are described in isolation from the technological and social contexts of workplaces in a number of policy reports (Darrah, 1992). Secondly, the conditions for transfer of mathematics knowledge between school and workplace or between different techno-logical contexts are unclear (Strässer, 1996; Evans, 1999; Wedege, 1999).

My interest in 'adults and mathematics' is that of an educational planner, but my point of departure as a researcher is that reforms in adult education must address the social nature of work, including the capacity to understand and modify technology. Thus my fundamental research question is formulated in the border area between adult education research and the didactics of mathematics (meaning the scientific discipline related to research and development in mathematics education): Could one imagine that mathematics teaching and learning provide semi-skilled workers with the possibility to develop technological competences which may place them as subjects in relation to technology in their workplace? i.e. a personal competence that changes inability to initiative and power. And, if the answer is in the affirmative, how should mathematics teaching and learning be organised? (Wedege, 1995a; 1995b)

Whereas the acquisition of mathematics as a school subject is the central issue in classical didactics of mathematics, technological competence is a math-containing competence and not pure mathematical knowledge. Thus, due to the hidden life of mathematics in technology, there is an underlying methodological-didactic question concerning the possibility of establishing the content of the mathematics learning having these competences as its aim. In the chapter on 'Adults and Mathematics', in the *International Handbook of Mathematics Education*, FitzSimons, Jungwirth, Maaß and Schloeglmann point out that "the question of which kind of mathematics is really necessary, and in which context, in order that people can cope with situations they encounter, or can alter them according to their needs" gives rise to problems (FitzSimons et al., 1996:761). This is the question I should like to address here. The context is semi-skilled job functions in the workplace, which might encompass several work tasks; and people who are the *adults* with brief formal schooling whose perspective with regard to education is about training themselves for the job on hand or for skilled work.

CONCEPTS OF COMPETENCE IN ADULT AND FURTHER EDUCATION

During the last decades, the classical theory/practice dichotomy has been questioned in adult education research and there has been growing interest in 'tacit knowledge'; knowing and learning in action/practice (Schön, 1986; Lave & Wenger, 1991). I regard the widespread use of the term 'competence', which includes both knowledge and skills, in educational studies as characteristic of our times.

The Danish noun 'kompetence,' as well as the English 'competence' and the German 'Kompetenz', are derived from the French noun 'compétence', which has two basic meanings: (a) authority, powers; and (b) capacity, professional and factual insight within a certain area, for example professional competence. 'Competence' occurs within each language area side-by-side with various everyday meanings and specific meanings in the world of education and also as scholarly concepts in the fields of linguistics, psychology, pedagogy, the law, and industrial sociology. The OECD is working towards achieving joint assessment and certification of occupational skills and competences in vocational education and training. The approach is technocratic as the interest is in planning, management and control but there are some interesting observations in the efforts of Gabriel Fragnière, a French-speaking Belgian, to clarify the concepts. He advocates making a distinction between qualifications and competences. Qualifications can be defined *a priori* and have to do with formal lines of education and certification while competences have to do with experience and informal recognition. In defining 'competences', he writes:

> These are composed by the *individual* and, one would think, *subjective* ability to use one's qualifications, know-how and knowledge to accomplish something. In fact, there are no "objective" competencies capable of being defined independently of the individuals in which they are embodied. There are no competencies in and of themselves; there are only competent people. (Fragnière, 1996:47)

Fragnière points out that, when discussing what the French call 'compétences transversales', English speakers 'core qualifications' and Germans 'Schlüssel Qualifikationen', there is a regrettable confusion between qualifications and competencies. 'Compétences transversales' are precisely those related to the individual, to his behaviour and his specifically personal abilities. They do not define gestures or know-how which are directly and objectively linked to a very specific task as 'qualifications'. This French language comment may also be interpreted as criticism of the British merging of 'competence' and 'qualification' in the National Vocational Qualification system (NVQ) where competence is closely linked to assessment, and competence is equated with performance (see Eraut, 1994).

Gail FitzSimons, in the Section Introduction and her chapter (this volume) points to the difference in Australia between the so-called 'Key Competencies' and the competency-based education and training curricula (CBT) deriving from a strong behaviourist tradition. We may find the notion of 'Key/core competencies' in a series of reports concerning the requirements of the technological change in industry. For example the transformation from Tayloristic work organisation to open autonomous work organisation. In Britain, Roseanne Benn is critical of the mechanistic competency-based approach, with qualification understood as practical skills, and is looking for ways "to promote engagement, understanding and creativity as well as competence amongst practitioners" (Benn, 1997:57). She proposes counteracting the mechanistic approach to the education of adults educators by examining the concept of the reflective practitioner as proposed by Schön (1983). However, each criticism should be viewed in its respective context of the British NVQ system and the Australian CBT system as, in its basic sense of 'capacity', competence unites the complex mix of knowing and doing. In adult mathematics education discourse, I propose rescuing the concept from the technocrats by insisting on the difference between competence and performance (as Chomsky did in linguistics) and remembering the will to perform.

Like other concepts used in education research (e.g. knowledge, skill, qualification), *competence* is given specific meanings in different problematiques. However, I think it is possible to formulate four common features across the lines of different educational contexts. Competence is:

— always linked to a subject (person or institution)
— a readiness for action and thought and/or an authorisation for action based on knowledge, know-how and attitudes
— a result of learning or development processes in everyday practice and/or education
— always linked to a specific situation context. (cf. Wedege, 2000)

These four features are also to be found in Oscar Negt's notion of competence in his ideal education for the worker of the future, which is made up of six different competences (Negt, 1989) The competences in question might be summarised as: (a) to see things in context; (b) to deal with people and nature in a caring manner; (c) to see one's own practice in the light of historical dynamics; (d) to handle problems of identity; (e) to show sensitivity in the face of exploitation and abuse; and (f) the competence to control technology at a level where the cohesion of general technological progress is visible. In my construction of a normative concept of semi-skilled workers' technological competences, I have chosen as my basis Negt's ideal of education.

NUMERACY AS A TRANSVERSE COMPETENCE ON THE LABOUR MARKET

It is a basic assumption in my research that it is possible to locate a math-containing competence that everybody on the labour market with a certain level of technology needs in principle, in other words that it is meaningful to speak of *labour market numeracy*. The term 'needs' should not be read as an expression of necessity, rather of relevance. Thus this is not just a matter of given labour-market demands concerning the individual's skills and understandings, but also whether needs can be relevant in relation to technological changes (in technique and/or work organisation), or the individual's perspectives in working life or further education.

The labour market's need for numeracy changes over time and place with the development of society and of technology. In the 1980s and 90s two contrary tendencies could be observed. On the one hand the presence of pocket calculators and information technology meant that the need for manual calculations, mental arithmetic, geometric construction work and so on had changed. This meant different demands on numeracy - fewer demands in the opinion of some. On the other hand the same technology made it possible to organise work differently. The need for an overview, coordination, and communication became greater. This made new demands on numeracy - greater demands in the opinion of others.

In the field of research that comprises 'adults knowing and learning mathematics', the construction and further development of a concept of 'numeracy' is a task that many researchers relate to (FitzSimons et al., 1996). The term 'numeracy' was introduced for the first time in the United Kingdom in the late 1950s as a parallel to the concept of 'literacy' (Cockcroft, 1982). The need was felt for a concept to cover necessary, basic arithmetical operations corresponding to the concept used for reading and writing skills. Several studies have subsequently examined the low level of numeracy in society. They represent, however, two different approaches to the subject area: an objective perspective (society's requirements of numeracy) and a subjective perspective (adults' individual need for numeracy).

The *objective perspective* is represented, *inter alia*, by a large-scale British study of the mathematical needs of adult life initiated in order to make recommendations concerning the curriculum in primary and secondary school. In 1982, in the so-called 'Cockcroft Report', numeracy is defined as having two attributes:

> The first of these is an 'at-homeness' with numbers and an ability to make use of mathematical skills which enable an individual to cope with the practical mathematical demands of his everyday life. The second is an ability to have some appreciation and understanding of information which is presented in mathematical terms, for instance graphs, charts or tables or by reference to percentage increase or decrease. (Cockcroft, 1982:11)

In the years since then there has been lively debate between educational planners and researchers in the English-speaking countries (the United Kingdom, the United States of America, Australia, etc.) about the content and meaning of the concept of 'numeracy'. The discussion has, *inter alia*, concerned questions such as: How broad is the competence? How deep? How general? How specific? Is numeracy also a matter of democracy?

The *subjective perspective* is represented by a large number of studies on 'adults and mathematics'. The research questions concern adults' ideas about and attitudes towards mathematics, mathematics anxiety and blocks, adults' competences as potential in the learning process, and so on. "Mathematics Counts" was the title of the Cockcroft Report; 15 years later a book entitled "Adults Count Too" was published (Benn, 1997). Each examine the low level of numeracy in society, but the two approaches are quite different. Benn, argues that mathematics is not a value-free construct but is imbued with elitist notions which exclude and mystify. She recognises but rejects the discourse of mathematics for social control where mathematical literacy is seen as a way of maintaining the status quo and producing conformist and economically productive citizens. Similarly, she rejects the approach where any problem with mathematics is located in the learner rather than the system (Benn, 1997).

Overall in this debate however, I find that numeracy appears with the four features formulated above that characterise 'competence' in relation to 'skill', 'knowledge' or 'qualification', in spite of the fact that neither the approach nor the linguistic usage are the same. In the British context, like Benn, Jeff Evans views 'competence' narrowly, almost as functional skills. In his comments on the numeracy definition in the Cockcroft Report, he writes: ". . . both attitudes - an 'at-homeness' - and skills are considered important: *confidence* counts, as well as competence" (Evans, 1989:203). I regard 'confidence' and 'the will to use one's knowledge' as something distinguishing competence as a readiness for action and thought from purely knowledge and skills.

But in contrast to a general concept of competence, any concept of numeracy is normative, as with other concrete manifestations of concepts of competence (professional competence, cultural competence, technological competence, etc.) (cf. Eraut, 1996). The need of society or the labour market for numeracy cannot be perceived directly:

> To be numerate is more than being able to manipulate numbers, or even being able to 'succeed' in . . . mathematics. Numeracy is a critical awareness which builds bridges between mathematics and the real world, with all its diversity. Being numerate also carries with it a responsibility: of reflecting that critical awareness in one's social practice. (Yasukawa & Johnston, quoted in Benn, 1997:69)

Numeracy as a basis for semi-skilled workers' technological competences involves this responsibility of critical reflection. We may find a concept of reflective knowledge in Ole Skovsmose's theoretical work concerning mathematics and democracy. His key concept is 'mathemacy', not 'numeracy', but I find his distinction between three types of mathematics knowledge useful and instructive:

1. Mathematical knowledge as such.
2. Technological [mathematics] knowledge, which is the competence to build and to use a mathematical model.
3. Reflective [mathematics] knowledge, to be interpreted as a more general conceptual framework, or meta-knowledge, for discussing the nature of models and the criteria used in their construction, applications and evaluations. (Skovsmose, 1994)

Skovsmose bases this distinction on two theses. The first thesis, which is concerned with the philosophy of technology, states that *the knowledge required to develop technology is different from the knowledge that is needed to analyse and assess technology*. The other thesis is about learning processes; it states that *by learning mathematics you do not automatically learn how to use it*. Or in other words: technological (mathematics) knowledge which, for pragmatic reasons, I prefer to denote 'practical (mathematics) knowledge', cannot be reduced to mathematical knowledge. It is Skovsmose's ambition to develop a notion of 'mathemacy' parallel to the notion of 'literacy' developed by Paulo Freire, meaning much more than just being able to read and write. 'Mathemacy' should become a kind of competence for acting in the world structured by mathematics (Skovsmose, 1998).

NUMERACY IS CONTEXTUALISED

As we have seen, numeracy as an everyday competence cannot be identified as a collection of skills and understandings alone, isolated from the contexts in which they are used.[3] It does not merely comprise the four basic arithmetical operations and other mathematical subjects. At the workplace, it is not enough to know the multiplication tables from 2 to 10 if this arithmetical skill cannot be applied to measuring and to calculating the materials necessary. For example, the formula for measuring the circumference of a circle, 2π x *Radius*, is mathematical knowledge that can only be used for calculating the materials that are necessary when converted to the formula π x *Diameter* when one is able, in the physical sense, to measure the diameter of the object but not the radius. Conversely, in practice one can go far with the 2, 5 and 10 tables if one merely can set up a sum to solve the practical task. Nor is numeracy just an ability such as 'calculating a dosage'. In the world of reality calculations are always influenced by what they are to be used for and how precisely they should be performed. At a hospital there is a difference between dosing medicine and detergent.

In order to identify and describe mathematics in semi-skilled job functions and to analyze how numeracy at work is interwoven with specific qualifications and social qualifications, I am investigating selected firms within four lines of industry: building and construction, the commercial and clerical area, the metal industry, and transport. In organizing my investigation I follow the systematics developed in the Australian project, "Rich Interpretation of Mathematical Ideas and Techniques". I shadow a worker for half a day to describe the action taking place. At the end of the day I interview the worker to explore any issues that have arisen. The observations are written up as a descriptive story with examples of particularly interesting incidents (Hogan, 1997). Furthermore, I photograph interesting situations and tools and collect written materials with figures, formulas, diagrams, and so on (e.g. working drawings, plans, and statistics). In processing the data I use an operational tool with four analytical dimensions which we have constructed to describe and analyze numeracy. One is *context*; what one knows and what one should know depends on whether one is in a supermarket, at work, or in a test situation. In my study the context is described in terms of work function and technology - and also what is produced. "There is a difference between a fault in an aeroplane and a television set," as an operative in the quality control section of a large electronics firm expressed it. *Media* is another dimension; the relevant numeracy depends on whether it is to be applied to oral information, a manual, the weekly production plan, or a pile of earth, even if the figures and the four basic arithmetical operations are the same. A third dimension comprises *personal intention*; it is crucial whether one wishes to obtain or to give information, to plan production, to check the quality of the product, to pass the time, and so on. The fourth dimension we are working with is *skills and understanding* such as geometric sense, rough estimates, competence in mathematical modelling and a sense of sizes (Lindenskov, 1997; Wedege, 1998). The examples in the following sections are from this study.

MATHEMATICS AND TECHNOLOGY

Technological development involves new techniques, work organisation and qualification. Figures abound at places of work but mathematics is hidden in the technology and there is a widespread feeling among adults that 'mathematics is important, but not for me.' Mogens Niss has called this phenomenon the contradiction between the objective social relevance of mathematics and its subjective irrelevance: 'the relevance paradox' (Niss, 1994).

Everyone on the labour market experiences and participates in technological development. While some people experience that they are in control of their situation at work, others do not. Many people speculate about development - politicians, philosophers and educational planners. The great question for philosophers is the possibility of humans being able to control technological development. The extent to which the education system should react exclusively to the qualification demand or whether it also should have an active function is a political question. One of the central educational questions is about the need for qualification. Both political and educational issues have to do with 'technology transfer' from mathematics education to the labour market, a metaphor used by Jürgen Maaß and Wolfgang Schlöglmann. They also point to the fact that the new technologies altering our life so radically are essentially mathematical technologies (Maaß, 1998).

600 years ago the first mechanical clock was constructed. With this invention, time was divided into random units (hours, minutes, seconds), and time gradually came to be perceived as the sum of these units. The mechanical clock extends the area for measurement and quantification: space, weight and time. Precise measurement of time became one of the central elements in the organisation of social and working life (Keitel, 1989). Although it would be several hundred years before the clock became an everyday possession, it gradually changed the relationship between human beings and reality. It introduced objective measurements and made possible

objective mathematical rules for dealing with time. Time became an authority.

15 years ago IBM released the first personal computers (PCs) onto the market. Today there is a PC in 40% of Danish homes and a simple pocket calculator is almost given away when one buys other products. In the space of less than a quarter of a century an infinite volume of calculation has been taken over by computers at the same time as adults' need to use mathematics has changed. While the clock, in its time, introduced and made visible figures for time, mathematics is now made invisible in the new information technology. When a spreadsheet has first been set up, the formula and calculations are hidden. It is only when conversions are necessary that formulas and mathematics knowledge become visible. It is only when the daily routine is broken by a new problem that the worker becomes conscious of his/her mathematics activity.

Example 1. At Copenhagen airport different task groups cooperate by means of computer. When the aircraft are being loaded and unloaded, the loading group and the load planner are in constant computer contact. In the loading instructions the planner has placed baggage, cargo and mail in the four cargo compartments in front of and behind the wings. The ideal balance factor (38.0) and the limits (5.9/51.6) also appear from these instructions. The balance factor of the aircraft can also be read on the screen during loading: in the loading report for one specific aircraft it is 28.2. The work team does not have to enter the figures for the distribution of weight between the four cargo compartments in the formula for the balance factor as this figure is automatically calculated when the cargo and the weight are entered.

When decisions are being made at the airport about loading an aircraft, the priorities are 1) safety, 2) keeping to the timetable, and 3) service. Time is often at a premium when an aircraft is to be unloaded and loaded, and keeping to the timetable can mean than some cargo may have to be sent on a later plane. As the first priority is safety, this can, however, mean that the flight may be delayed and the level of service may not be so high if the balance factor is not within the permitted limits. The authorisation to release the flight belongs to the foreman of the group but the decision not to follow the loading instructions can only be made after consultation with the loading planner.

This is also an example of the fact that the necessary qualifications are not only to be found in technique alone. The balance factor for the load in question can be read on the computer. This means that the foreman of the group, without any knowledge of the formula, has a means of measuring what happens if they leave some cargo out of the loading instructions. In principle he can make this type of decision but if there is extra cargo which does not figure in the instructions (and this was actually the case with a later plane), he cannot precisely predict what will happen to the balance factor if the cargo is placed, for example, in one particular compartment. If the work were organized in autonomous groups, knowledge of the formula for calculating balance would have been necessary to carry out the job function.

Calculating the balance factor is actually part of the courses of training for this work. All the companies where I made observations use Adult Vocational Training to qualify their workers. However, the invisibility of mathematics in work (Harris, 1991) combined with the learning perspective of adults (vocational qualifications and not mathematical knowledge) result in a lack of motivation to learn mathematics. The typical worker is of the opinion that there is too much mathematics in the courses. This may be because the connection between job and mathematics is not made visible in the instruction or because the mathematical tasks are not relevant despite their being constructed on the basis of authentic material.

> **Example 2.** Because of the importance of figures and time in production, any teacher of mathematics can generate very many tasks on the basis of written instructions for the work task of 'packing and control of covers' from a large electronics company. The following are two examples:
>
> > **A. Packing** (the four basic arithmetical operations)
> > 600 covers are to be checked and packed in boxes. There are to be 5 layers in each box. Each layer is to consist of 3 rows of 5.
> > - How many boxes are needed?
> > **B. Basis time** (the four basic arithmetical operations, percentages)
> > The basis time for the work operation (check and pack one cover) is calculated to 4.63 which means that you have to do the operation 1000/4.63 times per hour to keep the standard.
> > - How many pieces per hour does this correspond to?
> > The working time for checking and packing 248 covers is 1 hour.
> > - What percentage of basis time is the working time?

The context representing reality in these tasks, the task-context, is construed on the basis of authentic material, but the situation context for using mathematics in the work place has not been taking into account (Wedege, 2000). The operative who is to perform the work function, 'packing and checking covers', does not experience the need to carry out these calculations. The instructions state that each box should include 75 pieces.

When the operative fetches packaging material for the 600 pieces, she has to calculate the number of boxes to be used. When new objects appear, she must read, do a little calculation and count, but this quickly becomes routine. The computer carries out all calculations concerning working and basis time. However, the electronics company is in the process of introducing autonomous production groups, which means that the job of coordinator is performed for 14 days in turn by each of the members of the group. The working day of the coordinator starts by printing out the production plan. The company produces on order with a delivery time of 5 days and via the computer she is in contact with, *inter alia*, the orders office, the production department and sub-contractors. When planning and coordinating the work, there are several factors to be taken into account. A little later she takes part in a meeting with the production leader and planner, together with the coordinators of the department's other groups where they discuss production plans and service grades. The service grade is calculated in percentage and equals:

(number of items delivered) x 100/(number of items to be delivered according to the production plan)

More is demanded of the operative's numeracy in the autonomous groups than in the 'narrow job'. Cooperation and coordination with colleagues and departments requires understanding and conversion of information to figures in complex contexts as well as communicating about these matters.

In educational systems like the Danish Adult Vocational Training system, the objective is to qualify the workforce to meet the needs of the labour market and the individual in step with technological development. However, specific professional, general and social qualifications are necessary- but not sufficient - for technological empowerment.

TECHNOLOGICAL COMPETENCES IN THE WORKPLACE

It is a general trend on the labour market that semi-skilled workers now assume planning functions that previously were management tasks. The story in the following examples has been constructed on the basis of authentic material and situations from different companies. It illustrates the fact that attitudes to mathematics are just as much part of a worker's qualifications as skills and understandings. At the same time the story illustrates that both practical and reflective mathematics knowledge is needed of the worker when production is organized in autonomous groups. The mathematical subject is 'graphs.'

Example 3 Thomas is a CNC operative in an autonomous production group at a metal company. There is no job rotation at the lathe he operates and this suits him very well. When he is checking the objects that are turned, he **reads** a graph (or a 'chart' as he would probably say, cf. Evans, 1997) on the screen where he evaluates whether the finished object fulfils tolerance requirements. He can also see whether production is stable, which can have implications for the tools and the number of objects to be checked.

There is a graph on the notice board of the production groups showing the sickness statistics of the group. The graph also compares average absence due to illness for the department and for the company as a whole. This absence is up over 8% in Thomas's group while the average is below 4% in the month of October. During the break Thomas speaks with the other members of his group. He says: "That was me. That month in hospital. You can see it." A long term of illness for one person affects the average. The group as a whole understands this but it is of no interest to Thomas how the figures are calculated or the graph constructed. Actually, his attitude is that all these statistics are something the management sit doing in the office because they do not have anything else to do.

There are graphs showing the service grades of each of the groups on a joint notice board in the department. At the end of November Thomas's group is 45 hours behind. The service grade is down to 80. The production leader suggests that they should organise the work in shifts so that they can come up to 100 during December and not work between Christmas and New Year. Thomas takes no part in the conversation of the group about organising the work so that the service grade can be maintained, and he has no intention of doing so. He just knows that it is a matter of working hard.

In a Taylorised company with narrow job functions and a foreman who says how the work is to be organised, Thomas would be a qualified operative. At a place of work with autonomous groups he is not qualified to take part in decisions about work organisation caused by a low service grade. Thomas's participation in the community of practice of the production group is peripheral and he is not undergoing a learning process that can lead him to central participation (Lave & Wenger, 1991). Technological competence at the workplace is a personal competence which changes inability into resourcefulness. Such a competence, which may place semi-skilled workers like Thomas in a central position as subjects in relation to technology in their workplace, must comprise both a vocational and a democratic dimension.

I define a worker's *technological competence* in the workplace as a personal math-containing competence:

— to assess critically/constructively and adapt to (or alter) and handle new situations which imply social and professional challenges;

- to evaluate and take part in technological decision-making processes regarding new technology in the workplace.

The competence presupposes the following qualifications:

- to handle and develop techniques and labour organisation in the workplace;
- to come to grips with the principles and the knowledge basis of technology;
- to realise the relationships between such techniques and organisation and general technological development in society.

This description of qualifications implies that both specific professional qualifications, general qualifications, and social qualifications are involved. The democratic dimension encompasses my suggestion for a clarification and extension of perhaps the most sought-after qualification in today's labour market, that is, 'flexibility', combined with another personal competence for participation in democratic processes regarding technological transformations. Technological competences are based on numeracy and literacy.

To be technologically competent, the worker in **example 3** needs three kinds of reflective mathematics knowledge as defined by Skovsmose (1998). Mathematics-oriented reflection guided by questions like: Is the service grade calculated correctly? Model-oriented reflection guided by questions like: Is service grade a reliable model for productivity? Context-oriented reflection guided by questions like: What is the actual purpose and function of carrying out the mathematical modelling in this metal company? In this context, the statement 'power to the people' by means of job development and education takes on a different meaning from the one given it by leading industrialists. 'The power' becomes not only a means of increasing the productivity and improving the competitiveness of individual companies, but also a means of making it possible in general to make decisions and to act in solidarity with people and the environment.

ACKNOWLEDGEMENT

I want to thank Gail FitzSimons, and Helle Alrø for their critical and constructive comments to an earlier version of this chapter which is produced as part of the research initiated by the Centre for Research in Learning Mathematics, Denmark, and funded by the Danish Research Councils.

NOTES

1 The English term 'qualification covers both actual qualification(s) and the process of becoming qualified. I use 'qualification' in both senses.
2 Knowing that mathematics knowledge is always contextualised, "Building Bridges" between mathematics and the real world is a big problem — both in theory and practice (Evans, 2000; Wedege, 2000). However this issue is not a theme of this chapter.

REFERENCES

Benn, R. (1997). *Adults Count Too: Mathematics for Empowerment*. Leicester: NIACE.
Cockroft, W. H. (1982) *Mathematics counts*. London: Her Majesty's Stationery Office.
Darrah, C. N. (1992) 'Workplace Skills in Context'. *Human Organization, 51*(3), 264-273.
Eraut, M. (1994) *Developing Professional Knowledge and Competence*. London: The Falmer Press.
Evans, J. (1989) 'The Politics of Numeracy'. In P. Ernest, (Ed.) *Mathematics Teaching. The State of Art*. London: The Falmer Press, 203-220.
Evans, J. (1999) 'Building Bridges: Reflections on the problem of transfer of learning in mathematics', Special Issue of *Educational Studies in Mathematics, 39*(1-3).
FitzSimons, G. E., Jungwirth, H., Maaß, J. & Schlöglmann, W. (1996), 'Adults and Mathematics (Adult Numeracy)'. In A. J. Bishop, K. Clements, C. Keitel, J. Kilpatrick & C. Laborde (Eds.), *International Handbook in Mathematics Education*. Dordrecht: Kluwer Academic, 755-784
Fragnière, G. (1996). 'Problems of Definition'. In OECD, *Assessing and Certifying Occupational Skills and Competences in Vocational Education and Training*. Paris: OECD, 39-58.
Harris, M. (1991). 'Looking for the Maths in Work'. In M. Harris (Ed.) *Schools, Mathematics and Work*. Philadelphia: Falmer Press, 132-144
Hogan, J. (1997) *Rich Interpretation of Using Mathematical Ideas and Techniques (RIUMIT)*. Final Report to the Commonwealth Department of Employment, Education, Training and Youth Affairs. Adelaide: Australian Association of Mathematics Teachers Inc.
Keitel, C. (1989). 'Mathematics Education and Technology'. *For the Learning of Mathematics*, 9(1), 7-13.
Lave, J. & Wenger, E. (1991) *Situated Learning. Legitimate Peripheral Participation*. Cambridge: Cambridge University Press.
Lindenskov, L. (1997) 'Developing guidance material to uncover a mathematics profile of adult participants on a crane course'. In D. Coben, & J. O'Donoghue (Comps). *Adults Learning Mathematics - 4. Proceedings of the Fourth International Conference of ALM*. London: Goldsmiths University of London, 129-133.
Maaß, J. (1998) 'Technology Transfer - A Useful Metaphor for University Level Mathematics Courses for Engineers and Scientists'. In D. Coben & J. O'Donoghue (Comps) *Proceedings of Adults Learning Mathematics - 4 the Fourth Conference of Adults Learning Maths - A Research Forum*, 4-6 July 97. London: Goldsmiths College, University of London, 58-62.
Negt, O. (1989). *Die Herausforderung der Gewerkschaften*. Frankfurt/Main; New York: Campus Verlag.

Niss, M. (1994).'Mathematics in society'. In R. Biehler, R. W. Scholz, R. Strässer & B. Winkelmann. (Eds.) *Didactics of Mathematics as a Scientific Discipline*. Dordrecht: Kluwer Academic Publishers, 367-378.

Olesen, H. Salling (1996) 'A New Concept of Qualification'. In H. S. Olesen & P. Rasmussen, (Eds.) *Theoretical Issues in Adult Education - Danish Research and Experiences*. Roskilde: Roskilde University Press, 65-86.

Schön, D. A. (1983) *The Reflective Practitioner. How Professionals Think in Action. USA*: Harper Collins Publishers.

Skovsmose, O. (1994). *Towards a Philosophy of Critical Mathematics Education*. Dordrecht: Kluwer Academic Publishers.

Skovsmose, O. (1998) 'Linking Mathematics Education and Democracy: Citizenship, Mathematical Archaeology, Mathemacy and Deliberative Interaction'. In Hartmut Köhler *Mathematics and Democracy*. Special issue, *Zentralblatt für Didaktik der Mathematik*. 6,195-203.

Strässer, R. (1996). *Mathematics for Work - a Didactical Perspective*. (Regular Lecture at ICME 8, Sevilla)

Wedege, T. (1995a) Teknologi, kvalifikationer og matematik. *Nordisk Matematikkdidaktikk*, vol.3/2, Juni 95, 29-51.

Wedege, T. (1995b).'Technological Competence and Mathematics'. In D. Coben, (Comp) *Mathematics with a Human Face. Proceedings of ALM-2 the Second Conference of Adults Learning Maths - A Research Forum*, 7-9 July 95. London: Goldsmiths College, University of London, 53-59.

Wedege, T. (1998). 'Adults Knowing and Learning Mathematics. An introduction to a new field of research between adult education and mathematics education'. In Tøsse, S, Bergstedt, B. Puurula, A, Falkencrone, P. (1998) *Corporate and Nonformal Learning. Adult Education Research in Nordic Countries*. Trondheim: Tapir Forlag, 177-197.

Wedege, T. (1999). 'To know — or not to know — mathematics, that is a question of context'. In P. Boero, *Teaching and Learning Mathematics in Context*. Special Issue, *Educational Studies in Mathematics. 39*(1-3), 205-227.

Wedege, T. (in press). 'Mathematical knowledge as a vocational qualification'. To be published in A. Bessot, & J. Ridgway. (Eds.) *Education for Mathematics in the Workplace*. Dordrecht: Kluwer Academic Publishers.

Chapter 12

Mathematics and the Vocational Education and Training System

Gail E. FitzSimons
Monash University/Swinburne University of Technology, Victoria, Australia

THE VOCATIONAL EDUCATION AND TRAINING SYSTEM

Introduction

In many English-speaking countries of the world by far the greater part of the vocational education and training (VET) sector is isolated from mainstream education, although there is some blurring of boundaries in the upper secondary school years and in some university offerings. Mathematics education in the VET sector has a history of conservatism and is now in danger of being marginalised as rapid institutional reform impacts upon the sector within an agenda of wider social and economic reforms. The aim of this chapter is to investigate and analyse the situation of mathematics education[4] within the vocational education and training (VET) sector from an Australian perspective.

The first section provides a brief introduction to dual interpretations of competence with respect to VET (see Wedege, this volume, for a fuller discussion). In the second section I will present an industry perspective on mathematics in our society from a selection of reports about the mathematical skills required in the workplace and the effects of the constantly changing nature of contemporary work. These findings have implications for VET curriculum and teaching; an important debate concerns issue of transfer. The third section deals with the practical aspects of

D. Coben et al. (eds.), Perspectives on Adults Learning Mathematics, 209–227.
© 2000 *Kluwer Academic Publishers. Printed in the Netherlands.*

teaching mathematics in the VET sector: curriculum, flexible delivery, assessment, and the professional development of mathematics teachers. The issue of research into mathematics education in the VET sector cannot be ignored although it faces the dual problem of marginalisation in both mathematics education and vocational education communities.

The politics of competence

Mathematics in the VET sector has evolved historically as instruction in trade- and technician-based calculations for students in the second tier of post-compulsory education - technical and vocational education has generally, but not always, been attributed a status subordinate to academic education. Recent developments in policy formation giving control of curriculum determination to employers or spokespersons from industry together with restricted possibilities for policy discourse have contributed to near total absence of public debate about the mathematics taught in the sector. This is in marked contrast to the lively debates that seem to accompany prospective and actual changes to school mathematics curricula, and even the possibility of government interference in the higher education sector's teaching effort. One major outcome of VET policy formation has been the imposition of competency-based education and training (CBT) and, although there has been violent opposition by spokespersons from higher education to its introduction in their sector, in recent years it has profoundly influenced curriculum and teaching in the VET sector and is likely to continue to do so. In Australia it has formed a strategic part of the implementation of economic rationalist policies based on training reform through its stranglehold on curriculum and assessment practices.

The processes of teaching and learning in the VET sector have been severely constrained by the imposition of a modernist CBT model whose enduring popularity appears to be attributable to its structural formation, ensuring accountability in an era where what can be *shown* to have taken place is of prime importance (Jackson, 1993, 1995). The mathematics curricula have become atomised, reduced to the lowest common denominator of what can be specified, and tested accordingly. Although CBT was supposed to support the development in students of a set of generic competencies claimed to be essential for participation in the workplace and adult life generally (see, for example, Wedege, this volume), there is little genuine connection between the nationally accredited mathematics curricula and the range of generic or key competencies promoted in Australia. Research indicates further that these competencies themselves are heavily context-bound, and their transfer is neither automatic nor assured (Billett, 1998; Down, 1997). The human capital paradigm, which has replaced that of social and personal development over the last two decades, has clearly shifted the focus of VET away from the students to industry, although such shifts appear to be cyclic (Stevenson, 1995; White, 1995). In the contestation of knowledge as the goal of vocational education and training, educational values have been subsumed by industrial values.

MATHEMATICS AND SOCIETY: AN INDUSTRY PERSPECTIVE

In this section I will consider a selection from reports that enquired into the mathematical content and processes required in the workplace. Early reports appear to be based on a more or less static view of the workplace. However assuming a stance from the workplace site - amidst the rapid change which is characteristic of the information society - offers a different perspective on the mathematical skills and competencies which might be useful. Discussion of the implications of explicit and implicit mathematics in society, together with the importance of decision making abilities, suggest that current vocational education and training curricula may be out of touch with the actual needs of students and industry.

Mathematics in the Workplace

Over the last three decades there have been reports in many countries about the mathematics (or numeracy) skills required in the workplace. This period has also seen the development of glossy posters, designed to give encouragement to young students, listing mathematical skills deemed useful for various occupations. It is doubtful that such posters were successful in their intentions, possibly because they were based on an unproblematic "tool-box" notion of mathematics. However, the grid-like appearance and essentialist character of some posters lives on in the formulation of CBT curricula.

There is a widespread belief that mathematics underpins and enables the technologies of industry (e.g. NBEET, 1995). Although the relationships between mathematics and society are manifold and complexly interrelated, the prime focus of the vocational education and training sector is its relationship with industry. The Cockcroft Report (1982) noted that because of (a) the diversity of types of employment, (b) the variety of mathematical demands within each, and (c) considerable differences found to exist within occupations which might be assumed from their titles to be similar, it was not feasible to produce definitive lists of necessary mathematical topics for each. However a feeling for measurement was considered to be of major importance, with or without the use of measuring instruments. Foyster (1988, 1990) also observed that there were differences in mathematical requirements at various stages of any career path, and complex relationships between the worker's range of duties and degree of responsibility which could vary with the size of the enterprise. In other words, it is not possible to formulate a deterministic relationship between mathematics and any one occupation. The Cockcroft Report has been criticised (e.g. Noss, 1997) for its decision to adopt a narrower definition of numeracy than the 1959 Crowther Report, and for its adoption of an overtly utilitarian bias. Perhaps not surprisingly for its era, it failed to address seriously the issue of transfer. It did, however, appear to pre-empt the literature on situated cognition with its observations about learning on-the-job (cf. community of practice) and use of out-of-school methods of calculation. It also observed that affordances to calculations are provided by the tools at hand, and that the frequent repetition of mathematical tasks renders them as "commonsense" (see also Coben, Harris, this volume).

A New Zealand study by Knight, Arnold, Carter, Kelly and Thornley (1992) found evidence of the use of generic skills of problem solving, as well as the need for optimisation or determination of a 'best strategy' for a task. In addition, the use of technologies were clearly becoming very common in the workplace. In the United Kingdom these skills have all been incorporated throughout the General National Vocational Qualifications (GNVQ) core skills units in Application of Number (BTEC, 1995). Wedege (this volume) discusses workplace research based on work shadowing into the key competency of using mathematical ideas and techniques conducted by the Australian Association of Mathematics Teachers (AAMT) (1997).

In summary, research reports on mathematics in the workplace such as these sustain the view that mathematics is indeed an integral and important part of many activities, but nevertheless context-bound. However, in general, the notion of the workplace appears to be taken as unproblematic.

Mathematics and Changing Workplaces

The contemporary world of business and industry is beginning to realise the value of human capital, and expecting more from workers at all levels. In the case of numeracy, the old expectation of demarcated work roles is being superseded, and limited expectations associated with the procedural skills of specific numeracies are being complemented by the need for generic or higher order thinking skills. According to Buckingham (1997:vii) generic numeracy is taken to include "higher order thinking skills which imply a capacity to use the techniques of mathematical modelling to control, plan and predict with a critical appreciation of the many factors that make up a production environment." Nevertheless it is recognised that numeracy in practice is relative to time and space and cannot be explicitly determined as either specific or generic.

Noss (1997) argued that sophisticated mathematical skills are required for interpretation of results as well as error detection or retrieval from catastrophic technological breakdown situations. He observed that although in many work situations there is less reliance on traditional school mathematics skills which can be carried out more efficiently by computers, there is a greater reliance on an ability to think in a mathematical way. There are complexities in relations between professional and mathematical knowledge, and workplace decisions are based on an interplay of these in any given situation. Pozzi, Noss and Hoyles (1998) found that, with nurses and bankers, there is a need to represent models in non-routine situations, and that a workplace mathematics far broader than basic numeracy is required when decisions become contested or problematic. However, Noss (1997:5-6) observed that because of this apparent invisibility of mathematics in adults' working lives their mathematical needs appear "both insignificant in quantity and trivial in quality", with serious implications for curricula. The research with bank workers indicated the perpetuation of Fordist and Taylorist ideas that the "effective management of the labour process demands the separation of conception from execution, the removal of human intellect from the working process, and the fragmentation and gradual removal of skills and craft knowledge" (1997: 10). It may be concluded that different mathematics, rather than less, are required to meet the needs of changing workplaces, located as they are in compressions of time and space.

As the society we now inhabit heads towards a global knowledge economy, a premium is being placed on the development of human capital. Unlike the Taylorist management model, organisations value the relationship between people's skills, their culture (values and norms) and their processes. Team work, communication, continuous learning at both the organisational and the individual level are sought (Buckingham, 1997; Marsick, 1997). An Australian report (NBEET, 1996:74) described the competency of information literacy as:

> a literacy that combines information collection and analysis and management skills and systems thinking and meta-cognition skills with the ability to use information technology to express and enhance those skills. In a society of information 'glut' the ability to detect 'signal' from 'noise' will become increasingly valued.

This competency is resonant with international goals for senior school and post-compulsory mathematics (e.g., BTEC, 1995; Cohen, 1995; NCTM, 1989) and with the key or core competencies; it now applies to workers at all classificatory levels, from operators to managers. Marsick (1997), discussing the learning organisation, claimed that it is the learning of individuals, and subsequently the entire system, which serves to make the creation and use of knowledge meaningful. In knowledge management the concern for people and the development of an appropriate workplace culture are much more important than, yet inseparable from, the transfer of information alone, or the installation of technology for greater efficiencies.

Buckingham's (1997) study emphasises the importance and enduring power of workplace discourses in mediating and driving workplace processes. Access to these discourses depends on organisational philosophy and the possibility of training modules to negotiate spaces for participation by workers. Wedege (this volume) describes access to participation in workplace discourses and decision-making which have implications for the development through education and training of workplace competence. Thus it is argued that there is a need for recognition of a broader generic approach to vocational and workplace mathematics education, to which I now turn.

Implications for Vocational Education and Training

In the first part of this section I will consider the impact of the concept of explicit and implicit mathematics in society in general, and for vocational education in particular. I will then discuss briefly implications of workplace research on mathematics curriculum and assessment, before moving on to consider the related issues of transfer and of institutions versus workplaces as sites of learning.

In disputing the claim that the ultimate reason for teaching mathematics is for its utility in practical and scientific enterprises in society (arguing that it should rather be taught as a cultural initiation), Chevallard (1989) elaborated the differences between explicit and implicit mathematics. Although it is the explicit uses in business and industry that are valorised, they are mostly concealed from view and, with the exception of arithmetic, not encountered by the general public; they are generally held to be synonymous with school mathematics. On the other hand, implicit mathematics is ubiquitous in its penetration of social and cultural life, embodied, crystallised or frozen into social objects. Social objects (material and non-material) with greater amounts of implicit mathematics are becoming more powerful and efficient, and are more widely available. Chevallard asserted that little or no knowledge of the mathematics used to establish a theorem or method is needed to use them relevantly, and that the average mathematical expertise required to consume mathematical goods and services decreases as their mathematical grade (or the amount of crystallised mathematics within them) increases. However, as discussed above, contestation or catastrophic change in the workplace alters the situation profoundly, as mathematical consumption metamorphoses to interpretation, problem solving, and even new knowledge production.

The distinctions between explicit and implicit mathematics and between specific and generic numeracies, highlight the dilemma confronting the construction of VET mathematics curricula:[5] deterministic or essentialist curricula cannot be justified. Unless thought is given to these distinctions, they are likely to reflect the popular view that less and less (explicit) mathematics is needed in any occupation. The perpetuation of modernist ideologies results in fragmented, hierarchical mathematics curricula which tend to reinforce the tradition of giving workers at the lower qualification levels a diet of solely specific numeracies, albeit garnished with vocational examples of at times spurious validity. This process is not only demeaning (and at times threatening) to the workers concerned, as they are positioned once more as educational "infants," but it also fails to recognise the actual knowledges and skills they possess which are often quite sophisticated, and frequently invisible (e.g., Harris, Wedege, this volume; O'Connor, 1994).

In apparent ignorance of the arguments for the non-viability of a unique hierarchical structure for mathematics (formal or informal) or for the acquisition of mathematical concepts (Ernest, 1991), Australian VET mathematics support-material for assessment outcomes lacks epistemological and psychological validity. With the few exceptions, the impact of twentieth century developments in applied mathematics and of continually evolving work practices, increasingly interlinked with technology, seems minimal. That is, students are still spending much of the limited time available practising routine mathematical skills which may be more efficiently computed by the use of workplace artefacts or electronic devices. Students are being denied potentially more useful and interesting applications of practical estimation, interpretation, evaluation, and error detection from numerical or graphical data based on real problems. The three-step, recipe-like, teaching method (introduction, condensed solution process, and schematised problems), found in German vocational colleges (Sträßer & Zevenbergen, 1996) is arguably more universal and indicates an impoverished pedagogical process which fails to link vocational and profession situations to mathematical concepts. This contextualised inter-relationship should be the prime focus of vocational education which is uniquely situated to avail itself of such possibilities.

There is a large body of research, including that written from a sociocultural perspective (e.g. Lave, 1988; Lave & Wenger, 1991), which indicates that there is no evidence that what is taught in school (or vocational) mathematics classrooms will transfer directly to the workplace. Masingila (1993) asserted that the so-called contextualised applications of typical textbooks are of little use in aiding transfer because they ignore the complexities inherent in any workplace. However, to increase the complexity of textbook problems would also increase the complexity of the reading required, and still not provide all of the affordances contributed to the formation and solution of problems posed in authentic settings. Boaler (1993) has suggested that transfer would be assisted by more open-ended solution paths so that learners can personally identify with the problems and also by helping the learner to generalise from the specific situation to the general. However, it is difficult to reconcile open-ended solutions with the prescriptive intent of much vocational curriculum and assessment, especially those coming under the hegemony of CBT. Clearly there has to be a balance between content and process, but there is an urgent need at all levels of education for students to be able to realistically model practical situations at levels appropriate to their abilities, and then to sensibly evaluate their solutions and reiterate if necessary.

The problems arising from issues of contextualisation and authenticity suggest that institutional learning (or text-based learning in workplace sites) is not necessarily a productive path to follow (Straesser, 1998). Billett, Cooper, Hayes, and Parker (1997) considered the issues of workplace learning, as an alternative or complement to learning in institutional settings, as the changing nature of work increasingly demands the ability to go beyond the routine and predictable. According to Billett et al., there are strengths and weaknesses of workplace participation. For example, there are advantages in activities which provide authentic goal-directed activities that press workers into learning which extends and reinforces their knowledge. Disadvantages include inaccessibility or opaqueness of knowledge because of lack of access, expertise, or co-operation in the workplace. Regardless of how authentic an institutional education tries to be it is always removed to some degree from the exigencies of the workplace. On the other hand, knowledge for workplace performance is often highly complex and takes time for robust construction to develop. As Billett et al. (1997:47) noted, both trades and professions have mandated extensive periods of workplace experience as a requirement to develop vocational knowledge. They conclude that "it is the quality and combination of experiences and guidance that are furnished in each environment which are likely to determine the robustness of the constructed knowledge". This conclusion is supported by Brown (1998).

Collins (1997) addressed the problem of students' preparation for a changing workplace by recommending the adoption of cognitive apprenticeship methods as proposed by Collins, Brown and Newman (1989, cited in Collins, 1997). However, the authors' claim that the principles of cognitive apprenticeship could be applied in workplace or institutional settings has been criticised by Kirshner and Whitson (1997) as not having a strong claim to theoretical legitimacy as an educational model.

According to Kanes (1997a, 1997b: 264), a burgeoning literature suggests that mathematical knowledge is comprised of sets of socially organised beliefs and practices, and is not mind-independent, nor made up of pre-given essences. Whereas an essentialist perspective renders the assumption of transfer from classroom to worksite unproblematic, Kanes asserted that viewing mathematics as a construction of some kind opens the possibilities of synthesis of knowledges at the site of use. One approach to mathematical knowledge, as distinct from the information processing and constructivist models, is as socially situated. Kanes's (1997b) summary of the literatures sees mathematical knowledge as "distributed within collective practice relating to a particular set of work or other culturally related tasks"). Lave and Wenger (1991) proposed that learning is a process of participation in communities of practice, gradually increasing in engagement and complexity - legitimate peripheral participation. Knowledge use then, according to Kanes, is equivalent to such participation, rather than either the far transfer of specific content and procedural knowledge or the individual construction of local knowledge.

In order to gain a deeper understanding of mathematics in the workplace Kanes (1997b) drew on the work of activity theorists on the use of mediating actions and tools. Based on his analysis of transactions at an airlines check-in desk, using the theoretical framework of mediating artifacts Kanes (1997b: 269) made the following suggestions:

1. . . . the workplace itself has primacy within the organisation and implementation of workplace knowledge -- thus any approach to workplace task competency should proceed from a detailed knowledge of the particular occupational situation, not an abstract set of numerical knowledge statements.
2. . . . numerical knowledge does not enter the workplace as a pre-given entity.
3. . . . numerical knowledge is not used as a unitary mathematico-logical structure within workplace sites. Analysis . . . suggests that numerical workplace knowledge is better seen as a body of fragmented knowledge.
4. . . . the logic of this fragmentation is governed by the character of mediating artefacts within task performance.

This research brings into question the issue of transfer and the implicit essentialist underpinnings typical of much VET mathematics curriculum and assessment practice.

A revolutionary approach to mathematics curriculum formation is needed - not as the grand narrative of a national curriculum which makes prescriptions for all workers in an industry or complex of industries, but at a more or less local level so that students are able to gain some experience in transferring their knowledge as well as utilising in a practical sense their non-mathematical knowledge. A mathematically informed analysis of occupational needs is necessary, supplemented by detailed knowledge of the occupation or broader vocation (e.g. Noss, Hoyles, & Pozzi, in press). Rather than a traditional functional analysis (e.g. Blackmore, 1999; Johnstone, 1993), vocational and mathematics educators need to work in collaboration with each other and with people actually employed in such work. The seeds of this approach can be seen in team teaching between mathematics and vocational educators (see below), but clearly a continuing program of research is needed.

Achtenhagen (1994) detailed some of the findings of a lengthy German research project making vocational business courses more relevant to students and industry. One major shift is the replacement of the hierarchical curriculum model, depicted by linear grids of sequential curricula, with an interlinked concept-map model which reflects more accurately the actual needs and constraints of the workplace. In this way the curriculum can be integrated, in line with situated cognition theory, thus enhancing the possibility of transfer. Randall (1997) described an example of 'course-congruent' additional mathematical support for an engineering course where mathematics was relegated to 'underpinning knowledge.' Mathematical skills were taught as and when they were needed, providing immediate relevance, and students were surprised when enlightened with their own mathematical achievements. However, this approach also effectively camouflaged the mathematics, which Wilkinson (1991: 76) suggested could disadvantage those who "are destined to be users and developers of higher mathematics" - or any mathematics for that matter.

Of course it must be recognised that vocational education is not solely concerned with meeting the needs of industry; the social needs of students for democratic competence must also be addressed (Niss, 1996; Skovsmose, 1994). In any case, these cannot be entirely separated from the workplace as skills of negotiation and decision making are an integral part of workplaces (Buckingham 1997; Wedege, 1995; this volume).

In summary, the evidence from workplace research suggests that the present formation of vocational mathematics curriculum is not viable, premised as it is on an unproblematic notion of transfer and hierarchical, essentialist notions of curriculum and learning. In the reformulation of curricula, many goals need to be taken into account (Bishop, 1993; Niss, 1996); it is not simply a matter of matching the curricula to the perceived needs of the employer which would serve neither the interests of individual students nor society at large. In fact, from the literature on changing workplaces and the new work order, industry will not be well served by a reliance on epistemologies and pedagogies grounded in eras of the past. Ultimately the quality and robustness of learning outcomes is a reflection of the combination of curriculum, teaching, and environment(s) which facilitate transfer.

MATHEMATICS EDUCATION IN VOCATIONAL EDUCATION AND TRAINING

This section will provide a critique of aspects of the existing system. The first is teaching in relation to flexible delivery, assessment, and professional development. The second is the issue of educational research which has traditionally avoided this marginalised sector, but which has in recent years been encouraged by governmental resurgence of interest in the concept of lifelong learning.

Mathematics Teaching

Apart from the curriculum, the teacher's knowledge of mathematics together with pedagogical content knowledge and reasoning (Brown & Borko, 1992) are critical factors in mathematics instruction. In Australia at least it may be to assumed that a large majority of VET mathematics classes (in face-to-face or flexible delivery modes) are characterised by traditional pedagogies resting on transmission epistemologies typical of decades gone by.

The term *flexible delivery* as used here - rather than its connotation of teachers accommodating the times and locations required by the enterprise in industry-based teaching - implies the use of self-paced learning materials, generally print-based but sometimes utilising electronic media, together with some form of occasional personal interaction with a tutor. It shifts the balance of responsibility and often costs to the learner, presenting additional problems for those with literacy and/or language difficulties or time management problems (Misko, 1994), and is associated with the trend towards commodification of education. Also, when prime responsibility for production of educational materials shifts from discipline specialists to educational technologists the learning of students already at risk is likely to suffer. However, this is not to deny its obvious advantages for capable, well-motivated students, especially those with limited access to educational institutions for reasons of distance, time, institutionalisation, and so on. To date there has not been a great deal of research to determine the efficacy of this mode in relation to mathematics education.

Assessment to industry standards is now the prime focus of the Australian VET sector. The rhetoric addressed to teachers in support documentation makes general statements about assessment being fair, equitable and varied, but generally falls short of offering much practical advice as to how these may be achieved. Although CBT encourages the use of assessment which demonstrates what the student can do in a practical sense, there is a great difference between certifying competence in a practical scientific technique and a theoretical mathematical technique. The former is observable and hopefully supported by underpinning knowledge. The latter, in a classroom test situation, is likely to be a carefully rehearsed academic routine. There is of course no guarantee that what can be performed in a mathematics class will transfer when and where it is needed. On the other hand, Cumming (in press) foregrounded some of the difficulties inherent in an uncritical acceptance of authentic assessment.

However, it is likely that few teachers of mathematics subjects in the VET sector would have considered research on assessment of mathematics (e.g. Clarke, 1996; Galbraith, 1995a, 1995b; NCTM, 1995), and even fewer as part of formal pre-service, in-service, or post-graduate study. Whether they reflect on current practice and then actively seek to improve upon it will depend on a range of factors, one of which is their knowledge of recent findings of research. In this, as in their teaching practice, a vital factor is the availability of professional development in the formal provision of seminars, conferences, and post-graduate studies, together with informal reading of professional journals, discussion with colleagues, and so on. In comparison to other sectors of education, professional development specific to mathematics education in this sector seems to be a very low priority, apart from numeracy teachers.

Within the VET sector many teachers have little more mathematical background than contained in the mathematics subjects they teach. Although internationally there are documents which make recommendations for the initial and ongoing professional development of teachers of school mathematics (e.g. NCTM, 1991), there are few guidelines for teachers in the VET sector. Following the NCTM model, the American Mathematical Association of Two-Year Colleges (Cohen, 1995) made five research-based recommendations for pedagogy. However, changing teachers' practice involves more than rhetoric or one-day seminars, no matter how well intentioned.

In Australia the responsibility for the professional development of vocational teachers has been transferred from the systemic to the individual provider level. This devolution means that within an institute there is very little likelihood of teachers of mathematics subjects being: (a) offered professional development appropriate to their individual needs, (b) aware of the existence of any such professional development, or (c) encouraged (or even allowed) to attend. For teachers employed by other providers the chances are more remote. The intensification of teachers' working conditions, together with the devolution of previously centralised teacher support services has virtually isolated mathematics teachers within institutions and even within individual trade or vocational departments, following the demise of mathematics departments. Networks which existed previously have become defunct. There is little or no incentive for VET teachers to undertake post-graduate qualifications in (mathematics) education - especially as they are now required to meet some or all of the full cost.

Apart from critiquing one's own practice and the social and cultural institutions within which it is set, one of the important roles of professional development is the dissemination of the findings of recent research.

Research in VET

The issues associated with the teaching and learning of mathematics in the VET sector have been largely ignored by the mathematics education community, although the situation is starting to change in Australia (e.g. FitzSimons, 1996b) and internationally (e.g. FitzSimons (Ed.), 1997, FitzSimons & Godden, this volume; Strässer, 1994, 1996).

Sweet (1994) noted that in Australia in the past there has been a tendency for scholars to ignore the VET sector, although this has recently begun to change with targeted allocations of national and state research funding (see also Brown & Keep, 1999; and the Journal of Vocational Education and Training website, www.leeds.ac.uk/educol/jvet99.htm; in relation to the UK). There are several broad issues associated with research in the sector; for example the debate about the funding and control (Seddon, 1997). There is a need on one hand to overcome perceptions that research (especially government-funded) is to validate predetermined outcomes. On the other hand Seddon warned that there is also a need to avoid undermining the generalisation of research by tending towards the more specialist, exclusive practices characteristic of some academics.

Recent experience in Australia indicates that funded research is primarily concerned with managerial issues, and rarely focused on issues of teaching and learning - and even then only in the workplace. Mathematics is generally labelled as numeracy and often bracketed with literacy (Buckingham's 1997 research on workplace numeracies provides a notable exception.) The last major funding for a vocational mathematics curriculum project (ACTRAC, 1993; Pantlin & Marr, 1992) required neither critique nor problematisation of existing curricula - the focus was on rationalisation and appropriation by

CBT. This lack of discipline-based mathematics education research has, among other things, resulted in the limited impact of technology as an object in preparation for the demands of the changing workplace and as a potential tool for teaching - except in rhetoric! It is only recently that the actual mathematical requirements of changing workplaces are beginning to be researched internationally (e.g. Bessot & Ridgway, in preparation; Wedege, this volume).

CONCLUSION

This chapter has explored issues associated with the teaching of mathematics in the vocational education and training sector, focusing on the Australian situation but from which parallels may be drawn to varying degrees with other industrialised countries. It has attempted to provide some explanations for the present situation of mathematics education in the sector. It would appear that mathematics education *per se* is not valued, either in comparison to other educational sectors or within an industry-focused sector where the major preoccupation of management appears (especially to its teachers) to be financial accountability.

The simplest and most obvious explanation for the apparent lack of valuing of mathematics education by management in the VET institutional system is that it has no industry of its own within this vocational realm, that is no substantial support base - critical to this sector of education. Another possible area of explanation lies with the values attributed to the discipline of mathematics by the various stakeholders in the VET sector. Mathematics clearly has a high status in our society (Apple, 1992; Martin 1988/1997; Popkewitz, 1988) and yet the same values which establish its power and invincibility (e.g. Bishop, 1988) serve to alienate or intimidate many people among whom are those responsible for making decisions in vocational education and training (See FitzSimons, 1998a & b, for further discussion).

The sector is complex, continually evolving, and vulnerable to the political influences of the day. Over a quarter of a century ago Myer Kangan (1974/1979: 9) summarised his approach to vocational education and training:

> One thing, however, seems clear, and that is the acceptance of a belief that people do not exist for the good of industry, but rather the reverse, that industry and commerce exist for the good of society.

> Although society is much more than a collection of individuals, its level of sophistication can be no higher than the capacity - and, of course, the willingness - of individuals to contribute collectively.

> This is what education in our time should be about - increasing the collective capacity of individuals to contribute to the good of society - their own good.

In times of economic rationalism we must not lose sight of these ideals!

ACKNOWLEDGEMENT

I wish to thank Tine Wedege and John O'Donoghue and the anonymous reviewers for their critical and constructive comments on an earlier version of this chapter.

NOTES

1 A broad definition of mathematics education will be adopted which includes numeracy, trade calculations, and statistics, for example, whether formally identified as such or embedded within other vocational courses.
2 In Australia curricula are no longer prescribed in an assessment-driven system. Competence is to be judged against industry standards.

REFERENCES

Achtenhagen, F. (1994). 'How should research on vocational and professional education react to new challenges in life and in the workplace?' In W. J. Nijhof & J. N. Streumer (Eds.), *Flexibility in training and vocational education* . Utrecht: Uitgeverij Lemma, 201-247.

Apple, M. W. (1992). 'Do the Standards go far enough? Power, policy, and practice in mathematics education'. *Journal for Research in Mathematics Education, 23*(5), 412-431.

Australian Association of Mathematics Teachers (AAMT). (1997). *Final report of the Rich Interpretation of Using Mathematical Ideas and Techniques Key Competency Project.* Adelaide, SA: Author.

Australian Committee on Training Curriculum (ACTRAC). (1993). *National Vocational Mathematics Curriculum Project. Curriculum Framework (Draft).* Canberra, ACT: Commonwealth of Australia.

Bessot, A. & Ridgway, J. (Eds.) (in preparation). *Education for mathematics in the workplace.* Dordrecht: Kluwer.

Billett, S., Cooper, M., Hayes, S. & Parker, H. (1997). *VET policy and research: Emerging issues and changing relationships. A report for the Office of Training and Further Education, Victoria.* Melbourne, Vic.: Office of Training and Further Education.

Billett, S. (1998). 'Transfer and social practice.' *Australian & New Zealand Journal of Vocational Education Research, 6*(1), 1-25.

Bishop, A. J. (1988). *Mathematical enculturation.* Dordrecht: Kluwer.

Bishop, A. J. (1993). 'On determining new goals for mathematical education'. In C. Keitel & K. Ruthven (Eds.), *Learning from computers: Mathematics education and technology.* Berlin: Springer Verlag, 222-242.

Blackmore, P. (1999). 'A categorisation of approaches to occupational analysis'. *Journal of Vocational Education and Training*, 51(1), 61-76.

Boaler, J. (1993). 'The role of contexts in the mathematics classroom: Do they make mathematics more "real"?' *For the Learning of Mathematics, 13*(2), 12-17.

Brown, A. (1998). 'Designing effective learning programs for the development of a broad occupational competence'. In W.M. Nijhof & J.N. Streumer (Eds), *Key qualifications in work and education*. Dordrecht: Kluwer Academic Publishers, 165-186.

Brown, A. & Keep, E. (1999). *Review of vocational education and training research in the United Kingdom*. Warwick, UK: Institute for Employment Research, University of Warwick.

Brown, C. A., & Borko, H. (1992). 'Becoming a mathematics teacher'. In D. A. Grouws (Ed.), *Handbook of research on mathematics teaching and learning*. New York, NY: Macmillan, 222-242.

BTEC (1995). *Core skills units: Application of number (levels 1-3)*. London: National Council of Vocational Qualifications.

Buckingham, E. A. (1997). *Specific and generic numeracies of the workplace: How is numeracy learnt and used by workers in production industries, and what learning/working environments promote this?* Burwood, Vic.: Centre for Studies in Mathematics, Science, and Environmental Education, Deakin University.

Chevallard, Y. (1989).' Implicit mathematics: Their impact on societal needs and demands.' In J. Malone, H. Burkhardt, & C. Keitel (Eds.), *The mathematics curriculum: Towards the year 2000* . Perth, WA: Curtin University of Technology, 49-57.

Clarke, D. (1996). 'Assessment'. In A. J. Bishop, K. Clements, C. Keitel, J. Kilpatrick, & C. Laborde (Eds.), *International handbook of mathematics education* . Dordrecht: Kluwer, 327-370.

Cockcroft, W. H. (Chairman). (1982). *Mathematics counts: Report of the Committee of Inquiry into the Teaching of Mathematics in Schools*. London: Her Majesty's Stationery Office.

Cohen, D. (Ed.) (1995). *Crossroads in mathematics*: *Standards for introductory college mathematics before calculus*. Memphis, TN: American Mathematical Association of Two-Year Colleges (AMATYC).

Collins, A. (1997). 'Cognitive apprenticeship and the changing workplace'. Keynote address in *Good thinking - Good practice: Research perspectives on learning and work. Proceedings of the 5th Annual International Conference on Post-Compulsory Education and Training*. Brisbane, Qld.: Centre for Learning and Work Research, Griffith University.

Crowther Report. (1959). *15 to 18: A report of the Central Advisory Council for Education*. London: Her Majesty's Stationery Office.

Cumming, J. J. (in press). 'Towards a theoretical base for assessment in adult numeracy'. In J. Izard (Ed.), *Assessment practices in the mathematical sciences*. Melbourne, Vic.: Australian Council for Educational Research.

Down, C. M. (1997, July). *Tapping into commonsense and experience: Using the Key Competencies to enhance workplace practice*. Paper presented at the National Centre for Vocational Education Research 1997 Vocational Education and Training Research Conference. Melbourne, Vic.: University of Melbourne.

Ernest, P. (1991). *The philosophy of mathematics education*. Hampshire, UK: Falmer.

FitzSimons, G. E. (1996a).'Is there a place for the history and pedagogy of mathematics in adult education under economic rationalism?' In *Proceedings of the História e Educação Matemática conference* (Vol. 2). Braga: HEM Braga 96, 128-135.

FitzSimons, G. E. (1996b). 'Understanding the adult learner of mathematics'. In B. Atweh, K. Owens, & P. Sullivan (Eds.), *Research in Mathematics Education in Australasia 1992-*

1995. Campbelltown, NSW: Mathematics Education Research Group of Australasia, 151-180.

FitzSimons, G. E. (1997a). 'Gender issues in adult and vocational mathematics education' *Mathematics Education Research Journal, 9*(3), 292-311.

FitzSimons, G. E. (1997b). 'Research Perspectives on Vocational Mathematics'. In *Good thinking - Good practice: Research perspectives on learning and work. Proceedings of the 5th Annual International Conference on Post-Compulsory Education and Training* (Vol. 3). Brisbane, Qld.: Centre for Learning and Work Research, Griffith University, 163-174.

FitzSimons, G. E. (1998a). 'New times for mathematics in vocational education and training'. In C. Kanes, M. Goos, & E. Warren (Eds.), *Teaching mathematics in new times* (Vol. 1). Griffith University, Brisbane: Mathematics Education Research Group of Australasia, 194-200.

FitzSimons, G. E. (1998b). 'The Institution of Mathematics in Vocational Education and Training'. In *Vocational knowledge and institutions: Changing relationships. Proceedings of the 6th Annual International Conference on Post-Compulsory Education and Training* (Vol. 3). Brisbane: Centre for Learning and Work Research, Griffith University, 79-88.

FitzSimons, G. E. (Ed.) (1997). *Adults returning to study mathematics: Papers from Working Group 18, 8th International Congress on Mathematical Education, ICME 8.* Adelaide, SA: Australian Association of Mathematics Teachers.

Foyster, J. (1988). *Maths beyond the classroom.* Canberra, ACT: Curriculum Development Centre.

Foyster, J. (1990). 'Beyond the mathematics classroom: Numeracy on the job'. In S. Willis (Ed.), *Being numerate: What counts?* Melbourne, Vic.: Australian Council for Educational Research, 119-137.

Galbraith, P. L. (1995a). 'Assessment in mathematics: Developments, innovations and challenges'. In L. Grimison & J. Pegg (Eds.), *Teaching secondary school mathematics: Theory into practice* . Sydney, NSW: Harcourt Brace, 289-314.

Galbraith, P. L. (1995b). 'Assessment in mathematics: Purposes and traditions.' In L. Grimison & J. Pegg (Eds.), *Teaching secondary school mathematics: Theory into practice.* Sydney, NSW: Harcourt Brace, 271-288.

Jackson, N. (1993). 'If competence is the answer, what is the question?' *Australian & New Zealand Journal of Vocational Education Research, 1*(1), 46-60.

Jackson, N. (1995). ''These things just happen': Talk, text, and curriculum reform'. In M. Campbell & A. Manicom (Eds.), *Knowledge, experience, and ruling relations: Studies in the social organization of knowledge.* Toronto: University of Toronto, 164-180.

Johnstone, I. (1993). 'Models for competency and competency-based curricula for science technicians.' *Unicorn, 19*(4), 66-71.

Kanes, C. (1997a). 'An investigation of artifact mediation and task organisation involving numerical workplace knowledge'. In *Good thinking - Good practice: Research perspectives on learning and work. Proceedings of the 5th Annual International Conference on Post-Compulsory Education and Training* (Vol. 1). Brisbane, Qld.: Centre for Learning and Work Research, Griffith University, 79-91.

Kanes, C. (1997b). 'Towards an understanding of numerical knowledge in the workplace'. In F. Biddulph & K. Carr (Eds.), *People in mathematics education* (Vol. 1). University of Waikato, NZ: Mathematics Education Research Group of Australasia, 263-270.

Kangan, M. (1979). 'A comment on 'TAFE in Australia.'' In D. McKenzie & C. Wilkins (Eds.), *The TAFE papers.* Melbourne: Macmillan. 6-20. (Reprinted from a paper presented at a Conference of the Technical Teachers Association of Victoria, June 1974.)

Kirshner, D. & Whitson, J. A. (1997). 'Editors' introduction to Situated cognition: Social, semiotic, and psychological perspectives'. In D. Kirshner & J. A. Whitson (Eds.), *Situated cognition: Social, semiotic, and psychological perspectives*. NJ: Lawrence Erlbaum, 1-16.

Knight, G., Arnold, G., Carter, M., Kelly, P. & Thornley, G. (1992). *The mathematical needs of New Zealand school leavers: A research report*. Palmerston North: Massey University.

Lave, J. (1988). *Cognition in practice: Mind, mathematics and culture in every day life*. Cambridge: Cambridge University Press.

Lave, J., & Wenger, E. (1991). *Situated learning: Legitimate peripheral participation*. Cambridge: Cambridge University Press.

Marsick, V. J. (1997). 'Current thinking on the learning organization'. Keynote address in *Good thinking - Good practice: Research perspectives on learning and work. Proceedings of the 5th Annual International Conference on Post-Compulsory Education and Training*. Brisbane, Qld.: Centre for Learning and Work Research, Griffith University.

Martin, B. (1997). 'Mathematics and social interests'. In A. B. Powell & M. Frankenstein (Eds.), *Ethnomathematics: Challenging eurocentrism in mathematics education*. Albany, NY: State University of New York, 155-171. (Reprinted from *Search, 19*(4), 1988, 209-214)

Masingila, J. (1993). 'Learning from mathematics practice in out-of-school situations'. *For the Learning of Mathematics, 13*(2), 18-22.

Misko, J. (1994). *Flexible delivery: Will a client focus system mean better learning?* Leabrook, SA: National Centre for Vocational Education Research.

National Board of Employment, Education and Training (NBEET). (1995a). *Education and technology convergence: A survey of technological infrastructure in education and the professional development and support of educators and trainers in information and communications technologies*. Commissioned Report No. 43, Employment and Skills Council. Canberra, ACT: Australian Government Publishing Service.

National Board of Employment, Education and Training (NBEET). (1995b). *Mathematical sciences: Adding to Australia*. Canberra, ACT: Australian Government Publishing Service.

National Council of Teachers of Mathematics. (1989). *Curriculum and evaluation standards for school mathematics*. Reston, VA: Author.

National Council of Teachers of Mathematics. (1991). *Professional standards for teaching mathematics*. Reston, VA: Author.

National Council of Teachers of Mathematics. (1995). *Assessment standards for school mathematics*. Reston, VA: Author.

Niss, M. (1996). 'Goals of mathematics teaching'. In A. J. Bishop, K. Clements, C. Keitel, J. Kilpatrick, & C. Laborde (Eds.), *International handbook of mathematics education*. Dordrecht: Kluwer, 11-47.

Noss, R. (1997). *New cultures, new numeracies*. Inaugural professorial lecture. London: Institute of Education, University of London.

Noss, R., Hoyles, C. & Pozzi, S. (in press). 'Working knowledge: Mathematics in use.' In A. Bessot & J. Ridgway (Eds.), *Education for mathematics in the workplace*. Dordrecht: Kluwer Academic Press.

O'Connor, P. (1994). 'Workplaces as sites of learning'. In P. O'Connor (Ed.), *Thinking Work: Vol. 1. Theoretical perspectives on workers' literacies*. Sydney, NSW: Adult Literacy and Basic Skills Action Coalition, 257-295.

Pantlin, K. & Marr, D. (1992) *National Mathematics Curriculum Project: Stage 1 report*. Canberra, ACT: ACT Institute of TAFE.

Popkewitz, T. S. (1988). 'Institutional issues in the study of school mathematics: Curriculum research'. *Educational Studies in Mathematics, 19*, 221-249.

Pozzi, S., Noss, R. & Hoyles, C. (1998). 'Tools in practice, mathematics in use'. *Educational Studies in Mathematics*, 36(2), 105-122.

Randall, C. (1997). 'Additional maths support in vocational courses'. In *ALM-3: Proceedings of the Third Annual Conference of Adults Learning Mathematics - A Research Forum*. London: Goldsmiths College, University of London, 135-143.

Seddon, T. (1997). 'Good thinking, good practice: Institutional design for research in VET: Supporting interests or protecting disinterest?' Keynote address in *Good thinking - Good practice: Research perspectives on learning and work. Proceedings of the 5th Annual International Conference on Post-Compulsory Education and Training*. Brisbane, Qld.: Centre for Learning and Work Research, Griffith University.

Skovsmose, O. (1994). *Towards a philosophy of critical mathematics education*. Dordrecht: Kluwer.

Soucek, V. 'Is there a need to redress the balance between systems goal and lifeworld-oriented goals in public education in Australia?' In C. Collins (Ed.), *Competencies: The competencies debate in Australian education and training*. Canberra, ACT: Australian College of Education, 162-181.

Stevenson, J. C. (1995, October). *The metamorphosis of the construction of competence*. Inaugural professorial lecture. Brisbane: Griffith University.

Strässer, R. (1994).' Mathematics for work: Vocational education. Report of Topic Group 3'. In C. Gaulin, B. R. Hodgson, D. H. Wheeler, & J. C. Egsgard (Eds.), *Proceedings of the 7th International Congress on Mathematics Education*. Québec: Université Laval, 244-246.

Strässer, R. (1998). 'Mathematics for work: A didactical perspective'. In C. Alsina, J.M. Alvarez, B. Hodgson, C. Laborde & A. Pérez (Eds.), *8th International Congress on Mathematics Education: Selected lectures*. Sevilla: S.A.E.M. 'THALES', 427-441.

Sträßer, R., & Zevenbergen, R. (1996). 'Further mathematics education'. In A. J. Bishop, K. Clements, C. Keitel, J. Kilpatrick, & C. Laborde (Eds.), *International handbook of mathematics education*. Dordrecht: Kluwer, 647-674.

Sweet, R. (1994). 'Why isn't there more research on vocational education and training in Australia?' *Making research work for vocational education: Papers and proceedings of the Victorian Training Research Conference*. Melbourne, Vic.: Office of Training & Further Education in Victoria.

Wedege, T. (1995). 'Technological competence and mathematics'. In *Mathematics with a human face: Proceedings of the second international conference of Adults Learning Mathematics - A Research Forum*. London: Goldsmiths College, University of London, 53-59.

Wedege, T. (2000). 'To know - or not to know - mathematics, that is a question of context'. *Educational Studies in Mathematics*, 39(1-3).

Wilkinson, T. S. (1991). 'Mathematics education post-GCSE: An industrial viewpoint'. In M. Harris (Ed.), *Schools, mathematics and work*. Basingstoke, UK: Falmer, 71-76.

White, M. (1995). 'Youth, employment and post-compulsory education: Crisis policy making in three depression decades in Australia - the 1890s, the 1930s and the 1980s'. *Australian & New Zealand Journal of Vocational Education Research*, 3(1), 110-140.

Section IV: Perspectives in Teaching Adults Mathematics

Introduction

John O'Donoghue
University of Limerick, Limerick, Ireland

The first principle of adult education is that adults should be treated as adults in the educational enterprise. There is widespread agreement among adult educators, based on the work of Knowles, Rogers and others, that teaching adults calls for different approaches than teaching children (e.g. Knowles, 1990; Rogers, 1986). The simple truth that adults differ from children, is seen as having methodological implications for their education. There is evidence in this section and elsewhere, (e.g. FitzSimons, 1997), that practitioners and researchers in adults' mathematics education are taking methodological issues seriously.

Anyone engaged in teaching mathematics to adult learners will confront a variety of issues. Issues such as the design of the mathematics curriculum; learning environment and resources; mathematics content and activities; assessment; and learners' attitudes and prior experience of mathematics if any, must figure prominently in any debate on teaching. Adult learners bring a lot to the educational enterprise, for good or ill, as the case may be. Adult educators need to take cognisance of this in their practice. As regards mathematics, it is more often the case than not that adult learners bring with them poor perceptions of mathematics re-inforced by negative attitudes arising out of their experience of school mathematics and associated pedagogical practices. The inescapable reality for those working with adults is that mathematics as seen through the eyes of adult learners is the antithesis of what tutors would like. Mathematics for these learners is difficult to learn; evokes negative emotions; is associated with failure; presents an obstacle to job promotion; constitutes a bar to further education; and

D. Coben et al. (eds.), Perspectives on Adults Learning Mathematics, 229–234.
© *2000 Kluwer Academic Publishers. Printed in the Netherlands.*

perpetuates inequality in society. Already the educational die is loaded against success for a significant proportion of adult learners of mathematics.

School mathematics is intimately related to adult education in mathematics. It is the recognised vehicle for the mathematical preparation of children for adult life. It serves as a touchstone for adult education programmes in mathematics, and is implicated in adult learners' preparedness and disposition toward more study in mathematics at basic or higher levels. Not surprisingly, school mathematics is more notorious for its failures than its successes since the price of failure is high for adults and society. Failure is experienced as low levels of mathematical competence in the adult population, levels that are deemed inadequate for effective participation in future society (National Research Council, 1989; Bynner & Parsons, 1997). Reports citing low levels of numeracy in the adult population are common (Basic Skills Agency, 1997). This is puzzling for mathematics educators when one of the principal goals for school mathematics everywhere is to prepare school children for adult life (Cockcroft, 1982; NCTM, 1989). The evidence suggests that this goal is largely unrealized, and the legacy of school mathematics is not a good one for adult education in mathematics whether it focuses on adult numeracy or is concerned with adult learners higher up the education ladder.

These problems of adult numeracy are universal where organized education exists but they are exacerbated in developing countries by a variety of circumstances including extreme poverty, failure to implement universal elementary or secondary education, social and political struggles, and devastation due to war, famine and natural causes.

It would be wrong to assume that all adult education in mathematics is concerned with numeracy or adult basic education. This is patently not the case. Adults have been studying mathematics in colleges and universities for decades as adult returners or mature-aged students availing of part-time, evening and continuing professional programmes of one kind or another. By and large they have remained invisible because they were treated the same as traditional-age students. Consequently, their mathematics education posed no new methodological questions for these institutions or their teachers. But this state of affairs is changing. Adults are becoming visible in college and university programmes for a number of reasons, not least being the fact that mature-age students constitute a significant proportion of the student body in many countries worldwide e.g. UK, Australia, and the U.S. Programmes which give special attention to the mathematical needs of adult returners and mature-aged students are now relatively common (see FitzSimons, 1997). They include Access programmes, for disadvantaged groups in society; bridging programmes, and special foundation courses for first-time adult learners or adult returners. This work is gaining momentum worldwide as special interests groups are formed at national/international level to support and advance practice and research in this area of adults' mathematics education e.g. *Adults Learning Mathematics - A Research Forum (ALM), Bridging Mathematics Network (BMN)*, (Australia/New Zealand), *American Mathematical Association of Two-Year Colleges (AMATYC)*. This interest and activity is unlikely to abate in developed countries as governments increasingly are encouraging adults to return to study in higher education as demographic factors impact on economic policy, and for other social and educational reasons.

In this context, the challenge for mathematics educators is to find effective ways to teach mathematics to a diverse population of adult learners with mixed attitudes towards mathematics and different aspirations, who are underprepared for post-secondary education in mathematics. The work of the American Mathematical Association of Two-Year Colleges is very significant in this regard because it offers a framework for developing programmes, and deals with the special needs of adult learners (AMATYC, 1995). They make the case for a foundation course that is based more on adult learners needs and interests than on their mathematical deficiencies and in this way they purposely steer clear of a deficit model for adults' mathematics education. This stance is very much in keeping with practice and research discussed in these chapters. As contributors deal with what now appear to be universal problems in adults' mathematics education namely, teaching algebra, developing appropriate assessments, devising special transition programmes or shedding light on the transfer of skills debate, one is struck by the centrality of adults' interests and *their* needs.

Kathy Safford's research with adult students returning to study mathematics at university is the basis of her contribution to this section. In her chapter, Safford describes an experimental algebra course for adult returners at Rutgers University using multiple perspectives as member of the course design team, course tutor and mathematics education researcher. The course design and pedagogical methods of the Introduction to Algebra for Adult Students (IAAS) course were influenced by the recommendations of the National Council of Teachers of Mathematics *Standards* document (NCTM, 1989). Teaching methods were based on the constructivist paradigm of teacher as facilitator and learner as builder of his/her own knowledge and understanding. A truly purist approach was eschewed in favour of a more pragmatic one where the practitioner intervened occasionally in traditional ways. Class sessions were devoted to exploring problems collaboratively in small groups or as whole class exercises.

Safford, as part of her doctoral research, examined the course from four perspectives. Here she re-visits her work to give us the students' perspective. Students' views were collected using audio and video-taped interviews and later analysed using qualitative methods. The aim was to use authentic student voices to help with course evaluation. These students voices are a pillar of her research and this chapter. Safford lets the students speak for themselves, and she listens. Her conclusions are recorded.

In her chapter, Barbara Miller-Reilly describes her work with adults returning to study at the University of Auckland. She discusses a new mathematics programme for adult returners and those who were previously unsuccessful at mathematics (which was specially designed as a vehicle for their re-introduction to mathematics). The programme marks a significant departure from previous university practice which consisted mainly of content-based presentations of mathematics. The new programme aims to integrate process and content using appropriate pedagogical approaches. These approaches differ from normal university approaches in first year mathematics courses. Miller-Reilly's programme is based on the *realistic mathematics* model proposed by the Dutch mathematics educators Freudenthal and deLange. Mathematisation and working with real world problems are central to this philosophy of mathematics education. These principles guide teaching which recognises that learners construct their own understanding of mathematics by working together in groups on real world problems. They are encouraged to explore and model in a number of different contexts.

Miller-Reilly also examines the effects of this approach on the beliefs and perceptions of her students. She discusses a survey which shows interesting age-dependent differences in attitudes and perceptions. She concludes by suggesting that the success of the programme may be attributable to its alignment with adult learning styles.

O'Donoghue gives a retrospective account of his experiences as director of an Irish mathematics' project during the period from 1980 to the present. This project has as its *raison d'etre* the explicit aim of preparing youths for work and adult life. Although it is not discussed explicitly there is clear evidence that the evolving social, cultural, political, economic and education climate contributed to the project's metamorphosis into a programme for adult learners. It is as a mathematics programme for adult learners it merits attention here.

The chapter highlights a number of interesting features of the programme from the dual perspectives of mathematics education and adults learning mathematics. The programme is underpinned by a cultural approach to mathematics which looks modern in the context of current concern for the social and cultural dimensions of mathematics education. However, the principal focus of the chapter is the project's approach to numeracy assessment. The rationale for the development of design specifications for a numeracy assessment instrument is discussed. The outcome is a modified grid design with some novel features which was used to construct tests that were trialled in centres throughout Ireland. These results are discussed in the context of local/national needs of adult learners, educational developments and aspirations for the future.

The penultimate chapter in this section deals with a central problem in mathematics teaching; how to teach mathematics for transfer. Indeed, teaching mathematics so that learners can apply or use it subsequently in a variety of new contexts is at the heart of mathematics education at all levels. Research in adults learning mathematics has potential to shed light on this important issue - as Evans has shown.

Jeff Evans looks again at the issue of transfer of mathematics learning in the context of adults learning mathematics. He recognises the limitations of traditional approaches which expect transfer of learning to proceed in a straight forward manner, say from school mathematics to everyday life. But he knows, as every experienced teacher knows, that results are disappointing in this respect as many learners cannot apply their learned mathematics in new contexts. However, he is not prepared to accept the strong form of situated cognition which holds that transfer of learning is virtually impossible between different contexts. Evans proposes a re-formulation of the transfer problem in terms of different discourses as a way forward. He argues that the boundaries between discourses are permeable, and it is possible to build bridges between them for the learners by identifying points of inter-relation. He then shows how these points of inter-relation can be exploited to design pedagogic practices that facilitate transfer of learning between different practices e.g. school mathematics and workplace mathematics.

Finally, in their chapter, Diana Coben and Noyona Chanda give an overview of recent developments in the preparation, professional development and accreditation of adult numeracy teachers in England, with some reference to parallel developments in adult literacy teaching. Their review reveals a sorry situation, reflecting the lack of priority accorded to adult numeracy teacher development in England and a 'sidelong glance' at rather more positive developments in Australia. They argue that adult numeracy teachers have a vital contribution to make to raising the level of numeracy of the adult population and that professional development in adult numeracy teaching must have greater prominence if practice in this area is to continue to develop.

Broadly speaking, these chapters taken together show that practitioners and researchers engaged in the mathematics education of adults favour learner-centred methods; contextualize mathematics; value learners' life experience; and appeal to adults' critical faculties. This is borne out, if further evidence is needed, in the accumulated proceedings of *Adults*

Learning Mathematics - A Research Forum (1995-98) as even a cursory analysis will show (e.g. Coben & van Groenestijn, 1999).

REFERENCES

American Mathematical Association of Two-Year Colleges. (1995). *Crossroads in mathematics: standards for introductory college mathematics before calculus.* Memphis: American Mathematical Association of Two-Year colleges.

Basic Skills Agency. (1997). *International numeracy survey: a comparison of basic skills of adults 16-60 in seven countries.* London: The Basic Skills Agency.

Bynner, J. & S. Parsons. (1997). *Does numeracy matter? Evidence from the national child development study on the impact of poor numeracy on adult life.* London: The Basic Skills Agency.

Coben, D. & M. van Groenestijn (Comps), (1999). *Proceedings of the fifth International conference of Adults Learning Mathematics (ALM-5).* London: Goldsmiths College, University of London in association with ALM.

Cockcroft, W.H. (Chairman). (1982). *Mathematics Counts: Report of the Committee of Inquiry into the Teaching of Mathematics in Schools.* London: Her Majesty's Stationery Office.

FitzSimons, G.E. (Ed.) (1997). *Adults returning to study: Papers from Working Group 18, 8th International Congress on Mathematical Education, ICME8.* Adelaide, SA: Australian Association of Mathematics Teachers.

Knowles, M. S. (1990). *The adult learner: A neglected species* (4th ed). Houston: Gulf Publishing Company.

National Council of Teachers of Mathematics. (1989). *Curriculum and evaluation standards for school mathematics.* Reston, VA: NCTM.

National Research Council (1989). *Everybody Counts: A report to the nation on the future of mathematics education.* Washington, D.C. : National Academy Press.

Rogers, A. (1986). *Teaching adults.* Milton Keynes, U.K.: Open University Press.

Chapter 13

Algebra for Adult Students: the Student Voices

Katherine Safford
St. Peter's College, Jersey City, USA

INTRODUCTION

In 1983, the National Commission on Excellence in Education published *A Nation At Risk*, a short, provocative document which initiated a scrutiny of United States education in every field and at every level. A leader in the ensuing mathematics education reform movement was the National Council of Teachers of Mathematics (NCTM), an organization which is primarily, but not exclusively, devoted to promoting quality elementary and secondary mathematics education. Their *Curriculum and Evaluation Standards for School Mathematics* contained suggestions for changes in course content, emphasis, methodology, and the use of technology for the learning and teaching of mathematics at the primary and secondary level. On the undergraduate level, the American Mathematical Association of Two-Year Colleges (AMATYC) and the Mathematical Association of America (MAA) later published guidelines for mathematical achievement in their respective jurisdictions.

One central theme of these reform efforts was a perceived need for all students to study algebra. The NCTM Curriculum and Evaluation Standards for School Mathematics states five general goals for all students, one of which is the ability to communicate mathematically (NCTM, 1989). Elsewhere in the same document algebra is described as "the language through which most of mathematics is communicated. It also provides a means of operating with concepts at an abstract level and then applying them, a process that often fosters generalizations and insights beyond the original context" (NCTM, 1989: 150). The reform literature attempts to identify the essence of algebra, the role of technology, and effective teaching strategies for conveying the first and incorporating the second. Taylor is one

D. Coben et al. (eds.), Perspectives on Adults Learning Mathematics, 235–255.
© 2000 *Kluwer Academic Publishers. Printed in the Netherlands.*

of several mathematicians who have challenged the traditional placement of the subject in the ninth grade where it serves as a gate which either admits students to further mathematics study or terminates their participation. He proposes that:

> The opportunity to study algebra should always be available. One of the strengths of the educational system in the United States is the many opportunities it affords students who have not previously been successful. We must never give up on students or allow them to give up on themselves. With high expectations, encouragement, and effective instruction, the algebra course can be converted from a filter that screens people out to a pump that propels people forward toward opportunity. (Taylor in Edwards, 1990: 51-52)

In the United States, almost half the students pursuing undergraduate degrees are twenty-five years of age or older, students availing themselves of the opportunity of which Taylor speaks (Lally, 1995). It is commonplace for students in this category to require a first-time or refresher course in algebra, termed "developmental algebra", because they either never studied the subject or do not recall enough of the skills studied in secondary school to tackle college mathematics. An undergraduate research effort which attempted to incorporate many of the proposed mathematics education reforms into a developmental algebra course for adults is the subject of this chapter. The author gives prominence to the students' voices throughout.

INTRODUCTION TO ALGEBRA FOR ADULT STUDENTS: THE RESEARCH PROJECT

Soon after the publication of the NCTM Standards document, the dean of the adult college at a major US research university shared her concerns that students from her college worked at a disadvantage when placed in developmental algebra with traditional age students. The dean, herself a mathematics professor, suggested to mathematics education faculty at the university that an algebra course based upon the recommended K-12 reforms might be beneficial for those students. Several teachers of undergraduate mathematics were in the doctoral program in mathematics education at the time and they expressed an interest in designing and offering such a course. The resulting course, Introduction to Algebra for Adult Students (IAAS), was the product of that research project. The design team examined developmental mathematics at the university level in light of the NCTM Curriculum and Evaluation Standards for School Mathematics and at the same time grappled with the problems faced by adult students returning to mathematics study. It should be noted that during the planning stages of IAAS only the NCTM Standards were available in published form so it served as the principal planning tool. Classes of IAAS were already being conducted when MAA and AMATYC published recommendations for developmental mathematics standards at the undergraduate level. Later comparisons of the course with these documents, however, showed *post facto* compliance with their suggestions.

Introduction to Algebra for Adult Students has now been offered for six years. The author was a member of the team which designed the course and an instructor during the first two years that it was offered. Her doctoral dissertation was an examination of the course from four perspectives (Ramus, 1997). One of those perspectives is that of the students. At the end of the second year, the thirteen members of the experimental class were invited to be interviewed about the course. Eight students were able to participate in the interviews which were conducted by a third party using a formal protocol (Appendix). These interviews were audio and video taped and then transcribed. The transcriptions were analyzed using qualitative methods. It is these interviews which provide the student voices of this chapter. The interviewees ranged in age from thirty to fifty. The individuals identified as R, E, and L are males. J, S, A, G, and C are females.

In performing the analysis, the author was often in the difficult position of being the researcher and the subject, at least in part, of the research itself. In categorizing the students' comments every effort was made to separate remarks which described a generic, good instructor from traits particular to the researcher. Even when the student voice spoke of a personal trait, for example, a sense of humour, the author attempted to identify a teaching technique, the use of humour to enhance the comfort level, as the characteristic valued by the student. The reader should keep this in mind when listening to the voices as quoted in this chapter.

ALGEBRA FOR ADULT STUDENTS: THE COURSE

The creation and implementation of IAAS was a collaborative effort between the administration of the adult college, the Mathematics, and the Mathematics Education departments at the university. The target student population was humanities majors who had not fulfilled their mathematics requirement for graduation and who seemed least able to master algebra in courses at the university taught using a traditional approach and text. The representatives of the mathematics department asked that the content be roughly equivalent to the content of the parallel traditional course but the expected level of notational proficiency was relaxed to reflect the limited needs of the students. The mathematics education researchers asked for freedom to design a course which might turn out to be very different from what the mathematics department and, in fact the algebra students, was accustomed to experiencing. The adult college dean asked that her students complete the course with an ability to reason mathematically and to communicate using the language of mathematics, algebra, without losing heart in the process.

From the outset, the design team envisioned a problem-centered course where a central problem was explored in a collaborative way by students working in small groups or as a whole class exercise. Each class period would begin with the problem which the students would be asked to solve using any method they could devise. After a reasonable amount of time, the various solutions and strategies would be put on the blackboard and, in the ensuing discussion, commonalties would be identified and algebraic generalizations revealed. Often one student would pose a question which was answered by another student who might raise a different issue. This work would then be followed by additional problems similar to the "opener" and students would be encouraged to look for pattern among the solutions and try to generalize and find a rule which could then be applied in future problems. There would be no pre-ordained schedule and the student mastery of the material would determine the pace.

One book which served as a guide during the planning phase was a slim volume of essays entitled *Algebra for Everyone*. The topics to be covered by the course were suggested by one of those essayists:

> The concept, principles and methods of algebra constitute powerful intellectual tools for representing quantitative information and then reasoning about that information. The central concepts of algebra include variables, functions, relations, equations and inequalities, and graphs. (Christmas and Fey in Edwards, 1990: 62)

These concepts became the focus of the course. The course material was structured to present algebra as a generalized arithmetic. This allowed the students, adults who were proficient at accomplishing everyday mathematical tasks, to examine mathematics as they knew and used it and to attempt to develop abstract rules to explain their algorithms. In the words of the professor directing the research project, "Algebra is the way we talk about how numbers behave when we don't know the numbers" (Davis, private communication). Another of his maxims, "Never answer a question until it is asked," encouraged the teachers to lecture minimally and to function more like discussion leaders than instructors. Classes were conducted using a constructivist approach where the teacher is the facilitator and the student is the builder of his/her own knowledge base. While a single definition of the term has yet to be achieved, the guiding principles of constructivism are that knowledge must be actively constructed by learners, and that coming to know is a process of organizing and adapting to the world as experienced by the learner (Gadanidis, 1994). Perhaps the best metaphor to describe the conduct of the class would be that of playing a game of pinball. This game, popular in gaming arcades in the U.S., consists of propelling a small metal ball into a case filled with several levers which redirect the ball and cause points to be scored. Once the ball, in the case of IAAS the question, is released, the outcome is determined by a mix of chance and skill. This loose structure was tempered at times by student demand for direction from the instructor as well as for adequate practice of the constructed schema.

Introduction to Algebra for Adult Students did bear similarities to the traditional versions of the class. The instructor and students met for eighty minutes, twice a week, for thirty weeks. Standard university tutoring, offered to all developmental students, was available. The class met in a regular university classroom. There were no computer facilities available for the instructors or students. The location of the class was restricted because the students were accustomed to attending other classes in nearby buildings before and after IAAS met.

Points of dissimilarity were the composition of the class which was exclusively part-time, adult night students. Instead of instructors from the mathematics department, the course was staffed by graduate students from the mathematics education doctoral program. During the pilot year it was team taught. In the second year there was one instructor, the author. Graduate students from the mathematics education masters and doctoral programs observed class sessions. Some of these observers provided a limited amount of tutoring keyed to the teaching style prevalent in the class sessions offered to tutor students from the class outside of class meeting times.

IAAS FOR ADULT STUDENTS: STUDENT VOICES

Math Histories

When asked if they had had problems with mathematics in the past, the responses were polarized. Two of the students said that their memories were pleasant. S had taken 3 years of high school math, finishing with Algebra II and Trigonometry. Until that third year, she had liked and done well in math, but did not like all the formulas in trigonometry. Later in her interview, S shared the thought that she might have majored in math if she had encountered IAAS earlier in her collegiate experience. A, who was actually planning to major in mathematics at the time of the interview, described herself as "always good in math...never disliked it or struggled with it." She viewed mathematics as being "like a puzzle and there's a light at the end of the tunnel that you can see." A believed that once the work was explained she generally did not find herself struggling with it.

The other six interviewees had less favourable math histories. R reported a fair aptitude for math in elementary school and then a disastrous year in junior high school, when he was placed in an accelerated class. He felt that this had left him a little behind and created a phobia for math that culminated in his failing algebra. He attributes some of his problems in math classes to a reluctance to ask questions. L remembered always having problems with mathematics when he studied the subject in Hungary. He blames the heterogeneous grouping of students that placed him in the same class as outstanding mathematicians. He felt uncomfortable asking questions, because "Why should I prove I was stupid?"

C admitted avoiding math classes "like the plague." She attributed her avoidance to a fear of not understanding it because she could never get the concepts and felt that there were too many rules to memorize. While she managed to pass her high school courses, C never was really comfortable nor secure with the material. E described math as his weakest subject. He had "mostly negative feelings" about other math courses he had in the past and, like C, felt that he could pass a math course but his knowledge was marginal and he did not feel that he had accomplished very much.

J was within five courses of graduation when the math requirement caught up with her. She had attempted one of the traditionally taught courses at the university, Math 023, and felt that the pace and the presence of traditional students worked against her in the mainstream class. In her words:

> I tried to take an 023 course here. Um, I guess it's your basic algebra course, and they moved at such a rapid pace that I couldn't keep up. So, they would give you an assignment on maybe Monday, and we'd review it in the next class. And then they'd give you another series of problems, or another type of problem the next class and say, 'OK, we're moving on,' and for me, I can't do that. I need to sit and I need to think about it, and work a few problems out, maybe a week at a time.

G had perhaps the most traumatic math history of those interviewed. She recounted a tale of an introductory algebra course taken at a community college with an adjunct instructor who battled illness and ineptness throughout the semester, to the detriment of the students. G went on to attempt algebra five more times, encountering "massive anxiety attacks" fought off with biofeedback and medication, culminating with eventual withdrawal or failure each semester.

Differences in Introduction to Algebra for Adult Students

When asked to describe differences between this course and those which interviewees had taken, several points emerged. L cited the homogeneous nature of the student population as a significant difference of IAAS. He was willing to ask questions because the person next to him might have the "same question in his or her head." He said that this course had helped him to get rid of his shyness. In her interview, J alluded to the same feelings about questions, namely, that she felt free to ask them. She says, "I guess because we're all adults in the same boat, she doesn't make us feel uncomfortable about saying, 'O.K., I'm the dummy. Could you explain it to me again?' Because we don't all think we're the dummies, but we just haven't learned it yet." R said basically the same thing, but even more emphatically. He told the interviewer that "probably the most important thing I've gotten out of the class is strangely enough, and it had nothing to do with math, it's the fact that I've gotten over this feeling of not asking questions."

R attributed this change to the "non-threatening" atmosphere of the class:

> First of all, the atmosphere is very different. Kathy was extremely understanding. She goes out of her way to give a lot of positive reinforcement, ... she has enormous patience. Much more than I have... She doesn't take anything for granted in terms of what she thinks is important. She assumes that a fair amount of her students maybe don't understand what she just said and she'll ask, she always goes out of her way, she doesn't put you on the spot. I know I hated, as most people did, getting up at the board or being called on. She doesn't do that.

S felt that the class was "totally different than any other class I've ever had. Period." When asked to elaborate, she echoed the thoughts of her classmates and then added a discussion of clarity of explanations. S said that in other math classes the instructor "would not, or could not explain for me and some of the other students but they know what they were doing but they couldn't explain it, which made it very difficult." She felt that, in her past classes, she and other students had eventually stopped asking questions because of this situation. S contrasted that experience with her experience in IAAS:

> In her class, she can actually explain so that you understand. You know, which makes it pleasant to be there. It's nice to come here because it's like, this woman is not an ogre, whereas in the past, I've had some math teachers that would tell me well, if you don't understand it, just go over the samples in the book, and I would be, like, totally lost.

R felt that student confidence was fostered by a series of small successes based on incremental activities. J concurred and described the practice of tackling problems of incremental difficulty as a difference she saw in the course.

J saw her confidence carrying into her work life. She had changed jobs during the academic year and said that she had attempted algebra problems that she never would have touched in the past on corporate entrance exams. That idea was echoed by G who said that she now spoke up more at meetings and attributed this to confidence gained in IAAS. She listed the positive, success-oriented flavor of the class as the main difference she saw in this class. Rather than telling the students that half would be gone by the midterm (G's previous experience) the IAAS instructor told the students, in G's words, "We're gonna get through this."

Another difference that G reported was the exercises the instructor had assigned in the first classes to make the class work together. In her words:

> In the very beginning she started. I've had this in other classes where they have you work with a partner and you introduce that person, so you're already interacting with other students, and you kinda get to know each other on a different level. Where in the previous math classes it was almost set up that you stayed very separate. You know...so just by being comfortable in the class, you know, and being more, made aware that we're all here at the same level, and that we're all gonna get through it together. Um, that made a big difference.

The interviewees who commented on similarities of this class to other classes felt that the material was the same as that they had encountered in previous classes. E said that he had experienced some of the short-term memory problems he had in the past. G admitted to having minor panic attacks like those she had experienced in the past but being able to work through them because of strategies she learned in IAAS.

Differences Outside of Class Sessions

Students were asked if, outside of the class sessions, there was any difference in the way they related to the course. Both J and A reported that the assistance of one of the graduate student observers outside of the class sessions made a positive contribution to their first-semester experience. Both felt that the assistance of someone who had observed the class and understood the instructor's style of instruction was a real asset. J said that this provided consistency. For a previous math class she had gone to the campus Learning Center for help but had not been satisfied. In her words:

> The problem I have with that is that not all the students (the tutors) there are on the same level. And not all the students there understand an adult's concern about how they do problems.

She contrasted this situation with that of a graduate student tutor who "observed how our professor taught us. And then she said, 'This is what she wants you to do.' And it was easier."

G reported that, by contrast to her previous experiences, she now looked forward to the class and it had become her "source of sanity" in a chaotic life. She not only looks forward to coming to classes but participates a lot more than she has in the past. R saw a difference in his discourse with his children as a result of his coursework. In the past, his wife helped his daughter with her math and he would help with her English. He now felt that he had more interest in the subject and that taking IAAS had "enhanced my capability as a, quote, teacher of my own children."

Surprising Elements

When the students were asked if they found anything surprising about the course, several different responses surfaced. Three students were surprised that they could do the work. In C's words, "The biggest surprise to me was that I got it! That was just, that was just something that, I mean I sit there, especially first semester when I got the final I was like, this has to be wrong. This, I mean, I got it. I really think I got it." A repeated this theme, perhaps less exuberantly, when she said, "Well, it's not as hard as I thought it would be and that's surprising, you know,...when you hear the word algebra, most people kinda like cringe...you know, just to hear the word algebra, but it's, it's not that bad." E found his ability to ease into the math itself surprising because he had not thought that he would be able to adapt so easily.

G found the student interaction surprising. She said that this interaction, particularly working together, was encouraged more than in other classes. She felt it was manifested in both small-group and whole-class discussion and will be discussed at length in its own section.

S had been stunned by the size of the class. She had been told at registration that the class had 450 students and she had sought out an amphitheatre on the first night of class. One can only imagine the look on her face when she entered the correct room and found she was the sixteenth, and final, student to arrive.

S also commented on the instructor as a surprising element of the class. In her words:

> Most professors don't interact with their students like Kathy interacts. Most of them will not take the time to go over something over and over and over again even if it seems as though every one else has gotten it, she takes the time to make sure that everyone has gotten it, and she doesn't make anyone feel, 'That's a stupid question' or 'That's a foolish question.' You know, which is nice.

J also responded that the patience of the instructor surprised her, in her words:

She has a lot of patience. And even if we don't get it, we're not..we're not skipped over. She makes every effort for us to try to get it. And she'll say, 'Well, look at it this way.' She gives us other ways to look at it.

L was surprised by what he called the "humanity" of the course. He had attended university in Europe and felt that, while the American system was perhaps less rigorous, it was more human. He admitted that this might be attributed to his adult status, but that he felt a much closer connection with the instructor than with any he had studied with in Europe. In his words, "It was a good feeling. In education it is a good feeling."

Attitudinal Change

All of the interviewees felt that their attitude had changed as a result of taking the course, although the degree of change varied. Those who liked math before the course felt that their fear of algebra had been mitigated. Student A said that she had always thought algebra was different from math and now she sees that "It's not like it's something from outer space that is very, very difficult, it's math, it's [a] thing that I know." S said that she would not be afraid to take another math course now that she has completed this one. G, who has to take statistics for her degree program, said that she had previously felt intimidated by algebra but no longer does, and she feels she'll "be okay" in the statistics class.

For three students, an incremental gain in self-confidence measured their advancement. Both E and J shared a willingness to tackle a problem, an attitude that was absent before they took this course. In her own words, J's attitude toward math had been "horrible...I'd just make faces at you, oh, like, 'Get away from me.'...now I'll at least make an attempt to solve the problem." She attributed the change in her feelings to the fact that it was an adult class. J felt that the sense of community this evoked created an even playing field, a feeling that "We're all in the same boat."

E contrasted his increased confidence with old feelings of math avoidance and fright. He told the interviewer, "I definitely feel more confident now as far as if I am given a problem...I think I have a better chance than I ever had of solving [it]." L, the Hungarian student, had difficulty finding the right words to describe his improved attitude. He stressed his ongoing respect for the subject but the fact that he had never felt close to it because of personal fear. Now, although he would not characterize himself as confident, he did think that success at problem solving had resulted in some increase in happiness and confidence .

R took a philosophical stance when asked this question. He felt that an intangible like mathematics was not something about which one should have an attitude. He felt that his attitude towards math pedagogy had undergone a change. R said, "I think now that I feel that not enough has been done in terms of math pedagogy. And I think that you can teach people math in a different fashion."

The Instructor

R continued his discussion of the course by describing the pedagogical approach of the instructor, referring back to an earlier discussion concerning the way rules were taught and learned in the class:

> [Some instructors say] this is the way you, this is the formula for say, the quadratic equation, this is what you're going to do. But the way she does it, really helps to develop some understanding. In other words, trying to find a repeating principle and then after we've worked through it a while, um, then it's fairly successful at that, then, she'll state what the rule is. I find what that really does is, one, as she say, you really own the concept more. Also, from my standpoint, I just find it much more interesting that way.

C echoed R's response when she told the interviewer that it was the instructor's approach that set her apart. In her words:

> Probably the biggest part of it is not standing there and saying this rule applies to this type of problem situation. We work it out and then we go from there...It wasn't that, you know, she gave the rules first and said this is it, this is how you're going to know to determine it. We just worked problem after problem after problem until we got it. That kind of thing. Illustrations, handouts, problems from the workbook. And just keep working at 'em until you get 'em. And then she said, 'Okay, well here's some rules you can follow.

Three of the interviewees commented on the clarity of the instructor's explanations and her persistence in the face of student misunderstanding. Repeating a thought she had introduced earlier in her interview, S said:

> She can explain, and she will explain, as I've said in the past, I've had professors who knew what they were doing, but perhaps couldn't explain something to me so that I could understand. And, you know when you ask someone something over and over and over again, sometimes the professor can get a little irritable. … never gets irritable. She gives everyone an opportunity in the class.

C concurred with S when she discussed what she termed the "concern" of the instructor. She said:

> She's concerned. She wants to make sure that the message that she is trying to get across is understood, and not understood by one or two, by everyone. We'll go back over stuff if necessary. If she finds that we are not, we're clueless as to

what she's saying, she'll go a whole other route to try to get us to understand what it is she's saying. So I guess it's patience. It's the individual concern.

The third student who commented on this aspect of the class pedagogy said that "If you don't understand a problem, what she'll try to do, she'll ask you what it is you don't understand about it, and then she tries to explain it that way. That's very helpful." He said that, out of all his courses, this is the first time an instructor has done that.

G felt that the instructor was more insightful than instructors she had encountered in the past, a trait that might not be replicable. She said that the instructor could "read people" by picking up facial expressions and body language, so that even if students were saying that they understood, their body language told a different tale, and this instructor was skilled at recognizing that fact. G continued by saying that even when you "get caught" the class was in no way intimidating because the instructor did not put you down and say "Well you should know that by now" or "Well why are you here if you can't figure that out?" which are phrases she recalled from former instructors.

L alluded to his previous discussion of the humanity and adult nature of the class. He described the instructor as being more accessible than instructors he had studied with in Europe, but attributed this to the combination of the ages within the class and the differences in the American education system and mentality. He described the instructor as being "a part of the class." In L's words, "It is very nice. She knows the math. She gives some part of her knowledge but she is not a dictator."

Student Cooperation and Interaction

Students interacted within the class sessions in both large and small-group encounters. Specific tasks were assigned to be worked on cooperatively in small groups based on the work of Johnson et al (1984). When working in whole-class mode, the class frequently functioned as a "large co-operative group" volleying around questions, insights, and answers until an acceptable level of student satisfaction was attained. In the interview, the question was posed, "Some people feel that students can help other students to understand math. Do you think that this is true?" In every case, the response was an enthusiastic, "Yes."

Perhaps the most surprising finding, from the researcher's perspective, was the student responses concerning small-group work. Graduate student observers in their reports on the class had noted no effective group work. This, in fact, had been the perception of the instructor, namely that the students sat in small groups in acquiescence to her requirements, but that no classical cooperative group work took place.

The interviewees saw things differently. In response to this query, they said that, not only had they worked in small groups, but that it had been very helpful. Upon reviewing the testimonies, the difference probably hinges on the word classical. The instructor was accustomed to observing the structured groups frequently employed in elementary and secondary education settings. In those groups, members are generally assigned tasks such as group leader and recorder. Often the teacher determines the group membership based on criteria such as academic ability and personality traits. Groups in IAAS self-selected and functioned informally, as will be described by the students.

R was the most mathematically adept student in the class. His discussion of groups reinforces the educational theory that high-achieving students can benefit from group work. In comparing this math course to others he had taken, he said:

> We work in groups, which I had never done before. I don't care to work in groups, but I like the fact that you can talk to...Well, it seems to relax everyone else, too, it just seems to and I also find it a benefit to me of being in a group atmosphere is, in my case, that I can by talking to other students when they ask me questions I find it helps crystallize my thinking.

Later, when asked specifically about students helping one another, he responded, "It helps me when somebody asks me a question because it really makes, it forces me to concretize in my mind what I'm doing because I don't seem to be very good at that." R describes his approach to group work, which reflects the way that groups functioned within this class:

> When somebody asks me, I don't like when I'm asked until I've already worked it out because I find that is very distracting. I like to work on my own. I never, when we form groups, I just don't, I need a minute to...I find it distracting when someone says, 'Well how do you think?' I seem to have my own way of approaching it and I like that first minute or so to decide where I'm going. I don't tend to rely on other people because obviously in that situation, I mean the instructor, yes, but my assumption is that the person on my left and right knows as little as I do at that point so let me rely on me first and then I'm more than happy to discuss back and forth to see it they have a better way.

S frequently worked with R and gave her perspective on group work when she told the interviewer:

> Working in the groups,....it helps, you know, it's helped me a lot...getting views of other people. Because, even though I might think I have the answer, or sometimes I will do something and I'm not sure if I did it right, and getting someone else's point of view might remind me, well, we did such and such in

class or back then we might have blah-blah-blah, and this is how it should be done. And they will show me, it's not like, you know, you're all alone.

A alluded to R's desire to first work on tasks alone when she said:

> Sometimes it [working in groups] does help, and other times it, you know, sometimes you just wanna work alone. You wanna figure it out or if you stumble over something that you can't figure out then you prefer to work with someone else, but sometimes you just prefer just to do it alone, just to see if you can do it by yourself.

C justified the value of group work when she repeated the old adage, "Two heads are better than one." She said group work had been very helpful to her because she experienced different ways of getting the same answer to class problems and that was "Absolutely" a good thing.

This ability to help each other extended beyond the small groups and into whole-class discussion. When reviewing suggested solutions, students were encouraged to ask others to explain their answers. At times, the instructor would seek help from students to rephrase a student question or to couch an instructor explanation in peer language. C had experienced great difficulty mastering signed number operations. She referred to that difficulty when she shared:

> ...a good example with this negative number blockage that I had. When someone in the class, you know, they kept hearing me saying the same thing over and over because maybe I, and probably I didn't hear what I was saying and they noticed just by what I was saying where my problem was. And that's when, I can't think of her name, but that's when she said to me, 'Jot down these four rules.' About the negative numbers. and I wrote them on the top of the paper and then when I went back to the workbook to do the problems, I would go back and forth to them.

J said that she had benefited from peer assistance when struggling to understand some concepts. "Sometimes, one of the students that may be sitting next to you will say, 'No. You looked at it the other way. Look at it this way.' 'Cause someone in the class may understand it quicker, or find another way to make it work." L, too, had learned with the assistance of peers. He shared his experiences when he told the interviewer that he had not felt shy asking the student next to him to help him understand something difficult.

S spoke at length on this topic, stressing the fact that she welcomed students sharing different viewpoints or solutions because it helped her to see where she had gone wrong, although she emphatically asserted her unwillingness to back away from her solutions until others had won her over to their thinking. She shared:

You know, if this is what I have, I will tell you...this is what I have, now it may be wrong, but this is how I did it. And thus, I will explain the whole thing. Naturally, it could be wrong, but, you know, unless somebody shows me something else, I will stick to my answer. And normally, you know I, you know, another student will say 'It's done this way or such-and-such,' or Kathy will ask someone else, and they will explain it to me, so like, I don't feel bad.

J covered both small-group and whole-class interaction in her response to the interviewer's question. When asked if students could help other students she replied:

Yes, that can happen...some students do help a lot. There are students in our class who say, 'No, you're looking at it wrong. Look at it this way. This is what she really means.' Um, some students remember it from high school. Some people are more proficient...Sometimes we figure it out together. Whereas I may get one part of the problem, and they say, 'No, you're supposed to divide at the end, or you're supposed to subtract or multiply at the end.' I go, 'Oh, that's what I'm doing wrong.' and you combine the two and go, 'all right, let's see what we do,' and then work it out. Um, yeah, two students can help one another a lot, very much so.

G compared this class to the others she had taken and failed:

In the other classes we helped each other. There were, there's always somebody you can connect with in class. Outside of class we helped each other. But within the class...because of the mood of the class and the instructor...You really did not want to let on to other people that you didn't know what you were doing...Several of the instructors I had taught higher math, and that's where their mindset was. So they were very impatient if you, if you didn't know it. And they went very fast and, like I said it was like, you know 'If you can't do this, then, you know, you shouldn't even be here.' It [working together with other students] pulls you more together. You know, you don't feel like you're alone that you're the only one that doesn't know this. You know, in this class you realize that it's just the basic. You know, if I knew it, I wouldn't be here.

The interviewer asked G if she had experienced that helping in IAAS and she replied, "Oh, a lot! A lot! There, there's quite a few times where Kathy'll be working, trying to get us to understand something, and somebody'll verbalize it in their own way and I'll be like, 'Yeah, OK, I got that.'" And when asked if she had been in a position of learning from the other students, G said, "Yeah, but I would have never done that in another class."

And finally, E related a time when he was able to help some of the other students and said that it had made him feel good to do so. He said:

Recently we went over some geometry trying to find the area of a certain property or whatever. Some people don't feel too comfortable with it but, for some reason, I didn't have much of a problem at all understanding it and someone else did, and I just offered my help and they were able to see it more clearly.

Suggestions for Improvement

Five students could think of nothing that would improve the course. R summed up his feelings when he said:

I think, all things taken into consideration, the level of ability of the people in the class, I really couldn't, I think that it's really a pretty remarkable achievement. I think the class works really well and I'm sure that there is a way to improve it but I really couldn't speak to it, I'm not an educator. But my own experience...I find nothing.

Three students suggested ways they felt the course could be enhanced. G wanted more homework in the first semester. This reflected the problem discussed earlier by the instructor, who could not find a suitable text and was frequently writing and reproducing her text on the same day that the class met. It was only in the second semester, once signed numbers had been covered, that a commercial workbook could be used to relieve that pressure. G acknowledged that fact and said that she saw no way to improve the second semester.

A expressed a wish that the instructor was more available for private consultation. She suggested evening office hours. In her words:

Sometimes it would be nice if you could meet with your instructor. I mean it's good to work with the tutor, but if you could have the time to just sit down with your instructor...one-on-one, that would be nice.

This also reflected a problem recognized by the instructor but difficult to overcome. All of the students worked days, many only arrived on campus as class began at 6:00 p.m. Some went on then to another class immediately after IAAS finished. Those who did not go to another class generally just wanted to go home after a full day of work. The instructor agrees that, if offered again, "By Appointment" office hours should be an option and students should be encouraged to avail themselves of it.

J was of the opinion that small-group work had slacked off during the second semester and should be more strongly encouraged for the duration of the course. There were some difficulties in posing the question to L, the English as a Second Language (ESL) student. It would appear that he interpreted the question as "What would you tell a different instructor to do." and his response is, therefore, an affirmation of what he liked rather than a suggestion for change. He asked that future instructors continue the practice of "no question is stupid" because that policy had been "a big help to us."

Recommendations for Continuation

There was unanimous agreement that the course should continue to be offered for adult students. G answered enthusiastically, "Definitely. I don't know why they waited so long." E thought that the class "helped me tremendously" and should be continued for UC students. S felt that "...personally, they should have classes like this in every college." L felt that the course would even be useful for non-humanities majors in the calculus pipeline.

J spoke strongly in favor of a separate course for adult students. She said:

I think it should continue because it's at an adult pace...It fills a need here...for an adult trying to make it through Rutgers...you know, we don't have many classes where we're among our peers. Totally among our peers...It's intimidating sometimes, when you have this kid, like I said, sitting next to you, who hasn't been out of high school six months, and he whizzes right through.

C echoed J but incorporated elements of the course in her discussion:

It's the process and the method with which this class is taught which is very assuring, can be very comfortable. It was understandable, it was on a level that I could understand it yet she didn't make me feel like I was someone, that I was not smart enough and that's why I was there...You know that kind of a thing. You know, I felt much like I was an adult in the class.

It was R who supplied the most eloquent testimonial to, and argument for, IAAS:

I would say that, if you look at the practical results, and at least by my standard, the way I would judge it, it seems to work. The people seem interested, much more interested in a math course than people before and you have to realize that the people there are hard cases, people who had a strong distaste...a dislike of the subject. They don't, they seem to have less of it each week. In the first few weeks, there seemed to be a lot of resistance, there was a lot of fear...People come to class each week, they do the work, they feel, they're more empowered. And the fact of it is, people learn at different rates, people have problems with different subjects. So, if it takes a little longer to get the job done, it's a lot better than not getting the job done at all. these same people would be taking, this one woman in the class told me she took three or four algebra classes, failed them each time. And I really feel quite confident that if she had taken this course in the beginning, she wouldn't have wasted all that time and the resources of the

University. She would have gotten through it and she would have felt a lot better about it. That would be my argument.

DISCUSSION

Each of the collaborating parties who planned IAAS had their parochial goals for the course. The mathematics department was concerned that students would emerge from the course knowing the rules of algebra and possessing the capability to use algebra to communicate mathematically. While that was actually evaluated in a different section of the author's dissertation, clearly the students felt that the same material was covered. Those who had taken algebra prior to enrolling in IAAS all attested that this was the case.

The mathematics education agenda was far more ambitious. Representatives of that discipline conceived a course radically different from the traditional developmental algebra course which they were accustomed to teaching.   They wanted to re-order the sequence of topics, employ cooperative learning techniques, incorporate discovery learning strategies, and capitalize on the knowledge base which adult students bring to the learning experience.   In attempting to overcome math anxiety or even phobia, they hoped to offer a course which was so radically different from those previously experienced by the students that the students would not associate the class with negative experiences nor dredge up half-remembered, and possibly erroneous, ways of solving problems.

The change in topic sequence would seem to have had no negative effect nor did the student-established pace. By the end of the course, students could perform algebraic manipulations and successfully negotiate the translation of verbal problems into notation and find solutions. No one indicated in their interview that they felt shortchanged in mastery of the subject. Cooperative learning, although not the classic model, was approved by all the interviewees.   Research findings from other disciplines and other educational levels were echoed in statements by both skilled and struggling students that collaboration yields positive results.

Determined efforts to give all questions respect contributed substantially to an environment where learning could flourish and dissipated anxiety in the students, even those who had failed a traditional version of the same course. As the person who is described as "patient" I feel compelled to say that on occasion that patience took every bit of strength I had.   It is rewarding to know that students recognized and valued it.   The adult homogeneity of the class was credited as contributing to the ambience of the group. The possibility of looking foolish was more acceptable among peers.

Perhaps the most rewarding aspect of the interviews, from a designer viewpoint, was the successful incorporation of constructivist strategies into the course. Students felt ownership of the rules which they had constructed from observing patterns in their solutions. Oversight and vigilance must be maintained so that students who perceive incorrect patterns, and therefore construct erroneous rules, are guided in the right direction. Students did, however, request additional practice so that the rules would become routine. As an educator, I have come to value drill and practice more after discussions held with these students.

Finally, the dean who wanted a course which would capitalize on the strengths of adult students while overcoming their reservations about taking algebra need only read the endorsements for continuing the course at the university to know that she "backed a winner" when she gambled on Introduction to Algebra for Adult Students.

CONCLUSIONS

The findings suggested by the student voices might be categorized in three ways: the course, the instructor, and the students themselves. As far as the course is concerned, the students indicated that they felt the rules of mathematics had more meaning for them because they had developed the rules themselves. The homogeneity of the class encouraged an openness to ask questions and to offer solutions. They felt that the material was essentially the same as that which they had attempted to master in traditional courses. While they enjoyed discovering the rules themselves, some students felt that more practice in applying newly mastered concepts was needed for mastery. Students believed that they had benefited from interaction with other students in both small group and whole class discussions.

The profile of an effective teacher which emerged portrayed someone who was patient and treated the students with respect. Clarity of presentation and persistence in pursuit of student understanding of the course topics were valued by the students. Humor kept the atmosphere light and contributed to student comfort levels. The availability of tutoring by graduate students with teaching styles similar to the instructor enhanced student learning outside the classroom. Knowles (1978: 92), in discussing theories of learning in a democratic culture lists four basic characteristics of an educative environment: "1) respect for personality; 2) participation in decision making; 3) freedom of expression and availability of information; and 4) mutuality of responsibility in defining goals, planning and conducting activities, and evaluating." It would seem that students in Introduction to Algebra for Adult Students concurred with his opinion.

Students felt that their attitude towards mathematics and confidence in their ability to "do" mathematics had changed in a positive direction. This confidence carried over into other areas of their lives. Students recognized applications of algebra in their daily lives. All the students who were interviewed felt that the course should continue to be offered at the university as it filled a real need for the returning adult student.

APPENDIX

INTERVIEW PROTOCOL

Interview Protocol
Mission Algebra
April, 1995
Student's Name: _____
Occupation: _____
Approximate Age: _____
Gender: _____ **Ethnicity:** _____
Interviewer: _____
Date: _____

a. Introduce myself and thank the person for coming. Why are you taking this particular course?

1. Did you take any college level math classes before this one?
What classes?
(IF not) What was the last math class you have taken? How long ago?
2. Have you had any problems with math in the past?
(If yes) Are you able to identify those problems?
3. Describe your feelings about mathematics classes you have taken in the past.
What have you liked about them?
4. Do you find this class to be different from other math classes you have taken?
How is it different? How is it similar?
5. Outside of the class sessions themselves, are there differences in how you relate to this course (from other courses you've taken)?
Ways you prepare? Interactions with other people about the math? Homework? Tests? Other? Are there similarities?
6. What (if anything) have you found surprising about this class?
7. How would you describe your attitude toward math before beginning this class?
8. Do you think your attitude has changed over this year?
(If yes) In what ways has it changed?
To what would you attribute any change?
9. Do you think that the instructor is different from math instructors you have had before?
(If yes) In what ways?
10. This is an algebra class. If someone asked you what algebra is, what would you respond?
11. Can you think of a time when you have needed or used algebra in your daily life?

For instance?

12. Some people feel that students can help other students to understand math.
Do you think that this is true? Does this ever happen with this class?
Describe.
Has this involved you directly?
In what ways?

13. Are there things that you wish the instructor did differently in this class?
Explain.

14. If the head of the department asked you whether this class should continue to exist, how would you respond?

REFERENCES

Edwards, E.L., Jr., (Ed.). (1990). *Algebra for Everyone*. Reston, Va.:
   National Council of Teachers of Mathematics.
Gadanidis, G. (1994). 'Deconstructing Constructivism'. *Mathematics Teacher*, 87,
   91-94.
Johnson, D., Johnson, R. & Holubec, E. (1986). *Circles of Learning*. Edina,
   MN: Interaction Book Company.
Knowles, M. (1978). *The Adult Learner: A Neglected Species*. Houston, TX:
   Gulf Publishing.
Lally, R. (1995, January 22). On higher ground: Four-year schools meet students
   changing needs. Sunday Star-Ledger, Section 10, 3-9.
National Commission on Excellence in Education (1983). *A Nation at Risk: The
   Imperative for Educational Reform*. Washington, D.C.: U.S. Government
   Printing Office.
National Council of Teachers of Mathematics (1989). *Curriculum and Evaluation
   Standards for School Mathematics*. Reston, Va.: National Council of Teachers
   of Mathematics.
Ramus, K. S. (1997) *How the Mathematics Education Reforms Pertain to
   Undergraduate Curriculum: An Introductory Study of an Experimental
   Developmental Algebra Course for Adults*. Ann Arbor, MI: UMI Company.

Chapter 14

Exploration and Modelling in a University Mathematics Course: Perceptions of Adult Students

Barbara J. Miller-Reilly
University of Auckland, New Zealand

INTRODUCTION

Traditionally the Department of Mathematics at the University of Auckland has catered for students who successfully passed school examinations in year 12 (age 18 years) and who wanted to major in the mathematical or physical sciences. However, within the last two decades, the percentage of students without the background knowledge for this level of study in mathematics has risen. The reason for this is twofold – first, a much larger percentage of the school leaving age cohort is attending university and, second, the number of older students enrolling has risen. In the early 1990's the Department made a deliberate effort to meet the needs of these students by designing a new course (Mathematics 1), which forms part of a degree programme. (Studying seven courses is a normal full time study load in a year of study for a three-year degree.)

Mathematics 1 was taught for the first time in 1994. The approach is a significant departure from the more traditional content-based presentations of mathematics in that it aims to integrate mathematical process and content. The guiding principles underlying the teaching are based on research which suggests that students can learn mathematics very effectively when they construct their own understanding by working in groups and by doing mathematics in "real-world" contexts (de Lange, 1993). The topics are social themes, for example, environmental issues, maps, packaging and medicine. Wherever possible students are encouraged to work together on open-ended tasks or investigations of mathematical situations, learning to communicate mathematically in order to increase their mathematical confidence and their ability to mathematise.

D. Coben et al. (eds.), Perspectives on Adults Learning Mathematics, 257–269.

This study attempts to determine how effectively the investigative and interactive approach of Mathematics 1 moderates students' beliefs and builds their mathematical confidence and facility in investigating mathematical situations. Further, it considers whether their beliefs are affecting their reactions to, or performance in, the class. In order to compare two distinct age groups in Mathematics 1, we will compare students who have recently left high school (aged 20-24 years old) and older students coming back to mathematics after a reasonable period of time (aged over 30 years old).

THEORETICAL BACKGROUND

Students' beliefs about mathematics may influence their reaction to Mathematics 1 and, in addition, the teaching approach may change students' perceptions about the learning of mathematics. A Sydney study (Crawford, Gordon, Nicholas & Prosser, 1994), seeking to identify conceptions of mathematics held by beginning university students, found that the majority viewed mathematics as a necessary set of rules and procedures to be learnt by rote. McLeod (1994) points out that non-routine problems, which should lead to more enjoyment and more interest in mathematics, may not because of a conflict with students' beliefs, and Schoenfeld (1989) indicates that problem solving performance can be undermined by beliefs. Mathematics 1 is based on the *realistic mathematics* education approach in the Netherlands (de Lange, 1987). Its essential aspects are that of *mathematisation* and the role of context. Problems involve a "real world" context which is initially explored intuitively, to organise, structure and discover their mathematical aspects.

Issues about the use of context in mathematics problems are raised by many researchers. Helme (1994), in her study of adult mathematics students, finds that "contextual barriers" were imposed by contexts which were unfamiliar to the students and therefore alienating for them; that all students were not motivated by context; and that some preferred familiar contexts and some unfamiliar ones. In addition Lajoie (1995) emphasises that care must be taken in the development of real world problems to ensure no cultural bias is introduced.

FitzSimons (1994) suggests that adults returning to mathematics are often unaware of the amount of mathematical knowledge and experiences which they bring to their studies. Lehmann (1987) surveyed students, ranging in age from 17 to 63 years, who were enrolled in a basic algebra course in a large mid-western university in the USA. She finds that older students expressed more confidence that they would be successful on everyday mathematical tasks than did younger students. Based on a knowledge of adult learning, Rogers (1986) lists some practical suggestions for teaching adults. These suggestions include moving from concrete to general, making tasks relevant to students' needs for motivation, relating new material to existing experiences and knowledge, and the need for adults to be active and not passive learners.

Gibson (1994:7) collected mathematics "metaphors" from her students at the start of the school year, enabling them "to focus on their views of mathematics and of themselves as learners", and informing her about how they felt in previous experiences learning mathematics. For example, one student wrote "for me, maths is a giant jigsaw puzzle, with all the pieces the same colour". Gibson (1994) states that she is using "metaphors", as we will, in a "broad sense". Bowman (1995:206) says that, with the use of metaphor, an experience "can be described in terms of properties that belong to something more familiar". Metaphors can use language that is playful and flexible, and "help clarify understanding of experiences that are not easily described literally". Sims (1981:402) used metaphors during the evaluation of a bilingual education programme to take advantage of the metaphor's "projective properties, its synthesizing function, and its generality i.e. its remoteness from specific problems".

METHOD

An instrument containing attitudinal and belief statements and open questions was designed to explore students' reactions to Mathematics 1. This survey, which was piloted in 1994, was administered in 1995 during lectures and tutorials in late March (pretest, one month after lectures had commenced for the year) and October (posttest, in the final week of lectures). Demographic data was also requested and included the student's age, gender and mathematics background. Attitudinal variables measured included self confidence in mathematical ability and beliefs about mathematics. Open questions were part of both the pretest and the posttest (see Appendix). Additional qualitative data was collected by conducting interviews with a number of students. Gibson's (1994) technique using metaphors was modified and used during these interviews with students in Mathematics 1. The students were usually asked to interpret their own metaphors, which was deemed important by Gordon and Langmaid (1988) in their discussion of the use of this projective technique in qualitative market research.

Fifty-nine students (out of 84 initial enrolments) completed the pretest and 44 the posttest (of the 65 who sat the final examination). In the next two sections we present and discuss some of the findings from the 1995 survey, focusing on a comparison of the beliefs and mathematical confidence of students from two distinct age groups. A presentation and discussion of parts of in-depth interviews with three students follows, exploring their use of metaphors to describe their learning experiences in mathematics. Analyses of a pilot survey undertaken in 1994 were published previously (Miller-Reilly, 1995; Miller-Reilly, 1994). Further analysis of the 1995 data (Miller-Reilly, 1997) and another investigation of the use of metaphors as a research technique (Ocean & Miller-Reilly, 1997) are also available.

RESULTS FROM QUESTIONNAIRES

Each age group brings a different background in mathematics, defined by the level attained in formal mathematics study in the past, to Mathematics 1. Two-thirds of the older students, coming back to mathematics after a reasonable period of time (aged over 30 years old), have only completed two or three years of high school mathematics. The younger students who have recently left school (aged 20-24 years old) were more likely to have studied mathematics until age 16 or 17 in high school (70%), so their formal study of mathematics is not only more recent but also they have studied mathematics longer. It is interesting to note that the pass rate for Mathematics 1 is different in these two age groups; 78% of students aged 30 years and older passed, compared to 65% of the 20-24 year olds.

Beliefs About Mathematics

Six belief statements based on a study by Schoenfeld (1989) were included in the questionnaire, with response categories on a 5 point Likert scale. Responses to two of these beliefs are discussed and illustrate the different patterns occurring in the older and younger age groups, although the small sample sizes make a full statistical analysis difficult, and perhaps inappropriate.

Table 1 indicates that at the time of the pretest a smaller percentage of the younger students than older students Disagree or Strongly Disagree with the statement *Mathematics problems can be done correctly in only one way.* There is weak evidence in this data to suggest that responses to this statement at the pretest are not the same in the two age groups (Wilcoxon Rank-Sum Test, two-sided p-value is 0.106). The difference in these distributions may be because the life experience of the older group has led them to believe that there is usually more than one way to solve most (quantitative) problems. However these proportions for the two age groups are almost equivalent by the end of Mathematics 1, several younger students moving from an Undecided response at the pretest to Disagree or Strongly Disagree at the posttest.

Table 1. Responses to: *Mathematics problems can be done correctly in only one way*

30 years and older:	Disagree & Strongly disagree	Undecided	Agree & Strongly Agree
Pretest (n=9)	100%	0%	0%
Posttest (n=11)	91%	0%	9%
20-24 years:			
Pretest (n=20)	65%	25%	10%
Posttest (n=20)	85%	10%	5%

Statement from a questionnaire developed by Schoenfeld (1989).

At the pretest (see Table 2) there is no difference between the proportions of the older or younger groups of students who Disagree, or Strongly Disagree, with the belief *The best way to do well in maths is to memorise all the formulas.* At the posttest a higher proportion of the older students are in these response categories, several moving from the Agree or Strongly Agree categories; however the proportion in the younger group remains substantially unchanged.

Table 2. Responses to: *the best way to do well in maths is to memorise all the formulas*

30 years and older:	Disagree & Strongly disagree	Undecided	Agree & Strongly Agree
Pretest (n=9)	55%	0%	45%
Posttest (n=11)	82%	0%	18%
20-24 years:			
Pretest (n=20)	55%	20%	25%
Posttest (n=20)	60%	15%	25%

Statement from a questionnaire developed by Schoenfeld (1989).

Mathematical Confidence

There is an indication, in responses to several of the open questions given at the posttest, that many students now have increased confidence in their mathematical ability; however, the proportion of students signalling this change varies in each age group. This may reflect a conflict between students' beliefs about the learning of mathematics and the approach in Mathematics 1. Analysis of responses to two of the open questions in the posttest are now discussed.

There are differences between the older and younger groups of students in their responses to the open question, *Has this course affected your mathematical confidence? Explain please.* In the first instance, all of the older students answered this question compared to 65% of the younger group, and 82% of the older group indicated that their confidence had improved, compared to 25% of the younger students. These responses fell into two categories. The first was their new understanding of mathematics as important and useful – 27% of the responses from the older group and none from the younger group were in this category. Examples of comments older students made are:

It makes me realise how important (it is) to learn maths and it is a must for everyone to know.

Yes, I feel more confident about how mathematics plays an important role in every day living.

The second category contained students who indicated that they felt more capable of doing mathematics or that it had improved their attitude to mathematics; 55% of the older group and 25% of the younger students responded in this way. Older students comment:

It has indeed improved my confidence in mathematics.

Absolutely - it has greatly improved my attitude towards maths - ie I am not so afraid of maths - I could face another course.

Some - refresh my memory on mathematical problems that I have forgotten.

A younger student in this response category said:

Dramatically. I am going to be a teacher and I took this course specifically to gain more confidence. I'm not so scared now about finding ideas for teaching.

It would appear that the scores on the scale measuring a students' self concept in mathematics (Gourgey, 1984) reflect this result. Scores on this scale decrease from pretest to posttest (indicating less confidence at the posttest) but this change is statistically significant only for the younger students (t=3.44, p<0.0001 those aged 24 years or younger.

Another open question on the questionnaire was *Has the course affected your ability to investigate mathematical situations?* Thirty five percent (n=7) of the younger group did not respond to this question (only 43% of this group passed the course), as well as one older student (who passed). Fifty five percent of the older group indicated that the course had, either definitely or in a limited way, increased their ability to investigate mathematical situations, with 50% of the younger group responding in a similar vein.

Responses among those 30 years and older included the comments:

I developed a more critical approach.

Yes, in a very limited way.

Probably assisted me in the approach to problem solving (eg brain storming/ lateral thinking).

Among those 20-24 years old, responses included:

Yes, the idea of not to accept every mathematical problem on face value, to investigate a problem and maybe even come up with new answers.

Thirty six percent of the older group indicated that the course had not affected their ability (two thirds of these students passed the course), compared to 15% of the younger group (all passed). It may be that many of the younger students who may have responded in this category did not answer this question. A negative response from an older student indicated:

> I'm still lacking in basic arithmetic skills, basic algebra, basic geometry.

A student in the 20-24 year old group said:

> It was too basic to put any real effort into, so I haven't really learnt much.

DISCUSSION OF SURVEY RESULTS

The differences between the responses at the pretest of the two age groups to the statement *Mathematics problems can be done correctly in only one way* may be because the life experience of the older group has led them to believe that there is usually more than one way to solve most (quantitative) problems. The responses of both age groups are very similar at the posttest so, for the younger students, it appears that their experience in Mathematics 1 may have increased the proportion who believe there is more than one way to solve mathematics problems.

On the other hand, the proportions in each category of the younger group's responses to the statement *The best way to do well in maths is to memorise all the formulas* change little from pretest to posttest. This belief is more resistant to change for the younger age group, supporting the results of a study of beginning university students' conceptions of mathematics by Crawford et al (1994), where the majority viewed mathematics as a set of procedures to be learnt by rote.

Students' beliefs about how to learn mathematics effectively may have caused negative reactions (McLeod, 1994; Schoenfeld, 1989) to the attempts in Mathematics 1 to develop the art of mathematising by investigating mathematical situations (de Lange, 1993). This was possibly more noticeable for the younger students and may have led many of them to react adversely to the open-ended realistic approach in Mathematics 1. This reaction resulted in fewer younger students than older students reporting positive changes in their mathematical confidence. Reactions to Mathematics 1 could also be influenced by the contexts used in the investigations. The task contexts could have acted as a "contextual barrier" (Helme, 1994) or may have had a cultural bias (Lajoie, 1995).

Many older students indicated Mathematics 1 has improved their mathematical confidence, possibly because, as FitzSimons (1994) suggests, they are unaware of the amount of mathematical experience they bring to a mathematics class. Lehmann (1987) also found that older students felt more confident with everyday tasks, indicating that they may have approached the "realistic" investigations more confidently.

The philosophy of Mathematics 1 may also align well with the strategies for adult learning developed by Rogers (1986), which he based on characteristics of adults' self-directed learning activities. For example, his suggestion to use discovery learning, as adults are active rather than passive recipients of learning, might have been addressed in Mathematics 1 through students working on investigations of mathematical situations. In addition, since adults usually move from concrete to general in self-directed learning, starting from social topics and discovering the mathematics within these contexts may be appropriate for adult students. The contexts are likely to be related to the adult students' existing experiences and knowledge and meet the need for motivation - two other characteristics mentioned by Rogers.

INTERVIEWS

Data from interviews with three students, which include some of their experiences in the Mathematics 1 course, follow. In this discussion I will highlight the metaphors used by these students to describe their learning experiences in mathematics.

"Digging up as opposed to raking over": John's Story

At the time of the interview John is 44 years old. He studied mathematics up to age 15, in a small rural school. "We didn't get a good grounding in maths", it was "rote-learning", "not much application". He has 20 years work experience in the electrical and electronics trades, learning some specialised maths for these jobs. He is in his fourth year as a part-time student, having studied biology, geography, chemistry and geology. He saw the need to strengthen his background mathematics and so enrolled in Mathematics 1.

He was asked to imagine if Maths 1 was weather, what would it be like, and he replied "It would be a nice sunny day". I interpret this metaphor as illustrating his growth in mathematical confidence. He says that he is "not so hesitant about getting into a maths problem, trying to sort through it" whereas before he would have "walked away". Maths 1 "does help you build a lot of confidence in what you're doing in maths" which he attributes to the "continued learning process" encouraged in Maths 1. "With [the labs in Maths 1], where you've got to go away and finish them and develop them more, you tend to remember. That's one big advantage."

When John was asked to think of a kitchen utensil that Maths 1 was like, he replied "I don't know. Probably like an opener, can open up things". This metaphor succinctly symbolises his comments, such as, "I can see it opening up a lot of areas", "developing different angles", the "sorts of skills" you need in "geography labs", for example. He comments that the assignments are "open-ended" and you "more or less design a maths problem for it so it does open [the assignment] up quite a bit".

If Maths 1 were a tool, he describes it as "digging up as opposed to raking over". This metaphor seems to refer to the depth of understanding he has achieved in

Mathematics 1, as opposed to superficial knowledge. This is illustrated by his comparative comments that most people miss out on learning these skills and just learn to "manipulate figures" and that there is "more time to think about it, and also thinking from different angles as well, as opposed to a rote-learning type situation". You learn to "put things in the proper perspective, and think about what's happening. I've developed that through Maths 1."

John passed Mathematics 1 with a B grade and completed his BSc three years later, majoring in geography.

"Frypan - I use it often": Yuko's Story

At the time of the interview Yuko is 21 years old and this is her first year of study (full-time) at the University of Auckland. She arrived in NZ from Japan 2 years ago, attending language schools in Auckland for about 18 months. Her parents live in Japan so Yuko said "once I decided [the courses I wished to study] I told [my parents] I'm going to take these subjects and they said that's ok." She is hoping to major in languages. She studied mathematics right through high school.

I find it hard to understand and follow the meaning of much of what Yuko was saying during the interview. When I introduce the idea of using metaphors to describe her experiences, she becomes more animated and seems to enjoy this method. It helps to clarify my understanding of experiences that she does not easily describe literally (Bowman, 1995) because of the level of her oral fluency in English. It becomes a powerful tool for her to express her meaning, particularly as she interpreted most of the metaphors she used.

To the question "What if high school maths were an animal?" Yuko replies that her experience learning maths in Japan was like a lion. "Lion is cute animal but" it always "try to catch animal", kills them and eats some meat then kills another animal and "eats half of" that one. There is lots of "left-over meat". She "studied lots of maths [and] forgot lots of maths". It was "thrown away". Her experience in Maths 1 reminds her of "the cow - eating all the time". "Cows don't eat a lot because" they move food from "stomach to mouth" and eat it again. "I study mathematics and whenever I need some skills I remind of the cow and then chew again."

She is asked to think about the utensils she would use in a kitchen and decide what kind of utensil would be like maths in high school. She replies: "Dishes and tin opener - put away - forget where you put away. So many kinds of dishes and I don't know which ones to use, but I cook something. Tin opener? I don't use tin opener so I forgot where I put it and how to use it, but I know what it is." Yuko interprets this metaphor as "It's useful but forgotten how to use it, like the mathematics. There are so many skills around. Which skill I can use?" Maths 1 is like "knife, fork and spoon, frypan, I use them often. I know where it is, I know how to use them. I use them so many times so I remember where I put it. I know the formula, I know when I have to use it." She likes the approach in Maths 1 better, "because we can use this mathematics. I know when I think about things in a mathematics way and I like this thinking in mathematical way. When I study this course, ... you have to use mathematics to solve these [assignment] problems - [they] are likely to happen. I want to study mathematics more because I feel it's useful now.   I'd like to study mathematics next year as well."

Yuko achieved an A grade in Mathematics 1 and a B+ in Mathematics 2, in the second semester. After successfully completing all the courses she enrolled in for the year, she left the University of Auckland.

"A narrow and bumpy street": Keiko's story

Keiko is 21 years old and moved to NZ five years ago with her family. She completed all five years of high school, taking mathematics until age 15. At the time of the interview it is her first year at the University of Auckland and she is studying Mathematics 1, Korean and Chinese language and culture. She said "my parents ask me to do maths or science. ... If I have to choose between maths and language would choose language. This year I told my parents I can't do maths very well - I've forgotten everything." They replied that she should try as "maths is quite important in our life". But she said "actually, I thought myself as well I should study maths - a little bit - thought [this course] easy one for you".

When I ask "If your early high school experience were a way to travel, what would that way be?" Keiko replies "a straight road ... nothing there, just straight, a nice wide road". Her interpretation of this metaphor is "because easy to understand and easy to solve the problems. If hard, then teacher or friend always help you." If high school maths were a kitchen utensil, Keiko says it "must be a knife because useful, and everyday have to use ... easy to cut ...(to solve problem) although sometimes need to sharpen it, so need to think a bit first sometimes."

For her experience in Maths 1, the 'way to travel' would be a "very difficult way .... going to the wrong way and back again   .... a narrow and bumpy street ... lots of hills". In Maths 1, the 'kitchen utensil' is "an electric element (not oven) ... electric one is so inconvenient ... if busy and want hot water, it's not like gas, takes a long time to heat!" These metaphors seem to indicate that she found Mathematics 1 difficult, which is illustrated by her comparison "I think question not hard if I understand well but because in high school just question and answer, question and answer, so easy. But here you have to write why. Sometimes I just don't know why!" Maths 1 has been "Uncomfortable! Very!"

> The most important thing she has learned about maths in Maths 1 is that the "questions always about daily life so I think it's quite useful but at moment I don't need to use it." Keiko achieved a B pass in Mathematics 1 and completed her BA in three years of full-time study, majoring in Chinese and Korean. She studied Mathematics 2 in the final year of her degree and achieved a marginal pass.

DISCUSSION OF INTERVIEWS

Since Mathematics 1 has been a very different experience for each of the two young Japanese women, what has made the difference? Yuko seems to be less dependent on her parent's approval for the subjects she studied than Keiko, who still lives at home with her parents. Their scores on the Maths Self Concept Scale are different. Keiko's score decreases markedly from pretest to posttest (18/40 to 8/40), indicating a loss of mathematical self-confidence, whereas Yuko's scores are 23 and 21 respectively. Keiko has less high school mathematics background than Yuko, which may have affected her ability to handle the content of Mathematics 1. Keiko believes that she learned mathematics effectively by "memoris[ing] everything, all the formula and so on ... quite easy to" and agrees with the statement *The best way to do well in maths is to memorise all the formulas* at the pretest and also at the posttest. By contrast, Yuko is undecided about this belief statement at the pretest and disagrees with it at the posttest. Keiko's belief is similar to that of many beginning university mathematics students (Crawford et al, 1994), and has been resistant to change. This conflict between her belief and the approach used in Mathematics 1 is probably one factor which has caused her negative reactions to the course (McLeod, 1994; Schoenfeld, 1989).

The interviews gave some interesting, useful and rich results, particularly with the use of metaphors to provide a trigger for conceptualisation, and comparison, of their experiences learning mathematics (Sims, 1981). My experience conducting these interviews reflects that of Gordon & Langmaid (1988:89) who report that the use of metaphors "created new energy in the interviews". The metaphors used by these students illustrate the "synthesizing function" of a metaphor, "a metaphor's ability to compress a great deal of peripheral, intuitive and emotional content into one symbol" (Sims, 1981:402). Each student's metaphors enabled me to understand more clearly how their current and previous experience learning mathematics had affected them (Gibson, 1992). This technique appears to be a novel approach in this area of research in mathematics education.

APPENDIX

Open Questions for Mathematics 1 Posttest 1995
Instructions: Answer each of the following questions in a sentence or two. Write your answers in the space below each question.

1. *Explain, with reasons, whether you liked or disliked Mathematics 1.*
2. *What have you liked best about this course?*
3. *What have you liked least about this course?*
4. *Could you suggest ways that this course could be improved?*

5. *What topics did you like best?*
6. *What topics did you like least?*
7. *Are there other topics you would like to have learned about?*
8. *Explain why you liked or disliked the assigning of marks for participation in tutorial tasks.*
9. *What did you think of the tasks which were given out in tutorials?*
10. *What are your reactions to working with a group on the task in the tutorials?*
11. *What do you think about being able to redo term tests?*
12. *What comment do you have about the style of the term test questions?*
13. *Did you use the printed lecture notes? YES / NO (Circle one)*
14. *Comment on the usefulness of these notes.*
15. *Has this course affected your mathematical confidence? Explain please.*
16. *What do you think about the maths you have done in this course?*
17. *Has this course affected your ability to investigate mathematical situations? If so, in what way?*
18. *What did you think of the course's approach?*
19. *Do you intend to continue studying maths next year?*

REFERENCES

Bowman, R.P. (1995) 'Using Metaphors as Tools for Counselling Children'. *Elementary Guidance and Counselling,* 29, 206-216.

Crawford, K., Gordon, S., Nicholas, J, & Prosser, M. (1994). 'Conceptions of Mathematics and How it is Learned: The Perspectives of Students Entering University'. *Learning and Instruction, 4,* 331-345.

de Lange, J. (1987). *Mathematics, Insight and Meaning: Teaching, Learning and Testing Mathematics for the Life and Social Sciences*: Vakgroep Onderzoek Wiskundeonderwijs en Onderwijscomputercentrum, Rijksuniversiteit Utrecht.

de Lange, J. (1993).'Assessment in Problem-oriented Curricula'. In N. L. Webb & A. F. Coxford (Eds.), *Assessment in the Mathematics Classroom: 1993 Yearbook.* Reston, Virginia: National Council of Teachers of Mathematics, 197-208.

FitzSimons, G. (1994). *Teaching Mathematics to Adults Returning to Study*: Deakin University.

Gibson, H. (1994). "Math Is Like a Used Car: Metaphors Reveal Attitudes toward Mathematics" . In D. Buerk (Ed.), *Empowering Students by Promoting Active Learning in Mathematics.* Reston, Virginia: The National Council of Teachers of Mathematics, Inc., 7-12.

Gordon, W. & Langmaid, R. (1988). *Qualitative Market Research.* Aldershot; Brookfield, USA: Gower.

Gourgey, A. F. (1984). *The Relationship of Misconceptions About Math and Mathematical Self-concept to Math Anxiety and Statistics Performance.* Paper presented at the American Educational Research Association, New Orleans, LA, USA.

Helme, S. (1994). *Mathematics Embedded in Context: The Role of Task Context in Performance, Task Perceptions and the Solution Methods of Adult Women Students.* Unpublished Masters of Education Thesis, Australian Catholic University.

Lajoie, S. P. (1995). 'A Framework for Authentic Assessment in Mathematics'. In T. A. Romberg (Ed.), *Reform in School Mathematics and Authentic Assessment.* Albany, NY, USA: State University of New York, 19-37.

Lehmann, C. H. (1987). *The Adult Mathematics Learner: Attitudes, Expectations, Attributions.* Paper presented at the Annual Meeting of the American Educational Research Association, Washington DC.

McLeod, D. B. (1994). 'Research on Affect and Mathematics Learning in the *JRME*: 1970 to the Present'. *Journal for Research in Mathematics Education, 25*(6), 637-647.

Miller-Reilly, B. (1995). 'A New Approach for Students Returning to Mathematics', *Readings from the Mathematics Education Unit 1995.* Auckland, New Zealand: Mathematics Education Unit, School of Mathematical and Information Science, University of Auckland, 81-94.

Miller-Reilly, B. J. (1994). *Studying the Effects of an Innovative Instructional Approach in a New Bridging Paper.* Paper presented at the Australian Bridging Mathematics Network Conference.

Miller-Reilly, B. J. (1997). 'Reactions Of Adults To An Investigative Mathematics Course'. In G. FitzSimons (Ed.), *Adults Returning to Study Mathematics, Papers from Working Group 18, 8th International Congress on Mathematical Education (ICME8)*: The Australian Association of Mathematics Teachers Inc., 101-118

Ocean, J. & Miller-Reilly, B. (1997). 'Black Holes and Beginning Teachers: A Connected Approach to Teaching Mathematics'. *The Australian Mathematics Teacher, 53*(4), 17-20.

Rogers, A. (1986). *Teaching Adults.* Milton Keynes, England: Open University Press.

Schoenfeld, A. H. (1989). 'Explorations of Students' Mathematical Beliefs and Behaviour'. *Journal for Research in Mathematics Education, 20*(4), 338-355.

Sims, D. C. (1981). *Context-Sensitive Evaluation Technology in Bilingual Education.* Eastern Michigan University, Ypsilanti, MI (National Institute of Education (ED), Washington, DC.

Chapter 15

Assessing Numeracy

John O'Donoghue
University of Limerick, Limerick, Ireland

INTRODUCTION

The Applications Oriented Mathematics (AOM) project, initiated in 1979, is an on-going collaboration between the statutory county-based education authority, Tipperary (NR) Vocational Education Committee, and the Centre for Advancement of Mathematical Education in Technology (CAMET (Ireland)) at the University of Limerick, Ireland. The dynamic created by the evolving situation led to a rich vein of mathematics education research in adults learning mathematics. In this respect, the AOM project has spawned three fruitful lines of research viz.

— an assessment-led open learning system for adults learning mathematics (O'Donoghue, 1997)
— Look + See Poster Series for adult learners (O'Donoghue, 1997)
— numeracy assessment (O'Donoghue, 1995a, 1996).

This chapter gives a summary overview of the journey travelled by this project and the current state of work-in-progress. However, the principal focus of this chapter is the theoretical framework for numeracy assessment which evolved during the author's work with the project and influenced the design of a compatible numeracy assessment instrument for adults. Aspects of this work are detailed in papers presented at ALM conferences (O'Donoghue, 1995a, 1996).

The chapter begins with essential background information on adult education in Ireland, the mathematics education context and methodological issues. Salient features of the AOM programme are presented since they

D. Coben et al. (eds.), Perspectives on Adults Learning Mathematics, 271–287.
© 2000 *Kluwer Academic Publishers. Printed in the Netherlands.*

influenced the nature of the theoretical framework which evolved and had a direct bearing on the design of the assessment instrument. The AOM numeracy framework is then presented with associated definitions. This is followed by a detailed discussion of the numeracy assessment instrument. The chapter concludes   in traditional manner with   discussion and concluding remarks sections.

BACKGROUND

Adult education in Ireland

In Ireland "adult education is virtually invisible in contrast to other sectors of education" (Irvine, 1990:88).   Adult education has not been accorded any real priority in the context of national education provision until recently.   Expenditure on adult education is among the lowest in the OECD countries.   Participation in adult education in Ireland is very low (20%) and is about half of the average rate in the OECD countries.   (Minister of State, Department of Education, 1997).   Recent efforts by the government through the responsible minister (the first ever minister appointed with responsibility for adult education) are directed towards generating a discussion document by the end of 1998.   This will serve as a precursor to planned government initiatives in adult education including legislation.   It is envisaged that adult education will be given proper recognition and status; structured properly at local and national level; and adequately funded[1].

Meanwhile adult education in Ireland is organised and delivered through a variety of government and voluntary agencies.   These include second level schools, higher education institutes and an array of statutory and voluntary bodies and community groups.   The county-based statutory Vocational Education Committees (VEC's) are the main providers of adult education in Ireland through their local schools.   Each committee employs a full-time Adult Education Organiser (AEO) for its area.   A myriad of voluntary organisations provide courses for adults throughout the country mainly for their members.   Literacy provision is organised by the National Adult Literacy Agency (NALA).   There is no separate provision for adult numeracy.   An umbrella organisation for voluntary agencies exists and is called the National Association for Adult Education in Ireland (AONTAS). It was founded in 1968 to promote adult education in Ireland and receives state aid for that purpose.

The country is well served by the National Training and Employment Authority (FAS) which is responsible for industrial training of adults and the national apprenticeship schemes. Another agency, CERT, is responsible for education and training in the catering and tourism industry.

A further education sector has emerged in recent years and is running alongside provision at upper secondary level (15-18+) in the vocational education sector mainly up to and beyond the School Leaving Certificate level. This is further education very much along the lines of the UK model for further education (FE).This new sector is likely to have a major impact on adult education provision in Ireland in the future. A National Council for Vocational Awards (NCVA) was established in 1991 to rationalise and co-ordinate development in this area including certification.

Finally, it should be said that the vast majority of tutors in adult education in Ireland are employed part-time and have little or no professional training in adult education. They work for agencies for which the provision of adult education is secondary or subordinate to their main role (Irvine, 1990).

The mathematics education context

The Applications Oriented Mathematics (AOM) programme was developed as a lighthouse programme. It was designed to show what could be done for 15-17 year olds who were failing the official mainstream mathematics programme at upper secondary level in Ireland. It was a planned alternative to the then existing highly academic programmes at this level. In its design the programme anticipated several key recommendations of the Cockcroft Report (1982). Often these innovations were implemented contrary to official policy. The AOM philosophy is based on Wilder's (1973) view of mathematics as a cultural element and this in turn led to a treatment of mathematics as an organic whole characterized by skills, processes, abstractions, proofs and applications. In this scheme of things mathematics is meant to be useful and its usefulness is interpreted in a special way as providing a conceptual vehicle for organizing, interpreting and dealing with the real world. This approach has resonances with some views of numeracy especially those which emphasize aspects of mathematics such as critical thinking, problem solving and communication as well as computational skills (Crowther, 1959; Le Roux, 1979; Cockcroft, 1982; Chapman & Lee, 1990; Tout, 1996). In hindsight, it is easy to recognise these emphases and it should come as no surprise that the author's notion of numeracy (introduced later in this chapter) is closely linked to them. Published accounts of the project over the years show a surer and maturing conceptualization of the work-in-progress along these lines (O'Donoghue, 1982, 1990, 1995b).

The AOM programme attracted a variety of adult user groups from the outset. These included learners in formal and informal education settings. In particular there was a significant take-up by adult learners attending literacy centres, adult and community education centres and some of the prison population.   Later (from 1989) long-term unemployed workers wishing to avail themselves of second chance education under a government sponsored Vocational Training and Opportunities Scheme (VTOS) joined the programme in special centres throughout the country.   Some salient features of the programme are listed here for reference:

- the programme is underpinned by an educational philosophy which treats mathematics as a cultural element (O'Donoghue, 1978)
- it is targeted at young adult and adult learners
- it deals with learners in traditional and non-traditional settings
- applications are central to the programme philosophy
- the programme integrates technology including calculators and computers
- it attends to the pedagogical issues related to programme philosophy, content and learners.

Research methodology

The AOM project is a collaborative effort between researcher and practitioners.   At times the developmental aspect of the work dictated the pace for pragmatic reasons.   It is difficult to say whether those practitioners involved always saw themselves as researchers.   However, there was a definite reluctance to accede to pressure for numeracy tests until the issues had been 'researched properly' by the team.   Hence the drive to put the numeracy work on a research footing.   While it is true to say that the author always viewed the work as *research* in the *action research* tradition, it may not always have lived-up to that claim over the years due to various practical pressures.

On the other hand the assessment work was problem-led from the outset. It was conducted and managed on an action research cycle involving consideration of the situation and context, critical reflection as a source of insights and further action, critical trialling during a pilot phase and the use of appropriate evaluation procedures (McKernan, 1991).   The assessment work represents a deliberate intervention in adult education in the field of adults learning mathematics.

The author has collaborated at all stages with practitioners in the person of literacy, numeracy and adult education tutors and centre co-ordinators and mathematics teachers.   They have been advised at all stages and involved in an evaluative process of critical commenting, face-to-face try-outs, pilot tests and continuous monitoring. This interaction is very productive and has contributed in many ways to the overall goal. In particular, ideas about test design, length of test, language used, levels of difficulty, nature of test items, marking schemes, pass standard and reporting have greatly influenced the work-in-progress. It is proposed to continue the work in this mode of qualitative research as it suits the enterprise.

An effort is made throughout the chapter to locate various AOM activities in time and the following may further assist the reader in this regard: the AOM project began in September, 1979 and is still on-going only as regards numeracy work; numeracy assessment tests for adults were available from May, 1989 and are still available in January and May of each year; numeracy assessment work overlaps other AOM activities and may be viewed as progressing through two phases, the *ad hoc* phase (1989-95), and the research phase (1993-99) including a pilot study (1996) and full implementation (1997-99).The AOM open learning system including the poster series was developed in the period 1994-97.

DEVELOPING A NUMERACY ASSESSMENT FRAMEWORK

Early work and the ad hoc *phase*

While the project team was totally committed to devising new assessment methods which it did from the start, it did not involve itself in numeracy assessment. This is simply because the original aims were not construed in numeracy terms nor were they couched in the language of numeracy. But feedback from the learner base indicated a persistent demand for numeracy assessment and certification. In 1989 the first numeracy tests were offered in conjunction with the AOM programme. They were well-received with the numbers taking them increasing sharply in 1993, 1994 and continuing in 1995.

An attempt began in 1995 to re-conceptualise all the work of the AOM project in appropriate numeracy terms. This was driven in part by demand but also by wider educational issues in the Irish context such as an evolving further education sector (O'Donoghue, 1995b). This went hand in hand with efforts to put numeracy assessment on a better footing through research. Two distinct but overlapping phases are discernible since the AOM team became involved in numeracy assessment work: the *ad hoc* phase (1989-95), and the research phase (1993-99).

The so-called *ad hoc* phase is characterised by a naïve approach to numeracy assessment. This was based on first-hand experience of assessment in the AOM project and the combined resources of the team in terms of teaching and assessing experience. While this resource was not inconsiderable, it soon became clear that it was inadequate. It resulted in the use of a thinly adapted off-the-shelf model instrument based on the Institute of Mathematics and its Applications (IMA, 1977) basic skills tests. These early numeracy assessments which were offered in the period 1989-95 were timed, written tests and consisted of a set of open-ended tasks or problems. They were marked on an 'all-or-nothing' basis i.e. there was no partial credit. A pass required candidates to secure 50% of the available marks. They were replaced in January 1996, by specially developed numeracy tests.

Paradoxically, the tutors and learners were happy with this form of assessment while the project team always viewed it as an emergency measure. While the tests were programme-based (initially all candidates studied the AOM (Part 1) programme) the project team remained satisfied that they were adequate. But increasing numbers of candidates entering in subsequent years were prepared in different ways or had no specific preparation and simply availed of the test. This was a new development that required specific attention.

It should be said that early in the research phase which began in 1993 the naivety of the early work was confirmed. But valuable lessons were learned. A plan of action was devised and a programme (Table 1) of work initiated which is continuing today.

Table 1. Programme of Work

GOALS	APPROACH
Devise:	Exploit:
Working model of numeracy	AOM experience
Numeracy programme	AOM/Numeracy experience
Appropriate assessment	Wider experience
Materials	Research
Certification	
Training model/materials	

The research phase

This assessment work is predicated on the AOM project's working models of numeracy, numeracy programme and assessment. These models which are summarized below were developed through action research in response to a felt need for an indigenous numeracy programme. No such programme was available in Ireland at that time.

The author met with a small group of literacy/numeracy tutors under the aegis of the Tipperary (NR) Vocational Education Committee to advance this work. Over a period of many months (1993-94) and several meetings, these exchanges led to working definitions and approaches. These ideas were structured and given form by the author for presentation to a wider audience for critical reaction. A specially convened one-day workshop was used for this purpose (May 1994). Fourteen tutors engaged in literacy/numeracy work in a variety of centres around the country evaluated the work to date. The general approach was well received and much constructive feedback on the design of a numeracy assessment instrument was offered by tutors. A prototype numeracy assessment was constructed on the basis of a revised design and subsequently trialled in a national pilot study in January, 1996 (O'Donoghue, 1996).

The author's "working definition" of numeracy which was distilled from the work-in-progress, research and reflection is central to this assessment work. For the purposes of this project it seemed important to focus on five characteristics:
— scope of numeracy
— the mathematics of numeracy
— the societal aspect of numeracy
— the time-dependent nature of numeracy
— the individual and numeracy.

Briefly explained, this means that numeracy is a broad-based attribute comprising attitudes, mathematics, technology and process skills such as problem solving, communication and interpretative skills. It has a core of elementary mathematics which is broad-based and not confined to computational skills. The needs and conditions of society influence what numeracy encompasses e.g. process skills such as problem solving are more highly prized in the workplace than ever before. All this suggests that numeracy is a *dynamic* concept changing over time. Finally, we must not lose sight of the fact that numeracy is a human individual capability that is bound up with the individual's capacity to perform whatever roles may emerge in the future as worker, citizen, learner and others. (O'Donoghue, 1995b).

The purpose of this characterization of numeracy is to add clarity to our thinking about curriculum development and assessment as these professional activities relate to numeracy. This analysis and conceptualization suggests that the mathematics element of a numeracy programme should be broad-based, address the needs of the individual and society and integrate the use of available technologies. A programme of elementary mathematics which meets these requirements must include:

Number	Measurement
Percentages	Statistics

Ratio/proportion	Approximation/Estimation
Basic algebra	Calculators
Shapes	Computing.

Consistent with this conceptualization of numeracy is an assessment approach which focuses on:

— core knowledge and skills
— use/application of mathematics
— mathematics as a means of communication.

These competencies may be viewed loosely as indications of levels of understanding for assessment purposes at a particular stage e.g. Stage 1, Basic Numeracy,

These working models have been made explicit albeit in summary form because they underpin the work completed to date and the on-going research. All subsequent discussion in this paper is coloured by these ideas.

Assessment rationale

The development work was guided by practical, professional and academic considerations.   On a practical level, it was felt that any assessment instrument devised should focus *inter alia* on process   skills, incorporate levels of understanding and be robust enough to accommodate specific new emphases. A particular practical consideration was that centres would accept this mode of assessment and take ownership of it on behalf of their learners. This latter consideration has methodological implications for development work. The academic and professional concerns centred mainly on achieving appropriate standards in all aspects of our research and development work.

NUMERACY ASSESSMENT INSTRUMENT

Design of the assessment instrument
As a result of experiences with the AOM programme and the *ad hoc* numeracy work the team was pre-disposed towards:

— a comprehensive timed written test
— grid design based on content and behaviours
— criterion-referenced tests

– process skills (problem-solving, communication and interpretative skills).

There was a strong desire to stay close to the learners and tutors and involve them in the development phase. It was felt that this alliance would lead to improved assessment practices specifically in areas of instrument design such as validating test items, setting levels of difficulty and identifying important new emphases.

Grid design

A design grid evolved in this context that is robust enough to incorporate the various features identified. The grid is based on a standard content/behaviour grid (e.g. Ten Brink, 1974; Dean, 1982; Carter et al, 1994) but includes important additional features (Figure 1). The particular form of the grid was influenced by the work of others e.g. Brown (1992, 1993) and Romberg et al (1990) in that key competencies or understandings are identified and two over-arching considerations are introduced via screening.

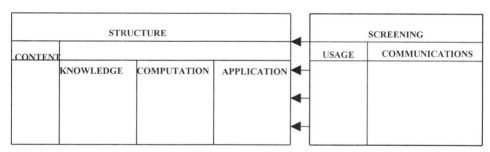

Figure 1. Design grid: AOM Numeracy Test

The behaviour dimension reflects the concern for levels of understanding as defined by the team above. It includes knowledge, computation and application.

The 'screening' aspect is introduced to avoid problems of assessing certain types of knowledge and ignoring others e.g. *knowing what v knowing how.* Both are included here. It also functions as a device to prevent strict compartmentalisation of content within rigid boundaries. Screening introduces two over-arching considerations viz *usage in context* and *communications skills.* These are central to the team's philosophy. Every item included in the test is 'screened'.

The team has adopted a particular approach to 'usage screening'. All items are judged against a list of contexts (Table 2).

Table 2. Provisional List of Usage Contexts

Usage Contexts
Employment/DIY
Household Budget
Consumer
Sport/Leisure/Recreation
Travel
Citizenship

This list is restricted because the team believes it has a bearing on difficulty of test and may be linked to levels of numeracy. For example, it may be that usage in additional contexts will help to define a higher level of numeracy. More empirical work needs to be done on this aspect of numeracy assessment.

Similarly all items are screened against the communications skills list (Table 3). Obviously this is a provisional list and needs more work. But at this point the team is convinced that the approach guarantees due weight and emphasis for communications skills.

Table 3. Provisional List of Communications Skills

Communications Skills
Reading (e.g. numbers, graphs etc)
Writing (e.g. numbers etc)
Extracting information/media
Translating information/media
Interpreting information/media
Presenting information (e.g. tables, charts, graphs)

As indicated each item included in the test is judged against content and behaviour dimensions, and screened appropriately. Relative difficulty is determined by reference to experience, other tests, and limited field tests. In addition each item is viewed as a separate task. Tasks are presented in two ways: by means of standard objective - type items or open-ended questions. This mix, it is felt, addresses the multi-dimensional nature of mathematical content. More extensive work in the area of validation is planned involving tutors and learners.

Test features

It is convenient to refer to this instrument as the *numeracy test*. A number of features are worth noting:

It is a timed test

While it is a timed test there is a relatively relaxed attitude towards the time factor. A number of devices are used to mitigate the effects of a prolonged single sitting. The time requirement for each section is deliberately overestimated by a small margin. A short break (30 minutes) is allowed after Section A. Candidates can start Section C before the time allowed for Section B has elapsed. Calculators are allowed for Section B and C.

Timed tests are traditional in Irish education and they are deeply rooted in the culture. For many Irish adults, success in mathematics means passing such a test and anything else runs the risk of being viewed as inferior and unacceptable.

The test comes in sections

The test is divided into three timed sections:

Section A: Mathematical Facts and Computational Skills

Section B: Problems in Context

Section C: Mathematical Communication

Each section assesses learners in areas singled out by the project for special attention.

The material in the sections is designed to overlap.

Test items

Test items in Section A are essentially criterion-referenced and presented in multiple formats. The format is selected that best fits the intended purpose. Each section is dominated by particular item format(s). In particular, Section B contains only open-ended tasks comprising single-step problems in context. In all, the test instrument uses four different item formats - multiple-choice, free response, fill-in-the-blank, or write a few sentences.

Technology

Candidates are invited to use calculators on Sections B and C but are forbidden their use on Section A. Candidates are expected to be prepared in the use of calculators.

The design grid (Figure 1) was used to develop the assessment instrument for the pilot phase which began in January 1996 and all subsequent sittings (6 in total).

Given the project's emphasis on context and communication perhaps it is not surprising that these aspects should be examined in separate sections (Sections B and C). However, some readers may be surprised that Section A is devoted entirely to what might be described as 'abstract sums'. The project view is that this kind of work is necessary and valuable for many adults and deserves an important place in any numeracy-type programme. This in no way detracts from the work of those who emphasise the role of context in learning mathematics e.g. Lave (1988). It is rather an attempt to maintain balance. There is no gain if the argument polarises around mathematics in context and decontextualized mathematics. The point is that *some but not all learners* are served in either case. Numeracy as an issue in mathematics education must treat these aspects as *complementary*. The test instrument recognises this situation in its design and construction.

Marks and Standards

Items in Section A are marked on an all-or-nothing basis. Each item has a single correct response. Correct responses attract one mark while incorrect responses receive zero marks. Marks are allocated for problems in Section B on the basis of correct identification of processes involved and the successful implementation of the process. Thus candidates can obtain partial credits in this section as indeed they can in Section C on a similar basis. All marks assigned are multiples of one.

The relative weights between sections A, B, and C are preserved in the proportions 4:5:3 approximately. The pass standard is meant to reflect the emphases valued by the project team. Since the project team takes the view that activities examined in sections A, B and C are not mutually exclusive, a simple aggregate score is not appropriate. A compromise between a simple aggregate and Boolean combinations is used to determine the pass standard. Basically candidates are required to achieve 50% overall (A+B+C) and not less than 50% of the marks in any two of the three sections A, B, C.

Results for each candidate are mailed to each centre within six weeks of the examination date. Individual marks are not disclosed. A profile of a candidate's performance is given using letter designations. Some typical profiles are shown in Table 4 where S represents a satisfactory outcome and U an unsatisfactory outcome.

Table 4. Typical Profiles

SECTIONS				
A	B	C	A+B+C	
S	S	U	S	PASS
S	U	S	U	FAIL
U	S	U	S	FAIL

DISCUSSION

The AOM programme produced a wealth of good quality assessment experience. It is hardly surprising that this experience had a major formative influence on the author's subsequent work in numeracy assessment. Allied with this was a determination to set the research work in the context of best practice in mathematics assessment. Among the concerns identified and issues raised the following deserve special attention.

Assessment principles

There was a clear concern that the research and development work should be guided by the following principles:

- mathematics assessment should seek to find out what learners know rather than focus on what they do not know (Cockcroft, 1982)
- different modes and types of assessments should be used (Cockcroft, 1982)
- care must be taken to align the assessment with the mathematics programme involved (NCTM, 1989).

The all-or-nothing marking scheme used in conjunction with aspects of AOM assessment had to be modified to reflect learners' work. While the tutors and learners using the AOM programme understood and accepted the marking scheme there was still a deep cultural resistance to it. The anticipated difficulty was avoided by devising a new marking scheme for the numeracy assessment instrument.

It became clear from our experience with numeracy assessment that the numeracy instrument would have to be robust enough to serve in a :

- programme mode (supported by a specific programme)
- programme-free mode (learners presenting for test only).

These issues received special attention as the theoretical framework for numeracy assessment evolved and in turn influenced the design of the numeracy instrument.

Monitoring and evaluation

There are no independent bench marks for this type of work in Ireland. This means that in the interim period results will have to stand on their own merits until a bank of comparable data can be accumulated over several sittings. Meanwhile we measure our expectations against the AOM experience over the years and anecdotal evidence from centres. This feedback is solicited from tutors and co-ordinators on the occasion of test sittings and other occasions. It usually comes in written form and is dealt with by the project director (author) in the first instance and then the project's Examination Committee. While the examination is in progress there is on-line telephone support to deal with queries and problems. So far it appears that the new format has been well received by centres and candidates. More importantly the pass rates/failure rates seem to be acceptable (See Table 5). The failure rates are inflated by the practice in some centres of entering candidates who have not been prepared in any way for the examination. We have discouraged this practice but cannot prevent it.

Table 5. Number of candidates and success rates

Sitting/Year		1996	1997	1998
Jan	Pass	175	159	98
	Fail	41	27	20
	Total	216	286	118
May	Pass	122	70	52
	Fail	37	36	7
	Total	159	106	59

However, it is evident from early results and an examination of scripts that some problems are deep-seated indeed. Difficulties with decimals, percentages and simple algebra that were evident throughout the whole AOM experience are still present. Another feature of AOM data - the contribution of clusters of failing candidates to the failure rate - still persists in the numeracy data A different but potentially more damaging feature is evident in these examination scripts. It appears that candidates are unable to use calculators. Even at this early stage there is much that requires careful attention.

CONCLUDING REMARKS

A number of points are worth making at this stage. In absolute terms the number of candidates looks quite small but the author can assure readers that it is significant in the Irish context. Again, while this study constitutes research for the author it is very much the *real thing* for candidates who are using it to secure certification. The project team is very conscious of this latter fact and much work was directed towards securing national certification for candidates by working out an equivalency relationship with the National Council for Vocational Awards (NCVA) Foundation Certificate in Mathematics. The project work in this regard received early approval from the NCVA but only on a once-off basis for the year 1996. It has since been decided that this approach to numeracy assessment using once-off timed tests is at odds with NCVA philosophy which favours portfolio assessment in their Foundation Level Certificate. However, the continuing steady demand for AOM-style assessment may indicate a need for wider choice for adults. The issue of choice for adults may have been under-valued by the NCVA as a means of improving participation by adults. As we write this paper there are signs of a re-think and the issue is likely to be re-opened in the near future.

The project team is satisfied that the programme has achieved its primary purpose as a lighthouse programme since the government has made available a similar programme within the mainstream provision and has widened the scope of official mathematics provision beyond what could have been envisaged twenty years ago. This is an entirely satisfactory outcome for the project team and would have led to its winding-up before now were it not for sustained demand from adult groups. This demand, in the future, should be met within the general education provision in the emerging Further Education sector. In view of this and after a careful assessment of developments and needs in this sector, the AOM team decided to phase - out the AOM programme from September 1997 because adult learners of mathematics will be catered for adequately by NCVA under their remit. Publication of the AOM open learning pack (in press) comprising text book, work book and poster set will be a suitable testament to the team's efforts and serve adult learners well for some years to come. The team viewed the assessment work in a different light and decided to continue with its work in this area of adults learning mathematics.

Recently the project group has been designated as a mathematics support group for the National Council for Vocational Awards. This association provides a vehicle for an on-going input into the mathematics education of adult learners in Ireland as programme developers, tutor trainers and researchers. Mathematics assessment research will be an integral part of on-going work but the direction it will take is not clear at the time of writing. The National Council for Vocational Awards emerged in the context of, and as a response to a growing further education sector in Ireland and policy decisions in relation to access to higher education and adult continuing education. It is likely to have a significant impact in this area of education in the coming years.

ACKNOWLEDGEMENT

I gratefully acknowledge the constructive comments of Diana Coben and Gail FitzSimons on an earlier version of this chapter. This revised version benefited from the perceptive comments of the anonymous reviewers.

NOTES

1   The Government published its Green Paper (discussion document) in Nov. 1998. This document lives up to the expectations of interested parties and sets the scene in Ireland for a final round of consultations before legislation.

REFERENCES

Brown, M. (1992). *GAIM Topic Criteria*. Edinburgh: Thomas Nelson and Sons Ltd.

Brown, M. (1993). 'Assessment in Mathematics Education: Developments in Philosophy and Practice in the United Kingdom'. In M. Niss (Ed), *Cases of Assessment in Mathematics Education : An ICMI Study*. Dordrecht:Kluwer Academic Publishers, 71-84.

Carter, D., Frobisher, L & Roper, T. (1994). 'Assessing Mathematical Achievement'. In A. Orton & G. Wain (eds), *Issues in Teaching Mathematics*. London: Cassell, 117-135.

Chapman, A & A. Lee. (1990). 'Rethinking Literacy and Numeracy'. *Australian Journal of Education*. 34(3), 277-289.

Cockcroft, W.H. (1982). *Mathematics Counts : Report of the Committee of Inquiry into the Teaching of Mathematics in Schools*. London : Her Majesty's Stationery Office.

Dean, P.G. (1982). *Teaching and learning mathematics*. London: The Woburn Press.

Institute of Mathematics and its Applications (1977). 'A Proposal for a National Standard of Basic Skills in School Mathematics'. *Bulletin of the IMA*, 13(3/4), 66 - 67.

Irvine, D.G. (1990). ' Initial and inservice training for tutors of adults : some implications for the status of adult education'. *Irish Educational Studies*, 9(1), 88 - 102.

Lave, J. (1988) *Cognition in Practice : Mind, Mathematics and Culture in Everyday Life*. Cambridge : Cambridge University Press.

Le Roux, A.A. (1979). 'Numeracy: An alternate definition'. *International Journal of Mathematical Education in Science and Technology*. 10, 343-354.

National Council of Teachers of Mathematics (1989). *Curriculum and Evaluation Standards*. Reston V.A. : NCTM.

McKernan, J. (1991). *Curriculum Action Research: A handbook of methods and resources for the reflective practitioner*. London : Kogan Page.

Minister of State, Department of Education (1997). *Launch of International Adult Literacy Survey Reports*. (Press Release, October).

O'Donoghue, J. (1978). *Educating and training mathematics teachers for Irish secondary schools : a new perspective on teacher education*, unpublished PhD thesis, Loughborough University.

O'Donoghue, J & L. Murtagh (1983). 'An exercise in school/scheme-based curriculum development : the Tipperary (NR) VEC Alternative Mathematics Programme'. *Compass*, 12(1), 41 - 53.

O'Donoghue, J & L. Murtagh (1990). 'Applications Oriented Mathematics : The Tipperary (NR) VEC Alternative Mathematics Programme for Senior Cycle'. In G. McNamara, K. Williams & D. Herron (Eds), *Achievement and Aspiration : Curricular initiatives in Irish post-primary education in the 1980s*. Dublin : Drumcondra Teacher's Centre, 111-123.

O'Donoghue, J. (1995a). 'Assessing Numeracy'. In D. Coben (comp.), *Mathematics with a Human Face, Proceedings of the Second Conference of Adults Learning Maths - A Research Forum (ALM-2)*. London: Goldsmiths College, University of London in association with ALM, 105-111.

O'Donoghue, J. (1995b). 'Numeracy and further education beyond the millennium'. *International Journal of Mathematical Education in Science and Technology, 26(3), 389 - 405*.

O'Donoghue, J. (1996). 'Assessing Numeracy 2'. In D. Coben (comp.), *ALM-3, Proceedings of the Third International Conference of Adults Learning Maths - A Research Forum*. London: Goldsmiths College, University of London in association with ALM, 78-91.

O'Donoghue, J. (1997). 'An assessment-driven open learning system for adults learning mathematics'. In G.E. FitzSimons (Ed), *Adults returning to study mathematics : Papers from Working Group 18, 8th International Congress on Mathematical Education (ICME 8)*. Adelaide : The Australian Association of Mathematics Teachers Inc., 119-128.

Romberg, T.A., Zarinnia, E.A. & Collis, K.F. (1990). 'A New World View of Assessment in Mathematics'. In G. Kulm (Ed) *Assessing Higher Order Thinking in Mathematics*. Washington, DC : American Association for the Advancement of Science, 21-38.

Ten Brink, T.D. (1974). *Evaluation: A practical guide for teachers*. New York: McGraw-Hill.

The Central Advisory Council for Education (England), (1959). *A Report of the Central Advisory Council for Education (England) (Crowther Report), Vol. 1*. London: HMSO.

Tout, D (1996). 'Some reflections on , Adult Numeracy Teaching: A course for teachers'. In D. Coben (comp.), *ALM-3, Proceedings of the Third International conference of Adults Learning Maths - A Research Forum*. London : Goldsmiths College, University of London in association with ALM, 166-171.

Wilder, R.L (1973). *Evolution of Mathematical Concepts: An Elementary Study*. London: Transworld Publishers Ltd.

Chapter 16

Adult Mathematics and Everyday Life: Building Bridges and Facilitating Learning 'Transfer'

Jeff Evans
Mathematics and Statistics Group, Middlesex University UK

INTRODUCTION

How should we teach mathematics so as to support adults' functioning satisfactorily in their work and everyday lives? We can draw on the range of activities that the typical adult[1] is involved in, but in the usual basic education or college pre-calculus course, different adults will vary in the activities they participate in. And further, each adult's activities vary over his/her lifetime. Thus, the mathematics taught must be *flexible* and *powerful,* that is able to be generalised or 'transferred' to other contexts.

Learning and thinking in school or college mathematics can be relevant to learning and thinking in 'outside' settings and activities, in several ways. This might involve:

(i) the *harnessing* of out-of-school activities and thinking in the teaching of college subjects;

(ii) the *application* of learning from college contexts to work or everyday activities; or

(iii) the use of a school subject like mathematics outside of its own domain, in nursing or business studies.

Thus, we might talk of the *transfer* or generalisation of learning in general - meaning the use of ideas and learning from one context in another. The possibilities for, and limits on, such processes clearly are

289

D. Coben et al. (eds.), Perspectives on Adults Learning Mathematics, 289–305.
© 2000 *Kluwer Academic Publishers. Printed in the Netherlands.*

especially important problems for mathematics since it is claimed to have wide applicability across the curriculum, and outside the school or college.

My aims here are: to describe an approach to these issues that provides an alternative, both to traditional learning transfer theories and to situated cognition; and to help learners and their teachers to build bridges between different practices, particularly between school or college and work.

VIEWS ON THE TRANSFER OF LEARNING IN MATHEMATICS

A variety of views on transfer proliferate in educational circles, as well as in psychology and sociology. The discussion has been especially vibrant in mathematics education in the last 10 or 15 years. Here traditional approaches include views favouring the use of behavioural learning objectives (e.g. Glenn, 1978), 'numerical skills' approaches (see Eraut, 1996), and 'utilitarian' views such as those of the Cockcroft Report (1982). They share several important ideas. Teaching and learning are seen as involving the transmission and internalisation of a body of knowledge (and skills), which is basically context-independent. A problem or 'task', and the mathematical thinking involved in addressing it, are seen as able to be described in abstract, e.g. as a 'plus', a 'percent', or a 'proportional reasoning' problem; hence it is claimed to be possible to talk about 'the same mathematical task' occurring across several different contexts. And contexts themselves are described 'naturally' e.g. as 'school mathematics' or 'business mathematics', apparently not needing any further description or analysis. Therefore these views expect that the 'transfer of learning', e.g. from school to everyday situations, should be relatively straightforward - at least for those who have been properly taught. And so it is - but only for a limited number of students.

However, in practice, transfer remains a difficult problem: one cannot *depend* on its being accomplished, by a particular adult, in a particular situation. There is much anecdotal evidence that teaching often has disappointing results in this respect, or put another way, that learners often 'fail' to accomplish transfer. In particular, recent research on adults has shown striking differences between performance in work, or everyday situations, on the one hand, and performance in school, or school-type tasks, on the other (e.g. Lave, 1988; Nunes, Schliemann & Carraher, 1993).

In recent years, strongly opposing positions have emerged. One example is the *strong form* of situated cognition: proponents of this view have often cited Jean Lave's (1988) *Cognition in Practice*. It argues that there is a *disjunction* between doing mathematics problems in educational settings, and numerate problems in everyday life, as these different contexts are characterised by different *structuring resources* - including ongoing activities, social relationships, cultural forms of quantity such as money. These worlds and the practices in play in them are *disjoint,* and subjects' thinking is specific to these practices, and these settings. Thus transfer of learning from school or college to outside contexts is pretty hopeless.

However, there are several problems and gaps in the account given by situated cognition. First, in its strong form, the view threatens a cul-de-sac (Noss & Hoyles, 1996b, Ch.2): it presents a *proliferation* of differently situated types of mathematical thinking, with high boundaries between them, and claims that the use of one type of thinking in another context is basically impossible. This hopelessness is refuted below. Second, this approach seems to assume that practices and communities of practice can be seen as 'natural' - whereas I argue that description and *analysis* of the bases of different practices (and communities) is required. In particular, although Lave and some others researching within broadly situated approaches mention 'sign systems', etc., they do not seem to consider in a systematic way the effects of different language (or 'discourse') underlying practices in different contexts.

The *strong form* of situated cognition is presented here as an 'ideal type', but it still has many proponents. The work of Jean Lave herself has moved on. Her more recent work (Chaiklin & Lave, 1993; Lave, 1996) acknowledges that no practice could ever be completely closed, or completely separated from other practices. Her approach consists of studying learning within communities of practice, and the bridges between them; in particular, the social relations, and identities across them.

This brief discussion (see also Evans, 1999) suggests a need for a reformulation of the problem of transfer. There are a number of issues or gaps in earlier accounts that need attention, including:

(1) how to characterise and differentiate the various contexts of thinking, activity and learning, and the related practices at play in them;
(2) how to describe the relations between practices, and between communities of practice, e.g. the boundaries or bridges between them;
(3) how to acknowledge the importance of affect, motivation, and so on; and
(4) how to design pedagogic practices that will facilitate transfer or generalisation.

Currently, a number of areas, besides mathematics education, are contributing to this, and seem to me to be converging in their analyses. These include developmental psychology - e.g. Nunes et al. (e.g. 1993), Saxe (e.g. 1991); cognitive psychology - e.g. Anderson et al. (1996), Pea (e.g.

1987); and approaches drawing on discourse theory (including poststructuralist insights) - e.g. Walkerdine (1988); Walkerdine and Girls & Mathematics Unit (1989); Muller & Taylor (1995); Evans & Tsatsaroni (1994, 1996); Evans (1999, 2000).

CONCEPTUALISING BOUNDARIES AND BRIDGES

Characterising and differentiating the various contexts of thinking, activity and learning, and the related practices at play in them

The approach I am proposing focuses on activities or *practices*: examples would be school mathematics, research mathematics, work practices such as nursing and banking, apprenticeship e.g. into tailoring, and everyday practices such as shopping. Each practice is constituted by *discourses*, and makes available different *subject-positions*.

Discourses are systems of ideas expressed in terms of *signifiers* and *signifieds*; signifiers are words, sounds, gestures, etc. and signifieds are conceptions, what is meant. These discourses give meaning to the practice by expressing the *goals* and *values* of the practice, and *regulate* it in a systematic way, by setting down standards of performance. Important practices are associated with a community of practice, a subculture of individuals with (some) shared goals, and a set of social relations (power, difference) - with different members of the community taking up different *subject-positions*. For example, the basic positions available in college mathematics are normally 'teacher' and 'student'; in shopping or street-selling, they would be 'seller' and 'buyer'. In a particular setting, we can analyse the practices *at play*, that would be involved in the positioning of participants.

This approach, like situated cognition, recognises different practices as in principle distinct, as discontinuous - e.g. school mathematics and everyday practices like street selling. But, using the approach recommended here, we can avoid the *cul-de-sac* (see above). Language and meaning in the discourses involved can be analysed by considering relations of signification - relations of *similarity, as well as difference*, between signifiers (terms) and signifieds, and also devices such as metaphor and metonymy. So far this draws on de Saussure's structural linguistics (see e.g. Walkerdine, 1988, Ch.1).

And we can go further. Walkerdine and others have shown how to use poststructuralist ideas about the inevitable tendency of the signifier to 'slip' into other contexts, thereby making links with other discourses, and producing a play of multiple meanings - to provide insight into meaning-making in mathematics (see e.g. the discussion of 'shopping with mummy' below); see also Walkerdine (1988, Ch.2) on children's use of language to indicate relations of size, Brown (1994) and Evans and Tsatsaroni (1994).

Thus, rather than attempting to specify the context of a college mathematics problem by looking only at its wording - or by naming the context as if simply based in 'natural' settings, as researchers we can describe it as socially constructed in discourse. This means:

(a) analysing the practices at play in the context (see below); and

(b) attending to particular signifiers and their relations of similarity and difference, as they are used in social interaction.

Describing the relations between practices, and communities of practice, e.g. what the boundaries between them might be like

Examining the relations among signifiers and signifieds enables us to analyse the *similarities and differences* between discourses - for example, between college and everyday mathematics. This is in turn necessary for understanding possible bridges between practices.

Contrary to the hopelessness of the strong form of situated cognition, I argue that it is possible to build bridges between practices, by trying to identify areas where out-of-school practices might usefully 'overlap' or inter-relate with school or college mathematics. This requires first of all that distinctions are made between those relations of signification in the learner's everyday practices that provide *fruitful* 'points of articulation' with school or college mathematics, and those that may be *misleading*. An example of a misleading inter-relation would be the problematical attempt to harness the use of 'more' in the home - where its opposite is *no more* (as in 'no more ice cream for you') - to help teach 'more' vs. *less* as an oppositional couple at school. The pupils are likely to be confused because what appears to be 'the same' signifier has a different meaning (signified) in the home and the school discourses (Walkerdine & Girls and Mathematics Unit, 1989: 52-53).

Sometimes pupils are confused by the rules necessary to ensure the pedagogic effectiveness of what is introduced as a 'game', for example a primary school 'shopping game' described by Walkerdine (1988, Ch. 7). There a boy made 'errors' in his sums because he did not realise that, in the game, one was allowed - indeed, one was *required* by the rules - to start afresh with a new 10p after each purchase. Though the child *called up* - that is, identified the task as - practical shopping, through which he 'made sense' of the apparent demands of the task, he nonetheless made errors because he was *positioned in*, and *regulated by*, the pedagogic shopping game.

While some aspects of everyday shopping practice were also useful in the game - say, remembering the familiar result that 'when you have 10p and buy something worth 9p, you will have 1p left', other aspects of shopping - for example, the idea that one must give up money to obtain the purchase - were not 'included' in the discourse of the school shopping game. Also, importantly, the goals and purposes were quite different in the two practices.

Thus, Walkerdine argues that activity within one discourse - say, playing a particular card game - will help with (i.e. can be 'harnessed' for) another - school mathematics - in those, and only those, aspects of the game which are both contained in school mathematics and which enter into *similar* relations of signification (Walkerdine, 1988:115 ff.). This would suggest that knowing the order of precedence among the 13 cards of a traditional deck (2,3,4, ... 9,10, Jack, Queen, King, Ace) would help someone to learn to count (1,2,3,, ...). But only up to a point: there are *similarities* in the identical orderings of cards and natural numbers between 2 and 10 - but, also, especially, the *difference* between the Ace and '1' must be made explicit. So we must broaden Walkerdine's stipulation of 'similar relations of signification' to mean 'similar or specifically different'.

Most of these illustrations relate to schoolchildren, many of whom are still learning everyday language, as well as school subject languages. Similar difficulties occur with adults. For example, many adults returning to study mathematics are puzzled by the idea that 'multiplication', which always means an increase in everyday language, can result in a diminution (when fractions are involved). Those used to the conventional binary meaning of 'probable' - either it is or it isn't - must reorient to its having a range of values between 0 and 1 in mathematics. And the term 'normal' has a range of meanings depending on which discourse is called up from among those of physiology, physics, statistics, or the everyday (Abercrombie, 1969). And the difficulties with any kind of mathematical modelling of 'real situations' are illustrated below.

Acknowledging the importance of affect, motivation, etc.

Many accounts of mathematical thinking, and even situated cognition, largely ignore the area of emotion. There are a few exceptions. Taylor has discussed the power of desire at the individual and the societal level (e.g. 1989). Walkerdine has emphasised the importance of the relations between cognition and affect: 'meanings are not just intellectual' (Walkerdine & Girls and Mathematics Unit, 1989:52). Nimier (1993) has discussed defences against mathematics.

Acknowledging affect or emotion for a given individual at a particular moment is not just an 'optional extra'. Other work shows that whenever a teacher reaches outside of mathematics for an example as illustration, the mathematics is *at risk*; e.g. when illustrating mathematics in the context of 'shopping with Mummy', when the mother 'has financial difficulties, ... is sick far away or deceased' (Adda, 1986:59). Similarly, adults' tutors must be wary of the emotional charges of examples, e.g. that of smoking and health frequently used in statistics - for many adults have lost family or friends to cancer or to heart disease (cf. Open University, 1983).

This problem flows from the fundamental character of language, its ability to produce *multiple meanings*: the signifier can always break with any given context, and be inscribed in new contexts without limit (Evans & Tsatsaroni, 1994).

Affect can be seen as the energy behind activity, as the power behind reason (Buxton, 1981). In this discussion, affect is understood as an emotional charge attached to particular words, gestures, and so on. These signifiers are linked together to make up *chains of meaning*. Thus the charge can flow from one signifier to another, by *displacement*. Indeed it can be argued that insights from psychoanalysis can allow us a fuller consideration of the affective (Walkerdine, 1988; Evans & Tsatsaroni, 1994, 1996).

An example comes from an episode with an adult interviewee in my research (described below), 'Ellen'. When asked to calculate a 15% tip for a meal she has 'chosen' from a restaurant menu, she hesitates, then makes a 'slip' (dividing by 15, rather than multiplying). In response to a 'context-sensing question' about how often she does this sort of calculation, she admits that she doesn't usually pay, but nevertheless, she habitually adds up the cost of her meal - since she 'doesn't want to be an expense'. It is possible to read 'expense' as a signifier on which meanings are *condensed*: it would signify for Ellen both the cost of, say, her meal obtained by summing the prices of individual dishes, and her being a burden within a relationship: these two ideas are *metaphorically* linked in her history. In this case the signifier 'expense' would be located at the intersection of two (at least) discourses (discourses on relationships, on eating out, and on school mathematics) The anxiety, guilt, pain of being an expense could be *displaced* onto the idea of the cost of her meal, and in turn onto any calculations entailed in producing that sum, including that of a tip. Here her displaced anxiety *may* influence her ability to transfer the calculation of 15% from school or college contexts (where she was a successful student) to everyday (eating out) or hybrid contexts (Evans & Tsatsaroni, 1996).

I would argue that the quality and intensity of affective charges may often be a major influence in the success or failure of many attempts at transfer - an influence that has so far been largely ignored in the mathematics education literature.

Thus another reason that a particular set of relations of signification may not be an apt source of fruitful articulations, in attempting to *harness* everyday life for school purposes, is that these relations may be *distracting* or *distressing* - and not only *misleading* (see above). I would expect similar issues to arise in attempts to *transfer* from school learning to work; see the case study below.

IMPLICATIONS FOR TEACHING

Designing pedagogic practices that will facilitate harnessing and transfer

Besides seeking out fruitful (non-misleading, non-distracting) points of inter-relation, we must structure the pedagogic discourse so as to work systematically through a process of what we usefully might call 'translation', taking account of both similarities and differences of signification. This involves a series of steps, where the signifiers and signifieds linked in one set of signs are *transformed* into a new set of signs, thereby creating new meanings. The several steps are held together through the construction of *chains of meaning* (Walkerdine, 1988).

A simple example is that of a mother who, in discussing with her child the number of drinks needed for a party of the child's friends, helps the child to learn to count - by the following transformations from one step to another (Walkerdine, 1988:129):

Step

1 Child (*signified*)
  Name (*signifier*)
2   Name (*signified*)
         Finger (*iconic signifier*)
3   Finger (*signified*)
                 Spoken Numeral (*symbolic signifier*)
4   Spoken Numeral (*signified*)
                        Written Numeral *(symbolic signifier)*

At the first step, the mother-teacher, encourages the child to form a sign linking the name of each child *(signifier)* with the 'idea' of that child *(signified)*. At each subsequent step, a new signifier (gesture, numeral) is linked to a new signified, which had been the signifier at the previous stage; each step thereby creates a new set of signs. The chain of meaning moves as follows: actual child (more precisely, *the idea of* the child) - name of child - iconic signifier - spoken symbolic signifier - written symbolic signifier.

Here, the different steps do not really represent different discourses, but they nevertheless show how a series of carefully constructed links between signifiers and signifieds could provide the bridges for crossing boundaries between discourses - here, between home practices and school mathematics. Thus the scheme may also suggest the form of a basic strategy for 'teaching for transfer'. Another example is provided by a teacher teaching children to add in Walkerdine (1988).

Schliemann (1995:49), in a paper concerned with the viability of harnessing mathematics from everyday settings to help with learning school or college mathematics, reaches a conclusion similar to Walkerdine's (above) about the necessary conditions for transfer or generalisation:

> ... mathematical knowledge developed in everyday contexts is flexible and general. Strategies developed to solve problems in a specific context can be applied to other contexts, *provided that the relations between the quantities in the target context are known by the subject as being related in the same manner as the quantities in the initial context are.* (my emphasis)

These views, from developmental psychologists, seem to converge with those of some cognitive psychologists, who argue that transfer between tasks is a function of the degree to which the tasks *share 'symbolic components'* (Anderson et al., 1996; Singley & Anderson, 1989).

They are also converging with a team of mathematics educators, with a special interest in computer representations, or modelling. Noss & Hoyles (1996a) give a fascinating account of research done as preparation for teaching a course in 'banking mathematics' (BM) to employees of a major investment bank. They aim thereby to bring about changes in the work discourse by challenging it with academic mathematics (AM) - that, is, by attempting transfer: '... to make sense of the world we were watching, we had to find a way to impose a mathematical gaze on it' (Noss & Hoyles, 1996a:9).

We can consider key points of their work in parallel with the discussion above. First, Noss and Hoyles recognised a number of ways in which work practices and academic mathematics discourses are distinct; for example, familiar representations, such as graphs, are 'read' differently: in BM, graphs tend to be considered as *displays of data* - whereas, in AM, they are read as a 'medium for expressing relationships' (1996a: 13-15). They were able to locate fruitful points of inter-relation in the learner's everyday practices, and also potentially misleading links. One example of the latter is the care that is required in discussing interest calculations (using percentages), where the conceptual priority (in AM terms) of simple interest (prior to compound interest) conflicts with its relative rarity in BM practice. But a key point was found where work practices usefully overlap with academic mathematics: the idea of a function was used as a 'bridging concept' between BM and AM. And programming was used as a way of building models, so that their students would learn

> what it means to construct a mathematical relationship, and how and why the language of mathematics assists in conferring expressive power to the description of relationships.... programming is a way by which learners can express the state of their current understandings symbolically while holding on to the meanings which can all too easily become lost in the passage to conventional mathematical discourse.   (Noss & Hoyles, 1996a:8)

In addition, Noss and Hoyles show usefully how to generate new ideas on building bridges, by developing a deeper mathematisation, by posing problems that appear 'innocent' in BM, but which are 'provocative' or deeply significant in AM. For example, they use their knowledge of the meanings within the practical context (BM) to seize on the idea of 'continuous compounding', where the periods over which interest is calculated continually shrink (from yearly to monthly, to daily, etc.) and which is normally considered only as an 'exotic' topic in financial mathematics texts (Noss & Hoyles, 1996a:20).

Thus Noss and Hoyles's work illustrates and helps to develop our ideas of transfer, by focussing on similarities and differences among signifiers. They show how to enhance curriculum development with research, and to carefully construct the pedagogic discourse, so as to facilitate 'transfer'.

Let us sum up by producing a set of useful guidelines for teaching and learning for transfer, based on the analysis above and on Anderson et al. (1996) (see also Pea, 1987):

(a) Show the learners how to perform a detailed analysis of the shared or similar components - *and the different aspects* - of the initial and target tasks. For example, the aim may be to transfer the use of the derivative to find a maximum or minimum value of a function, from the modelling of the height of a ball thrown upwards over time, to the expression of the value of profits depending on output. Similarities may include the 'inverted U' quadratic form of both functions, and the finding of a maximum by setting the derivative equal to zero, in both cases.

Height   **Profit**

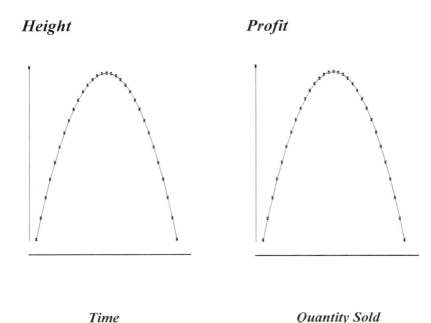

Time   *Quantity Sold*

Figure 1a *Ballistic Motion*   *Figure 1b Profitability*

But there are several differences. In the ballistic motion example, the time variable is continuous, whereas the number of units of output is discrete. This difference is important: in the business economics case it undermines the use of the calculus, which is assumed to be about infinitesimal changes - though, if the relevant levels of output are high, the infinitesimal model may 'fit' acceptably. There is also the issue of the justification of the model: the quadratic form of the motion example follows from the assumption of the constant value of the acceleration due to gravity, whereas the form of the profits model lacks such a firm theoretical basis, and hence depends on empirical testing and is liable to change.

There are also evocative differences in language in the discourses around the two problems. In the 'college mathematics and physics' example, the key terms are 'distance', 'velocity', 'acceleration'; in the business economics example, the key terms include 'marginal' revenue and 'marginal' cost.

(b) Include the ability to transfer as a specific, and explicit, goal. This would be done by establishing links between the two situations, and the related discourses and practices, by *translating* between the terms / languages used, and by *generalising* the methods used across contexts.

(c) In teaching the initial task, seek to incorporate a balance of generality and situational features. That is, anticipate what will come to be seen as *similarities* across situations, and *differences*, respectively.

(d) Teach the initial task in more than one context. For example, use examples of both a child throwing a ball vertically into the air, and of a goaltender in football kicking the ball into the air and down the field.

(e) Allow practice in recognising the *cues* that signal the relevance or 'applicability' of an available skill. In mathematics these cues are recurrent features of pattern, structure, or relationship. For example, in the above, both situations have been analysed (and simplified by *assumptions*) to depict a quadratic relationship between two variables (that holds independently of place and time). This is the sort of analysis we would hope our students could do as the basis of mathematical, statistical or business economics modelling[2].

(f) Allow repetition or practice on the target task.. This will help the student to appreciate the possible range of generalisation, and the constraints on it, resulting from crucial differences in discourses.

For further discussion of the problem of transfer in mathematics teaching, see e.g. Boaler (1997) and Masingila (1996).

IMPLICATIONS FOR RESEARCH

In the discussion above, I pointed to the need to specify the context of a school mathematics problem by:

(a) analysing the practices at play in the setting; and

(b) attending to particular signifiers and their relations of similarity and difference, as they are used in social interaction.

Thus at least some of our research effort in this area can usefully be involved in producing and reading interview transcripts.

As an illustration of sensitivity to ways of promoting transfer - but also to the barriers and pitfalls - I include a reference to a case study from my own research (Evans, 1999, 2000). 'Donald' was a mature student in his 40s, who had worked on the money markets in London and was now studying urban planning. Here I consider his responses of to one of the problems presented to a sample of social science undergraduates for solving, concerning a graph showing how the price of gold varied over one day's trading in London (Figure 2).

This graph shows how the price of gold (in dollars per fine ounce) varied during one day's trading in London. Which part of the graph shows where the price was rising fastest? What was the lowest price that day?

The London Gold Price - January 23rd 1980

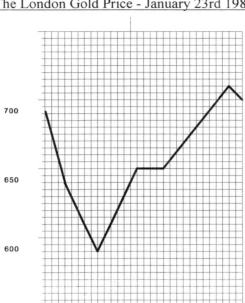

This graph shows how the price of gold (in dollars per fine ounce) varied during one day's trading in London.

Source: Evans (1998), based on Sewell (1981)

Figure 2   Question 3 in the interview

In the context of an interview indicated to the subjects as being for research purposes, and done by one of their 'mathematics' tutors in his office, two practices were judged to be 'at play' - on the basis of the setting of the interview, the language used in the letter of invitation, the interviewer's scripted talk, and the student's likely expectations. These two discursive practices were 'college mathematics' (CM) and 'research interviewing' (RI). In addition, I judged, mostly from the particular subject's talk, what was the 'predominant positioning' of each during each crucial episode of their interview.

This case study (see Evans, 2000, Chapter.10) shows several things:

(i) Donald is apparently able to focus on *discursive similarities and differences*: he seems able to read the diagram as a 'chart' (business mathematics) or as a 'graph' (college mathematics), and to recognise the connections between a 'trend' and a 'gradient' (respectively).

(ii) He is also aware of the different goals of the two practices, that relate to different objectives in using the graph. In *business*, the objectives are implicitly competitive, to make comparisons across personnel or groups, as well as growth-orientated, to make comparisons over time; in *college mathematics*, the objectives are less comparative, focused on the qualities of the curve, including the rate of change. He is aware of *different values and standards of regulation*, in particular of *precision*, required in the two discourses of college mathematics, and business mathematics.

(iii) He is also open about the *different feelings* evoked by the two practices. For example, his awareness of the different goals of the two practices, business or college mathematics, is sometimes painful.

(iv) He shows himself able and willing to use both college mathematics and money-market mathematics. Further it appears he is able to choose which practice to use to address the problem in the interview, to decide whether or not to apply his (more precise) college mathematics methods of calculating gradients to the problem of saying during which period of the day the relevant price was rising faster. Though not certain, it also appears that Donald is able to bridge the two practices, i.e. to transfer his college mathematics methods to deal with a problem involving charts - assuming he accepted the need for this - on the basis, say, of a notion of *economy of cognitive effort* (cf. Pea, 1987).

CONCLUSION AND DIRECTIONS FOR RESEARCH

In this chapter, several of my examples relate to school mathematics and pupils. At the same time, other illustrations show how very similar processes are relevant for adults. Indeed, the experience of coming to grips with new meanings is common to all learners, regardless of age.

Here I set down a general set of conclusions concerning the transfer - or translation - of learning.

1. Continuities between practices (e.g. school and out-of-school activities) are not as straightforward as traditional views assume - and hence scepticism is in order about the idea that transfer of learning between practices is itself straightforward.

2. We can accept the views of researchers in situated cognition and others that there is a *distinction* - but not necessarily a *disjunction* - between doing mathematics problems in educational settings, and numerate

problems in everyday life. Thus we can acknowledge that transfer is not dependable and often difficult. But it is not impossible, and hence we can be more optimistic than these other approaches suggest.

3. In teaching and learning, bridges between practices can be built, by (a) describing the practices involved (in the transfer relationship), and analysing the related discourses as systems of signs; and by (b) analysing the *similarities and differences* between discourses (e.g. college vs. everyday mathematics), so as to identify fruitful 'points of articulation' between mathematics in educational settings and outside ('target') activities.

4. The inter-relationships of thought and feeling have received insufficient emphasis in most earlier discussions of transfer. They must be allowed for, because of the risks of attempts to inter-relate practices in ways that may distract the learner, and because of the involvement of emotion in (5).

5. The inevitable tendency of language to flow in unexpected ways and generally to assume multiple meanings within different practices, constitutes a severe limitation on the possibilities of any intended transfer. Yet this ability of a signifier to form different signs also provides the basis for any transfer possibilities. Thus, though the successful crossing of bridges cannot be guaranteed 'risk-free', this paper has sketched some steps it is *necessary* to follow. For anything like transfer to occur, a 'translation' across discourses would have to be accomplished through careful attention to the relating of signifiers and signifieds in particular chains of meaning. This translation is not straightforward, but it often will be possible.

6. Ways of designing pedagogic practices can be developed that will facilitate transfer, including: task analyses based on (3) above; incorporating a balance of generality and situational features in teaching the initial task; and providing practice in recognising cues for the applicability of a specific idea or method.

7. To develop the study of transfer from school to work, we need research programmes including a focus on sign systems and meanings, as outlined above, and more widespread workplace studies in the styles of Recife (e.g. Nunes *et al.*, 1993) and the London Institute (e.g. Noss & Hoyles, 1996b).

8. Given the links between the notion of transfer and the traditional views criticised above, as well as widespread dissatisfaction with the notion (e.g. Lave, 1988, 1996), I propose that the term should be replaced by 'translation'.

NOTES

1   In this chapter, *adults* are understood as people who: participate in a substantial range of
    everyday activities and social relations; have at least the opportunity for paid or voluntary
    work; and are conscious of having social or political interests.
    Thus, I would include many 'adolescents', and virtually all 'mature students'; in the UK
    the latter are 21 or over, and usually have previous work or child-care experience.
2   These recurrent features come under what Nunes et al. (1993), following Gerard
    Vergnaud, call 'invariants'.

REFERENCES

Abercrombie, M.L. (1969). *The Anatomy of Judgement*. Harmondsworth: Penguin.
Adda, J. (1986). 'Fight against academic failure in mathematics'. In P. Damerow *et. al.* (Eds.),
    Mathematics for all. Paris: UNESCO., 58-61.
Anderson, J. R., Reder, L.M. & Simon, H.A.(1996). 'Situated Learning and Education',
    Educational Researcher, *25*, 4, 5-11.
Bernstein, B. (1996). *Pedagogy, Symbolic Control and Identity.* London: Taylor & Francis.
Boaler, J. (1997). *Experiencing School Mathematics*. Buckingham: Open University Press.
Brown, T. (1994), 'A Post-structuralist Account of Mathematical Learning', Ch.11. In P.
    Ernest (Ed.) *Mathematics, Education and Philosophy: An International Perspective*,
    London: Falmer, 154-161.
Buxton, L. (1981), *Do You Panic about Maths? Coping with Maths Anxiety*. London:
    Heinemann.
Chaiklin, S. & Lave, J. (Eds.) (1993). *Understanding Practice: Perspectives on activity and
    context.* Cambridge: CUP.
Cockcroft Committee (1982). *Mathematics Counts* (The Cockcroft Report). London: HMSO.
Eraut, M. (1996). *The new discourse of Vocational Education and Training: a framework for
    clarifying assumptions, challenging the rhetoric and planning useful, theoretically
    informed research*. Paper given at European Conference for Educational Research, Seville.
Evans, J. (1999). 'Building Bridges: Reflections on the problem of transfer of learning in
    Mathematics', *Educational Studies in Mathematics: Special Issue on the Contexts of
    Teaching and Learning Mathematics*, 39, 1/2/3.
Evans, J. (2000). *Adults' Mathematical Thinking and Emotions: a Study of Numerate
    Practices* . London: Falmer Press.
Evans, J. & Tsatsaroni, A. (1994). 'Language and subjectivity in the mathematics classroom'.
    In S. Lerman (Ed.), *The culture of the mathematics classroom*. Dordrecht, NL: Kluwer.
Evans, J. & Tsatsaroni, A. (1996). 'Linking the cognitive and the affective in educational
    research: Cognitivist, psychoanalytic and poststructuralist models'. *British Educational
    Research Journal: Special Issue on Poststructuralism and Postmodernism*, 21(3), 347-
    358.
Glenn, J. (1978). *The Third R*. London: Harper and Row.
Lave, J. (1988). *Cognition in practice: Mind, mathematics and culture in everyday life.*
    Cambridge: Cambridge University Press.
Lave, J. (1996). 'Teaching as Learning, in Practice'. *Mind, Culture, Activity, 3*, 3, 149-164.
Masingila, J.O., Davidenko, S. & Prus-Wisniowska, E. (1996). 'Mathematics Learning and
    Practice in and out of School: a Framework for Connecting these Experiences',
    Educational Studies in Mathematics 31, 175-200.

Muller, J. & Taylor N. (1995). 'Schooling and everyday life: knowledges sacred and profane'. *Social Epistemology, 9*, 3, 257-275.

Nimier, J. (1993). 'Defence mechanisms against mathematics' (transl. C.Hoare & D.Tahta). *For the Learning of Mathematics, 13,* 1, 30-34.

Noss, R. & Hoyles, C. (1996a). 'The visibility of meanings: Modelling the mathematics of banking', *International Journal for Computers in Maths Learning, 1,* 1, July.

Noss R. & Hoyles C. (1996b). *Windows on Mathematical Meanings.* Dordrecht: Kluwer.

Nunes, T., Schliemann, A. & Carraher, D. (1993). *Street Mathematics and School Mathematics.* Cambridge: Cambridge University Press.

Open University (1983). 'Smoking, statistics and society', Unit C4 in *MDST242: Statistics in Society.* Milton Keynes: Open University Press.

Pea, R. (1987). 'Socialising the Knowledge Transfer Problem'. *International Journal of Educational Research,* Special Issue on Acquisition and Transfer of Knowledge and Cognitive Skill, *11,* 6, 639-663.

Saxe, G. (1991). *Culture and Cognitive Development: Studies in Mathematical Understanding.* Hillsdale, NJ: Lawrence Erlbaum Associates.

Schliemann, A. (1995), 'Some Concerns about Bringing Everyday Mathematics to Mathematics Education'. In L.Meira & D. Carraher (Eds.), *Proceedings of the 19th International Conference for the Psychology of Mathematics Education (PME-19),* Recife, Brasil, 1, 45-60.

Singley M.K. & Anderson J.R. (1989), *The Transfer of Cognitive Skill.* London: Harvard U.P.

Taylor, N. (1989). 'Let them eat cake'. In C.Keitel *et al.* (Eds.) *Mathematics, Education and Society,* Proceedings of Day 5, ICME-6 . Paris: UNESCO, 161-163.

Walkerdine, V. (1988). *The mastery of reason: Cognitive development and the production of rationality.* London: Routledge & Kegan Paul.

Walkerdine, V. & Girls & Mathematics Unit (1989). *Counting girls out.* London: Virago.

Chapter 17

Teaching "not less than maths, but more": an overview of recent developments in adult numeracy teacher development in England - with a sidelong glance at Australia

Diana Coben & Noyona Chanda
School of Continuing Education, University of Nottingham, UK / London Language and Literacy Unit, London, UK

THE PROBLEM: THE 'CRISIS' OF ADULT INNUMERACY

In January 1997 two reports were published in Britain to coincide with the BBC numeracy campaign, 'Count Me In'. These were a survey of the numeracy skills of adults in seven countries undertaken by the Opinion Research Business (ORB) (Basic Skills Agency, 1997) and a study of the impact of poor numeracy on adult life (Bynner & Parsons, 1997). Both reports paint a sorry picture.

In the first report UK respondents came bottom of the international league. On questions covering the addition and subtraction of decimals, simple multiplication, the calculation of area, calculating percentages and using fractions, only 20% of people tested in the UK completed all twelve tasks accurately. The corresponding figure was 33% in the country which came second from the bottom, Australia.

But, in the words of the title of the second report, by comparison with literacy, *Does Numeracy Matter?* The authors conclude that it does matter. In their study of evidence from the National Child Development Study, involving 1714 adults aged 37, on the impact of poor numeracy on adult life they found that:

D. Coben et al. (eds.), Perspectives on Adults Learning Mathematics, 307–327.
© 2000 *Kluwer Academic Publishers. Printed in the Netherlands.*

People without numeracy skills suffered worse disadvantage in employment than those with poor literacy skills alone. They left school early, frequently without qualifications, and had more difficulty in getting and maintaining full-time employment. The jobs entered were generally low grade with limited training opportunities and poor pay prospects. Women with numeracy difficulties appeared especially vulnerable to exclusion from the clerical and sales jobs to which they aspired. Men's problems were less clearly differentiated between occupations. (Bynner & Parsons, 1997:27)

The UK government's recent major report on adult literacy and numeracy, the Moser Report (DfEE, 1999a), uses evidence from Bynner & Parsons (1997, 1994) as well as the British part of the International Adult Literacy Survey (IALS) (Office for National Statistics, 1997). The Report's stark conclusion is that:

1.4 The situation for numeracy is both worse [than that for literacy] and more confusing because the tests are weaker and the evidence is controversial. Estimates of the percentage of adults having some numeracy problems range from 30% to 50%. We regard 40% as a reasonable figure to have in mind in this report. But we also adopt a division often used (even if arbitrary) between "low" and "very low" numeracy, the latter category being those with very severe difficulties. On this basis something like one in five adults have very low numeracy. The following are survey findings about numeracy:
  • one in three adults in this country cannot calculate the area of a room that is 21 by 14 feet, even with the aid of a calculator;
  • one in four adults cannot calculate the change they should get out of £2 when they buy the goods displayed in Figure B.
1.5 What is clear from research is that very limited numeracy can be as serious as poor literacy for the individual, in certain jobs and indeed for the economy. (DfEE, 1999a: Summary and Recommendations)

The weakness of tests for numeracy and the controversial nature of the evidence that Moser refers to, mean that one must be circumspect in drawing conclusions from survey evidence. A further, fundamental problem is that there is no agreement as to what 'numeracy' is: it is a deeply contested concept, subject to major shifts of definition (Withnall, 1995; Baker and Street, 1994; Evans, 1989). As a result, evidence from different surveys is not readily comparable. There is a tendency, also, for surveys to be based on somewhat restricted notions of numeracy. For example, the international ORB survey is based on a notion of numeracy as consisting solely of computational skills, while Bynner & Parsons (1997) report that the National Foundation for Educational Research (NFER) designed the assessments used in the research to fit the levels of competence indicated in The Basic Skills Agency's standards - standards which are based on a functionalist notion of numeracy. As has been argued elsewhere (Coben, in press), both the computational and the functionalist models of numeracy ignore other important aspects of mathematics, in particular, mathematics as a means of communication.

Furthermore, research on adults' mathematics life histories (Coben & Thumpston, 1996; Coben, this volume) indicates that some adults undervalue the mathematics they can do, dismissing it as 'just common sense', while regarding as mathematics only that which they cannot do. Further research is needed on this, but it is possible that this phenomenon may have a bearing on adults' underperformance in numeracy tests.

However, while one might argue about the notion of numeracy informing the research, the picture painted by recent surveys is undoubtedly bleak. The publicity surrounding their publication feeds a widespread sense of disquiet about educational standards, particularly in mathematics. As the *Times Educational Supplement* (24 January 1997) put it bluntly: UK adults are at the bottom of the maths league.

Nor is the 'problem' a new one. These are only the latest in a series of alarming revelations in recent years (ALBSU, 1987; ACACE, 1982; Sewell, 1981). For example, Brigid Sewell's enquiry into adults' use of mathematics in daily life (Sewell, 1981), commissioned for the Committee that produced the Cockcroft Report (Department of Education and Science 1982), together with the associated national survey (ACACE, 1982), found an equally sorry picture. Approximately 30% of those questioned could not handle simple subtraction, multiplication, division or percentages, or understand a simple graph; almost half the adult population could not read a simple timetable and over half did not understand the meaning of the rate of inflation (ACACE, 1982). Nor is innumeracy without cost in society: in 1993 the government-funded Adult Literacy and Basic Skills Unit[1] (ALBSU) estimated that poor basic skills, including inadequate levels of numeracy, cost British industry £4.6 billion a year (ALBSU, 1993), a concern which runs through the government's 'Competitiveness' White Papers[2].

Whatever the truth about the extent and nature of adult numeracy, there is certainly a perception of a crisis of adult *innumeracy*.

ONE SOLUTION: ADULT NUMERACY TEACHING

While much of the public agonising occasioned by reports of adult innumeracy focuses on alleged falling standards in schools and proposes schools - and to a lesser extent parents - as instruments for the remediation of the 'crisis', a more immediate solution also presents itself: what Bynner and Parsons (1997:28) call "remedial teaching" of numeracy to adults. Some adults, of course, are also parents, so this solution neatly kills two birds with one stone.

But just as alarm about adult innumeracy is not new, neither is the provision of numeracy classes for adults. These developed in Britain in the wake of the BBC adult literacy campaign of the mid-1970s and took root as part of the expansion of adult community education provision for the 'disadvantaged' encouraged, in England and Wales, by the Russell Report (United Kingdom, Department of Education and Science, 1973)[3].

However, in the 1970s and 1980s public and government concern about adult illiteracy overshadowed that about innumeracy. Accordingly literacy provision was prioritised, a situation exacerbated by the reluctance of many literacy tutors to teach mathematics. Despite changes in the forms of provision and the practice of teaching in basic skills since the 1970s, it is still the case that responsibility for organisation, co-ordination and staff development in this area is likely to be in the hands of staff from a subject background in literacy, English or communications skills. Nonetheless, despite its 'poor relation' status, the development of numeracy provision proceeded, indeed flourished in enlightened areas, but it did so in the shadow of adult literacy and was often subsumed within literacy in official reports.

Numeracy became no more visible as terms such as 'adult basic education' (ABE), 'basic skills', 'adult essential learning', 'foundation learning' and 'core skills' succeeded each other. The plethora of terms used to describe work in this area was not just a cosmetic device: sometimes a change in terminology signified a marked shift in policy and in focus.

This was the case in the early 1980s when 'adult basic education' (for that quasi-mythical state already colonised by adult literacy education, 'everyday life') gave way to 'basic skills' (for employment). Basic skills provision was increasingly funded through the government's Manpower Services Commission (MSC) schemes for the unemployed. The demand for numeracy was increasingly linked to a need for certification to prove job-worthiness or satisfy entry criteria for further training and education.

PROFESSIONAL CULTURES IN ADULT NUMERACY TEACHING

It was against this background that professional cultures in adult numeracy teaching developed from the 1970s on, in a period of increasing - but uneven - professionalisation of adult education (Jarvis, 1995).

Professionalisation of adult numeracy practitioners was especially problematic since some worked unpaid as volunteers. The professional cultures that emerged reflected this situation and the complex, changing and vexed relationships between conceptions of mathematics and numeracy on the one hand and between conceptions of good practice in adult literacy and adult numeracy on the other.

Although adult numeracy teaching was - and to a large extent remains - undertheorised, this professional culture was imbued with humanistic ideas of student-centredness. These sat more or less comfortably with socialist, feminist and anti-racist affirmations of the right to education of working class people, women and members of minority ethnic groups and drew inspiration from the late Brazilian radical adult educationalist, Paulo Freire. Process was regarded as at least as important as product, education was political, the empowerment of women and of minority and disadvantaged groups was an especial concern.

Methodology developed in adult literacy work was the nearest to the new-style thinking and this further distanced numeracy work from mainstream mathematics teaching. Adult numeracy practice aspired to: start from where the student is; enable students to work at an individual pace; base work in contexts relevant to the adults concerned; base content on what the students need or want to know in the short term; an absence of examinations. Thus 'good practice' in numeracy, as in literacy, was judged in terms of relevance to the learner's needs and fidelity to the learner's context. The importance of a negotiated curriculum, familiar in liberal adult education, was stressed, in contrast to approaches based on Piagetian notions of the staged development of mathematical concepts derived from children's education, or approaches in which the formal hierarchies of Western mathematics dictated the curriculum content. Indeed, hierarchies of any kind were viewed with suspicion in a culture which aspired to egalitarian ideals.

To this extent, adult numeracy appeared to fit more comfortably into the 'literacy mode' than the 'mathematics mode' but the relationship was always uneasy. There were differences in philosophy, objectives and experience between literacy and numeracy practitioners and between numeracy practitioners themselves which have yet to be researched. An additional complication was that in the majority of adult education centres, adult numeracy provision and practice was organised and supported by staff whose experience and training were in literacy rather than numeracy. To the hard-pressed Adult Basic Education Organiser, numeracy often represented the addition of a problematic facet to her (it usually was 'her') already demanding role.

Tension between conceptions of numeracy and mathematics arose out of the perceived need to raise the status of numeracy as an important and independent field of practice, thereby affording status to numeracy practitioners as well as motivating adult learners. The latter was particularly important: adult learners' often fraught childhood experiences of attempting to learn mathematics in school needed to be countered if their second chance at learning were to succeed.

A polarisation resulted, with some numeracy practitioners consciously defining themselves in contradistinction to school mathematics teachers, eschewing school mathematics teaching methods, curricula and materials, along with the examination-driven study of mathematics, and questioning the contexts through which mathematics was taught. These practitioners were questioning some fundamental issues concerning mathematics teaching to adults but that fact tended to be lost in the distraction of the 'mathematics versus numeracy' debate and undoubtedly fed an isolationist tendency not uncommon in other areas of adult education.

The early 1980s saw the emergence of the short, sharp numeracy course in training programmes for the unemployed funded by the MSC. This model, derived from punishment regimes for young offenders and promoted on grounds of increased efficiency, was in marked contrast to that developed in adult literacy work. Many adult numeracy teachers distanced themselves from such short-term expediency and continued to develop student-centred, holistic approaches to adult numeracy.

In the 1990s, debates have centred around the importance of numeracy for work, for citizenship and lifelong learning, and the role of parents in children's achievement in numeracy. However, in recent years, such topics have been difficult to explore through the avenue of numeracy staff development because of changed priorities and consequent funding reallocation.

But what are the skills, knowledge and understandings required by those who undertake adult numeracy teaching? What form should teacher development in adult numeracy take? We turn now to look at attempts in England and in Australia to answer these questions.

TEACHER DEVELOPMENT IN ADULT NUMERACY IN ENGLAND

Numeracy teacher education in England has developed on a decidely *ad hoc* basis. Provision of numeracy staff development in the 1970s and 1980s was patchy and reflected the practice-based, atheoretical focus of numeracy teaching - questions of 'how' took precedence over questions of 'why'. While adult numeracy was in the pioneering phase this was arguably as much a strength as a weakness, since it enabled experimentation, innovation and creativity to flourish, unhindered by accreditation frameworks, received notions of the right way to proceed, or rigid notions of the nature of mathematics. Before 1990, training opportunities for numeracy tutors in England and Wales were funded by Local Education Authorities (LEAs) and through the ALBSU Regional Training Grants programme. Less training was available (or demanded) for numeracy than for literacy. In some areas there was an attempt to develop customised numeracy training schemes under the auspices of the RSA (Royal Society for the encouragement of Arts, Manufactures and Commerce) Customer-Specific Accreditation Scheme. However, with the emergence of the national accreditation framework, such initiatives faded into extinction.

The development of a national accreditation framework for teachers of basic skills to adults came about as a response to a perceived need to rationalise teacher development in this area. Adult basic education was under pressure to become accountable through the ability of its practitioners to design and deliver appropriate curricula and through the introduction of measurable outcomes for students, such as examination passes.

In 1983, ALBSU consulted nationally in England and Wales on the issue of the format and funding of its Regional Training programme. The result was widespread consensus on the need to develop greater coherence in staff training in basic education, particularly as many practitioners had by that time attended a substantial number of training events but received little recognition for their efforts (ALBSU, 1988).

The process of developing greater coherence began in 1985 with ALBSU sponsorship of three major pilot projects aimed at exploring approaches to accreditation as well as describing occupational standards for work in adult literacy. The intention was: to confirm and develop good practice that was already in the field rather than to prescribe ideal practice; to acknowledge the varied starting points of experienced ABE tutors; to develop an accreditation framework rather than an examination-based course; and to facilitate different routes to accreditation (for example, through the accreditation of prior experiential learning).

It was intended that the accreditation framework, when finalised, would be less demanding than the RSA *Diploma in Teaching and Learning in Adult Basic Education*. The new accreditation was intended in the first instance for practising, experienced tutors and later for those who had successfully completed a period of initial training recognised by ALBSU. It was also hoped that the accreditation framework would harmonise with the findings of the pilot projects.

In 1990, ALBSU's first version of an accreditation scheme for practising adult basic education tutors, validated by the City and Guilds of London Institute, was launched. The framework comprised accreditation at two levels: the in-service *Certificate for Teaching Basic Communication Skills to Adults* (CG9281) for practising tutors and the pre-service *Initial Certificate in Teaching of Basic Skills to Adults* (CG9282 *Literacy* and CG9283 *Numeracy*) for potential tutors and newly appointed volunteers.

The *Certificate for Teaching Basic Communication Skills to Adults* (CG9281, hereinafter called the CG9281 Certificate) was novel in many respects. It was competence-based, not directly linked to a training programme or course of study, and it offered flexibility in routes to accreditation, including the opportunity to accredit prior experience in the field. Most importantly, it relied on mentors to facilitate the process of evidence-gathering and assessment of competence. The role of the mentor was not that of a trainer but rather an advisor in the portfolio-building process. Indeed it was emphasised that mentors did not need to be experienced or qualified in the same field as the candidate.

Funders made simple choices between the expense of a training course and the seemingly cheaper option of supporting individuals towards accreditation. ALBSU funded the training of the first tranche of mentors, but at institution level mentors found it difficult to fulfill their roles for a variety of reasons, not least of which was a lack of relevant experience and subject specialism. Candidates for accreditation wishing to specialise in numeracy, sometimes found it difficult to find a suitably experienced mentor within the same institution, or even in the same region. Those organisations which chose the new award as a cheaper option to running taught training courses found it difficult to manage and operate. The assumption that this was the most effective (and most economical) approach for the accreditation of experienced teachers was to be proved wrong. Indeed, some very experienced teachers are still in the process of achieving the accreditation after five years' effort at compiling a portfolio of evidence of competence!

ALBSU's internal review of the scheme at the end of its pilot year pointed to an unwieldy system, wide open to differences in interpretation and difficult to steer towards successful completion. Surprisingly, some of the most experienced teachers had the greatest difficulty in providing evidence of competence, and assessors seemed reluctant to accredit their prior experience at face value. After more than a decade of adult literacy and numeracy teaching, this was a silent statement about the need for structured professional upskilling, rather than simply rubber-stamping the status quo.

The negligible take-up of the scheme by numeracy teachers (less than 20 nationally) was further proof that either such teachers did not see the relevance of this accreditation to them or that their current competence fell far short of the standards required and therefore their need was for training first and accreditation second.

In the light of the ALBSU review, and in tandem with the contemporary development of the national Training and Development Lead Body (TDLB) Standards for Training and Development, the CG9281 Certificate was revised in 1992 to more closely match the competence-based National Vocational Qualification (NVQ) format[4]. The revised version that emerged was the CG9285 *Certificate in Teaching Basic Skills to Adults* (CG9285-020 *Literacy* and CG9285-021 *Numeracy,* hereinafter called the Certificate. Although the revised Certificate was more detailed in terms of performance criteria and more prescriptive in terms of evidence requirements, the problems in implementation remained formidable. A more long-term and wide-ranging review of the scheme might have resulted in a different agenda, focusing on mathematics-related teaching and learning theory and practice, including, for example, error analysis, ways of explaining, dealing with misconceptions, mathematical literacy, all of which are applicable to any adult mathematics learner in any context.

The CG9285 Certificate was later revised in November 1995 to correspond to the standards of the *Further and Adult Education Teachers' Certificate* (CG7306), for which it represents the element of contextualisation of teaching in either numeracy, literacy or English to Speakers of Other Languages (ESOL).

The Initial Certificate, also, was based on national consultations about the format and content of the training of volunteers in adult basic education, rather than on an analysis of what the starting teacher in adult literacy and numeracy should know and be able to do. This pre-service level of certification was intended, in the short-term, to allow for national standardisation of volunteer training programmes and, in the future, to be the entry qualification for work in literacy and numeracy in post-compulsory education and training provision. But in trying to satisfy conflicting agendas - such as how much responsibility a volunteer should be expected to take on, or whether the Local Education Authority should pay for teaching placements - the scheme lacked cohesion and rigour. Crucially, for an entry-level qualification, it failed to provide the detailed knowledge and skills base that could pump-prime professional development of teachers and improve the quality of provision. Whereas the background research into the development of the Initial Certificate focused on the training of volunteers, ALBSU should have anticipated that motivation for take-up of entry-level qualifications was more likely to be linked to employment prospects in the field and thus focused more on developing a strong foundation of mathematics-specific knowledge and skills.

An examination of the Initial Certificate scheme components shows clearly that the prime aim is to provide a new tutor's toolkit for survival in adult education generally (i.e. generic competence) and that consideration of numeracy is secondary. As a preparatory accreditation scheme for entry into adult numeracy teaching, this is surely inadequate. The contextualisation of generic competence is certainly important for someone needing a licence to practice as a numeracy practitioner, but it cannot be a substitute for the acquisition of a body of underpinning theoretical knowledge and understanding.

The scheme pamphlet for the Initial Certificate makes passing reference to the importance of teaching concepts, but little depth can be expected, given that the entire taught element is only 16 hours. The practical aspect of the course relates to needs analysis, programme design and delivery to one student - hardly an adequate preparation for teaching groups that are diverse in terms of needs, abilities and learning styles.

Further examination of the support materials for the Initial Certificate (Brittan, 1993) reinforces the survival toolkit idea - especially the 'Further Reading' section at the end of the book. The course *does* introduce the trainee to some kinds of adult numeracy provision, but does not prescribe the study of pedagogy or the analytical development of teaching strategies with reference to adults learning numeracy. Indeed, while the content of the Initial Certificate looks back to the age of adult basic education and volunteer tutors working one-to-one with students, the reality is more likely to be work with groups of adults and young people in further education colleges on a variety of programmes which include numeracy.

However, assuming that a numeracy practitioner, armed with a CG9283 Initial Certificate, were to gain employment as a teacher of numeracy to adults, there is, in the current climate of cutbacks and preoccupation with management and assessment qualifications, only a slim chance of being trained on the job as a teacher of numeracy to adults. There may not be a numeracy colleague or mentor available, there is even less likely to be a numeracy-specific skills development programme. Part-time tutors may not have access to any training that is available and will probably be expected to undertake professional development in their own time.

After six months on the job, the CG9285 Certificate in Teaching Basic Skills is suggested as next-step professional development for the individual member of staff, a step which also helps the organisation to satisfy the staff training profile of The Basic Skills Agency's Quality Kitemark. The problem is that this is a competence-based accreditation scheme which assumes that underpinning knowledge and understanding have already been acquired and can be demonstrated in practice. As such it is vulnerable to the criticisms made of other competence-based assessment and accreditation schemes (principally NVQs/SVQs) that they are: based on a behaviourist model, ruthlessly applied; 'jargon-heavy' and 'content-light'; bureaucratic and time-consuming in operation, and hence expensive; variable in assessment standards; inadequate as a tool for the assessment of knowledge and theory.

There is no requirement for training to be available or undertaken to ensure that candidates have access to underpinning knowledge and understanding. In the real world of implementation of such schemes the requirement to demonstrate knowledge is all too easily glossed over. Through the achievement of the CG9285 Certificate, practitioners gain experience of portfolio preparation and *(de facto,* but not *de jure)* a licence to continue to practice. But they have not been exposed to the richness of relevant knowledge, neither do they have the opportunity to reflect on their own practice with a view to growing and developing as professionals.

With hindsight (since one of the present authors was a member of the consultative group concerned in the revision of the accreditation framework), it could be argued that the accreditation framework for work in adult numeracy has much more to do with the licence to practice than with the preparation and development of the knowledge and skills of professionals and experts in this area. An important omission in the developmental stages of the accreditation framework was consideration of the implications of national standards such as those embodied in the National Curriculum for schools and in Core Skills for the General National Vocational Qualification (GNVQ) in the numeracy and mathematics teacher training curriculum. To some extent, this was due to a conflict of interest arising out of the fact that ALBSU was both responsible for developing national standards as well as promoting its own products in the field (for example its *Numberpower* Certificate in basic numeracy for adults). Another problem was that these products had already been developed and there was pressure to present them as national standards.

Table 1. Numbers achieving adult numeracy teaching qualifications compared to those achieving adult literacy teaching qualifications

YEAR	NUMERACY	LITERACY
Initial Certificate in	Teaching Basic Skills to	Adults:
	CG9283 Numeracy	*CG9282 Literacy*
1994 – 1995	1478	4310
1995 – 1996	1288	4041
Certificate in	Teaching Basic Skills	to Adults:
	CG9285-021	*G9285-020*
	Numeracy	*Literacy*
1994 – 1995	57	302
1995 – 1996	48	251

Source: City and Guilds of London Institute Annual Statistics

Although ALBSU's financial support for those endorsing the accreditation scheme provided a kick-start, by the mid-1990s the low take-up at both pre-service (Initial Certificate) and in-service (Certificate) level (shown on Table 1) pointed to a lack of confidence in the potential of the scheme to meet either the training needs of newly-appointed staff or to act as a route to employment. The figures also starkly reveal the relative unpopularity of certification in numeracy teaching by comparison with literacy. Given that the majority of attendances on Initial Certificate courses and Certificate accreditations are initiated by funders, rather than on the basis of demand from individual practitioners, this would suggest that even those responsible for planning and implementing staff development have a lesser interest in certification for numeracy than for literacy.

Research by Joy Joseph (1997) amongst UK members of *Adults Learning Mathematics - A Research Forum* (ALM)[5] confirms this picture of the relative unpopularity of the qualifications in numeracy teaching by comparison to literacy teaching amongst paid staff, and of the relative unpopularity of the CG9285 Certificate, by comparison to the Initial Certificate. Using ALBSU/Basic Skills Agency Reports for 1993-94 and 1994-95 and information from the City and Guilds of London Institute, Joseph calculated the ratios of qualifying paid and volunteer tutors in literacy and numeracy per 1000 students on programme in that subject (see Table 2). Interestingly, she found more volunteers achieving the Initial Certificate in numeracy than in literacy, in contrast to the position amongst paid staff.

Table 2. Ratios of qualifying tutors per 1000 students on programme in numeracy and literacy

	NUMERACY	LITERACY
Initial Certificate Volunteers	33	25
Initial Certificate Paid staff	9	13
CG9285 *Certificate* Paid staff	0.8	1.9

Source of data: City and Guilds of London Institute and ALBSU/Basic Skills Agency Reports 1993-94 and 1994-95. (Joseph 1997:176)

Joseph found a fairly evenly mixed reaction to the Initial Certificate. However, the majority of respondents condemned the CG9285 Certificate. Comments included:

'With little support, the 9285 is a nightmare!' [current candidate]

'We all hate it! Assessment takes priority over development and learning is cumbersome, time consuming and expensive.' [assessor]

'I gained very little as far as learning was concerned.' [qualified tutor]

But condemnation was not quite universal. One uninvolved tutor said that the CG9285 Certificate "seems of considerable value" while a qualified tutor said that it "focuses on the importance of providing a structured learning programme for each student, ensuring that the best possible outcomes can be achieved." (Joseph, 1997:181).

Joseph concludes that accreditation is now driving rather than following the curriculum for both tutors and students and that the pressures of the current climate militate against good practice in adult numeracy work. She suggests that all trainee adult basic education tutors should be encouraged to follow training courses in both literacy and numeracy, since so many students have difficulty in both areas. Most importantly, the decline in numeracy teacher development amongst paid staff, particularly at the higher levels, must be reversed. As she says, "Low numbers in training lead to poorer quality training, and a downward spiral could easily develop." (Joseph, 1997:182).

THE NEED FOR RESEARCH AND THEORY TO INFORM THE EMERGING FRAMEWORK

Strikingly absent from the accreditation scheme documentation is any reference to specific research or theory. As we have said, the theoretical base for adult numeracy work - and hence also for adult numeracy teacher development - is largely lacking and it could be argued that the documentation merely reflects this. It is also the case that none of the surveys of numeracy levels in the adult population has questioned the role that adult numeracy teaching might play in adult numeracy learning. Certainly those charged with the development of the national accreditation framework did not analyse the findings of research into numeracy teaching as a preliminary to planning what should be included in the occupational standards.

The low level of research into adult numeracy teacher education reflects that into numeracy generally, as we see from the *Bibliography of Research in Adult Literacy and Basic Skills* (ALBSU, 1994), which reveals the paucity of research activity in adult mathematics/numeracy education prior to 1992. Although funded research is still rare, research in this area is now taking off, particularly through the development of *Adults Learning Mathematics - A Research Forum* (ALM). ALM is an independent international research forum bringing together researchers and practitioners and encouraging practitioners to be aware of research and practice around the world, and, where appropriate, to undertake research themselves. But this is a fairly recent development (since 1994) and adult numeracy is still a relatively under-researched and under-theorised field by comparison with other areas of education

Add to this lack of a theoretical and research framework the recurrent uncertainties over funding in further education in recent years, and the application of literacy teacher training models to numeracy teacher training and you arrive at the current unsatisfactory situation, where an accreditation framework for numeracy teachers exists, but one which appears not to enjoy the confidence of either teachers, managers or staff developers, as shown by the statistics on take-up (see Table 1).

The present accreditation framework for numeracy teachers has developed in isolation from developments in adult numeracy education (and adult numeracy teacher education) outside the UK. It has been divorced from parallel developments in Initial Teacher Education and in mathematics education in schools. It suffers from the incoherence that is a feature of teacher education in the post-compulsory further education (FE) sector, where teachers are not required to hold a teaching qualification and "there is no coherent pathway or framework for their ongoing professional development" (Ecclestone, 1996:146).

Against this background, basic skills teaching is described in the Moser Report as "marginalised, remaining something of a Cinderella service" (DfEE, 1999a: Summary and Recommendations, 1.2). But Moser has decided that it is high time that Cinderella should go the ball: the Report accordingly recommends that a new qualification for teachers should be developed (DfEE, 1999a: Summary and Recommendations, 1.38).

This recommendation is timely, since a national framework for teacher training in the FE sector is currently emerging (Atkin, 2000, forthcoming). The Department for Education and Employment recently announced that the National Training Organisation for the FE sector (FENTO, 1999) and the Basic Skills Agency have begun developing a new initial training framework and qualification for new entrants to basic skills teaching, which will be closely aligned to the new training framework being developed for FE teachers in general. In addition, a tool-kit for basic skills teachers will be produced which will include details of the new standards and curriculum for literacy and numeracy as well as guides to effective pedagogy and approaches to basic skills education. Furthermore, an intensive training programme is to be introduced for all existing basic skills teachers (DfEE 1999b).

So – the sorry situation outlined above is about to change out of all recognition. But will it change for the better? It remains to be seen what form the new framework, with its associated training and 'tool kit' will take, but, like the outgoing accreditation framework for numeracy teachers described above, it has developed largely without benefit of research and underpinning theory. There has been little involvement of universities, which are, after all, institutions where educational research is undertaken.

Universities also provide postgraduate training, but postgraduate courses specifically geared to helping adult numeracy teachers develop their ideas and their skills are still rare and perhaps a handful of students are currently registered in UK universities for research degrees at Masters or Doctoral level directly concerned with adult mathematics education. Links urgently need to be forged between the 'licensing' and professional development of practitioners in the new accreditation framework, encouraging both practical teaching skills and academic study and research leading to higher academic qualifications. It is to be hoped that the emerging framework will facilitate this. More study and research - both theoretical and empirical - is required into all aspects of adult numeracy and adult numeracy teacher development.

A useful initial step would be an international review of arrangements for adult numeracy teacher development: it is one thing to recognise the shortcomings in one's own situation, another to be able to compare it with efforts by practitioners in other countries to deal with similar issues. At present there is no international comparative study of adult numeracy teacher development. As a first step towards such a review, we end this paper by taking a sidelong glance at one country where adult numeracy teacher development has been taken seriously for some time: Australia.

POSTSCRIPT: TEACHER DEVELOPMENT IN ADULT NUMERACY IN AUSTRALIA

The contrast between teacher development in adult numeracy in Australia and the 'Cinderella service' in England could hardly be greater. With a comparable 'problem' of adult innumeracy, as judged by the recent ORB international survey (Basic Skills Agency, 1997), Australian adult numeracy educators have, especially since 1995, the staff development tools with which to tackle it. That year saw the publication of *Adult Numeracy Teaching - Making Meaning in Mathematics* (National Staff Development Committee for Vocational Education and Training and the Commonwealth of Australia, 1995), also known as (and cited here as) ANT. ANT is described by three members of the team which produced it, Betty Johnston, Beth Marr and Dave Tout, as

> an 84-hour professional development course designed as a continuation and further development of existing professional development packages, such as *Breaking the Maths Barrier* (Marr & Helme, 1991) leading in turn to postgraduate study (Johnston, Marr & Tout, 1997:166).

The primary purpose of ANT, as described in the 'Information for Presenters' (ANT, 1995:viii), is

> to blend theory and practice about teaching and learning adult numeracy within a context of doing and investigating some mathematics, whilst developing a critical appreciation of mathematics in society.

The project team began with the question: "What should numeracy teachers be able to do after this course?". Their answer was:

After this course a teacher
1) should have a critical appreciation of mathematics in society, and
2) should be able to initiate appropriate learning activities by identifying the numeracy needs of students and responding from a variety of approaches to teaching and a range of appropriate mathematical resources and knowledge. (ANT, 1995:x)

The structure of ANT accordingly tries to weave together three strands: "knowing about maths; learning (and teaching) maths; and doing maths. This last strand is central to the course: clearly to teach numeracy you must know how to do mathematics" (ANT, 1995:x). The ANT team thus tackle head on the question of the teacher's own grasp of mathematics, a question which parallel British initiatives have signally failed to address.

In their conference paper for the third ALM conference, Johnston, Marr and Tout (1997) point out that ANT was an initiative of the National Staff Development Committee for Vocational Education and Training, which works under the Australian National Training Authority. The Committee awarded the project jointly to the Centre for Language and Literacy at the University of Technology, Sydney (UTS) and the Adult Basic Education Resource and Information Service (ARIS) at the National Languages and Literacy Institute of Australia (NLLIA) (Johnston, Marr & Tout, 1997:166). The ANT project thus embodied the link between research and practice, between a university and a training and staff development organisation that we have argued is greatly needed in the UK. It did so on the basis of interstate consultation with educators and a search of the relevant literature. The project sought the advice of individual consultants, a National Reference Panel and an international Academic Reference Panel (one of the present writers served on the latter Panel). ANT was piloted in two states and on completion, its publication by a national organisation ensured that it was widely disseminated throughout Australia.

Nor did the project team shy away from theory, describing their "critical constructivist" approach as follows:

A critical constructivist approach starts from the experiences and perspectives of the learners and the local community, learning and evolving mathematics that is relevant to their needs - helping students to become strong within their own culture and to learn at the same time how to critically appropriate knowledge from a wider range of experiences. (Johnston, Marr & Tout, 1997:168)

Whether one agrees or disagrees with the ANT approach, it has undoubtedly opened up areas for discussion on which the present English adult numeracy teaching accreditation system is silent. On the vexed question of 'what is numeracy?', they conclude that "numeracy is not less than maths, but more" (Johnston, Marr & Tout 1997:167) and ANT reflects this positive view.

By 1997, the ANT course had been run about ten times and in most Australian states. Johnston, Marr & Tout (1997) report that it has generated much enthusiasm and many questions. Independent evaluation would, of course, be necessary to endorse that view, but it appears from this distance as if, on every count, the Australian project puts the English numeracy teacher development system comprehensively in the shade.

One member of the ANT team, Dave Tout, made a telling comment on the adult numeracy teacher development he encountered (or failed to encounter) on his trip to Europe in 1996 to attend the ALM-3 and ICME-8 conferences[6]. He stated that

I was looking forward to hearing about training or professional development courses and resources, as again this has been a priority in Australia. However, I was surprised that the development of training and professional development opportunities in adult numeracy seemed to have had little prominence and I came away with very little knowledge in this area. (Tout, 1997:14)

This is a sad reflection on the lack of priority that has been accorded to adult numeracy teacher development in England over decades. Adult numeracy teachers have a vital contribution to make to raising the level of numeracy of the adult population. Professional development in adult numeracy teaching must have greater prominence if practice in this area is to continue to develop. Teaching numeracy as "not less than maths, but more" requires teacher development worthy of the name. The signs are that this issue is at last beginning to be taken seriously at the highest level and this is very welcome; it remains to be seen whether the form of adult numeracy teacher education that emerges will rival that developed in Australia.

ACKNOWLEDGEMENTS

This chapter is a revised and updated version (reproduced with permission) of our article with the same title in *Teacher Development: an international journal of teachers' professional development*, Vol. 1, No. 3 (Special Issue on Literacy and Numeracy), 1997, 375-92.

The authors are grateful to Gill Jullings and Joy Joseph for their helpful comments on points raised in this chapter. The opinions expressed - and any flaws remaining - are our own.

NOTES

1. On 5 April 1995 the Basic Skills Agency replaced the Adult Literacy and Basic Skills Unit (ALBSU) as the national development agency for literacy, numeracy and related basic skills in England and Wales. By 'basic skills' the Agency means:
   the ability to read, write and speak in English and use mathematics at a level necessary to function and progress at work and in society in general.
   In Wales basic skills includes the ability to read, write and speak in Welsh where Welsh is the first language or mother tongue.
   Source: The Basic Skills Agency
2. The 'Competitiveness' White Papers referred to here are:
   Department of Trade and Industry (1998) *Our Competitive Future: building the knowledge economy*. White Paper (Cm 4176) December 1998. London: The Stationery Office, Great Britain
   Great Britain. Cabinet Office (1996) *Competitiveness: Creating the Enterprise Centre of Europe*. White Paper (Cm.3300) June 1996. London: The Stationery Office, Great Britain. Department of Trade and Industry, Treasury, Department of Transport (1995) *Competitiveness: forging ahead*. White Paper (Cm.2867) May 1995. London: Her Majesty's Stationery Office Great Britain.
   Department of Trade and Industry (1994) *Competitiveness: helping business to win*. White Paper (Cm.2563) May 1994. London: Her Majesty's Stationery Office
3. As the title suggests, this paper focuses primarily on teacher development in adult numeracy in England. In Scotland, the Alexander Report (United Kingdom, Scottish Education Department, 1975) also encouraged the development of adult community education around this time.
4. The British system of vocational qualifications based on the assessment of competence comprises National Vocational Qualifications (NVQs) in England and Wales and Scottish Vocational Qualifications (SVQs) in Scotland. Competence-based assessment has generated a considerable literature, both 'for' and 'against' (see, for example: Wolf 1995; Smithers 1993; Jessup 1991). The TDLB has now become part of a larger Employment National Training Organisation.
5. *Adults Learning Maths - A Research Forum* (ALM) is an international forum founded in 1994 to promote research in this field. Membership is open to individuals and institutions. For details, please contact: Professor John O'Donoghue, ALM Chair, Department of Mathematics and Statistics, University of Limerick, Limerick, Rep. Ireland; email: john.odonoghue@ul.ie

6. The Third International Conference of *Adults Learning Maths - A Research Forum* (ALM-3) took place at the University of Brighton, England, 5-7 July 1996 (see Coben, comp. 1997). The International Congress on Mathematics Education (ICME-8) took place in Seville, Spain, July 14-21 1996. ICME-8, for the first time included a Working Group (WG-18) on 'Adults returning to study mathematics'. Papers from WG-18 are in G.E. FitzSimons, ed., (1997).

REFERENCES

Adult Literacy and Basic Skills Unit (1994) *Basic Skills Research: Bibliography of Research in Adult Literacy and Basic Skills.* London: ALBSU

Adult Literacy and Basic Skills Unit (1988) *Editorial ALBSU Newsletter,* Vol. 28, Winter 1988. London: ALBSU

Adult Literacy and Basic Skills Unit (1987) *Literacy, Numeracy and Adults: evidence from the National Child Development Study.* London: ALBSU

Advisory Council for Adult and Continuing Education (1982) *Adults' Mathematical Ability and Performance.* Leicester: ACACE

ANT (see: National Staff Development Committee for Vocational Education and Training and the Commonwealth of Australia, 1995)

Atkin, C. (2000, forthcoming) 'Training the Trainers: a review of teacher training in England for the further education sector'. In *Europa Handbuch Weiterbildung.* Neuwied: Luchter Hand Verlag

Baker, D. A. & Street, B. V. (1994) 'Literacy and Numeracy Concepts and Definitions' *International Encyclopedia of Education.* Oxford: Pergamon Press

Basic Skills Agency (1997) *International Numeracy Survey: a comparison of the basic skills of adults 16-60 in seven countries.* London: The Basic Skills Agency

Baty, P. (1997) 'Revamp for NVQ mooted' *Times Higher Education Supplement,* 24 January 1997

Brittan, J. (1993) *An Introduction to Numeracy Teaching.* London: Adult Literacy and Basic Skills Unit

Bynner, J. & Parsons, S. (1997) *Does Numeracy Matter? Evidence from the National Child Development Study on the impact of poor numeracy on adult life.* London: The Basic Skills Agency

Bynner, J. & Parsons, S. (1994) *The Basic Skills of Young Adults.* London: The Basic Skills Agency

Coben, D. (forthcoming) 'Numeracy, Mathematics and Adult Learning'. In I. Gal, (Ed.) *Numeracy Development: A Guide for Adult Educators.* Cresskill, NJ: Hampton Press

Coben, D. (Comp.) (1997) *Adults Learning Maths - A Research Forum - 3, ALM-3 Proceedings of the Third International Conference of Adults Learning Maths - A Research Forum (ALM),* 5-7 July 1996 at University of Brighton. London: Goldsmiths College, University of London in association with Adults Learning Maths - A Research Forum

Coben, D. & Thumpston, G. (1996) 'Common Sense, Good Sense and Invisible Mathematics'. In T. Kjaergaard, A. Kvamme, N. Lindén (Eds) *PDME III Proceedings: Numeracy, Gender Class, Race.* Landås, Norway: Caspar Publishing Company, 284-97

Dfee (1999a) *A Fresh Start: Improving literacy and numeracy. The report of the Working Group chaired by Sir Claus Moser* (The Moser Report). London: Dfee

Dfee (1999b*) Better Basic Skills: Improving Adult Literacy and Numeracy.* Leaflet. London: Dfee.

Department of Education and Science, (1973) *Adult Education: A Plan for Development,* Report by a Committee of Inquiry appointed by the Secretary of State for Education and Science under the Chairmanship of Sir Lionel Russell CBE (The Russell Report). London: Her Majesty's Stationery Office

Department of Education and Science (1982) *Mathematics Counts,* Report of the Committee of Inquiry into Mathematics in Schools under the Chairmanship of Dr W.H. Cockcroft, (The Cockcroft Report). London: Her Majesty's Stationery Office

Ecclestone, K. (1996) 'The Reflective Practitioner: Mantra or a Model for Emancipation?' *Studies in the Education of Adults* 28 (2), 146-161

Evans, J. (1989) 'The Politics of Numeracy'. In P. Ernest (Ed.) *Mathematics Teaching, the State of the Art.* Lewes: Falmer Press, 203-19

FENTO (1999) *Standards for Teaching and Supporting Learning in Further Education in England and Wales.* London: Further Education National Training Organisation (FENTO)

FitzSimons, G. E. (Ed.) (1997) *Adults (returning to) study mathematics: Papers from the 8th International Congress on Mathematics Education (ICME 8) Working Group 18.* Adelaide, SA: Australian Association of Mathematics Teachers

Jarvis, P. (1995) *Adult and Continuing Education (2nd edition).* London: Routledge

Jessup, G. (1991) *Outcomes: NVQs and the Emerging Model of Education and Training.* London: Falmer Press

Johnston, B., Marr, B. & Tout, D. (1997) 'Making Meaning in Maths. Adult Numeracy Teaching: a course for teachers'. In D. Coben (Comp.) *Adults Learning Maths - A Research Forum - 3, ALM-3 Proceedings of the Third International Conference of Adults Learning Maths - A Research Forum (ALM),* 5-7 July 1996 at University of Brighton. London: Goldsmiths College, University of London in association with Adults Learning Maths - A Research Forum, 166-171

Joseph, J. (1997) 'Numeracy Staff Development for Basic Skills Tutors'. In D. Coben (comp.) *Adults Learning Maths - A Research Forum - 3, ALM-3 Proceedings of the Third International Conference of Adults Learning Maths - A Research Forum (ALM),* 5-7 July 1996 at University of Brighton. London: Goldsmiths College, University of London in association with Adults Learning Maths - A Research Forum, 172-82

Marr, B. & Helme, S. (1991) *Breaking the Maths Barrier.* Canberra, Australia: Department of Employment Education and Training

National Council for Vocational Qualifications (1995*) Review of 100 NVQs and SVQs. A Report submitted to the Department for Education and Employment by Gordon Beaumont.* London: NCVQ

National Staff Development Committee for Vocational Education and Training and the Commonwealth of Australia (1995) *Adult Numeracy Teaching - Making Meaning in Mathematics* (ANT*).* Melbourne, Australia: National Staff Development Committee or Vocational Education and Training

Office for National Statistics (1997) *Adult Literacy in Britain.* London: Office for National Statistics

Scottish Education Department (1975) *Adult Education: The Challenge of Change,* Report by a Committee of Inquiry appointed by the Secretary of State for Scotland under the Chairmanship of Professor K.J.W. Alexander (The Alexander Report). Edinburgh: Her Majesty's Stationery Office

Sewell, B. (1981) *Use of Mathematics by Adults in Daily Life.* Leicester: Advisory Council for Adult and Continuing Education

Smithers, A. (1993) *All Our Futures: Britain's Education Revolution.* A Dispatches Report on education. London: Channel 4 Television

Tout, D. (1997) 'Some Reflections on Adult Numeracy'. In D. Coben (Comp*.) Adults Learning Maths - A Research Forum - 3, ALM-3 Proceedings of the Third International Conference of Adults Learning Maths - A Research Forum (ALM)*, 5-7 July 1996 at University of Brighton. London: Goldsmiths College, University of London in association with Adults Learning Maths - A Research Forum, 13-15

Withnall, A. (1995) 'Towards a definition of Numeracy'. In D. Coben (Comp.) *Adults Learning Maths - A Research Forum, ALM-1, Proceedings of the Inaugural Conference of Adults Learning Maths - A Research Forum, (ALM)*, 22-24 July 1994 at Fircroft College, Birmingham. London: Goldsmiths College, University of London in association with Adults Learning Maths - A Research Forum, 11-17

Wolf, A. (1995) *Competence-based Assessment.* Buckingham: Open University Press

Chapter 18

Postscript: Some Thoughts on Paulo Freire's Legacy for Adults Learning Mathematics

Diana Coben
School of Continuing Education, University of Nottingham, UK

These chapters, taken together, bear witness to a community of practitioners and researchers engaged in research and practice in adults learning mathematics. One view of what constitutes mathematics education research (Ellerton & Clements, 1998:154) is that "it is an enterprise conducting careful studies that are informative, in the sense that they generate share-able knowledge that is simultaneously non-trivial, applicable, and not obvious".

The editors believe that these chapters meet these criteria for scholarly work in a research domain. In addition, there is ample evidence here to show that they are, in the words of Ellerton and Clements (1998:154), bent on creating "more equitable forms of mathematics education around the world". If, as Kilpatrick (1992:31) says, mathematics education can be described as "a conversation with thousands of voices speaking on hundreds of topics", then surely this book raises a voice for adult mathematics education which must be heard in this conversation.

One voice that consistently argued for more equitable forms of education around the world was that of the Brazilian educationalist, Paulo Freire, who died in 1997. Given the extent of his influence worldwide, it seems fitting to end this book with some thoughts on Freire's legacy for adults learning mathematics.

INTRODUCTION

Paulo Freire was a contradictory and charismatic figure who seems to have both resisted and exploited his status as a guru of radical education. His 'pedagogy of liberation' has had a tremendous impact in many parts of the

D. Coben et al. (eds.), Perspectives on Adults Learning Mathematics, 329–342.

world, but often without much clarity as to what the political purposes of education should be, except in the most general and rhetorical terms. As a result, his ideas have often been honoured more in the breach than in the observance. He is of huge symbolic importance to the marginalised field of adult education but he is a symbol interpreted in very different ways by his many admirers and by those who resist his appeal. Discussion about Freire is both polarised and very personalised, he is often discussed in terms of his personal qualities - his sincerity, his humility - and commentators seem either to love him or hate him. His work has been translated - and sometimes re-translated - into many languages. His best known book, *Pedagogy of the Oppressed* (Freire, 1972a; 1995a), is regarded by many as inspiring and by many others as unreadable and obtuse. Freire's life has been mythologized - indeed the word 'myth' has been used of Freire by several commentators. Pierre Furter (1985:301) describes him as "a myth in his own lifetime" and Kathleen Weiler (1996) has written a perceptive article entitled 'The Myths of Paulo Freire'. The most authoritative 'reading' of Freire to date, Paul V. Taylor's critically sympathetic 'bio-text', indicates areas of myth, hiatus and conflicting information in a variety of published sources, some apparently sanctioned by Freire himself (Taylor, 1993).

Given that Freire had little to say about mathematics, what does his 'pedagogy of liberation' mean for adults learning mathematics? If we turn to the literature for help we find little discussion in this area. An honourable exception is Roseanne Benn's book *Adults Count Too* (Benn, 1997), which draws on Freire in a wide-ranging, passionate and critical exploration of 'mathematics for empowerment'. From a different perspective, I have explored the complexities and contradictions of Freire's work in my book, *Radical Heroes: Gramsci, Freire and the Politics of Adult Education* (Coben, 1998), in the final chapter of which I discuss Gelsa Knijnik's work in ethnomathematics (see Knijnik, this volume), a field which has some engagement with Freire's ideas. In this 'postscript', while drawing on that book, I shall focus on Freire's legacy for adults learning mathematics through an analysis of two very different developments in adults' mathematics education, both of which take Freire as a starting point. These are Marilyn Frankenstein's work with adults learning mathematics in the USA and the REFLECT programme of development education in what Freire would call the 'Third World'. Finally, Munir Fasheh's moving and powerful account of his changing understanding of mathematics and of his role as a teacher in the West Bank and the Gaza Strip in the 1970s, in which he draws on Freire amongst others, is reprinted here as a coda.

FREIRE'S IDEAS AND EDUCATIONAL PRACTICES

First, a brief overview of some of Freire's ideas and educational practices. Perhaps the best known term, and the one most immediately associated with Freire (although not invented by him) is *conscientização*, usually translated as 'conscientization'. Conscientization is an elusive concept in Freire's writing, often - although wrongly, in my view - equated with the second-wave feminist practice of consciousness raising. Freire uses it to denote his education process, stating that it "represents the development of the awakening of critical awareness" (Freire, 1976:19) in oppressed people initially trapped in what he calls "the culture of silence". This 'awakening' he envisages as the outcome of guided progress through various stages of consciousness (described in Freire, 1976 and Freire, 1972b). The goal of conscientization is a more fully human state of being, which Freire calls 'critically transitive consciousness'.

In the classical Freirean educational process (described in Freire, 1976; Freire, 1972a; 1995a), investigators work with groups of people they judge to be oppressed to analyse their situation and identify 'generative themes' and 'generative words'. These are themes and words which are particularly meaningful and words which are syllabically fruitful (i.e. they can be deconstructed into their separate syllables and reconstructed in new combinations to form new words, exploiting the fact that Portuguese words are composed syllabically). The information is then 'decoded', culminating in the presentation of 'codifications' - slides depicting representations of the 'people's reality', which form the basis of the educational programme. Thus it is intended that the content through which literacy is acquired should be familiar, relevant and challenging.

Freire insists that education is political praxis, and that his is a 'pedagogy of liberation', necessary for the victims of oppression to achieve critically transitive consciousness. He counterposes his pedagogy of liberation with the repressive pedagogy of domestication - an example of a device that recurs throughout his work, that of presenting pairs of opposing elements. In a related pair of opposites, 'banking' education is set against 'problem-posing' education - banking education indicating an approach in which the teacher 'deposits' knowledge in the student, rather as one might deposit money in a bank vault, and problem-posing education indicating active engagement on the part of both teacher and student. The latter is characterised by dialogue, a term Freire uses to mean a deep spiritual communion between teacher and learner, inspired by love. In order to achieve dialogue, love and hope, the educator must commit 'class suicide' and go through what Freire calls an 'Easter experience' - 'die' (at least metaphorically) and be born again on the side of the oppressed.

Freire's use of Christian imagery here is not accidental. I believe Freire should be seen in the context of the movement from which his thought and his practice emerged: the coming together of forms of Marxism and forms of Catholicism in the movement known as Liberation Theology in Latin America in the 1950s and 1960s. Indeed, Freire's 'pedagogy of liberation' may be understood as analogous to the 'theology of liberation'. While making people more fully human, Freire also aims to bring them closer to God. His is a pedagogy of hope - the title of one of his later books (Freire, 1995b) - hope for the 'wretched of the earth', to use Frantz Fanon's phrase (Fanon, 1967); as much a pedagogy of redemption as a pedagogy of liberation. It is a coming together of religion and politics that many find inspiring but in which, for me, the politics are compromised by the religion, just as, for others, his religious stance may appear to be compromised by his politics.

In my view the fundamental problem with the political aspect of Freire's work is the inadequacy of his notion of power. His simple model of oppressor/oppressed; powerful/powerless (again, note the oppositional pairs) takes no account of the fact that an individual may be both oppressed *and* oppressor. If education really is to be empowerment, a far more sophisticated model is needed, one that takes full account of such issues as gender, culture, class, language and ethnicity, amongst others. It would need also, to engage with the contradictions inherent in the teacher/student relationship, which cannot simply be resolved through sacrifical love on the part of the teacher.

Often called an eclectic - with much justification, as he draws on a wide range of thinkers from very different philosophical traditions - Freire is in fact a deeply syncretic thinker, in keeping with that aspect of his Catholic heritage. Perhaps this explains why his disciples are able to take from him what they like - the left takes the parts that sound Marxist and Christians take the parts that sound Christian. Small wonder then that comment and debate on Freire's work is so fragmented and that he has inspired such markedly diverse practice.

So what is Paulo Freire's legacy for adults learning mathematics - and for teachers of adults learning mathematics? I shall turn first to the work of one such teacher, Marilyn Frankenstein, in the USA.

DEVELOPMENTS FROM FREIRE IN
MATHEMATICS/NUMERACY EDUCATION

A glance at some of the headings in Frankenstein's book *Relearning Mathematics: A Different Third R - Radical Maths* (Frankenstein, 1989) tells us something about her approach: Part One is headed "Mathematics: anxiety, anger, accomplishment", with a sub-heading "Mathematics anger: mathematics is not useless and boring", Part Two covers, "The meaning of numbers and variables". The focus on affective, emotional responses to mathematics, on meaning in mathematics and on mathematics as a tool for understanding the world, are all strong features of Frankenstein's work, as is her refusal to duck politically sensitive issues. She makes extensive use of material from newspapers, advertising and official reports to explore contentious issues such as arms control, racial discrimination and the unequal distribution of wealth, and her book includes many sharply satirical political cartoons.

There is much in Frankenstein's book which is quite a long way from Freire - including the cartoons - these are not the products of Freirean investigations - but she acknowledges her debt to Freire, in her book as well as in her article, 'Critical Mathematics Education: An Application of Paulo Freire's Epistemology' (Frankenstein, 1987) and her chapter, written with Arthur B. Powell, 'Toward liberatory mathematics: Paulo Freire's epistemology and ethnomathematics' (Frankenstein & Powell, 1994). In her chapter with Powell, the strong points of Freire's epistemology are encapsulated as: his insistence that "knowledge is not static, that there is no dichotomy between objectivity and subjectivity, or between reflection and action; and knowledge is not neutral"; thus, "Knowledge does not exist apart from how and why it is used, and in whose interest"; for Freire, "people produce knowledge to humanize themselves" (Frankenstein & Powell, 1994:75,76).

Frankenstein's work seems to me an important contribution to Freire's legacy in three major respects: first her insistence that knowledge is not neutral is a necessary counterbalance to the prevailing view of mathematics as objective, fixed, immutable; second, her use of challenging, politically sensitive material as a vehicle for teaching mathematics is a necessary counterbalance to the prevailing functionalist approaches, based as they all too often are, on a very limited view both of the nature and functions of mathematics and of the roles of adults in the modern world; third, and perhaps most importantly, in her passionate commitment to the values which suffuse Freire's work - his concern for the oppressed, his commitment to education for the liberation of human potential and for social change. Freire, then, may be seen as lending legitimacy to Frankenstein's outspoken, creative and oppositional approach to teaching mathematics to adults. But could other authorities be cited for her work? I think they could. Freire, after all, did not originate the idea that knowledge is not neutral; he is not alone in insisting that education is political; his view of education as a humanising process is common in the romantic tradition from Rousseau onwards. Freire's dualistic political vision and his glamorisation of the teacher are as unhelpful in mathematics education as they are in literacy work and neither features in Frankenstein's work, which is original and exciting in its own right.

Why, then, does Frankenstein cite Freire in support of her approach? She is certainly well aware of criticisms of Freire, for example by feminists such as Kathleen Weiler (1994). I think the fact that she does so is a reflection, at least in part, of Freire's symbolic importance to adult educators: he is a beacon - a 'radical hero', as I have argued (Coben, 1998) -- for oppositional practitioners and theoreticians alike. In such a diverse field, riven with internal dispute, it becomes imperative to situate oneself politically in relation to Freire. It is also, I think, a reflection of the syncretic nature of Freire's thought, referred to above, since that enables Frankenstein to take from Freire the ideas that suit her purpose and leave the rest. My concern is that the theoretical weaknesses in Freire's work, some of which I have outlined above, may undermine the development of theory and polarise debate in the field of adults learning mathematics, as, arguably, has already happened in the wider field of adult education. Freire's very syncretism, while enabling his followers to 'cherry-pick' the ideas that suit them, also makes it very difficult to conduct a cogent discussion of his work, since people often find themselves at cross-purposes. A measure of the range of interpretations that result may be gauged by my second example of a Freirean development in the field of adult mathematics education: the REFLECT programme.

REFLECT

REFLECT stands for 'Regenerated Freirean Literacy Through Empowering Community Techniques'. It is an approach to education amongst the poor of the world developed by the British non-governmental organisation (NGO), ACTIONAID and launched in 1996 by Linda Chalker, Minister for Overseas Development in the then Conservative UK government. REFLECT brings together some aspects of Freire's techniques and rather more techniques from Participatory Rural Appraisal (PRA), a process developed by Robert Chambers (1983; 1993) which is well-established in the field of development education. While not specifically a mathematics education programme *per se*, REFLECT techniques highlight mathematics, unlike 'classical' Freirean literacy techniques.

The idea in REFLECT is that people come together with a coordinator (someone from outside – as are Freire's 'investigator/teachers', at least in his early work in Brazil) and map their geographical location, their 'community'. This raises all sorts of questions about what is meant by 'community', but REFLECT does at least offer a set of techniques which could be used to explore that question and other questions of power: race, gender, etc., on which Freire is weak. The REFLECT approach also involves participants *as co-investigators*, rather than as consumers of the codifications prepared by outsiders, as in Freire's approach.

The REFLECT technique brings people together in order to look at where they are, who they are and what resources are available to them (reflecting its roots in PRA). It involves mathematics at the heart of the process, since, for example, counting and measuring will have gone on in order to establish how many people live in a particular village, where the river flows, and so on. Similarly, a health calendar records seasonal variations in health and disease, plotted over a year, alongside a record of cropping patterns and a grid shows sources and uses of credit - a hot topic in poor rural communities, for obvious reasons. For each of the graphic images represented in the manual there is a section on numeracy and this is very welcome, since, as I have said, numeracy is often subsumed within literacy or ignored altogether.

Nicola Foroni and Kate Newman (1998), in their perceptive article on 'Numeracy in REFLECT', argue for a radical re-definition of approaches to adult numeracy. They set out a number of principles which I quote in full here because of their cogency and potential for helping us to think through new approaches to theory, research and practice in the adult numeracy field. The principles may strike a chord with other work discussed in this book. They state that:

- the knowledge and logical operations that illiterate adults possess are essential elements to take into account, and the foundation on which all programmes should be based;
- mental calculation should be seen as a valid form of operation and this should be the point of departure for the acquisition of new knowledge;
- it should also be recognised that various options/paths exist when approaching a particular situation and that all these are equally valid (as long as they work reliably);
- the daily experience of the participants must be used as a starting point, along with the systems of measurement and calculation that belong to the specific context;

- the learning process should be structured using maths to work in real situations to solve real problems;
- the process should be designed so that the participants find and control the logic, understand a problem and are able to identify the steps necessary to resolve it;
- the process should be designed to enable participants to perform these steps to arrive at a solution mentally and/or in writing;
- mathematics [education] should concentrate on strengthening, rather than replacing, the mental arithmetic ability that people possess. It should improve this skill in such a way that they can use the operations required in their daily life and reinforce their faith in their own ability, constantly recognising their own knowledge and practices;
- we should respect and use the local measurement system, as this is a cultural expression tied to context and daily life;
- prejudices embedded in the formal system should be challenged, such as the opposition inherent in the written system to any form of estimation. Estimates are effectively regarded as 'incorrect' and therefore inappropriate in formal mathematics. However, in 'real life' an estimate is often more useful than strict, precise calculation. (Noroni & Newman, 1998:111)

Freire, Frankenstein and REFLECT all use graphical representation, although in different ways, which I think in itself is interesting. Many people, when they hear the word 'mathematics' or 'numeracy', probably think of 'sums', but one would not immediately think of 'sums' when looking through the *REFLECT Mother Manual* (Archer & Cottingham, 1996) - or, indeed, Frankenstein's (1989) book, both of which contain a wealth of visual material. Frankenstein also makes good use of images of artwork, including sculpture and painting. The graphics in the REFLECT manual are rather more prosaic - it contains representations of diagrams, maps and calendars made in the course of mapping the environment and resources available to any given community.

But the Freire who inspired REFLECT is very different from the one who inspired Frankenstein's book. REFLECT is hardly oppositional and certainly not Marxist, neither is it particularly Christian: it is about helping poor people to gain a better foothold within the existing capitalist system, not about changing the system. Like any other approach, it could no doubt be subverted for oppositional ends, but that is clearly not the intention of ACTIONAID or the British government. It is, however, open to the same accusations of naivety that I have levelled against Freire. As Kathy Safford pointed out in the discussion at the ALM-4 conference, the technique raises the question "why does this person want me to reveal information about my household?". I agree.

It seems to me that what is missing in REFLECT, at least in its first incarnation, as in Freire's own work, is an understanding of power. Without it, educational intervention based on his ideas will be ameliorative at best and invasive and irresponsible at worst. Without an understanding of power it is all too easy to view as one homogeneous 'community' a group of people who may be divided in many important ways.

But REFLECT is an evolving approach, and such criticisms seem to have been heard. In their 'Reflections on REFLECT', Phnuyal, Archer and Cottingham (1998:29) present a 'renewed definition' with empowerment at its heart:

REFLECT is a structured participatory learning process which facilitates people's critical analysis of their environment, placing empowerment at the heart of sustainable and equitable development. Through the creation of democratic spaces and the construction and interpretation of locally-generated texts, people build their own multi-dimensional analysis of local and global reality, challenging dominant development paradigms and redefining power relationships in both public and private spheres. Based on ongoing processes of reflection and action, people empower themselves to work for a more just and equitable society.

Elsewhere, Phnuyal (1998:37) insists that "Through a critical analysis of power structures in society, REFLECT promotes 'political literacy', an understanding of how power relations work" and notes that power relationships overlap, so that, for example, "without addressing both gender and racial discrimination, poverty and illiteracy may not be improved". In his discussion of the importance of Freire's ideas to REFLECT, he points out that REFLECT is broadly in agreement with Freire's view that illiteracy is a social product and the result of an oppressive and unjust social mechanism, but he stresses that it is not enough simply to teach this 'fact' (a point with which Freire would surely agree, but one for which his literacy technique makes little provision). Instead, REFLECT participants must internalise learning in their own context. It is a distinction, as Phnuyal says, between teaching theories and practising theories and, for me, it takes REFLECT 'beyond Freire'.

But whatever the strengths and weaknesses of REFLECT or any other Freire-inspired programme, the striking fact is that Frankenstein's work and the work of the REFLECT teams are very different. Given the syncretic, eclectic quality of Freire's thought, perhaps it should not surprise us.

Coda

It seems fitting to give the last word to one who knows only too well that politics is about power: Munir Fasheh. His moving account of his work as a mathematics educator in the West Bank and the Gaza Strip in the 1970s is quoted in Marilyn Frankenstein's book (1989: 57-9). It is reprinted here as a fitting coda to this discussion - and to this book.

When structures fall people rise

When I returned to Birzeit in 1971, I was filled with energy in two different directions: the one, to expand the use of logic and science in the world through teaching, and the other, to deal with what we experienced as an attempt to dismantle the Palestinian community as a viable entity. Opportunities in mathematics presented themselves almost immediately. While the Arab countries had already introduced the 'New Math', the West Bank and the Gaza Strip, being under military occupation, had been left out. Birzeit organized a course for all the High School teachers in the West Bank in the summer of 1972. I ran that programme and helped to incorporate cultural concepts, independent exploration and effective engagement into the syllabus, to overcome the fundamentally dry, and alien abstraction of the math. Both teachers and students were enthusiastic about this revitalization of the teaching but it did not yet lead me to question hegemonic assumptions behind the math itself.

The Palestinian community I went back to was self-confident, energized, idealistic, and already involved in its own renewal, largely as a result of the development of the Palestinian movement. A group of us began children's programs in drama, arts, crafts, mathematical games, simple science experiments, poetry, music and literature, which developed and expanded quickly. We also began working voluntarily in other community projects. While these activities in the community involved joyousness, spontaneity, cooperation and freedom, they were not yet fully articulated for me as education and were not yet fully a praxis in Freire's sense.

While I was using mathematics to help empower other people, and while I was being empowered by the voluntary work, mathematics itself was not empowering me. It was, however, for my mother, whose theoretical awareness of mathematics was completely undeveloped. Math was necessary for her in a much more profound and real sense than it was for me. My illiterate mother routinely took rectangles of fabric and, with few measurements, and no patterns, cut them and turned them into beautiful, perfectly fitted clothing for people. In 1976 it struck me that the mathematics she was using was beyond my comprehension; moreover, while mathematics for me was the subject matter I studied and taught, for her it was basic to the operation of her understanding. What kept her craft from being fully a praxis (in Freire's term), and what limited her empowerment, was a social context which discredited her as a woman and uneducated, and paid her extremely poorly for her work. Like most of us, she never understood that social context and was vulnerable to its hegemonic assertions. She never wanted any of her children to learn her profession; instead, she and my father worked very hard to see that we were educated and did not work with our hands. It was a shock for me to realise, in the face of this, the complexity and richness of her relationship with mathematics. Mathematics was integrated into her world as it never was into mine.

My mother's sewing demonstrated another way of conceptualising and doing mathematics, another kind of knowledge, and its place in the world. The value of my mother's tradition, of her kind of mathematical knowledge, while not intrinsically disempowering, however, was continually discredited by the world around her, by the culture of silence and cultural hegemony.

The discovery of my mother's math was a discovery about the world and relationship between hegemony and knowledge. Hegemony does not simply provide knowledge; it substitutes one kind of knowledge for another in the context of a power relationship. While I had been struggling to make the mathematics I had learned meaningful, the embodiment of what I was seeking was in front of me, made invisible to both my mother and me by the education I had been given, which she desired for me. It had been, in Freire's terms, an education for oppression, domestication and dehumanization. While I was not yet ready to question the theoretical bases of Western science and math themselves, the discovery allowed me to recognize the greater need for liberated education, to respect all forms of knowledge and their relation to action.

For me, this powerful statement has resonances that are as much Gramscian as Freirean, but insofar as they are Freirean, they are enormously strengthened by Fasheh's understanding of power relations and his deep respect for his mother's mathematical knowledge. His recognition that the latter was "not intrinsically disempowering [but] continually discredited by the world around her, by the culture of silence and cultural hegemony" indicates a conception of the 'culture of silence' which is different from Freire's in that it is an active concept: Fasheh is talking about the process of *silencing*, not the state of *being silent*. It is the difference between the noun and verb forms, the significance of which Taylor picked up in his critique of Freire's literacy process, referred to above.

Ultimately, Freire's legacy will be judged by the use that is made of his ideas by those inspired by his vision and by the extent that his ideas contribute to, rather than inhibit, the development of theory and practice in adult education, including adult mathematics education. The jury is out.

ACKNOWLEDGEMENTS

This is an edited and updated version of 'Paulo Freire's Legacy for Adults Learning Mathematics', first published in D. Coben and J. O'Donoghue (comps) (1998) *Adults Learning Maths-4: Proceedings of ALM-4, the Fourth International Conference of Adults Learning Maths -- A Research Forum held at University of Limerick, Ireland, July 4-6 1997.* London: Goldsmiths College, University of London in association with ALM. I am grateful to all those who took part in the discussion which took place at ALM-4. The discussion was taped and this chapter draws on the edited transcript. My thanks also to Marilyn Frankenstein for permission to reprint Fasheh's 'When structures fall people rise'.

REFERENCES

Archer, D. & Cottingham, S. (1996) *REFLECT Mother Manual: Regenerated Freirean Literacy Through Empowering Community Techniques.* London: ACTIONAID

Benn, R. (1997) *Adults Count Too: mathematics for empowerment.* Leicester: NIACE

Chambers (1993) *Challenging the Professions: Frontiers for Rural Development.* London: IT Publications

Chambers, R. (1983) *Rural Development: Putting the Last First.* Harlow: Longman

Coben, D. (1998) *Radical Heroes: Gramsci, Freire and the Politics of Adult Education.* New York and London: Garland Publishing Inc./Taylor and Francis

Ellerton, N.F. & M.A. Clements. (1998). 'Transforming the international mathematics education research agenda'. In A. Sierpinska and J. Kilpatrick, (Eds) *Mathematics education as a research domain: a search for identity.* Dordrecht: Kluwer Academic Publishers, 153-173.

Fanon, F. (1967) *The Wretched of the Earth.* Trans. C. Farrington. Harmondsworth: Penguin

Foroni, N. & Newman, K. (1998) 'Numeracy in REFLECT'. In, *PLA Notes participatory learning and action,* International Institute for Environment and Development, 32, June 1998, 109-115

Frankenstein, M. (1989) *Relearning Mathematics: A Different Third R -- Radical Maths.* London: Free Association Books

Frankenstein, M. (1987) 'Critical Mathematics Education: An Application of Paulo Freire's Epistemology'. In I. Shor (Ed.) *Freire for the Classroom: A Sourcebook for Liberatory Teaching.* New York/London: Heinemann

Frankenstein, M. & Powell, A. (1994) 'Toward liberatory mathematics: Paulo Freire's epistemology and ethnomathematics', chapter 4. In P. L. McLaren & C. Lankshear (Eds), *Politics of Liberation: Paths from Freire.* London: Routledge, 74-99

Freire, P. (1995a) *Pedagogy of the Oppressed,* New Revised 20th-Anniversary Edition, translated by M. Bergman Ramos. New York: Continuum

Freire, P. (1995b) *Pedagogy of Hope: Reliving Pedagogy of the Oppressed,* translated by R.R. Barr. New York: Continuum

Freire, P. (1976) *Education: The Practice of Freedom,* translated by M. Bergman Ramos. London: Writers and Readers

Freire, P. (1972a) *Pedagogy of the Oppressed*, translated by M. Bergman Ramos. Harmondsworth: Penguin

Freire, P. (1972b) *Cultural Action for Freedom*. Harmondsworth: Penguin

Furter, P. (1985) 'Profile of Educators: Paulo Freire'. *Prospects*, 15 (2), 301-10

Kilpatrick, J. (1992). 'A history of research in mathematics education'. In D.A. Grouws (Ed) *Handbook of research on mathematics teaching and learning*. New York: MacMillan Publishing Company, 3-38.

Phnuyal, B., (1998) 'The organic process of participation and empowerment in REFLECT'. In, *PLA Notes participatory learning and action*, International Institute for Environment and Development, 32, June 1998, 36-39

Phnuyal, B., Archer, D. and Cottingham, S. (1998) 'Reflections on REFLECT'. In, *PLA Notes participatory learning and action*, International Institute for Environment and Development, 32, June 1998, 27-30

Taylor, P.V. (1993) *The Texts of Paulo Freire*. Buckingham: Open University Press

Weiler, K. (1994) 'Freire and a Feminist Pedagogy of Difference'. In P. McLaren & P. Lankshear (Eds) *Politics of Liberation: Paths From Freire*. London and New York: Routledge, 12-40

Weiler, K. (1996) 'Myths of Paulo Freire'. *Educational Theory*, (Summer 1996) 46(3), 353-71 .

Index